Africa's Ogun

African Systems of Thought

General Editors
Charles S. Bird
Ivan Karp

Contributing Editors
James Fernandez
Luc de Heusch
John Middleton
Roy Willis

AFRICA'S
OGUN
OLD WORLD AND NEW

Second Expanded Edition

Edited and with a
New Introduction
by Sandra T. Barnes

INDIANA UNIVERSITY PRESS
Bloomington & Indianapolis

Library of Congress Cataloging-in-Publication Data

Africa's Ogun : old world and new / edited by Sandra T. Barnes. —
  2nd, expanded ed.
     p.   cm.—(African systems of thought)
  Includes bibliographical references and index.
  ISBN 0-253-33251-6 (cl : alk. paper).—
  ISBN 0-253-21083-6 (pbk. : alk. paper)
  1. Ogun (Yoruba deity)—Cult—Africa, West. 2. Ogun (Yoruba deity)—
Cult—America. 3. Yoruba (African people)—Religion.
4. Blacks—America—Religion. I. Barnes, Sandra T. II. Series.
BL2480.Y6A46   1989
299'.63—dc20   96-43166

1 2 3 4 5 02 01 00 99 98 97

Contents

ILLUSTRATIONS

PREFACE

This enlarged version of *Africa's Ogun* comes at a special moment—a time when the flow of ideas and peoples from one continent to another is producing a crescendo of reinvented traditions, novel representations, and fresh ideas about how the world has been and, perhaps more important, should be making itself. The second edition captures the spirit of these accelerated processes with five new essays and a new introduction—all centered on Ogun, and for the most part written to portray his new meanings and expressions at their creative peak.

The impetus for a larger volume emerged from the pleas of critics and readers for more descriptions and analyses of Ogun's late-twentieth-century florescence and for more insights into Ogun's nineteenth-century manifestations in West Africa. Originally, the ideas in this volume began to take shape in 1971 when I first began field research in Lagos, Nigeria, and they were periodically reinforced during subsequent research periods in the 1970s and 1980s. Each time I was struck by the vitality of certain religious ideas and practices and their adaptation to contemporary African life. Ogun, the ancient god of iron, warfare, and hunting, stood out in this respect, for his cult and the ideas espoused in it were alive, expanding, and flourishing. In present-day Nigeria his realm had extended to embrace everything from modern technology to highway safety—anything, in fact, that involved metal, danger, or, not incompatibly, political resistance.

In searching for an explanation for Ogun's vitality, I was led to his past, which, upon investigation, and certainly not surprisingly, revealed that Ogun embodied a core of Pan-African themes about human nature, conflict, and change that were basic to the construction of the world view of many peoples. In the Guinea Coast region of West Africa these ancient ideas remained as mere concepts in some societies whereas in others they eventually crystallized in the god Ogun and his cult. Later, as a result of the slave diaspora, some of these ideas were given a place in the reconstructed traditions of African descendants in the New World and, in time, in the lives of the peoples with whom they were coming in contact.

Ogun thus presented a challenging vehicle for examining issues that are categorized under the heading of continuity and change. Given the overwhelming dominance of global religions such as Islam and Christianity, how does a deity such as Ogun survive? How is it that he can appeal to an expanding audience? What does he mean to his followers? Is he the same in all contexts and at all time periods, or does he mean different things to different peoples?

These were the guiding questions in an earlier study, *Ogun: An Old God for a New Age* (Philadelphia, 1980), and at an Ogun colloquium held at the annual meeting of the African Studies Association in Los Angeles in 1979. The idea and encouragement for the colloquium and this volume came from Paula Girshick Ben-Amos and Dan Ben-Amos, who suggested that the international vitality of Ogun was in need of further exploration. Inasmuch as my early work came out of a mainly Yoruba experience, the obvious challenge was to examine Ogun elsewhere in West Africa and in the Caribbean and Latin America. In many places not only was Ogun a key figure in contemporary religious settings that had clear connections with the past, but he also was incorporated into new ideological systems and what might be called popular religions. Needless to say, it became increasingly clear that Ogun and others like him were not part of a disappearing world. In fact, Ogun and other divinities were beginning to play the same role that classical deities of the Greek and Roman world have long played in literature, drama, painting, and sculpture in Western civilization.

From its inception, putting together the essays about the *international* Ogun was a collective enterprise. It began with presentations by colloquium participants which became a core around which other contributions could be added. The U.S. Embassy in Lagos kindly provided a travel grant to Adeboye Babalọla so that he could participate in the colloquium. Others who gave papers and generously shared their own research and ideas about Ogun, but whose work is not included here, were William Bascom, who witnessed an Ogun festival in Ile-Ife, Nigeria, in 1938; Dan Ben-Amos, who studied the modern cult of Ogun in Benin, Nigeria; and Deirdre LaPin, who examined the extensive use of Ogun in the writings of Nobel laureate Wole Soyinka. Soyinka, moreover, attended the colloquium to offer his moral support. Finally, Ivan Karp met with participants to suggest further avenues for analysis and investigation.

The guiding principles for contributors were that their essays be original and based on their own research. With this in mind, some of the authors suggested others who they felt should be included, and in this respect John Pemberton deserves particular thanks. For other suggestions I am indebted to Deirdre LaPin, Candace Slater, Peter Frye, and Diana Brown.

A number of other people also contributed to the ideas that went into shaping the volume and its introduction. Miguel Barnet and Patricia Alleyne kindly helped me understand Ogun in Cuba and Trinidad, respectively, and Pierre Verger generously offered the benefit of his expertise in the People's Republic of Benin, Nigeria, and Brazil. Ivan Karp and Roy Sieber invited me to share my initial thoughts on the metaculture of Ogun with their Africa Seminar at Indiana University. Since then, at various stages and in various ways, I have benefited from the advice of Arjun Appadurai, Gregory Barnes, Paula Girshick Ben-Amos, Carol Breckenridge, Nancy Farriss, Ward Goodenough, Clifford Hill, Igor Kopytoff, Simon Ottenberg, and John Peel.

SANDRA T. BARNES

A NOTE ON ORTHOGRAPHY

Several West African languages, but primarily the Yoruba language, are used in this volume. Spelling conventions make use of subscript markings (as in ẹ, ọ, and ṣ) and the tone markings (as in à = low, ē = mid, or ó = high). Because conventions vary, each chapter is consistent unto itself. For the most part, subscript and tone markings are included in chapters where translations are important to the analysis, and omitted where they are not.

Sandra T. Barnes

Africa's Ogun Transformed:
Introduction to the Second Edition

I n recent decades there has been a virtual explosion on the world's religio-cultural landscape. New ideas, new practices, and new symbolic objects are traveling from place to place with relative ease and rapidity. They are borne by people whose movements are increasingly frequent and far-reaching, and by the media and communications networks that envelop the globe irrespective of people's physical comings and goings. As a result, some cultural traditions are neither spatially bound nor historically continuous, but instead flow in disembodied ways, only to be seized upon and integrated into the repertoires of a diverse range of peoples in a wide range of places and time periods.

If anything characterizes this explosive process, it is the fragmentation of traditions. Elements of belief and ritual—thought to have been historically embedded in cohesive and identifiable social systems—are adapted, reconstituted, and rearranged in new patterns of belief and worship. A plethora of new religiously oriented groups emerge; tiny sects mushroom into movements; sacred traditions are invented and reinvented; and, importantly, various aspects of global faiths and locally specific ones are borrowed and pieced together so as to render new configurations. This process gives the notion of *pastiche* a normative rather than marginal place in providing a conceptual understanding of the dynamics of late-twentieth-century religious experience.

The African heritage is providing critical elements in these innovations, borrowings, and blendings, and it appears not only in religious contexts but also in the arts, popular culture, and public discourse. The first edition of *Africa's Ogun* captured some of these developments, especially the kaleidoscopic manner in which knowledge surrounding a single West African deity was perpetually and contextually reconfigured. It also explained in considerable depth the meanings attached to Ogun—as deity and as concept—and their compelling qualities.

The second, expanded edition of *Africa's Ogun* continues this exploration of Ogun in motion, again using him as a lens through which to view the creative and adaptive processes that shape the ways people experience, define, and construct the sacred aspects of existence, represent them in human life, and make them manifest in religious practice. As before, the variations on Ogun themes are shown to be as much the result of intentional creativities and imaginative interpretations as they are the unintentional remains of the past. Today, however, the extent to which variations occur and, just as important, are *perceived* to be occurring, is dramatically expanding. What were in relatively recent times thought to be isolated, small-scale enactments of the African legacy are attracting a larger share of public notice and acceptance. This is especially true in the New World, and therefore the Americas receive greater emphasis in this volume than in the last (see the chapters by Drewal and Mason, Cosentino, Mason, and Scher). More emphasis also is placed on historical contexts of West Africa, where Ogun was nurtured and where Peel (Ch. 11) shows that the deity's manifestations varied significantly from place to place. Finally, Scher (Ch. 13) adds a fresh perspective by focusing on the instrumental agendas undertaken by the religious groups in which Ogun is embedded, especially agendas concentrating on the politics of heritage.

The explosive changes in religion are not confined to the Americas but are equally profound in Africa itself. A recent estimate suggests that there are 7,000 new religious groups in sub-Saharan Africa, with 32 million members (Jules-Rosette 1989:147). These groups are strongly influenced by Christianity and Islam, yet at the same time elements of indigenous practice and belief are retained to varying degrees. Certainly Ogun remains. More than many other precolonial supernatural powers, he has adapted to contemporary life and become increasingly visible to the public. A new military governor of Ogun State, Nigeria, insisted on taking his oath of office not on the Bible or Koran, as had become the custom in colonially introduced institutions, but on the traditional implement for taking oaths: a cutlass symbolizing Ogun in his role as god of iron and warfare and guardian of justice.[1] Ogun is prominent in the visual arts, including an outpouring of cinema,[2] video, and television programs, and in literature, such as the play *Ogun Lakaaye,*[3] in which the mortal (but soon to be deified) Ogun is presented as a successful warrior who vanquishes enemies of his town but is incapable of maintaining a peaceful home life. He also is the subject of a widely publicized festival in Lagos that is covered in newspapers and on television and calls on public figures and all users of iron implements and motor vehicles to attend "for their own good."[4] In the neighboring People's Republic of Benin, motorcyclists look out for their own good by protecting themselves with iron Ogun figurines attached to their fenders.[5]

The variability in form and meaning in the few examples just given is not recent. Peel's warning (Ch. 11) that Ogun can be neither essentialized nor considered in isolation is amply borne out in the historical record. In the first edition of *Africa's Ogun* and repeated in this edition, Armstrong's linguistic evidence (Ch. 2) reveals that in ancient times the concept *ogun* referred to rituals performed by blacksmiths to purify individuals after they had killed other human beings. A written account from 1604 described a deity—quite probably Ogun, given the symbolic evidence—to whom soldiers sacrificed a dog before mounting attacks on their enemies (Jones 1983:24). Now Peel takes us much further in elucidating variations associated with the precolonial Ogun. He provides a broad contextual and comparative portrayal of Ogun using missionary writings from the second half of the nineteenth century. These texts show that the same ancient occupational characteristics—hunting, smithing, and soldiering—were embodied by Ogun, but other characteristics, such as agriculture and snake handling, were salient then but are lost now. Furthermore, the amount of emphasis on one characteristic or another varied significantly from place to place. Of the 779 *orisha* groups mentioned in mission documents, Peel found that Ogun was strong in civic ritual in eastern Yorubaland, where iron was scarce, but more grounded in mundane activities in the west, where ironworking was widespread. Each historical context thus favored and reproduced a separate set of meanings and representations in the same way that context shapes religious expression in the present.[6]

As for variability in the New World, mass intercontinental migrations of people brought with them numerous strands of religious knowledge—strands that would merge and give rise to a variety of new faiths. Traditions that coalesced and flourished in Brazil included Candomble, Macumba, and Umbanda—a large and influential national religion that draws on Roman Catholicism, Afro-Brazilian Candomble, Kardecian spiritism, and native American beliefs (see Ortiz, Ch. 5). The Caribbean gave birth to a diverse range of religious groups: Voudou in Haiti, Santeria and Lukumi in Cuba, Shango and Spiritual Baptists in Trinidad, Tobago, and Grenada, Kele in St. Lucia, and Santerismo in Puerto Rico.[7]

Receiving societies for people of African descent from the sixteenth to the nineteenth centuries became the sending societies of the twentieth century. Brazilian immigrants began to make their way to Argentina and other nearby Latin American countries; large numbers of Caribbean migrants sought work and other opportunities in Canada, the United States, South America, and Europe; to a lesser extent there continued to be movements and contacts across the Atlantic between peoples of the Americas and West Africa. All of these cross-fertilizations have promulgated and given rise to even more African-based religious expressions. In this respect North America is experiencing an African renaissance. Many new groups are collectively known as the "Orisha" tradition, while others retain an independent identity such as the recent Yoruba Temple in Harlem (Brandon 1993:107); the well-known Oyotunji Village in South Carolina, with close ties to Cuba and Nigeria; the latter's clones, such as Archer, Florida; Neo-Voudou in various locations, most notably New Orleans; and a host of smaller celebratory traditions such as the annual Odunde festival in Philadelphia.

Possibly the most visible Afro-Caribbean religious florescence has been the result of the politically inspired Cuban exodus beginning in the late 1950s that took hundreds of thousands of people to Puerto Rico, Venezuela, and North American urban centers. Dade County, Florida, became home to 550,000

Cubans by 1980, and with them came a multitude of shrines and *botanicas* supplying the faithful with religious objects such as beads, pots, charms, candles inscribed with prayers and images, packets of herbal remedies, and a large array of books and relevant writings (Brandon 1993:6). Followers of Santeria had established fourteen spiritist centers in the Bronx by 1966–67, and by the 1980s there were estimated to be as many as a million devotees in the U.S., including some 50,000 to 100,000 in southern California alone (Mitchell 1988:16–17, 30). Afro-Cuban religious practices are complex. Rather than being a mono-lithic religion, they have over the decades splintered into several groups, of which the best known are Lucumi, Santeria, Santerismo, Espiritismo, and Ori-sha-Voudou; they have spread from Cubans to Puerto Ricans and Dominicans so that in New York, for example, many centers are multiethnic (Mitchell 1988: 30). The mix is not new. The first Santeria priest known to have existed in the U.S. in 1946 initiated priests in New York City as well as Venezuela, Argentina, Colombia, and Mexico (Brandon 1993:106).

Haitians found their way to the U.S. much earlier, as a result of the 1791–1804 slave revolution against the French, and had even founded an interracial Voudou group in Louisiana that was known to be functioning between 1822 and 1830 (Mulira 1990:49). The later, twentieth-century exodus of Haitians to North America brought some 450,000 people to New York City by the early 1980s (Brown 1991:4), with hundreds of priests and priestesses keeping Voudou tra-ditions alive, including Ogun, who is considered one of their primary North American deities (Mulira 1990:64). Entire ceremonies were dedicated to "Papa Ogu" in Le Peristyle Haitian Sanctuary, a group that functioned privately in Philadelphia for more than a decade,[8] and to "Ogoun La Flambeau," god of war and fire, by a New Orleans interracial group intent on driving dope peddlers and criminals from their community.[9]

Significant numbers of Trinidadians also moved to New York, California, and Canada, with even larger numbers commuting several times a year from their homeland to North America (Glazier 1983:128). As with the Cubans, a rich spectrum of religious options has been established—including Spiritual Baptist, Orisha, and Shango groupings—and devotees affiliate with several of them by means of overlapping memberships (Houk 1993:162).

In each of these traditions, insider-intellectuals play a key role in increasing their visibility and public acceptance. As practitioner-priest of the Yoruba Theo-logical Archministry in Brooklyn, a Lucumi-inspired group, John Mason writes prolifically and movingly of the historical and contemporary meanings of re-ligious experience taken from his own training in Afro-Cuban and African-American faiths. In this volume (Ch. 15) he portrays Ogun as a heroic figure who does not deplete the resources of the earth but takes only what he needs to subsist. The environmentalist image is profoundly significant in the American context because, in Mason's view, it once provided a necessary script for slaves who needed Ogun-type "survival" skills should they escape to the forest, just as today their descendants need a vision of hope and a strategy for existing in a world of hardship and deprivation.

Cosentino introduces another insider-intellectual in this volume (Ch. 12), the colorful Ysamur Flores, a Puerto Rican who writes about and places his Ogun in the experiential context of his new residence, Los Angeles. Flores is a busy man: proprietor of his own *botanica,* Ph.D. student at UCLA, frequent guest on local media programs, and full-time philosopher-priest whose successful practice has earned him the rubric "Santero to the stars." Although he considers his congregation a modest one, it is cosmopolitan. Flores has initiated more than 100 devotees from Venezuela, Puerto Rico, Miami, and Los Angeles, and from Vietnamese and African American backgrounds (Mitchell 1988:18). Flores speaks knowingly of Ogun as an archetypal "divine tough guy" who has been portrayed on the screen in *The Believers* and on television's *Miami Vice,* invoked on CNN as a "divine presence" at the ritual murders in 1989 in Matamoros, Mexico, and presented in pulp fiction as a ritually possessed, therefore involuntary, killer. In his portrait of Flores and his description of the outpouring of media interpretations of Ogun, Cosentino captures numerous ways the deity is being transformed into a startlingly hip, New Age hero.

On a larger scale, a substantial middle-class intelligentsia has played and is playing a major role in disseminating knowledge and promulgating the doctrines of Afro-based religions in Brazil (Ortiz, Ch. 5). Umbanda is the main beneficiary of an outpouring of books, conferences, and theological writings that explain Umbanda's theological premises and thereby systematize and legitimate this faith in ways that are characteristic of world religions. In the process Umbanda has become a national religion that embraces racially mixed congregations, including white-collar, service, and technically employed people, and that spills over Brazilian boundaries to incorporate nationals of an increasingly large territorial span. That Umbanda and other Afro-based religious groups draw on an eclectic range of ideological positions, blending the fragments of diverse traditions, is both symptomatic and definitive of the processes that are intrinsic to what we have come to gloss as "globalization."

Such processes are dramatically captured by Umberto Eco in his *tour de force* of contemporary connectivity, *Foucault's Pendulum.* In a lengthy section of the book, the principal characters are introduced to Afro-Brazilian religions that, the narrator informs his readers, are melting pots of ideas, peoples, and "age-old, unbridled hybridization." At the *terreiro de candomble* (religious centers) of northern Brazil they find chapel-like houses of African *orixas* (deities) that are unexpectedly fronted by corresponding images of Roman Catholic saints. Puzzled, the hero tries to understand the arrangement and presses his guide on whether the chapels are for deities or for saints.

> Don't ask embarrassing questions. . . . It's even more complicated in an umbanda. Saint Anthony and Saints Cosmas and Damian are part of the Oxala line. Sirens, water nymphs, caboclas of the sea and the rivers, sailors, and guiding stars are part of the Yemanja line. The line of the Orient includes Hindus, doctors, scientists, Arabs and Moroccans, Japanese, Chinese, Mongols, Egyptians, Aztecs, Incas, Caribs, and Romans. To the Oxossi line belong the sun, the moon, the caboclo of waterfalls, and the caboclo of the blacks. In the Ogun line we come upon Ogun

Beira-Mar, Rompe-Mato, Iara, Mege, Naruee. . . . In other words, it all depends. (Eco 1988:138–58)

The coming together of local belief and global religions—blendings that provide an esoteric core of mystery in Eco's novel—constitute a vast zone of metaphysical tension.[10] Such a zone is a context or site where multiple codes of knowledge meet and where homogenization and differentiation simultaneously take place. There is an unending Hegelian spiral: a new tradition comes up against an existing tradition, thereby producing another. Umbanda is therefore not alone in blending West African, pre-Columbian, and European traditions; the Espiritismo pantheon incorporates a mix of Hindu, Congo, and Gypsy representations (Brandon 1993:109); and Trinidad has Kabbalah groups that draw on arcane elements of Jewish mysticism, medieval alchemy, and Gnosticism (Houk 1993:164).

For Eco, as for other intellectuals who write about the religions described here, the dynamics of human interaction, human need, and human ingenuity are too complicated to be relegated to unidimensional, unidirectional, modernist predictions of how the world is making itself. The so-cálled great traditions— Christianity, Islam, Buddhism, and Judaism—have not dominated the contemporary global scene at the expense of "other" smaller traditions. Religious communities that for centuries have relied on written texts and professionally trained and bureaucratized priesthoods to communicate and promulgate their ideologies have not replaced communities that reproduce themselves primarily through oral means. Rather, the two modes have come to parallel one another, and simultaneously contribute to one another.

In a perceptive analysis of the consequences of today's globalizing and blending of religions, Wuthnow underscores the fact that increasingly individuals draw on several systems of meaning to construct their separate and unique understandings of the "sacred" (1992:3, 23–24). Religion is from one standpoint an increasingly subjective experience. This does not, however, negate the fact that doctrine is embedded in collective texts. The paradox is that institutionalized religions totalize their content, and in so doing establish screens that, by virtue of totalizing and systematizing theological discourse, effectively hide what is happening at more subjective levels—levels where people themselves perceive and invoke multiple codes. The subjective is thus the level at which synthesis begins.

The subjectivity of experience is beautifully captured in Drewal and Mason's examination of the multisensorial basis of meaning, and the literal embodiment of the ways information about a deity such as Ogun is individually understood, communicated, and perpetuated (Ch. 14). The two examine practices associated with the ritualization of body art in Yorubaland, where one has conducted research for many years, and in Cuba and Brooklyn, where the other is a priest and participant. They argue that the ritualized embodiment of meaning is a critical way knowledge is reproduced and remembered, and that Yoruba have long understood and utilized this means of facilitating subjective experience so as to maximize human potential in the struggle to make sense of the world and answer the ultimate questions humans face alone.

If globalization and acceleration in the flow of knowledge and the uses to which knowledge is applied show anything, it is that cultural heritage is put to purposeful ends, be the ends subjective or collective, inspirational or instrumental. At one remove we analyze the fragmented and recombined traditions that are proliferating throughout the Americas and giving rise to new religious faiths. At another we can examine the same traditions as grist for politically motivated, intentional activities. In Trinidad, Africa-derived religious groups compete among themselves to represent the largest number of supporters and, as Scher puts it (Ch. 13), gain a "dominant voice in the public sector." Some Trinidadian groups use an exclusivistic strategy, harking back to a pure, authentic heritage of Africa as a way of legitimating their claims to representation in various political arenas. Other groups use an ecumenical strategy, incorporating Roman Catholic or Hindu elements, to attract a substantial following. Still others take an inclusive position, declaring that what is relevant to the here and now is the way to bring followers together. Each group finds an ideologically separate way of mobilizing bias so as to negotiate a position in the ongoing competition for legitimacy and thereby primacy. The pieces of culture represented by Ogun and other deities are tools in these ongoing struggles, and the variations we see in interpretation are as instrumentally calibrated to heighten people's places in the opportunity structures of contemporary society as they are to express a relationship to the supernatural.

For many, the so-called authenticity of heritage is not the issue. Rather, it is the symbolics of heritage that are important, for they form part of a larger rhetorical strategy for energizing the politics of identity. Knowledge from the African diaspora has taken long to move from a world of unseen practice to the sphere of public action and discourse. The realignments of ideas, practices, beliefs, and traditions derived from or inspired by diasporic knowledge are not random, for at base they provide the texts, intellectual debates, and rationales for activating emotions and sentiments and, more than anything else, bringing people together to work toward purposeful ends.

We may wonder why Ogun appears in supermarkets on votive candles, in Voudou ceremonies to reclaim crime-ridden streets, or as an environmentally correct role model. And there are no single answers. What can be said is that the world is experiencing a religious transformation involving the flow of numerous beliefs and practices across international landscapes. The global reach of print, digital, and visual media knows no boundaries, and thus the most remote and the most cosmopolitan communities are equally exposed to representations drawn from multiple religio-cultural traditions. This leaves the question of meaning as the central issue to be ascertained and understood, for meaning is vastly complex and contextually unique. Questions of meaning, by which I mean the ways strands of knowledge are internalized and used to explain the unknown, are daunting in their variety. As quickly as we decode some, others emerge out of them. This is the age-old process of homogenization and differentiation.

The genius of historical and creative imagination finds expression in the realm of religio-political possibility. With this expression we are witness to a global transformation that challenges us to examine and learn from the new and intriguing agendas that reveal themselves when we seriously examine component parts such as Ogun, the larger narratives in which the Oguns of the world are embedded, and the sometimes overwhelmingly urgent ends to which they are employed.

NOTES

1. Adeboye Babalola, personal communication.

2. In the film *Egun Ogan* (the running prickly plant's thorn), hunters and warriors sing praises to Ogun and sacrifice to him before they set out for battle (Adeboye Babalola, personal communication).

3. The author is Olatubosun Oladapo.

4. Adeboye Babalola, personal communication.

5. Sally Scott, personal communication.

6. Bastide made the same observation years earlier, arguing that Afro-Brazilian religions adapted to each "structural niche" in a unique manner (1978:155).

7. A few recent studies of these groups include Brown (1986), Brumana and Martinez (1989), Pereira de Queiroz (1989), and Wafer (1991) on Brazil; Glazier (1983), Houk (1993), and Yelvington (1993) on Trinidad; Murphy (1988) and Brandon (1993) on Cuba; and Dayan (1995) and Desmangles (1992) on Haiti.

In this volume see Brown and Cosentino on Haiti, Ortiz and M. T. Drewal on Brazil, Mason on Cuba, and Scher on Trinidad.

8. *Philadelphia Inquirer,* July 31, 1992. Priestess of the group is Mambo Angela Movanyon.

9. Priestess of this group is Sallie Ann Glassman (*New York Times,* August 18, 1995, p. A10).

10. I am indebted to Hannerz for his discussion of zones of tension (1989:207).

REFERENCES CITED

Barnes, Sandra T. (ed). 1989. *Africa's Ogun: Old World and New.* Bloomington: Indiana University Press.

Bastide, Roger. 1978. *The African Religions of Brazil.* Baltimore: The Johns Hopkins University Press.

Brandon, George. 1993. *Santeria from Africa to the New World.* Bloomington: Indiana University Press.

Brown, Diana DeG. 1986. *Umbanda: Religion and Politics in Urban Brazil.* Ann Arbor, Mich.: UMI Research Press.

Brown, Karen McCarthy. 1991. *Mama Lola: A Voudou Priestess in Brooklyn.* Berkeley: University of California Press.

Brumana, Fernando G., and Elda G. Martinez. 1989. *Spirits from the Margin: Umbanda in Sao Paulo.* Uppsala, Sweden: Uppsala Studies in Cultural Anthropology.

Dayan, Joan. 1995. *Haiti, History and the Gods.* Berkeley: University of California Press.

Desmangles, Leslie G. 1992. *The Faces of the Gods: Voudou and Roman Catholicism.* Chapel Hill, N.C.: University of North Carolina Press.

Eco, Umberto. 1988. *Foucault's Pendulum.* New York: Ballantine.

Glazier, Stephen D. 1983. *Marchin' the Pilgrims Home: Leadership and Decision-Making in an Afro-Caribbean Faith.* Westport, Conn.: Greenwood Press.

Hannerz, Ulf. 1989. "Culture between Center and Periphery: Toward a Macroanthropology." *Ethnos* 54(3–4):200–16.

Houk, James. 1993. "Afro-Trinidadian Identity and the Africanisation of the *Orisha* Religion." In *Trinidad Ethnicity,* K. A. Yelvington (ed.). Knoxville: University of Tennessee Press, pp. 161–79.

Jones, Adam. 1983. *German Sources for West African History, 1599–1669.* Weisbaden: Franz Steiner Verlag.

Jules-Rosette, Bennetta. 1989. "The Sacred in African New Religions." In *The Changing Face of Religion,* J. A. Beckford and T. Luckman (eds.). London: Sage, pp. 147–62.

Mitchell, Rick. 1988. "Power of the Orishas." *Los Angeles Times Magazine,* Feb. 7.

Mulira, Jessie Gaston. 1990. "The Case of Voodoo in New Orleans." In *Africanisms in American Culture,* J. E. Holloway (ed.). Bloomington: Indiana University Press, pp. 34–68.

Murphy, Joseph M. 1988. *Santeria: An African Religion in America.* Boston: Beacon Press.

Pereira de Queiroz, Maria Isaura. 1989. "Afro-Brazilian Cults and Religious Change in Brazil." In *The Changing Face of Religion,* J. A. Beckford and T. Luckman (eds.). London: Sage: 88–108.

Rigaud, Milo. 1953. *Tradition voudoo et le voudoo haiten: son temple, ses mysteres, sa magie.* Paris: Niclaus.

Sahliyeh, Emile. 1990. "Religious Resurgence and Political Modernization." In *Religious Resurgence and Politics in the Contemporary World.* E. Sahliyeh (ed.). Albany: SUNY Press, pp. 3–16.

Shupe, Anson. 1990. "The Stubborn Persistence of Religion in the Global Arena." In Sahliyeh, pp. 17–26.

Wafer, Jim. 1991. *The Taste of Blood: Spirit Possession in Brazilian Candomble.* Philadelphia: University of Pennsylvania Press.

Wuthnow, Robert. 1992. *Rediscovering the Sacred.* Grand Rapids, Mich.: W. B. Eerdmans.

Yelvington, Kevin A. 1993. *Trinidad Ethnicity.* Knoxville: University of Tennessee Press.

Africa's Ogun

Sandra T. Barnes

1

The Many Faces of Ogun: Introduction to the First Edition

Th ere is a privileged class of supernatural and mythic figures who consistently grow in their renown and complexity. One thinks of such figures as Oedipus or Siva, each of whom plays a significant role in the traditions of many groups of people, to the extent that they have become metacultural, or international in scope. The contributors to this volume focus their attention on another such figure: Ogun,[1] an African deity, who thrives today in a number of West African and New World contexts, including the Caribbean, South America, and, more recently, North America.

Ogun was one of many deities carried to the New World by Africans during the slave diaspora which took place between the sixteenth and the mid-nineteenth centuries. More recently he, and the complex ideological systems of which he is a part, have been carried from Brazil to its neighboring countries and from the Caribbean to North America. In this more recent, twentieth-century movement of peoples and their belief systems, Ogun's appeal has transcended the boundaries of ethnicity, race, and class so that today's adherents are not simply people of African descent but people representing many walks of life. The story is equally dramatic in West Africa, where Ogun's popularity also has flourished and expanded.

As a consequence, more than 70 million African and New World peoples participate in, or are closely familiar with, religious systems that include Ogun, and the number is increasing rather than declining. Yet the claim that a god from a comparatively small religious faith, particularly one stemming from a nonliterate tradition, flourishes in spite of the overwhelming dominance of such large global religions as Islam and Christianity jars our expectations. Why does a deity like Ogun survive? How can he grow in popularity, especially when deities of global faiths are themselves gaining strength? Furthermore, how can we say that Ogun of the New World is still the same as Ogun of West Africa, given the limited interaction of peoples between hemispheres in the past century or more and the markedly different cultural influences that have obtained in each place during this period? Clearly, if we are to understand the Ogun phenomenon as more than a mere anomaly, a reassessment is needed of the way we view contemporary religious processes. This is a primary concern of my essay. As a first step, let me introduce Ogun in his more obvious manifestations.

Ogun is one of many gods and goddesses in West African pantheons. As such, he is embedded in belief systems of great complexity. It is not the intention of this volume to dwell on these systems in their totality, but it is important to know that, like the religions of the ancient Greeks and Romans or contemporary Hindus, Ogun always is one part of a larger whole. Perhaps because he has an uncanny ability to stay abreast of the times, Ogun has been a major figure in this larger picture for as long as historical records reveal.

Ogun is popularly known as the god of hunting, iron, and warfare. Today, however, his realm has expanded to include many new elements, from modern technology to highway safety—anything involving metal, danger, or transportation. In the minds of followers, Ogun conventionally presents two images. The one is a terrifying specter: a violent warrior, fully armed and laden with frightening charms and medicines to kill his foes. The other is society's ideal male: a leader known for his sexual prowess, who nurtures, protects, and relentlessly pursues truth, equity, and justice. Clearly, this African figure fits the destroyer/creator archetype. But to assign him a neat label is itself an injustice, for behind the label lies a complex and varied set of notions. As his devotees put it, "Ogun has many faces."

The many meanings of Ogun are revealed in a vast array of rituals, myths, symbols, and artistic representations. The same is true of other deities in the pantheon, who formulaically number from 201 to 401 and even more. Each deity has different features; for example, only Ogun devotees wear iron emblems, display fiery red eyes when possessed, and dance with swords. Such differences do not prevent deities from interacting with one another in the spirit world; they reproduce, have kinship relationships, and generally quarrel, love, help, and harm just as humans do. Rather, the differences perform a valuable service by separating one deity's meanings from another's.

The interactions of humans and deities take place in a varied range of contexts. They often involve several deities or groupings of deities. A devotee who venerates Ogun alone may retire to a private household corner to offer prayers and simple food sacrifices to his iron tools (see H. Drewal, this volume, Ch. 10). By contrast, communities stage public spectacles that are as complex in their staging as European opera; indeed, they are grander in scale than opera, since entire towns, from the king to the lowliest servants, participate for days and even weeks in their dramatic pageantry (Pemberton, Ch. 6). Between the extremes lie ritual encounters with divinities that take place during rites of passage and in a bewildering variety of family, occupational, and cult groups. These encounters are neither as solemn nor as standardized as those of Western missionary Christianity. Neither are they similar in substance. West African adherents put emphasis on sacrifice, divination, and possession as ways of communicating with deities, and they stress pragmatic, everyday concerns as the content of such communication.

Finally, ritual encounters put emphasis on emotions and personality traits. Ogun's devotees display fiery outbursts of anger to the extent that they may heedlessly injure bystanders; just as easily, they may dwell on Ogun's humanitarianism and self-reliance with poignant recitations of heroic deeds that require outstanding levels of courage and leadership. To a great extent, whether it is in thought, deed, or mood, humans and deities mirror one another in West African philosophies. Therefore, character strengths and character flaws are as divine as they are human.

Ogun plays a central role in these philosophies. Like all deities he advances understanding, unifies knowledge, and, as Durkheim and Mauss put it, creates "a first philosophy of nature" (1963:81). Stated more succinctly, he represents a theory of what life or part of life is about. To uncover this theory, however, we must return to a concern which I introduced earlier on.

If we are to appreciate Ogun's significance in contemporary religious life, any reassessment of that life must depart from past approaches that, by implication, relegated figures like Ogun to a dying tradition. The thesis here is that a deity's capacity to survive, flourish, and expand depends on the meanings he projects and, perhaps equally important, on the way those meanings are "packaged." Within the meanings of Ogun resides a philosophy of the human condition that can be stated as a theoretical proposition. The theory in Ogun embodies a profound and compelling observation of human nature. This theory enables us to examine a realm of ideas that explain, in deeply moving terms, certain strengths and weaknesses that are universal to the human condition. Still, there is no one source for these ideas.

The many manifestations of Ogun yield many meanings. Multiple meanings inevitably give rise to multiple interpretations and, by extension, multiple anomalies. Can we then claim there are common threads in Ogun traditions, particularly when these traditions are so geographically and historically separated? Clearly, if we are to understand what is unique to Ogun—or whether, in fact, he *is* unique—a reevaluation is needed of the way we treat meanings, particularly as they are reflected in a single cultural figure.

I will begin this endeavor—explaining why Ogun survives and by necessity what he means, since my thesis is that meaning and survival are connected—with a look at the scant but instructive historical evidence. The value of history lies in its ability to provide baselines from which to measure the deity's ongoing permutations. My excursion into Ogun's past is followed by a brief examination of the historical and contemporary processes that shaped, and continue to shape, his meanings and that also account for his expansion.

Any study of meanings, especially when they are attached to a deity whose history spans centuries and whose devotees span continents, is incomplete without a discussion of methods. This will form the next part of the essay. How can we uncover the deepest meanings of a metacultural figure? More particularly, how can we expect to uncover common meanings when there are wide variations in them? Fortunately, analytical tools for this kind of endeavor are beginning to reach a state of some refinement. By combining several of them we can grapple with complexities that previously stood in the way of our ability to generalize about culture on a grand scale and yet retain cultural uniqueness as part of that generalization.

Finally, I will return to Ogun's meanings, this time in search of his philosophical principles and how they are put together in ways that are easily but profoundly communicated. There is no single myth, ritual, or other context that captures his meanings in a comprehensive, unified way. Therefore, the theory of human nature that we encounter through Ogun and, I suggest, the thing that accounts for his survival, is drawn from the rich body of evidence provided in each of the chapters that follow.

The History of Ogun

No date can be assigned to the birth of Ogun, nor can a place be assigned to his origins. The ideas out of which Ogun emerged are undoubtedly ancient ones. In an earlier study it was proposed that many of the themes surrounding Ogun are rooted in a set of Pan-African ideas that probably accompanied the spread of iron-making technology throughout sub-Saharan Africa as far back as 2,000 years (Barnes 1980). I call these ideas the *sacred iron complex*. The three most commonly held ideas in the complex are that iron is sacred, that ironworkers are exceptional members of society with particularly high or low status (since their work makes them either feared or revered), and that iron workplaces (smelters and smithies) are ritual shrines or sanctuaries for the dispossessed (e.g., warrior refugees). A recent study suggests that sacred ritual and its attendant ideology may have been essential to iron-making as a formulaic way of remembering and perpetuating the steps and ingredients involved in the iron-making process (van der Merwe and Avery 1987:143). This being the case, the ideology attached to iron technology needed to be sufficiently flexible and general to be communicated easily and then adapted to various local cosmologies.[2] H. Drewal (Ch. 10) describes just such an adaptation in the iron-smelting ritual of a Yoruba community and shows how local ideology symbolically plays on the notions in the sacred iron complex.

Lévi-Strauss suggests (1966:16–22) that ideas such as those in the sacred iron complex are randomly distributed notions until people collectively join them together in ways that fit their own cultural contexts. He calls the people who engage in this collective enterprise *bricoleurs*, people who work with materials at hand. Each group of *bricoleurs* creates new patterns with random materials, making it difficult to compare cross-culturally the common denominators in the patterns without decontextualizing them and thereby reducing them to truisms. Although I return to this problem, it should be said here that in the forest-belt kingdoms of West Africa, a conventional pattern for dealing with extraordinary ideas, culture heroes, or anomalies in nature was to deify them. The genesis of Ogun, therefore, quite likely involved a deification that grew out of a set of commonly held notions about the mystical properties of iron and the powerful people who made or used it. But Ogun's beginnings need not have relied exclusively on iron-related notions.

Armstrong (Ch. 2) provides evidence to suggest that several equally fundamental, metaphysical ideas may have been involved in the genesis of Ogun. They center, first, on an association between pollution and killing—killers must be purified before they can be reintegrated into society—and, second, on the mystification of disorder—misfortune is supernaturally determined. These ideas are attached to a widely shared set of cognate concepts, *Ògún-ògwú-ògbú*, meaning "kill." Armstrong found that cognates of the term *Ògún* exist in six neighboring language groups in West Africa. Linguistic evidence led him to propose that the concept is at least as old as the beginning of the Iron Age and probably older. In two of the language groups, an *Ògún*-related term is the name of a ritual that is held to resocialize a dangerous hero—hunter or headhunter—by honoring his deed and, at the same time, cleansing him of the pollution of death with water from a blacksmith's forge.[3] Thus Armstrong takes issue with the hypothesis that Ogun arose out of Africa's iron revolution and its accompanying sacred iron complex. He proposes, instead, that earlier themes—hunting, killing, and the resultant disorder that killing brings—are more likely foundations on which an *ogun* concept, and later an Ogun deity, were constructed.

The actual apotheosis of Ogun—that is, transforming the concept into a divine being—appears to have occurred in a much later period than the creation of an *ogun* concept. The earliest reliable date that can be fixed to the existence of an Ogun deity is the latter part of the eighteenth century. The evidence comes from Haiti, where the cessation of slave imports from Africa by this date acted as a cutoff point for the introduction of the slaves' home culture. Brown (Ch. 4) indicates that Ogun had to have been firmly entrenched in Haiti by this time inasmuch as today he is a significant figure in its religious culture, and oral traditions tie him to a long series of Haiti's historical events. Clearly the god Ogun existed, and was widespread, before the 1700s in the West African societies whose peoples contributed to the slave diaspora, or he could not have emerged as strongly as he did in Haiti and elsewhere in the New World.

Yet dates for the emergence of this deity in West Africa must be inferred. One suggestion is that Ogun arose in eastern Yorubaland in the sixteenth century, when there was an increase in the supply of iron and an expansion of warfare (Williams 1974:83). The hypothesis is based, in part, on the fact that ritual objects made of iron, which can be dated because of their use of imported metal and which are commonly used by Ogun devotees, began to proliferate at that time. This hypothesis is pictorially reinforced by a brass plaque depicting a Benin warrior wearing miniature iron tools—the almost universal symbols of Ogun—that dates to the fifteenth or sixteenth century (fig. 3.1). An even earlier date for the emergence of Ogun is suggested by an annual ceremony, also in the Kingdom of Benin, which dates to the thirteenth or fourteenth century and which featured ritual battles and sacrifices of the type that today are appropriate only to Ogun (Barnes and Ben-Amos, Ch. 3). Both of these suggestions pin the emergence of an Ogun deity to activities associated with warfare. Furthermore, they pin the geographic area of his emergence to eastern Yorubaland and to the Kingdom of Benin, where ritual reenactments of battle between kings and town leaders have long figured in large civic pageants dedicated to Ogun. Ritual battles featuring Ogun also became significant in Dahomean kingship ceremonies, especially those honoring the military, and they have continued to the present day on a smaller scale elsewhere in eastern Dahomey (now People's Republic of Benin), western Yorubaland, and throughout the New World where Ogun appears.

A third suggestion is given by Babalọla (Ch. 7), who finds that songs and legends link the deity's origins to hunting. There are, of course, no dates for such mythological explanations, but the traditions themselves are concentrated within central and western Yorubaland, especially in the territory occupied by the Kingdom of Oyo, West Africa's largest precolonial empire. Their performance was tied to hunting and, by extension, to the military, since hunters were the vanguard of the army. A German surgeon aboard a Dutch merchant ship described a prewar sacrificial ceremony for a deity, specified only as "the Devil," that took place in 1603 and included seven dogs; today dogs are sacrificed exclusively to Ogun. The rites took place near Lagos (Nigeria), which at that time was under the Kingdom of Benin (Jones 1983:24). Oyo factors were present in the area, however, for Oyo controlled nearby trade routes linking its inland territory to the lucrative European sea trade.

As can be seen, all of the evidence for the emergence of Ogun is circumstantial. The suggested dates and regions for the genesis of this deity all rely on symbolic and ritual evidence that today is appropriate only to Ogun. But none of the evidence specifically names Ogun and therefore the connection between it and the actual deity cannot be confirmed.

Furthermore, because the evidence is fragmentary, no interpretation can be right or wrong. Little profit is to be gained from deciding whether sacred iron weapons from a blacksmith's forge or a successful yet polluted headhunter comes first as an ideological building block in the making of an *ogun* concept. Similarly, little profit can be gained from trying to pinpoint the deity's origins to a specific geographical region. Great profit can be realized, however, from combining all pieces of evidence, for they strongly suggest that there is an extraordinary tenaciousness in the themes attached to both Ogun as a deity and *ogun* as a concept. For instance, the sacred iron theme is kept alive by Cuban migrants in the United States who, like their compatriots at home, sacrifice to cauldrons (*caldera de ogún*) filled with iron objects, and to which in 1979 New York devotees added a real pistol (Thompson 1983:55). Likewise, the purification/killing theme is reworked in Brooklyn when a Haitian devotee who feels responsible for her son's death is consoled by a priestess who is possessed by Ogun in an elaborate ceremony (Brown, Ch. 4).

The way to think about the beginnings of a deity such as Ogun, then, is to view his origins, *by necessity*, as indeterminate. At any historical point, the ideas reflected by Ogun, or the ideas out of which he is created, are a cultural assemblage. Rather than assign any one set of ideas to the genesis of Ogun, it is instructive to view his origins in a *bricoleur* idiom: many available notions were pieced together into patterns that began as a concept and eventually emerged in a cult group with Ogun as its symbolic figurehead. Taken together, the ideas associated with Ogun represent an ongoing process that, in human history, has consisted of the working and reworking of available themes—be they sacred iron, pollution from unnatural death, or a host of others that are uncounted and unrecoverable. There is neither a beginning nor an end to these reworkings, and for these reasons it is well to speak of historical processes rather than historical beginnings.

Historical Processes That Shape Ogun

The history of Ogun is made up of additions and subtractions. In the extensive areas where Ogun is a significant part of the religious culture, there are many contexts in which he is salient. Over time these contexts are layered, one on another, so that what appears today as a bewildering variety of beliefs, legends, and rituals is an historical accumulation.

Additions leave behind a kind of "stratigraphy," as Obeyesekere vividly puts it (1984:284–5). Unfortunately, cultural stratigraphy does not reveal principles of order in the ways geological or archaeological stratigraphies sometimes do. Rather, layers of ideas are combined in any way. If there is logic in cultural stratigraphy, it is not chronology, but patterns in the ways additions and subtractions come about. One way of making additions is through paradigmatic transfers. When Nigerians changed from driving on the left to driving on the right-hand side of the road in 1972 it was interpreted as an "Ogun"-type event. Radio and television stations alerted the public by broadcasting an Ogun chant, written in traditional style by a popular musician, that advised people to pay tribute to Ogun before going out on the dangerous highways, and transporters and mechanics gathered in motor parks to offer sacrifices so that they might avoid accidents caused by the change (Barnes 1980:41). In essence, there was an available paradigm to signal an unusual event. Once it was applied to the event, it became a layer in the history of Ogun's performance as an appropriate actor.

New layers also come about through fusions. This happens when the attributes of two figures overlap in significant ways. Nigeria's Nobel laureate Wole Soyinka merges Ogun with Sango, the god of lightning and thunder, in a poem drawing on the imagery of electricity. The union can be seen, he writes, "during an electric storm when from high-tension wires leap figures of ecstatic flames" (1967:86). This is a temporary fusion in that it works in some contexts and not in others. Other fusions, say the historically common mergers of heroic warriors or hunters and Ogun, may be permanent. Whether temporary or permanent, the merger legitimates new symbols, themes, or legendary tales (say of a warrior's prowess) that thereafter can be added to the repertoire of features that is attached to the deity in question.

Fusions also account for loss. A Xhosa praise singer once explained that acquiring skills involved learning the ways in which events that occur to prominent people recall events of past eras: "And then you just begin to join those things" (Scheub 1975:22–23). Babalọla's analysis of Ogun's character (Ch. 7) treats this blending of past with present. Legends attribute to Ogun the founding of many communities and royal dynasties, especially when they are the result of conquest or civil war. At first an historical founder's name is linked to that of Ogun, the supernatural founder. One example is Ogundahunsi, the founder of Ire Town. Eventually the founder's personal name is dropped and only the title Ogun survives. This case and others like it constitute an ongoing process: what is once expanded eventually is compressed, obscured, then lost.

Other processes that are significant to the history of Ogun involve his perpetuation and spread. Possibly the most important mediums for transmitting information are rituals and oral traditions such as myths, songs, legends, or prayers. A relatively high level of intercommunity mobility in precolonial West Africa fostered the exchange of information (Barnes and Ben-Amos, Ch. 3). Trade, of course, was the most notorious vehicle for interaction. In addition, artists traveled explicitly to augment their repertoires (H. Drewal, Ch. 10). Hunters moved through wide territories spreading their Ogun chants (Babalọla, Ch. 7 and Ajuwọn, Ch. 8). Ogun devotees, in fact, were among the more mobile sectors of the populace, and thus Ogun was the patron deity of the road, the deity who "showed the way," and the founding father of new settlements. Needless to say, his followers spread their traditions as they moved. So, too, did itinerant priests, herbalists, and diviners, who were expected to introduce new religious practices and deities from one place to another. Ritual specialists were hosted by the more notable members of communities, who, as part of their strategy to increase their local power, adopted foreign mystical powers.

Oral traditions repeatedly tell of journeys undertaken by ordinary people to attend ritual festivals in far-off places. Native sons and daughters returned to their homes on these occasions, and representatives of rulers and chiefs also were delegated to attend them. In fact, representatives of the King of Ila, whose Ogun festival Pemberton describes (Ch. 6), had traveled fifty years earlier to the town of Ife (sixty miles away) to attend an Ogun festival. Their presence was noted by anthropologist William Bascom, who had just arrived in that city in 1938 for his first research. Bascom was struck by the stylized sword battles that were part of the rite (Bascom 1987), just as Pemberton was struck by similar battles staged, he was told, so that a town might have peace.

Ritual thus serves as a mnemonic formula for keeping knowledge alive and relatively predictable. Just as Africa's preindustrial ironworkers used sacred ritual as formulae for making iron, Ogun devotees use ritual as formulae for promulgating and perpetuating their deity. Reenactments of battle are foremost among these formulae today and are probably many centuries old.

All of these historical processes have been central concerns of researchers who study the African heritage in the New World. In one way or another their writings also ask to what extent the encounters between indigenous, European, and African systems of thought are obliterating the latter and to what extent such encounters leave them intact or altered. The transfer of African culture to the New World brought about the disappearance of many deities. In the slave trade, African populations were mixed together, and many were deprived of sufficient numbers to perpetuate their traditions; oppression and intolerance prevented many more from expressing them. As a result, some observers came to believe that the New World experience had virtually wiped out the African heritage.

In an influential study, Melville Herskovits attacked this position. "We have a tendency," he wrote, "to emphasize change and to take stability for granted." While Herskovits felt that it was essential to take account of both, he took a firm stand on the side of the "tenaciousness of tradition" (1958:xxxvii and 1937). To buttress his position he argued that the West African heritage was kept alive through the syncretic blending of Christian saints and West African deities. Thus in Brazil, Ogun was understandably merged with St. George the Warrior (Ortiz, Ch. 5), and in Cuba he became San Juan (Barnet 1968:80). Although Herskovits felt that West African meanings remained attached to the syncretized deities, he failed to give those meanings more than cursory attention in his writings and instead placed emphasis on the persistence of forms. Nevertheless, his emphasis on the tenaciousness of African culture left its mark on a generation of scholars.

One of them was Roger Bastide, who pointed out that African culture does not survive randomly, but only if there is a niche for it in the new society (1978:160). To his mind there is a dialectical relationship between the material conditions of life and the ideology that survives. Brown (Ch. 4) puts Bastide's notions to work on her Haitian case, where she points out that Ogun's roles as hunter and blacksmith have no favorable niche, since neither is a significant occupation in this Caribbean society. Instead, she shows that there is a functional relationship between the leader/warrior aspects of the *ogun* concept and the highly visible and powerful place military and political affairs have in Haitian life, and that this is the relationship that is elaborately worked out in Vodou traditions.

Not until recently have scholars who compare Old and New World Africanisms called for a significant shift of focus in the studies of continuity and change. The most explicit agenda comes from Mintz and Price, who feel that the study of African culture is empty until we uncover and then compare similar cognitive orientations in the world views of people on both sides of the Atlantic (1976:5–7). For them, comparing the form or function of super-natural elements does a disservice to our understanding of historical pro-cesses as these processes apply to human ideology. Rather, they suggest we compare not the structural aspects of cultural representations but what the representations mean, intend, and express. A byproduct of their approach is that once carried to its logical conclusion—which is to understand cognitive meanings—the findings can be used to explain why certain deities grow in popularity. The key to making convincing comparisons thus rests with the methods that are used to uncover the meanings of the cultural representations in question. I will return to a discussion of those methods below.

Ogun in the Present

One of the unanticipated processes in Africa and the Western hemisphere is, as indicated, that African-derived religious beliefs prosper rather than de-cline.[4] In Brazil alone, religious groupings that include Ogun have more than 30 million adherents, and they are spreading rapidly to Uruguay and Argen-tina, where there are scarcely any African descendants. The South American cults are neither class-, race-, nor ethnicity-bound (Ortiz, Ch. 5), and the same is true of Santería cults in Cuba (Barnet 1968:80). For instance, 100,000 Umbanda congregations have emerged in Brazil's southernmost state settled largely by Polish, Italian, and German immigrants.[5] Ogun also moves along with Haitian and Cuban populations to New York, Florida, Cali-fornia, and Texas (Brown, Ch. 4 and M. Drewal, Ch. 9). Participation in Santería, Cuba's African-derived faith, is believed to be stronger since the Cuban Revolution than Roman Catholicism, and it is especially strong in North America, where it also serves as a support system for newcomers (Hageman 1973:15). In fact, Miami police are briefed so as not to misinter-pret some of the sacrificial rites of Cuban-American Santería devotees (*Wall Street Journal* 18 Oct. 1984). Finally, Caribbean and West African religious practices are spreading to a growing body of English-speaking North Ameri-cans, and these new devotees hold ceremonies and have produced, after in-struction by Cuban adherents, a theological treatise on African deities (M. Drewal, Ch. 9).

The growth and vitality of a deity such as Ogun do not take place at the expense of other faiths or other supernatural forces. Ogun does not coexist with them in an either/or relationship. All of the societies where Ogun flour-ishes are culturally and religiously plural societies wherein religious faiths par-allel one another.

The coexistence of several traditions poses few if any cognitive problems for members of plural societies. What does pose problems to the Western mind is that people often take part in and profess several faiths simultaneously. To some extent, the Western predisposition to think about deities in a monotheistic framework is extended into a monethetic way of classifying membership in cults, churches, temples, mosques, or shrines: a person is a Muslim or a Christian, not both. To many Western observers of West Africa, its peoples should be faithful either to their precontact religious systems or to Christianity, and either to precontact systems or Islam, but not to both. Participation in several religious faiths violates the Western tenet of exclusivity: thou shalt have no other gods before me. Dual or even multiple participation is not, however, contradictory to polytheistic thought, which by definition has an open, inclusive orientation to religious experience. In reality, dual participation is more common than studies of religion indicate, and the concept of "popular religion" also offers a vehicle for its study. Similarly, a category of bi-religiosity offers another vehicle for capturing many people's religious behavior. Many investigations fail to pick up dual participation, mainly because they focus on the faith itself rather than on the members and their practices, choices, or individual beliefs. The essential point about religious systems that parallel one another is that each of them is like an arena: participants come and go. People ordinarily assign one religious label to themselves, but there are no sanctions levied on those who move among several arenas simultaneously. Certainly, in many New World societies, exclusivity is not the norm. Ortiz (Ch. 5) offers many insights into the roles of Candomblé, Umbanda, Spiritism, and institutionalized Catholicism and their abilities to parallel one another and draw on one another's adherents. As in West Africa, Brazilian participants of all backgrounds move in and out of these arenas in increasing numbers.

Today's religious practices also give birth to new ideologies. In a classic study of religion in Java, Geertz (1960:355ff) shows the ways, despite the inevitable ideologic antagonisms that exist in any religiously plural society, in which boundaries between religious world views are blurred and new views come into being. The nub of his argument is that religion cannot be limited to certain times and places. Hence, social interchanges among peoples in Javanese society lead to interchanges of values and behaviors. The same is true in the societies discussed here. Among Yoruba-, Fon-, and Edo-speaking peoples, who figure so prominently in the West African cultural systems presented in this volume, Christianity and Islam have come to play strong parts in people's lives. Yet the blending of Christianity and precontact religious orientations is so marked that new forms have emerged that can loosely be described as African Christianity—a generic label that glosses a proliferation of well-developed and institutionalized, independent churches and their overarching governing bodies. The same is true of African Islam. The blendings range on a continuum that moves from the indigenous precontact religious systems to orthodox European, mission-type systems of Christianity or orthodox Islamic brotherhoods. There are even triple blendings of Christianity, Islam, and indigenous systems. To classify them would be to misrepresent the nature of the phenomena or the abilities of adherents to layer ideas on one another, make analogies, or otherwise subtract and add in a variety of ways. Better to say that the present religious landscape is in flux—more complicated than this brief summation indicates—and that the elements that make up ritual and belief overlap and intertwine in a bewildering complexity.

Be that as it may, the outcome so far as Ogun is concerned is that he remains firmly embedded in a repertory of mystical ideas that perpetuate ancient themes, yet contribute to the making of new combinations, new religious groupings, and new interpretations of the ultimate questions that have puzzled humans since the beginning of time.

Methods for Uncovering the Meanings of Ogun

Earlier I indicated that devotees see Ogun as having a host of meanings and that they came about historically through continued layerings, fusions, and so on. In one West African community alone at least six separate Ogun themes are developed by as many separate cult groups.[6] If we were to compare meanings in various cult groups on both sides of the Atlantic, a more daunting number of themes would emerge. Suffice it to say here that the variations in meanings and themes are sufficiently marked that we may well ask if Ogun is one god or many. The answer to dealing with variation lies in two propositions. First is the insistence by Durkheim and Mauss (1963:78) that a deity collects and classifies information. The second, by Lévi-Strauss (1966:36), is that information of this sort is not collected randomly.

Attributing certain things to a deity is like placing these things under the same rubric or in the same class. Each class (or "domain" as it should be called when one is dealing with a polytheistic religious system) is ordered according to logical principles. A typical one is the single common denominator principle whereby phenomena are classed according to one feature. Using this principle, one might propose that all things relating to iron belong in the Ogun domain, and therefore this is *the* diagnostic principle for deciding whether or not something is Ogun-related. In some New World contexts, however, iron has receded compared to other elements (Brown, Ch. 4). Likewise, at Yoruba hunters' funerals iron is not a featured symbol (Ajuwọn, Ch. 8). How, then, do we find logic in the way Ogun classes information?

The principle by which Ogun information is classed accepts variation in meanings. Rather than being an exclusive principle, it is inclusive. The technical term for this kind of classification is polythetic.[7] In a polythetic system of classification, no one feature gives definition to a domain. A polythetic system identifies a domain through combinations of features. Again, no one thing need be present to make a deity Ogun. Rather, a sufficient number of features should be present to allow an identification to be made (Douglas 1978:15). A useful way of dealing with polythetic classification is to think, as Wittgenstein proposed, of a chain of "family resemblances," where the

defining attribute changes from one link to the next (Needham 1975:350).
Take, for example, the following sets:

ABCD
AB DE
A CDE
   BC EF.

There is no one monotypic feature that gives definition to all of the sets.
Yet there is sufficient overlap in the features of each set to establish a family
or a chain of overlapping resemblances. In polythetic classifications, stress is
laid on each set's having a simple majority of the defining features, and not
on assigning decisive weight to any one of them.

   Thinking of Ogun as a system of classifying information—according to an
inclusive, or polythetic, principle—shifts the discussion of meaning from singular to plural. It therefore relieves us of finding a single common denominator with which to identify and then compare this divine figure. Taken as a
domain of related ideas, diversity and unity in meaning can then be thought
of as being simultaneously present. One of the most useful implications of
being able to think of meanings in the plural is that we can, by extension,
visualize the processes by which some meanings remain unchanged while, at
the same time, other meanings can be added, subtracted, or altered, little
by little, over time and space. It allows us, further, to make order out of what
seems to be contradiction, diversity, and unevenness. Needless to say, the
logic used by insiders in assigning meanings to a deity's domain is intuitive.
For the outsider, it is artificial and done mainly for heuristic purposes.

   A problem for the outside analyst comes in drawing boundaries, since a
chain of overlapping resemblances can, theoretically, extend indefinitely.
Drawing lines around a domain is like giving a medical diagnosis: a certain
amount of indeterminacy must be accepted. Nevertheless, when certain clusters of symptoms are present, there is a strong indication that the diagnosis
is correct. The rule of thumb when dealing with cultural representations is
to think of a deity's domain as sufficiently porous and adaptable to allow for
creativity, but sufficiently stable to reject distortion.

   Still, a deity does not absorb information randomly. The meanings in a domain do not shift and adapt to new stimuli without consequences. When the
weight of distinctive features in any one domain tips too far in the direction
of another domain we can say that a transformation has taken place. Orpheus
may well have presided over the prototypical domain from which Christ
emerged (Goodenough Vol. IV 1953:36), but over time the Christian messiah
developed his own distinctive features to the extent that a new deity, and with
it a new domain, emerged. Ortiz (Ch. 5) indicates a transformation may be
occurring in the ideology of Ogun in Brazil's fifty-year-old Umbanda religion.
Unlike the older (150 years) Candomblé, which adheres closely to its West
African antecedents, Umbanda represents an authentically Brazilian world
view—a coming together of African, European, and native American ideolo-

gies. As part of this synthesis, Ogun has gained sufficient stature to become a symbol of Brazilian national identity. Ogun of Umbanda is familiar: an aggressive, violent defender in the fight for a just and balanced social order. But more and more he represents the positive side in what Umbanda adherents see as a clear division between good and evil, something that is not done in Candomblé or West African world views. The transformation of the Umbanda Ogun into a force for good is not complete, for he is the only deity in the new Umbanda pantheon who can still move freely between both evil and good forces. Whether or not he will retain an ability to mediate between the two sides, or be compelled to represent only one side, and thus represent a major shift in cognitive orientations, only time will tell.

Given the problems with drawing boundaries, how can we, analytically, delineate domains? A first step is to find *redundance*. Needless to say, we are looking for redundant clusters of meanings, not a single cluster of meanings. A pioneering, but neglected, study that stresses the search for redundance is Erwin Goodenough's twelve-volume examination of religious symbols common to the Mediterranean world in Greco-Roman times that derived from the Old and New Testaments. In it Goodenough is deeply concerned with the problem of bringing objectivity to the task of interpreting the value and meaning of sacred symbols. He suggests that by accumulating scores of repeated cases, we establish a probability, a hypothesis, for assigning meanings, in his case, to symbolic representations (1953 V.I:31). Since this study, but independently, others have followed the same route. In his study of the meanings in Chinese systems of geomancy, Feuchtwang searches for *constant* symbols (1974:13). Obeyesekere's monumental work on the goddess Pattini, found in Hindu, Buddhist, and Jain systems of belief, concentrates on *agreement* (1984:334). And Turner, in his study of the many legends and historic and literary accounts of the twelfth-century tragedy of Thomas Becket, seeks out sequences of events that add up to a *redundant paradigm*, which, he believes, is ultimately drawn from early Christian traditions (1974:60ff) to explain the meaning and experience of martyrdom.[8]

The studies mentioned share the decided advantage of relying on written texts. Ogun is not, or was not until recently, associated with written traditions. His religious systems do not have priests, monks, or other specialists who have regular channels for contacting one another or exchanging ideas. They do not have overarching institutional bodies that standardize, perpetuate, or promulgate the ideology of Ogun. The redundancies that we see in the representations of Ogun, whether Old or New World, are transmitted primarily by word of mouth, among cult priests, priestesses, and adherents, through the repeated telling of traditions, the performance of rituals, and the production and reproduction of emblems and icons. In this, Ogun defies Weberian predictions which suggest that for global expansion to take place, a religious system must have systematic and depersonalized modes for disseminating its ideology. The unities that exist in the diverse body of Ogun representations—as revealed by redundant themes found in many societies

of the two hemispheres—are achieved not with the help of a supporting bureaucratic, codified apparatus, but through the power of custom.

The study of custom in unwritten traditions, while conventionally the preserve of anthropologists, is concentrated in what is now more broadly known
as the symbolic school. Like those who work with texts, humanist and social
scientist adherents of this school try to do two things: interpret cultural representations found in oral traditions, rituals, metaphors, symbols, and artifacts
in ways that are faithful to the actors and, then, translate their findings into
terms that can be appreciated by outsiders. The foundations were laid by
French structuralists, whose well-known work on myths erred in the direction
of interpretations that were so general as to be truisms, and American
ethnoscientists who in studying systems of classification remained too faithful
to cultural context to generalize about what may be universal to these systems. For symbolists, the key to a middle-level analysis has come to rest primarily in their use of methods, recommended above, that elicit redundancies
in cultural meanings and, thanks to the redundance, intepretations that can
be verified.

M. Drewal's study (Ch. 9) of Ogun ritual dance is faithful to the symbolic
school. She demonstrates that the meaning of Ogun is clearly displayed in
the repeated qualities of movement—quick, direct, and forceful, with an explosive release—of dancers and devotees. Not content to limit the analysis
to one level of experience, she also describes the ways performers bombard
the senses—sight, sound, touch, and in some cases taste—with recurring reminders of their deity's distinctive qualities. Dancers carry iron weapons, especially sharp-bladed ones, and refer to a species of snake that is quick and
deadly. The poetic chants that accompany performances contain percussive
sounds and word-images—"he kills with one blow"—that evoke swift destruction. Over and again images of Ogun are impressed upon the observer.

In contrast, a pacific, not to say, poetic—"death has cut off our flower"—
dimension of Ogun is revealed in Ajuwọn's presentation (Ch. 8) of Yoruba
hunters' funerals. Ajuwọn, too, draws on a wide range of ethnographic evidence: chants of funeral musicians, actions of hunting-guild leaders who pre-
side over the ceremonies, and items from the deceased's hunting kit that are
conspicuously displayed. The portrait that emerges is not a ruthless figure,
but a social role model from whom "the wise will draw inspiration." In funeral dirges Ogun is heroic leader—"lion of the thick forest"; provider—
"one who never runs away on sighting a beggar"; protector—"my breadwinner alone"; and so on. An almost limitless repertoire plays on the nurturing
side of the deity, repeatedly presenting the same themes to stress the
point.

Clearly, eliciting the patterns from one context does not reveal the full
meaning of a cultural representation. Thus, a second step is to ask *what* things
people put together, *how* they are put together, and *why*. These questions
are asked by O'Flaherty in an exhaustive study of the mythology of the Hindu
god Siva, who, like Ogun but for different reasons, also is labeled as a

creator/destroyer. These questions, she stresses, allow the outsider to comprehend a deity as subjects comprehend him or her (1973:2, 12). At the risk of oversimplifying a complex argument, it may be said that O'Flaherty asks why Hindu traditions consistently present Siva as erotic, virile, and passionate, on one hand, and as ascetic, pious, and withdrawn on the other. Earlier explanations of these seemingly contradictory traditions were that they either were anomalous or that one set of traits had been imposed on another and therefore was unfaithful to the ancient meaning of Siva. O'Flaherty argued, to the contrary, that both sets of traits are put together for a reason. Like love and hate, the "act of desire and the conquest of desire" are brought together to show that erotic and ascetic impulses are constantly interacting. Each set of impulses produces its own form of "heat" and each presents an unending play on the destructive and creative potential in desire (1973:5, 35).

Accordingly, when we look at Ogun it is not sufficient to extract one set of redundant patterns. If we elicit only the violent qualities of Ogun that are portrayed in the possession-dance context (M. Drewal, Ch. 9), our understanding of Ogun is incomplete. The same is true if, in analyzing Ajuwǫn's funeral context (Ch. 8), we stress only the nurturing and protective side of Ogun. Almost every context presents or in some way alludes to several dimensions of a deity. Babalǫla's study of Ogun songs (Ch. 7) uncovers themes that reveal many sides of the same unity, particularly the strengths and weaknesses that inevitably exist in a single being. And Pemberton's study of kingship ritual (Ch. 6) shows that Ogun is used as a symbol of political life and of many competing, but coexisting, agendas involving order and disorder.

Still in all, no single context explores all possible combinations of meanings that exist in Ogun's domain. Neither do they display the important creative dynamic that leads one set of combinations to generate another set.

When the several interpretations of Ogun in this volume are brought together and compared we find that each of them presents varying insights into the philosophy of life that Ogun embodies. Again, each interpretation is incomplete in some respect, for only in their totality do meanings and intentions become clear to the outside observer and, in some cases, to the insider as well. Drawing on the essays, then, let me offer an interpretation of the complete Ogun.

Interpreting the Meanings of Ogun

It is clear by this point that Ogun is repeatedly linked to positive and negative deeds. As a consequence of his harmful or beneficial acts he is viewed either as a lonely, isolated figure—the quintessential marginal man (Armstrong, Ch. 2)—or, in almost complete contrast, as a central force whose revolutionary and creative acts give birth to new social forms (Barnes and Ben-Amos, Ch. 3). Ogun kills and he creates. The two attributes are joined, for devotees are fully aware that all actions, especially those of leaders, warriors, or benefactors, are as advantageous to some as they are harmful to others.

One of the fundamental thematic combinations, therefore, is that Ogun is both destroyer and creator. These qualities are put together like two sides of an equation: destroyer = creator, or the obverse, creator = destroyer. From these equations it is possible to generate a series of permutations that are all faithful to Ogun. For instance, as a blacksmith, Ogun creates the tools and weapons that, when put to use by some occupational groups, increase productivity, but that also, when put to use by others, destroy the innocent. As a revolutionary warrior he eliminates an old order so that a new one can be established. To aid the powerless members of society, he takes from the powerful. Finally, as a hunter he depletes the natural world in order to nurture his own cultural world.

Rather than resolution, an unending tension is maintained between the two sides of either equation: destruction is creative and creation is destructive. The notion of an equation must be used here, rather than that of paradox or opposition, since the concept of opposition distorts the way devotees perceive their god. In African cosmologies where Ogun is a central figure, destruction and creation are two aspects of a unity that cannot be broken into opposing parts.

On a more abstract level, it can be said that Ogun is a metaphoric representation of the realization that people create the means to destroy themselves. He stands for humans' collective attempts to govern, not what is out of control in nature, but what is out of control in culture. He represents not so much what is inexplicable, unseen, or unknown, as what is known but not under control. He is a symbolic recognition of human limitations—human frailty, as Babalọla (Ch. 7) puts it in his exploration of Ogun's character—and it is this kind of limitation that accounts for his lack of control.

Still the combinations are unfinished, because Ogun also represents human triumphs over limitations. This facet of the deity is exposed by many West African peoples who employ Ogun imagery to mark and celebrate each stage of their societal development. Ogun taught humans to use fire, make iron, build cities, centralize government, conquer neighbors, and create empires. At each step of the way, in this folk model of social change, Ogun is the metaphoric representation of a transformation brought about by human effort (Barnes and Ben-Amos, Ch. 3).

The meanings of Ogun are as rich in philosophy as they are in metaphor. The philosophic wisdom found in Ogun ideology treats the inner experience associated with both destructive and creative acts, and it is particularly poignant in its portrayal of the loneliness that inevitably accompanies either one of them. In a well-known legend and its many variations—all of which focus on civil war, rebellion, and other forms of political conflict—the warrior Ogun sentences himself to eternal isolation, in some versions going so far as to commit suicide, after unwittingly slaying his own people in a frenzy of rage over their lack of "hospitality" (Babalọla Ch. 7). The plight of the human condition is the punishment inflicted by self-insight and self-recognition. Humans realize that their actions have consequences that they cannot predict and, as a result, that no perfect balance can be brought between being in control and being out of control. The sole corrective comes in maintaining vigilance through self-contemplation, and inevitably this is an isolating experience. The message is reinforced in a popular Trinidadian myth in which a warrior-prince kills his favored, invalid brother in a fit of jealousy. As a punishment he is sentenced to guard forever the gates (meaning the morals) of his town and to serve as a solitary reminder to himself and others of the consequences of allowing power to fall out of control.[9]

The inventor or artist, like the warrior or leader, also lives on the margins of society in order to realize sufficient freedom to make the kinds of connections that lead to innovative expression. The dilemma is captured in H. Drewal's discussion (Ch. 10) of Yoruba body artists who struggle to avoid psychic and social isolation. Moreover, it is a recurring theme in the work of Soyinka, who identifies with Ogun and, in a series of essays, poems, and other writings, explores the meaning of the predicament posed by his alter ego. For him, Ogun is a tragic figure because he presides over humans' struggles to master themselves. The Ogun artist either labors to create explanation where there is none, or dooms himself to live in an unbearable void. The predicament is posed as an existential battle between being and nothingness. Balance is achieved through willpower. For Soyinka, *Will* triumphs when the individual is reconciled with "the paradoxical truth of destructiveness and creativeness in acting man" (1969:126).

We could not be humans, so the philosophy of Ogun goes, seeking control of ourselves and our social existence, if we did not experience the out-of-control phases that are necessary parts of reproducing and expanding the powers that make human existence possible. This is the constructive/destructive cycle that must be appreciated if we are to grasp the meanings of Ogun. In the Old World, one of the emblems of Ogun is a snake biting its tail, feeding on itself, and thereby engaging in an unending repetition of destruction in order to regenerate. The image of the snake is consistent with the Ogun world view, wherein what we do to ourselves in a self-destructive way is an inevitable aspect of the self-constructive process. This is our fate. This is what isolates us as a species and as individuals. We know ourselves as others never do. The helplessness that comes from self-knowledge coexists with the power—Soyinka's *Will*—to overcome that helplessness.

The Power in Meaning

The power in the Ogun philosophy of life resides in its plasticity and its transportability. Through a host of related notions, layered and fused onto one another, yet packaged as a single concept, the various creative/ destructive potentials of human existence are recognized and given force. Ogun is a profoundly satisfying symbolic expression of a human dilemma: how to balance the need for constraint against the need for freedom. In belief systems of West African origin, this dilemma is reconciled through a supernatural transformation. The power of the idea is given form, a named identity, for example Ogun, so as to control it and then draw inner strength from that control.

Ogun, and appropriately so for a deity, has an ability to bring together notions from worldly and spiritual realms. So in the old Kingdom of Ila, civic unrest brought about by competition among powerful segments of the community is interpreted as divine anger. Pemberton (Ch. 6) aptly sums it up as the sacrality of violence. The notions from each realm are presented as extremes, for this is the way, well-known to students of myth, that a people's preoccupations are heightened, given weight, remembered, and passed on. Extremes make the point. The universe, as we view it through a deity's eyes, is revealed by the ways in which extreme thoughts and extreme deeds complement and balance one another.

The meanings of a deity are revealed, in great measure therefore, by knowing which extremes are put together and why. In the case of Ogun, the notions of control/lack of control, sacrality/violence, or protection/destruction are brought into a perpetual state of interaction for a reason. Only when the pairs are complete is a balance of power reached.

In the world view of the peoples who include Ogun in their cosmic realm, power is a single, neutral force. There is a marked contrast here between West African and Western Christian modes of thought. In the West, positive and negative—familiarly glossed as evil and good—can be divided into opposing parts and symbolized by Satan and God. In West Africa, positive and negative power is not separate. Power is singular, and therefore what we in the West see as dual and capable of being divided into two mystical notions cannot be divided in African thought. For the latter, power exists in a single supernatural representation.[10]

Indeed, it is unthinkable that superhuman figures—mirroring as they do the human condition—display only one side of their character. The duty of devotees is not to appeal to one aspect of their divine benefactors. Their duty is to bring all of their aspects—their full supernatural equations, as it were—into balance through sacrifice and other ritual ministrations, just as they try to bring balance and harmony into everyday life.

In bringing together ideas from different levels of experience, and showing their complementarity, the African world view is designed to balance what is otherwise out of balance. In this way, a divinity suggests a theory of the way the world works. A theory of this type is significant in that it is stated metaphorically, viz., a creator is a destroyer.

Ogun is a metaphor, but not a simple metaphor. Simple metaphors liken one thing to another: "screaming headlines" or "heart of stone." They are applied for a specific purpose to a specific event, person, or thing. Thus they do a one-time job; they are ephemeral. They cannot be changed, for to change them is to lose them. Perhaps this is the reason that simple metaphors are used mainly in studies of world view that are limited to local, monocultural situations.[11]

Ogun is a root metaphor (see Pepper 1966:91–92). A root metaphor *names* the things that are likened to one another. The name gives the root metaphor permanence and therefore it can do its job many times over. When a psychiatrist says his patient is suffering from an *Oedipus* complex he can name and summarize what otherwise might take pages to explain, and he can use the label repeatedly. By the same token, when Haitian devotees call a despotic leader *Ogun Panama*, after a real figure, they condense into one label a complex historical essay on the uses and abuses of power (Brown, Ch. 4). *Ogun Panama* was first applied to one person; later other despotic leaders were given the same label. By naming the metaphor, Haitians were free to adjust or augment its content.

The concept of root metaphor is a middle-level analytical tool. Other such concepts are *emphatic symbol*, which is applied to the Christian cross; *root paradigm*, applied to Christian martyrs; *conceptual archetype* and *archetype*, applied elsewhere to Ogun himself.[12] Root metaphor, like the other concepts, focuses on cultural representations by hovering between two levels of analysis: one that stays close to the empirical ground, as does ethnoscience, and another that soars to the language of universal principles such as deep structures of the mind, as does structuralism. Root metaphor operates on a middle level because it is an abstraction. Yet it is an abstraction formulated by the minds that are being explored. As such, a generalization about the phenomenon under consideration already has been made. Furthermore, this generalization lends itself to interpretations that can be confirmed either by the actors or, on the basis of recurring patterns, by the analyst. Because it is created by the actors, the generalization retains its cultural uniqueness. But because it is an abstraction, it lends itself to being translated from the terms of one culture into those of another.

Ultimately, once a root metaphor is named it becomes a protected category within which many ways of replicating, restating, or reformulating an idea can be tried out. The greater its ability to incorporate and adapt to new experience, the more powerful it becomes. This is why a root metaphor such as Ogun has the power to operate cross-culturally. The meanings contained in the root metaphor are the result of interactions that, once energized, are capable of acting on their own to incorporate an ever-wider range of insights and meanings (Turner 1974:28–29). Hence the permanent, named quality of the metaphor is the package that makes a domain of ideas dynamic, and that allows the ideas to expand, spread, and change over time.

Discussion and Conclusion

I opened this chapter with the suggestion that reorientations are needed if we wish to explain the popularity of an African deity, and the growing strength of the religious systems in which he is a significant figure, in light of predictions that global deities and global faiths would eliminate small ones. Let me summarize the responses to this challenge by first indicating why previous orientations lead us astray.

One of the stumbling blocks in the study of contemporary religious processes comes from the fact that religious systems are still typologized. By now this is an implicit act. Perhaps the best known explicit typology was brought to life by Weber (1946:292–97; 1963:1–19) and elaborated by his followers as the great and little religious traditions (e.g., Marriott 1955:171–72). Because these categories were grounded in an evolutionary perspective, the tendency when the two types of system were studied in the same frame of reference was—and here is where the legacy persists—to give the great traditions, such as Islam or Christianity, a central position and the little traditions a peripheral one. The rationale for the dominance of great traditions is that they have highly developed bureaucratic organizations, standardized and written doctrines, institutionalized methods for promulgating beliefs, and highly developed systems of ethics. In comparison, little traditions are characterized as fragmented, localized, and largely associated with illiteracy. When these attributes are compared, global ideologies are seen to influence; little ideologies, to respond. Given the evolutionary bias, the very act of typing religious systems has the effect of predetermining the direction of change: participants of small systems are converted to, or their ideologies are merged with, or replaced by, world systems. As Weber put it, the stronger systems vanquish the weaker (1963:17).

Although I have reduced the arguments to their stark essentials—for they are more subtle in their totality than can be indicated here—I have done so to call attention to the role typologies continue to play in shaping our thinking about religious change. The kind of weighted typology that stems from Weber and great and little tradition writers clearly obscures the vitality of small religious ideologies even when they do survive and thrive. At least one scholar has attempted to rectify the problem by calling attention to an extraordinary migration and fusion of ideas, taken from all types of religious systems, which he goes so far as to call a contemporary worldwide religious revolution (Wilson 1976:42). We know that the changes associated with this revolution have no correlation with the types of system that are spreading or the types of ideologies that are mixed together. But in other respects, actual investigations of these recent ideological migrations and their implications are still in their infancy.

There is a need, then, to shift the point of reference away from studies that take as a starting point the fact that global faiths and their deities dominate the religious landscape. Instead, we need to start from the premise that several religious traditions may coexist in one context, and that participants may be bi-religious, and to work through the complexity that ensues from these reoriented perspectives.

Typologies offer a second challenge, in that they also classify deities according to the systems of which they are a part. Weber thought of them as urban and pagan (1963:xli). The stumbling block in this case is that deities are categorized according to the sphere in which they operate (universal or parochial) or their functional relationship with followers (personal or impersonal), but not according to what they mean. In an influential series of articles, Horton (1971 and 1975) takes a similar approach. He argues that the efficacy of the high gods of universal faiths derives from their being sufficiently abstract, all-explaining, all-knowing, and all-encompassing to provide ideological bridges between diverse peoples who seek a common code for their interactions. By contrast, the lesser deities are limited by their specificity. They fail to link diverse peoples together, because they are concrete, because they are parochial and therefore tied to concrete places and groups, and because they represent only part of the cosmos. They are like the ancient Roman god Mercury, who represented a few parts of the universe—commerce, manual skill, eloquence, cleverness, travel, and thievery—and who therefore depended on a full pantheon to provide a complete cosmological explanatory system for Rome's faithful. Finally, the deities of parochial religious systems focus on pragmatic functions, and in this they differ from most Western religious systems. African religions tend to dwell on predicting, explaining, and controlling day-to-day circumstances such as illness, poverty, infertility, or bad luck; Ogun followers focus particularly on their fear of accidents and other dangers. Stress on pragmatism is a part of non-Western traditions to a greater degree than in Western religious traditions, which put strong emphasis on transcendental functions, such as preparing for the hereafter or helping devotees gain faith or inner "grace."

While Horton's typology and others like it can be faulted in their inability to capture a vast middle range of supernatural types, or to explore the degrees to which transcendental or pragmatic levels of involvement are truly meaningful, the more fundamental problem is that the qualities used to compare and contrast divinities are inappropriate to the levels of explanation that are sought.

The power of an ideology or a deity to gain a privileged place in the world resides, in large part, in what it explains and in the way the explanation is communicated. This is the second point to which we need to be reoriented. The measure of universality of a supernatural figure need not be ascertained from qualities that define, say, a deity's impersonal or personal relationship to a follower, or a deity's ability to function in all or part of the cosmos, or even a deity's pragmatic or transcendental relationship with a devotee. The ability to appeal to a universal, by which I mean culturally plural, audience rests on what a deity means: what, in fact, a deity signifies, symbolizes, suggests, and intends and the ways these elements are expressed. As with many world figures—Oedipus, Siva, Aphrodite, or Thor—the abilities to capture and then communicate one part of the human experience are the very qualities that give such figures a metacultural appeal.

All deities provide a theory of what life is about and resolutions to the problems life raises. The more economically and profoundly a theory of life is expressed, the more likely it is to transcend the limitations of one place or one culture, that is, the more likely it is to become a world theory (Pepper 1966:92). Some theories of human nature, like scientific theories, are more profound than others in the ideas they bring together. The theory of relativity is one of them. Some theories, like metaphors, have great powers to explain life's mysteries because they combine notions from different levels of experience. They fill voids. They explain the ways the world works, in succinct, easy-to-comprehend and easy-to-apply ways. When it comes to the Oguns of the world, we need to know from what philosophical principles they derive, and what they express and do for the people concerned. Meanings can bring them to the forefront of our consciousness. The meanings attached to a divinity determine which explanations of life we reject and which explanations, to return to the point with which this essay began, we elevate to a privileged class.

NOTES

1. To be consistent, I use the Nigerian spelling of Ogun throughout. He is Gu in the People's Republic of Benin (formerly Dahomey), Ogum in Brazil, and Ogou in Haiti. Other variants are given in Armstrong (Ch. 2).

2. Local and general (metacultural) ideology need not be homogeneous, as Tambiah shows in his study of Thai Buddhist spirit cults. There is a constant interaction between the two levels, but there are quite specific, local ways of working through an idea. Looking at local traditions is useful, he suggests, for illuminating ancient ideologies, although the conclusions are never more than "inspired guesswork" (1970:369–72).

3. This ceremony is held by Igala and Idoma peoples, who live near the confluence of the Niger and Benue rivers in today's Nigeria. A similar ceremony was performed in Abomey, capital of the Old Kingdom of Dahomey. For a discussion of the latter, and a map showing locations of the three groups of people in question, see Map 3.1.

4. Evidence for Ogun's growth comes primarily from southwestern Nigeria. In 1939 a Yoruba scholar felt Ogun was one of the four or five most widespread deities (Fadipẹ 1970:261). By the 1960s researchers felt Ogun was possibly the most widely venerated national deity (Parratt and Doi 1969:112). It is significant to note in this respect that Ogun's popularity did not decline, but grew, at the same time there was a sharp decline in the numbers of hunters, smiths, smelters, and warriors, who were the core of Ogun's following in precolonial times but who were replaced by the introduction of Western technology and colonial restrictions on internal warfare. See also Barnes (1980:36–37).

5. The popularity of Umbanda is discussed by Hoge 1983, Pressel 1980, and Lerch 1980.

6. Deirdre LaPin, personal communication. See also Barnes (1980:20).

7. I am indebted to Ivan Karp for suggesting that the polythetic principle is applicable here.

8. Others who stress similar approaches are Keyes, who focuses on the ideology of Karma (1983), and Friedrich, who examines the goddess Aphrodite (1978).

9. I thank Patricia Alleyne for bringing this myth to my attention. See Elder (1972:25–26).

10. Watts treats the Western tendency to make separations and suggests that the illusion of opposition interferes with our ability to grasp essential continuities (1963).

11. Rosaldo and Atkinson (1975) make use of metaphors to show the relationship between beliefs about human health and principles of nature in Ilongot (Philippine) world view.

12. For more detailed discussion and application of these concepts see Firth (1973:91), Turner (1978:248), Black (1962:241), and Verger (1982:32–33).

References Cited

Barnes, Sandra T. 1980. *Ogun: An Old God for a New Age*, Philadelphia: ISHI.

Barnet, Miguel (ed.). 1968. *The Autobiography of a Runaway Slave*, by Esteban Montejo, New York: Pantheon.

Bascom, William. 1987. "The Olojo Festival at Ife, 1937," in *Time Out of Time: Essays on the Festival*, A. Falassi (ed.), Albuquerque: University of New Mexico Press, pp. 62–73.

Bastide, Roger. 1978. *The African Religions of Brazil: Toward a Sociology of the Interpenetration of Civilizations*, H. Sebba (trans.), Baltimore: Johns Hopkins University Press.

Black, Max. 1962. *Models and Metaphors*, Ithaca: Cornell University Press.

Douglas, Mary. 1978. *Cultural Bias*, Occasional Paper 34, The Royal Anthropological Institute of Great Britain and Ireland.

Durkheim, E., and M. Mauss. 1963. *Primitive Classification*, Chicago: University of Chicago Press.

Elder, J. D. (ed.). 1972. *Ma Rose Point: An Anthology of Rare Legends and Folk Tales from Trinidad & Tobago*, Port-of-Spain: National Cultural Council of Trinidad and Tobago.

Fadipẹ, N. A. 1970. *The Sociology of the Yoruba*, Ibadan: University of Ibadan Press.

Feuchtwang, Stephan D. R. 1974. *An Anthropological Analysis of Chinese Geomancy*, Ventiane, Laos: Vithagna.

Firth, Raymond. 1973. *Symbols: Public and Private*, London: Athlone.

Friedrich, Paul. 1978. *The Meaning of Aphrodite*, Chicago: University of Chicago Press.

Geertz, Clifford. 1960. *The Religion of Java*, New York: The Free Press.

Goodenough, Erwin R. 1953. *Jewish Symbols in the Greco-Roman Period*, 12 vols., New York: Pantheon.

Hageman, Alice. 1973. "Santería in Black Experience," *Cuba Resource Center Newsletter*, V.2(6):15–20.

Herskovits, Melville. 1937. "African Gods and Catholic Saints in New World Negro Belief," *American Anthropologist*, XXXIX(4):635–43.

———. 1958. *The Myth of the Negro Past*, Boston: Beacon Press (first pub. 1941).

Hoge, Warren. 1983. "Macumba: Brazil's Pervasive Cults," *New York Times Magazine*, Aug. 21, pp. 30–33, 75–82.

Horton, Robin, 1971. "African Conversion," *Africa*, 41(2):85–108.

———. 1975. "On the Rationality of Conversion," Pts. I and II, *Africa*, 45(3):219–35 and (4):373–99.

Jones, Adam. 1983. *German Sources for West African History, 1599–1669*, Weisbaden: Franz Steiner Verlag.

Keyes, Charles F. 1983. "Introduction: The Study of Popular Ideas of Karma," in *Karma: An Anthropological Inquiry*, C. F. Keyes and E. V. Daniel (eds.), Berkeley and Los Angeles: University of California Press, pp. 1–24.

Lerch, Patricia B. 1980. "Spirit Mediums in Umbanda Evangelizada of Porto Alegre, Brazil: Dimensions of Power and Authority," in *A World of Women*, E. Bourguignon (ed.), New York: Praeger.

Lévi-Strauss, Claude. 1966. *The Savage Mind*, Chicago: University of Chicago Press.

Marriott, McKim. 1955. "Little Communities in an Indigenous Civilization," in *Studies in the Little Community*, M. Marriott (ed.), Chicago: University of Chicago Press.

Mintz, S. W., and R. Price. 1976. *An Anthropological Approach to the Afro-American Past: A Caribbean Perspective*, Philadelphia: ISHI.

Needham, Rodney. 1975. "Polythetic Classification," *Man* NS V.10(3):349–69.

Obeyesekere, Gananath. 1984. *The Cult of the Goddess Pattini*, Chicago: University of Chicago Press.

O'Flaherty, Wendy D. 1973. *Asceticism and Eroticism in the Mythology of Siva*, London: Oxford University Press.

Parratt, J. K., and A. R. I. Doi. 1969. "Syncretism in Yorubaland: A Religious or a Sociological Phenomenon," *Practical Anthropology*, 16(3):109–13.

Pepper, Stephen C. 1966. *World Hypotheses: A Study in Evidence*, Berkeley and Los Angeles: University of California Press.

Pressel, Esther. 1980. "Spirit Magic in the Social Relations between Men and Women (São Paulo, Brazil)," in E. Bourguignon (ed.), *A World of Women*, New York: Praeger.

Rosaldo, M. Z., and J. M. Atkinson. 1975. "Man the Hunter and Woman: Metaphors for the Sexes in Ilongot Magical Spells," in R. Willis (ed.), *The Interpretation of Symbols*, New York: John Wiley & Sons, pp. 43–75.

Scheub, Harold. 1975. *The Xhosa Ntsomi*, Oxford: Oxford University Press.

Soyinka, Wole. 1967. *Idanre and Other Poems*, London: Methuen.

———. 1969. "The Fourth Stage," in D. W. Jefferson (ed.), *The Morality of Art*, London: Routledge & Kegan Paul, pp. 119–34.

Tambiah, S. J. 1970. *Buddhism and the Spirit Cults in North-East Thailand*, Cambridge: Cambridge University Press.

Thompson, R. F. 1983. *Flash of the Spirit*, New York: Random House.

Turner, Victor W. 1974. *Dramas, Fields and Metaphors: Symbolic Action in Human Society*, Ithaca: Cornell University Press.

———. 1978. *Image and Pilgrimage in Christian Culture*, New York: Columbia University Press.

van der Merwe, N. J., and D. H. Avery. 1987. "Science and Magic in African Technology: Traditional Iron Smelting in Malawi," *Africa* 57(2):143–72.

Verger, Pierre F. 1982. *Orisha: Les Dieux Yorouba en Afrique et en Nouveau Monde*, Paris: Editions A. M. Métailié.

Watts, Alan W. 1963. *The Two Hands of God: The Myth of Polarity*, New York: Collier Books.

Weber, Max. 1946. *From Max Weber*, H. H. Gerth and C. Wright Mills (ed. and trans.), New York: Oxford University Press.

————. 1963. *The Sociology of Religion*, E. Fischoff (trans.), Boston: Beacon Press (first pub. in German, 1922).

Williams, Denis. 1974. *Icon and Image: A Study of Sacred and Secular Forms of African Classical Art*, London: Allen Lane.

Wilson, Bryan. 1976. *Contemporary Transformations of Religion*, Oxford: Oxford University Press.

PART ONE

The History and Spread of Ogun in Old and New Worlds

Robert G. Armstrong

2

The Etymology of the Word "Ògún"

The cult of Ògún is highly elaborated in Yoruba country and shows amazing vitality among people directly concerned with modern technology. In 1974, for example, the drivers of the Ibadan University Motor Transport system performed a sacrifice to Ògún in the presence of the Vice-Chancellor and a dozen or so of the other high officials of the university. One of the drivers, who came from Igara, an Igbira (or Ebira) town in the northwestern extension of Bendel State, was a particularly enthusiastic participant in the dances that followed the sacrifice of a dog. I cite this case as an illustration of the point made by Barnes that the Ògún cult continues to appeal to socially rather marginal men who are directly involved in the use of modern machines constructed largely of iron and steel. She goes so far as to call the Ògún cult "the cult of revolution," i.e., "the technological revolution brought about by the introduction of iron-making and the occupational specialization necessitated by that innovation" (1980:44).

As a deity, Ògún (and his cult, which is very male-oriented) was traditionally especially concerned with the smelting and forging of iron, with war, and with hunting. As Barnes says, it seems likely that the Yoruba cult is an amalgam and synthesis of originally separate cults. It has long been known that the cult is by no means restricted to the Yoruba. Indeed, an examination of the cult as it appears outside the Yoruba area (see Map 3.1) may well clarify its origins and some of the deepest meanings attached to it.

In Dahomey, now the Republic of Benin, Gŭ is the god of iron and of war. Herskovits (1938:105–107), in discussing the cult, does not mention a connection with hunting but says Gŭ is the god of metal, himself a smith, and the god of war. He is the third-ranking member of the pantheon, coming right after Mawú and Lísa. Fr. Segurola, a missionary with many years experience

with the Fon of Dahomey, writes: "Gŭ, fétiche des forgerons, dieu des armes
et de la guerre. C'est la déité de ceux qui travaillent le fer ou qui l'utilisent.
On lui réserve la ferraille ainsi que les animaux tués accidentellement par le
fer" (1963:194). I translate: "Gŭ: fetish of the blacksmiths, god of weapons
and of war. The deity of those who produce iron or who use it. Scrap iron
is reserved for him as well as animals accidentally killed by iron."

According to Herskovits (ii, 107), the god of hunters and the bush is Agè,
who ranks immediately after Gŭ in the sky pantheon. Herskovits says of an
earlier writer, "Le Hérissé . . . errs in making Agè the Earth god" (1938:107,
note). On linguistic grounds we suspect that le Hérissé may not be wrong.
In Idoma, which is a very conservative Kwa language, Earth is àjè or àgyè,
and its cult is directly and basically concerned with the hunt. Segurola
(1963:21) says: "Àgé, la Terre, divinité née de l'union de Lisa avec Mawu:
on honore ensemble ces trois divinités," "Àgé, the Earth, divinity born of
the union of Lisa with Mawu: these three divinities are honored together."[1]
In Dahomey, it would seem, the cults of iron and of the hunt are separate;
and the hunt is associated with the cult of the Earth, as in Idoma, east of
the Niger.

In Benin, according to Melzian (1937), Ògún is "the god of iron, smiths,
hunters and warriors; one of the highest gods in rank. . . . The sacrifices consist mainly of dogs, tortoises and snails, and oil must be used in them." This
set of ideas and symbols is closely similar to the Yoruba cult.[2]

Barnes, after recognizing the role of "the hunter tradition" in the Ògún
cult, speaks of "the earth tradition" as well. The main source is an old one
(Ellis 1894), but this report, from Offa, seems well-founded. It fits with the
myth of Ògún's disappearance, by sinking into the earth, and with the close
association of the Idoma Earth cult with hunting. There is also the association
of elephant symbolism with Ògún. Erinlè, "elephant of the earth," is regarded as the god of the bush (Williams 1974:91). He is also a hunter deity,
and according to one story, he too disappeared into the earth, after turning
himself into an elephant. Pa Adeniji (personal communication) says Erinlè
was a follower of Ògún. A warrior who was a hunter too, Erinlè was also
interested in agriculture, especially as a fertility god. He became an elephant
and sank into the ground, reemerging as a river. Barnes (1980:23) thinks of
him as a possible source of the elephant symbolism associated with Ògún.
For an example of this, one may consider the myth of the hunter Tìmọyìn,
who founded the city of Oshogbo. He was a priest of Ògún, and one day
killed a female elephant who was in the act of giving birth—a very serious
breach of taboo. Tìmọyìn established a shrine for the worship of the elephant
calf and became Ògún Tìmọyìn, himself an incarnation of Ògún (Wenger
1980:134–38). (The artist Susanne Wenger created a large batik wall hanging
on this theme, in which the elephant in parturition forms the central figure—a
very bold artistic theme indeed!) It is interesting that at the central town of
the Ògún cult, Ìré, no objects of Ògún worship are fashioned of iron (Wil-

liams 1974:84). It would appear that as we go east, the hunter symbolism becomes relatively more important in the Ògún cult.

East of the Niger, there is a quite different set of ideas and practices that, nevertheless, seem related to the Ògún cults of the Yoruba and the Edo peoples (including Benin). A fundamental difference is that groups like the Idoma, Tiv, and even the Igala do not have gods hierarchically arranged in pantheons like those of the Yoruba or the Bini. The really ancient Idoma religion consisted of Earth and Ancestors, rather like the religion of the Tallensi of northern Ghana, as described by Fortes (1945, 1949). The idea of a high god (Qwọicō) came from the Moslems, according to one very knowledgeable elder. There are local spirits and "medicines" or charms, but these have restricted fields of effectiveness. We do not find gods with personalities and histories who interact with each other, who are represented in works of art, and who govern whole areas of life. It is perhaps fair to say that pantheons are more typical of hierarchically organized states than of stateless societies or societies where the state is a creature of the lineages.

A key concept in Idoma male society is ògwú (Armstrong 1968:122). It has not proved easy to define, but its various uses may be illustrated. The crowing of a cock is ògwú, used with the verb tá, "to throw": ó gē tógwú, "he is crowing." There is a special ògwú call accompanied by a handflap over the mouth. Using it is the privilege of a successful hunter or someone who has killed a man and taken his head. Such a person has "made his ògwú" (yógwú). When a man has killed a fierce animal, like a lion, a leopard, a bush-cow, or an elephant, or has taken a head, he must undergo the ceremony called èōgwóōnà, "washing ògwú from the face." For a long time we translated this as "washing pride from the face," since ògwú, or "making ògwú," is a high honor, rather like getting a medal for valor in European or American armies. Another reason for the ceremony is that without it, the spirit of the slain enemy or animal may trouble the victorious warrior or successful hunter, and he may cause trouble at home. From a sociological point of view, èōgwóōnà may be regarded as the resocialization of a dangerous hero, the acclamation of his brave deed, accompanied by the cleansing of the spirit of the dead animal or man from his face. It is significant that the washing is usually done by a blacksmith at his forge.

From a linguistic point of view, the word ògwú is as similar to "Ògún" as it can be, given the different sound systems of Yoruba and Idoma. The vowels and tones are identical, given the fact that Idoma has no nasal vowels. Both have the consonant "g"; and the "w" after "g" is inevitable before "u" in uncompounded words in Idoma. Both words are intimately connected with war, hunting, and ironworking. In other words, there is a strong case for regarding "ògwú" and "Ògún" as cognates.

The word ògú, in the same sense as Idoma ògwú, also occurs in Igala, according to my Igala colleague, Dr. Ìdáchàbá, of the Ibadan Department of Agricultural Economics. The near-mad behavior of a successful killer is called *é-dógū*: *é-*, infinitive prefix, *dá*, "to cut," *ògú*. The water of a blacksmith's forge is used to cool him down. Tom Miachi, an Igala postgraduate student of anthropology, adds that the Igala word may be *ògú* or *ògwú* in different subdialects. He too says the ceremony of "washing *ògwú* from the face" is practiced in Igala for the same reasons as in Idoma. He gives me the Igala phrase "*é-gwèjóògwú*": analytically *é-*, infinitive prefix; *gwè*, "wash"; *éjú*, "eye, face"; *ògwú*. He agrees that an Igbo origin for the word seems plausible, and that "killing," as an abstraction, is a good translation for it. He also agrees that the Igala do not have "gods" in the Yoruba sense of "*òrìṣá*."

Sidney Kasfir has suggested (personal communication) that Idoma "*ògwú*" may derive from Igbo "*ògbú*," "killer." The verb "to kill" in Igbo is "*gbú*," probably cognate with Idoma "*ŋmó*."[3] Williamson, in her Igbo-English Dictionary (1972:153), says, "*ògbú ḿmādù*, 'man-killer'; a much coveted honour in the olden days; conferred on anyone who possessed a human head." The "*ò-*" prefix is for the agent, the doer of an act. The vowels and tones are identical with those of "*ògwú*"; the consonant, "*-gb-*," is a lightly imploded "*b*." It is produced by a movement of the back of the tongue toward the velum in combination with lip closure and is therefore to be regarded as a labio-velar consonant. The different articulation of Idoma "*-gw-*" is also labio-velar. The prima facie case for regarding Igbo "*ògbú*" as cognate with Idoma "*ògwú*" is strong, since both are used in the context of killing and taking a head.

Accepting this hypothesis, we may proceed to retranslate "*èōgwóōnà*" as "washing the killing from the face." Three Idoma informants agree that this translation makes excellent sense. The late King of Otukpó Land, speaking of the Lion Shrine (*Idu*) in the bush, said that it is the place where, "When one kills a person they wash it [i.e., the killing] from his face." He does not actually use the word "*ògwú*," but it is quite clear from the context that that is what he is talking about (unpublished tape-recorded interview, 1973, paragraph 24).

If we accept the hypothetical chain of cognation "*Ògún-ògwú-ògbú*," then in Igbo we arrive at a form that can be analyzed into other morphemes: *ò-gbú*, "killer," a verbal noun. Neither the Idoma nor the Yoruba forms can be analyzed further into meaningful parts.

Returning to the Idoma, we should also note that "*ògwú*" is an abstraction, not a god. It refers to hunting, to war, and to iron. Its relationship to iron-working is seen in the fact that it is usually the blacksmith who "washes the killing from the face" of the hunter or the warrior. He does it with medicinal leaves that have been dipped into the wooden trough of water in the forge which is used in the quenching of red-hot iron or steel implements after they have been heated, in contact with charcoal, to harden them. The following text was written, at my suggestion, in Idoma by a postgraduate student at the University of Ibadan, Ádā Ọkau, who comes from the Ọgllɛwu district of central Idoma (Otukpó Local Government Area). He had inquired about *ògwú* at home. I have edited it linguistically and translated it. One can see

from this text both the differences and the underlying similarities between
the Idoma concept of *ogwú* and the Yoruba cult of the god *òrìṣà* Ògún. Ọkau
says that this ceremony is not secret.

Eyī kÓgwúōna[4]

Ogwú wucē bɔ̄bí nɔ̄cɛ gboóōya eko nó lɔ̄cɛ ŋmó ámāŋ eko nó lɛbé
kíijile ŋmó. Ẹbé nōo webé kíijile ā wɛyī, ɛjɛ, mlaágábá. Ucē bɔ̄bi
nɔ̄coŋmɔ́ɔ̄cɛ gē yá ā wɛ ka hínīī: ó gē kɛlā lɛ bɔ̄cɛ nōo le jɛɛ́lɛ́ āa. Ó
gé yɔ̄ ī hīyē kɔ́ɔ̄cɛ nó ŋmó ɔ́māa (ɔ́dāŋ nó jíyē kúnū). Ó káa gē máācɛ
dóodu lɛ bɔ̄dā né lɔfú bɛ̄ɛ kanúṁ māa. ĀcĪdɔ̄ma gē ka ka hínīī: Ọ̄cɛ ɔ́māa
yɔ̄ ī jogwú. Eko dóodu nɔ̄cɛ gboóōjogwú lɛ āa, ācɛ géē ka kéē lɔ̄cɛ
ɔ́māa bī nyɔ̄ kéē lɔ́ eyī kógwú na céé kóō gboóōyúcōolɔhi. Ọdā nōo yá ɛ́ɛ́
nēeyī kógwúōna ī wā ā yɔ́ɔ̄.

Ẹdɔ kɔ́ɔ̄cɛ nōo gē naācɛ eyī kógwú ā waóonɔ̄wá (ábíije). Ọdā nūuwá
gē bī le neyī ā wɛ: ēpū kókōpī, ɔbúgwū ámāŋ́ kidaŋgbɔ, eŋ́ŋkpɔ̄. Uwá
géē neyī nyāa ɛgɛ nábíije gē yúkĪlɔ́ āa (ɔwá).

Eko nábíije gaáā neyī nyā ó le yɛ tɔ́ɔwá mlɔɔ̄cɛ nōo ŋmɔ́ɔ̄cɛ ámāŋ́ kɛbé
āa. Ó leŋ́ŋkpɔ̄ tāagbada nōo yīipɔ́wá āa. Ipéŋ́ŋkpɔ̄ nyā ó kwéēpū kókōpī
í tá gɔɔ́. Ó lɔbúgwū ámāŋ́ kidaŋgbɔ hɔ́ɔkɔ céé kóoyī kóō pé típéŋ́ŋkpɔ̄
āa. Eŋ́ŋkpɔ̄ nōo yɔ̄ nyā nábíije gē bī ɛ́ɛ́ nó gē noŋmɔ́ɔ̄cɛ eyī á. Ó géē
bī eŋ́ŋkpɔ̄ nyā i nɔɔ́ eī (igbɛtá ɛ̄cēéi) jāā lɛ bɛ̄ŋ kɛ̄cɛ̄ɛnɛ ámāŋ́ kɛ̄cāhāpa.
Ẹplĺéeko nōo yɔ̄ nyāa, ɔ̄cɛ nōo ŋmɔ́ɔ̄cɛ ā géē gboóōyúcōolɔhi.

Ọdā nōo bī onɔ̄wá ipéyī kógwúōna ā wɛ ka hínīī: anú wɔ̄cɛ nōo gē
niyó kágbe nācɛ gē bī tɔ́té ámāŋ́ koōŋmɔ́ɔ̄cɛ ā á.

Washing *Ògwú* from the Face[5]

"*Ogwú* is the bad behavior that a person begins to display when he
has killed a person or when he has killed a fierce animal. The animals
which are fierce are the African buffalo ["bush-cow"], the leopard, and
the lion. The bad behavior that the killer of a person displays is that he
talks like a person who is crazy; he calls the name of the person he has
killed (if he knows his name); and he regards everybody as not being
as strong as he is. The Idoma people [then] say, 'That man is crazed
by *ogwú*.' Whenever a man begins to be crazed with *ogwú*, people say
that *ogwú* must be washed from his face so that he may begin to behave
properly. It is this that brings [the ceremony of] washing *ogwú* from the
face.

"The sort of persons who wash *ogwú* from a person's face are the
blacksmiths (*ábíije*).[6] The things that they use for washing the face are
leaves of the *okōpī* [meni[7] oil tree], a cock or a duck, and water. They
will wash this face at the place where the blacksmith works [the forge].

"When the blacksmith is about to wash this face, he goes to the forge
with the man who has killed a person or an animal. He pours water into

the trough[8] that is in the forge. Into this water he dips the leaves of *okōpī*. He cuts off the head of the cock or the duck so that blood may flow into the water. This water is what the blacksmith uses when he washes the face of the killer. He will use this water to wash his face (three times a day) for four, or even seven days. At that time, the man who has killed a person will begin to behave well.

"The thing that brings the blacksmith into the washing of *ogwú* from the face is the fact that it is he who forges the weapons that people use in hunting or in killing a person."

A Yoruba authority, Pa Adeniji, reports that water for quenching iron is similarly used in Yorubaland to "wash Ògún" (*Ó wèGún*, "He washed Ògún"; and *Ògún wíwè,* "washing Ògún"). The washing strengthens the hunter or warrior and protects him from the spirits of the animals or enemies he has killed. The water is kept at the forge in a basin called *ọpọ́n omi* or *ọpọ́n àgbèdè.* The distinction between quenching and tempering (by air or sand cooling) iron is well understood, as is also the case in Idoma—and in Tiv, for that matter (Steve Tilley, personal communication).

Hunting is one of the oldest human activities, going far back into the Lower Paleolithic. War probably comes in the Neolithic with agriculture, which provides the surpluses that make the organization of war possible and give it a worthwhile target. Ironworking comes much later and produces the end of the Neolithic. Each of these occupations is present in the Ògún concept, which appears to be very ancient—given the presence of the cognate in Fon, Edo (Bini), Idoma, Igala, Igbo, and Yoruba languages, although these must be regarded as an ancient set of culture words associated with the spread of the cultlike syndrome of ideas, probably westward from Igbo to Yoruba and Fon. The forms "*ògbú - ògwú - ògú - Ògún - Gŭ*" are cognates by borrowing. They are paralleled in all these languages by a series of older genetic cognates for "kill," all of which begin with a labio-velar consonant: Igbo *gbú,* Idoma *ŋmó, ŋmgbó,* Igala *kpa,* Benin *gbé,* Yoruba *kpa,* Fon *hù* (cf. the related Ewe *wù* and *hù*; "*w*" and "*h*" before "*u*" are labio-velar articulations).

My point is that the hunting, and later the warrior, aspects that are so significant in the Ògún cult of the Yoruba are not sufficiently emphasized by Barnes, who looks to the more recent iron-making revolution (ca. 2,000 years ago) as an event that may have stimulated the cult's beginnings. On linguistic grounds, 2,000 years is not a bad guess for the phonetically eroded *ògbú-Ògún* set. These words may be compared with such early Christian words in English as "priest," from Greek "*presbyteros,*" and "bishop," from Greek "*epíscopos.*" The symbolism of washing with the blacksmith's quenching water gives us a kind of *terminus a quo.* The amalgam and synthesis of ideas and practices that are found in the Ògún cult, however, may well have roots that extend far more deeply into the past.

It would be interesting in the examination of Ògún's past to study the relation of hunting in the Ògún-ògwú syndrome to hunting in the various earth cults, since the latter are probably among the most ancient cults in this part of the world. In Yoruba culture, the Ògún cult has an earth aspect. In Idoma, the earth cult is concerned with the hunting of all animals and with the social relations of organized hunting activity. Ògwú, and very likely Ògún in Yoruba, are related to hunting as a masculine exploit—the hunting of fierce animals. Adeniji's comment that Erinlẹ̀ was concerned also with agriculture and fertility suggests a complex of ideas similar to that of the Idoma earth cult. The main Yoruba earth cult is controlled by the Ogboni Society. It is so secret that little is known publicly about it, but Adeniji says that it is not particularly concerned with hunting.

The meaning of all of this is cultural and psychological. Professional hunters are marginal men in any agricultural society, including Idoma. The best description of their marginal position that I know of was written by an Idoma poet, Samson O. O. Amali (1968:86–88), when he was still a Sixth Form schoolboy; it is reprinted below. The marginal position of hunters derives from many factors. They are wanderers and traditionally the founders of new settlements. Their interests, within limits, are worldly rather than domestic. They suffer from fatigue and loneliness, and in times when hunting is not very successful they may be hungry too. They achieve only a partial and temporary separation from village or town society, yet they may bring new ideas back home. Much of this pattern underlies the Yoruba Ògún cult and can be counted as additional psychological preparation for the latter-day transformation of Ògún into the god of vehicles and long-distance transportation. The implication is that in concentrating on the hunting aspects of Ògún, and by extension the marginal attributes of this occupation, the search for his origins can be broadened and, thereby, take a significant step forward.

The Hunter
by
Samson O. O. Amali

His weapons?
A dane gun
A product of
The village's blacksmith
A bottle of gunpowder
A tin of cartridges
His attire?
A piece of black cloth
Covering only his loins
He hung his cutlass
On his loins
He rubbed his protective

Charm upon his chest
And face.
Recited thrice
The blessing and protective
Incantations
He opened his door gently,
Peeped out gently
The night was still
It was very dark
No sign of any living being
Wind was blowing lightly
He walked backward
Out of his room
Raised his face
Into the sky,
The sky had no stars
A good omen.
He alone was awake
He stood still
In the still night
Studied the direction
Which the wind blew
And he began.
So he went alone
To hunt animals
In thick forest
In the heart
Of the still night.
This was his work.
He was a hunter
He followed
The foot-path
That passed
Through the forest
With his dane gun
Across his shoulder
All alone
In the dark still night.

He blew his
Hunting horn
Calling animals
In their tones
As he went along
Alone.

He arrived very close
To the hunting spot
Climbed the tree
Which stood very close
To the hunting spot
He had prepared
The spot
For the animals
To visit.
He clutched his gun
Ready to release
The trigger
At a moment's appearance
Of any animal
Sometimes he killed animals
Sometimes he killed no animals.
His was a tedious job
He had been beaten
By the rain
Many times
As he squatted
On the tree top
Armed
Awaiting his game
He had heard the voices
Of spirits.
Had met dangerous spirits
He could talk
With the animals
He was the mystery man
Of his land.

NOTES

1. The spellings of *Agè* and *Àgé* differ because neither is based on a modern linguistic analysis.

2. See also Bradbury (1973:257–58, 265).

3. The suggestion is that the *-gwú* syllable, with the sense of "kill," does not have an Idoma origin. Comparativists are likely to agree that *gbú* and *ŋmó* are cognate because both have a labio-velar consonant and a high, back vowel with a high tone; and they mean the same thing. The case is strengthened by the form *ŋmgbó* in the southernmost Idoma dialect, Yala (near Ikom on the Cross River), and by the form *ŋmgbέ*, "kill," in the closely related Ẹloyi language in Nasarawa. The ligature means that the "*gb*" is prenasalized, and the "*ŋm*" does not form a separate syllable.

4. High tone á; mid tone ā; low tone unmarked.

5. Literally, "washing the face of *ogwú*." (Dialect of Ādɔ́ká, which differs slightly from that of Otukpó.)

6. "*Ábüje*," the Igala word for "iron," used here as a blacksmith's title.

7. Meni appears to be *Lophira lanceolata*, a hardwood. The leaves have other medicinal and symbolic uses, such as cleaning the face of the gravedigger who has just buried someone who has died a "bad death."

8. "*Agbada*," the trough containing the water into which red-hot iron is plunged in order to quench it.

REFERENCES CITED

Amali, Samson O. O. 1968. *Selected Poems*, Ibadan: Privately published.

Armstrong, R. G. 1968. "Onugbo mlOko," *African Arts*, Vol. 1, No. 4.

Barnes, Sandra T. 1980. *Ogun: An Old God for a New Age*, Philadelphia: ISHI.

Bradbury, R. E. 1973. *Benin Studies*, London: Oxford University Press for International African Institute.

Ellis, A. B. 1894. *The Yoruba-Speaking Peoples of the Slave Coast of West Africa*, London: Chapman and Hall.

Fortes, Meyer. 1945. *The Dynamics of Clanship among the Tallensi*, London: Oxford University Press for International African Institute.

———. 1949. *The Web of Kinship among the Tallensi*, London: Oxford University Press for International African Institute.

Herskovits, Melville J. 1938. *Dahomey, an Ancient West African Kingdom*, New York City: J. J. Augustin.

le Hérissé, A. 1911. *L'Ancien Royaume du Dahomey*, Paris.

Melzian, Hans. 1937. *A Concise Dictionary of the Bini Language of Southern Nigeria*, London: Kegan Paul.

Segurola, Révérend Père B. 1963. *Dictionnaire Fon-Français*, Cotonou: Procure de l'Archidiocèse.

Wenger, Susanne. 1980. *Ein Leben mit den Göttern*, Wörgl, Austria: Perlinger Verlag.

Williams, Denis. 1974. *Icon and Image*, London: Allen Lane.

Williamson, Kay. 1972. *Igbo-English Dictionary, based on the Onitsha Dialect*, Benin City: Ethiope Publishing Corporation.

Sandra T. Barnes and Paula Girshick Ben-Amos

3

Ogun, the Empire Builder

During the years between 1400 and 1700 a cluster of conquest states rose to power along the Guinea Coast of West Africa and dominated large areas of this forest-belt region for several centuries. The expansion of these states was based on their many advantages, the most obvious of which was that each had a well organized and heavily equipped army, using a highly developed iron technology and, in a few cases, a mounted cavalry. The states included the Edo Kingdom of Benin, the Fon Kingdom of Dahomey, and a series of Yoruba kingdoms, the largest of which was Oyo (see Map 3.2). All of these states owed their political dominance to a policy of aggressive militarism.

It is no accident, we think, that each of these polities shared a symbolic complex which incorporated the three elements of iron, warfare, and state-building. This complex centered on Ogun (also known as Gu). For centuries there was close interaction between citizens of these states, thanks to migration, trade, warfare, and the itineracy of craftsmen and other specialists. Through this ongoing and intensive interaction, knowledge of a deity such as Ogun could easily have diffused.

It is well understood that symbols are adapted to, and then elaborated in ways that are unique to, or consonant with, the culture of the adopting groups. Certainly this was true in the cases discussed here. What is of interest, then, are not the differences but the similarities of underlying symbolic meanings which Ogun retained in each place. Basically, the Ogun concept encapsulated the progression from hunting to agriculture and the mastery of metallurgy, to urbanization and, ultimately, in these peoples' own view, to the development of empire. In one symbolic complex there existed a recapitulation of each kingdom's stages of growth and a statement about its basic nature.

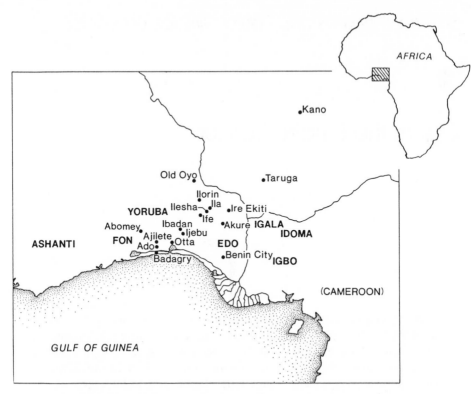

MAP 3.1. Significant linguistic groups (e.g., FON) and locations (e.g., Benin City) mentioned in chapters 2 and 3.

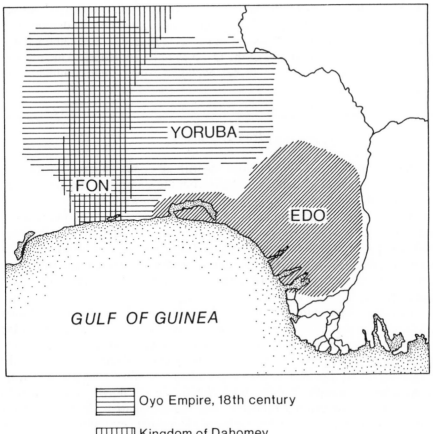

Oyo Empire, 18th century

Kingdom of Dahomey,
  19th century

Kingdom of Benin,
  c. 15th-16th centuries

MAP 3.2. Three precolonial conquest states on the eastern Guinea Coast
of West Africa where Ogun was a prominent deity.

In what follows, we examine some of the material and historical conditions that were relevant to the spread of a regional symbol. Then we demonstrate the ways in which basic symbolic meanings were shared, and, finally, we suggest that the myths and rituals of the Ogun complex served as a kind of "ideology of progress," devised by these peoples to explain their dominant position in the world.[1]

Iron Technology

The advent of iron in West Africa, as with all of sub-Saharan Africa, was "a catalyst which woke half a continent from the slumber of the Stone Age" (van der Merwe 1980:464). The diffusion of ironworking techniques was swift. If current calculations are correct there was a mere 800-year interval—500 B.C. to A.D. 300—between the earliest sub-Saharan smelting sites and the spread of iron to most areas of the subcontinent. During the early Iron Age, ending c. A.D. 1,000, population densities increased, and by its conclusion towns, kingdoms, and armies had emerged (Oliver and Fagan 1975:65).

The earliest known iron smelting in Western Africa is now believed to have occurred in what today is central Nigeria.[2] At the site of Taruga (see Map I for this and other places mentioned), an advanced iron technology existed as early as 600 B.C. (van der Merwe 1980:478; Calvocoressi and David 1979:10–11). By the end of the first millennium A.D., iron use and iron-making were widespread throughout Nigeria: in the northern savannah by the first or second century (Connah 1981:146–47; Shaw 1978:96–97), and in the southern forested area by the ninth (Shaw 1970:67, 260). Certainly at Benin by the thirteenth to fourteenth centuries iron smelting was well established (Connah 1975:34–35).

While the lateritic soils in much of West Africa made possible small-scale smelting of iron, large-scale smelting depended on the occurrence of rich ore-bearing sites. Several of the well-known sites in Nigeria, significantly, were concentrated around the capital city of Old Oyo and in more southerly parts of the kingdom, near the Awori and Egbado towns of Otta and Ajilete, respectively. In 1890, the Ajilete mine (20 miles north of coastal Badagry and the same distance west of Otta) was producing "excellent" ore from a series of many holes 8 feet in diameter and 50 to 60 feet deep (Mabogunje 1976:13). Ore deposits also lay nineteen-days' walk north of Abomey, capital of the Dahomean kingdom. During his travels in 1845–46, Duncan found that the hills north of Abomey "abound with iron," and that nearby smelters were willing to demonstrate their operations to him (1847:130–31). Similar sites occurred in western Nigeria and western Cameroon. The scale of smelting in these areas was impressive. At the end of the nineteenth century, for example, one Oyo site still had a smelting population of 100 to 120 (Bellamy

1904:101) and one Cameroon area had 270 smelters, whose production, exceeding the famous northeast Sudanic site of Meroe, was traded into Nigeria (Warnier and Fowler 1979:331). Whether or not these were the actual smelting sites which were producing iron when the forest-belt empires were formed is unknown. The point is that both the raw materials for large-scale production and the technical know-how for iron-making were in existence when the Guinea Coast kingdoms began to rise.

There has been considerable debate concerning the conditions necessary for the expansion of West Africa's large states. Some scholars believe that iron was an essential element (e.g., Davidson 1959:82–83; Goody 1971:46). This view coincides with folk ideology, for in speculating on their past political prominence, as represented in the ideology surrounding Ogun (discussed below), descendants of the Guinea Coast empires also equate state-building with the introduction and use of iron. Other scholars, however, hold that trade, a slow increase in population densities, or the control of labor and the subsequent ability to amass wealth and concentrate it in the hands of a privileged few were the conditions necessary to bring about state formation (e.g., Curtin et al. 1978:35–36; Horton 1976:103–113). This debate has been misleading, for two reasons. First, writers often confuse the search for conditions producing states with the search for origins of political centralization, whereas these are separate issues and must be examined separately. Second, they fail to take scale into account when comparing one case with another. Hence, arguments intended to apply to the building of kingdoms are countered with arguments that apply to the coalescing of sufficient power to operate a market center. Our concern is with the conditions necessary for the creation and expansion of states, that is to say, multi-community, stratified polities capable of centralizing the control and use of force.

Certainly iron was one of the elements that facilitated state building in West Africa. The weaponry that made territorial expansion possible was almost without exception made in whole or in part with iron and steel.[3] Iron production was concentrated in specific families or guilds that could be regulated and, therefore, as Goody points out (1971:46), the control of iron sources or its manufacture meant that military force also could be controlled. But iron was not solely responsible for the rise of large states in this part of the world. In addition to controlling weapons technology, it was essential that state-builders be able to organize and support large armies. Thus, in our view, iron, organization, and wealth were interdependent conditions, all necessary to the building of states.

Iron, Warfare, and Kingship

By the time Portuguese explorers arrived in Benin in the late fifteenth century, it was already an expanding warrior kingdom. According to an account by the Portuguese sailor Duarte Pacheco Pereira, "The Kingdom of Beny is about eighty leagues long and forty wide; it is usually at war with its neighbours and takes many captives" (Hodgkin 1960:93). While the Portuguese traded with the Benin kingdom intensively during this period, they sold it neither guns nor iron, possibly due to a papal ban (Ryder 1969:41), leaving Benin to continue its military expansion without the aid of imported weaponry or raw materials. Locally produced iron goods were not lacking, as this late sixteenth- or early seventeenth-century Dutch account indicates:

> They also have severall places in the Towne, where they keepe their Markets; in one place they have their great Market Day, called Dia de Ferro; and in another place they hold their little Market, called Ferro. . . . They . . . bring great store of Ironworke to sell there, and Instruments to fish withall, others to plow and to till the land withall; and many Weapons, as Assagaies, and Knives also for the Warre. This Market and Traffique is there very orderly holden. . . . ('D.R.' in Hodgkin 1960:121–22)

With their army using a variety of weapons—shields, javelins, spears, assegais, rapiers, bows and poisoned arrows—the Edo expanded their empire. The variety of weapons used by Benin warriors, and indeed their glorification of military prowess, were well represented in their sculpture. One example was a fifteenth/sixteenth-century brass plaque (fig. 3.1) from the royal palace illustrating the triumph of the Benin army over an enemy. The warriors are using shields, spears, and a variety of swords.

Seventeenth century Dutch sources indicate that the king of Benin could "mobilize 20,000 to 100,000 men. Thus he is the terror of his neighbours and an object of fear to his own peoples." Headed by a general, noble warriors and common soldiers were well disciplined and brave; "they never leave their posts, even when they have death before their eyes" (Dapper in Hodgkin 1960:128–29).

The motivations behind Benin's aggressive militarism are unknown, but it is clear that warfare was an accepted, ongoing aspect of the political system. It apparently was the custom for kings to declare war in the third year after their succession to the throne. Ruling princes of the empire who refused to pledge their allegiance at that time were considered rebels, and war was declared against them and their towns (Egharevba 1949:35). Economic factors were undoubtedly central to Benin's expansion, since, as Bradbury suggests, the Edo were intent on increasing their income from tribute, protecting and developing trade, and augmenting their army with captives and allies (1973:48). In Benin oral traditions, the commencement of their empire-building was associated with King Ewuare (c. fifteenth century), who was believed to have introduced major changes in the political structure of the kingdom, including centralizing royal authority, shifting the pattern of succession, organizing the urban population into corporate wards, and otherwise appropriating "a large measure of control over the means of administration" (Bradbury 1973:139).

FIGURE 3.1. Benin, Nigeria. Royal brass plaque from the palace at Benin. Warrior at far left wears miniature iron implements around his waist. 15th–16th century. H. c.17″. Photograph courtesy of the Museum für Völkerkunde, Leipzig.

The control of weapons production in Benin was part of this overall pattern of centralization. Iron craftsmen worked primarily for the king, but also for the nobles and, of course, for profit in the open market. There have been five guilds of smiths (sing. *ogun*; pl. *igun*) in Benin. The senior guild, Igun Eronmwon, consisting of brass-smiths, created the cast sculpture for which Benin is famous. Their objects decorated the royal palace and ritually enhanced the power of the king. Title-holders in this guild controlled great supernatural powers, which were used to protect the kingdom during important annual rituals. The other four, all ironworking guilds, produced herbalists' staffs, ceremonial swords, miniature emblems of Ogun, and assorted tools. All smiths were believed to control arcane knowledge, which they used for the enhancement and protection of the nation.

At its height, during the fifteenth and sixteenth centuries, the Benin kingdom reached its natural boundaries at the River Niger to the east and the sea to the south, and established suzerainty over Yoruba areas to the west and southwest up to the border of what was to become Dahomey. In the late sixteenth century it reached a common boundary with the Kingdom of Oyo.[4]

It is not known when the famed Yoruba Kingdom of Oyo got its start. Its foundation is variously set in the tenth to early fifteenth centuries, with the thirteenth being the most favored. We do know, however, that as a military power and empire it became important around 1600, and by 1780 it had attained its greatest size—greater than any other coastal African state—stretching from the Niger River to the sea and from Dahomey to the Benin border in the east (Law 1977:89; Obayemi 1976:255). Clearly Oyo's military policies were related to the desire for wealth, largely produced through commerce, especially long-distance trade. Not unrelated to Oyo's desire to expand and enlarge trade was its need for human labor to produce agricultural surpluses, and thus its need to take slaves both for domestic use and for foreign sale. Oyo's wealth also came from taxes on trade and from tribute, both of which were increased through expansion (Law 1977:202–236).

Like Benin, Oyo's power was dependent on military force; it was customary to stage expeditions every other year (Morton-Williams 1971:91). And like Benin, it expanded without the aid of firearms, which were not used effectively until sometime between the 1820s and the 1840s. Instead, Oyo's effectiveness in its military drives rested on two forces: a mounted cavalry numbering in the thousands, and a huge arsenal of iron weapons. So powerful was Oyo's military might that it defeated Dahomey in the 1720s, despite the latter's use of muskets, and forced it to pay tribute for nearly a century thereafter (Law 1977:164). The importance of cavalry, especially in savannah zones such as those occupied by Oyo, was captured by artists in many Yoruba kingdoms who idealized the equestrian warrior, and in fact portrayed Ogun as a mounted, spear-bearing soldier.[5] Edo artists, too, made extensive use of the horse and warrior theme in their bronze figures (Karpinski 1984). Yet the use of horses in both Benin and Dahomey was probably ceremonial and not military (Law 1980:22), since in the latter's forested environments horses were often subject to tsetse fly, and the expense of importing continuous replacements was high.

Oyo's army was well organized and led by a coterie of warrior chiefs whose senior members directly advised the king and acted as a strong check on his power. The size of its armed forces has been variously estimated at 10,000 to 100,000, with the lower number, even in the early nineteenth century, being the most reasonable (Law 1977:196–97). Its major eighteenth century adversary, Dahomey, was believed to have had no more than 12,000 warriors (Argyle 1966:89). The bulk of Oyo's army was made up of temporary recruits, although there were semiprofessional specialists, and its major strength came from the capital and not the provinces, tributary, or client states (Law 1977:183–97).

The main weapons of Oyo's cavalrymen and foot soldiers were spears, axes, and a variety of swords.[6] Special divisions of archers made use of bows and arrows (including crossbows), and both spears and arrows had iron heads that were often barbed. Other weapons included lances, cutlasses, daggers, knives, fighting bracelets, iron and wooden clubs, javelins, and even slings. To our knowledge, the only steel blades found on these antique weapons were on swords and knives (Smith 1973:232–33).

The government appears to have been less centralized in Oyo, where there was a separation of powers, than it was in Benin and Dahomey, and thus the relationship between that nation's highest civil authority and its smiths also was less centralized. In the nineteenth century, and no doubt before that time, the Alaafin (king) controlled his own weapon-producing smiths, who also supplied an allied power (Ajayi and Smith 1964:40). Additionally, a council of war chiefs led Oyo's military branch of government and, although the evidence is indirect, these chiefs probably had blacksmiths under their control (cf. Awẹ 1973:70). The official who commanded Oyo's citizen army and acted as prime minister of the kingdom, the Bashorun, worshipped Ogun; this god of warriors and smiths was his family deity, indicating that smithing was probably a family occupation (Johnson 1969:71; Morton-Williams 1967:54). The Bashorun presided over the Oyo Mesi, a council of state which not only advised the king but forced him to leave office (often by committing suicide) if his reign became unacceptable. Sitting with the Bashorun on the same council was the Ashipa, the official head of the Ogun cult in Oyo and his country's "minister of external affairs" (Morton-Williams 1964:254).

Dahomey, to the west of Oyo, traced its foundations to about 1625, and it became an important power near the end of that century. The unyielding pursuit of war was the hallmark of this kingdom, earning it the reputation of the Prussia of West Africa (Smith 1976a:51, 190). Yet Dahomey expanded gradually, not throwing off Oyo's yoke until 1818 and only then becoming the foremost power along the coast. In its rise to supremacy, Dahomey made use of guns, which it had received in trade as early as the late seventeenth century, and a few cannons, which were transported to the coast in the eighteenth century. The king monopolized trade in firearms and local production

of iron weapons. Likewise, the highly centralized army was under the immediate authority of the king, and included the famous divisions of women who
lived on the palace grounds and who, along with other powerful and well organized divisions of male warriors, brought Dahomey international fame as
a military power.

Dahomey's economy was based heavily on slave raiding and thus it
launched a fresh campaign each dry season on surrounding territories with
the intention of capturing as many slaves as possible for internal use and sale
to European merchants. Indeed Dahomey's fate was intimately bound up
with its militaristic, slave-raiding endeavors, and its oral traditions, which
looked back to earlier times, stressed this characteristic:

> The King has said that Dahomey is an enemy of all the world, and that his
> chiefs must use as much force in killing an ant, as they would to kill an elephant,
> for the small things bring on the large ones.

> The King has said that Dahomeans are a warrior people, and that, in conse-
> quence, it must never come to pass that a true Dahomean admit before an
> enemy that he is vanquished. (Herskovits and Herskovits 1958:480)

Dahomey's all-pervading interest in its militaristic mission was epitomized in
the motto of kings who saw war as the way to "make Dahomey always
greater" (Lombard 1967:72).

Dahomean traditions held that iron was the basis for its militaristic prowess. Iron must be looked after, said the king, or the careless owner would
become a lizard with a black tail (i.e., he would die), whereas the careful
owner would become a lizard with a red tail (i.e., he would live) (Herskovits
and Herskovits 1958:479–81).

The reliance of Dahomey on iron weaponry also was explicit in the relationship between smiths and the crown. All iron craftsmen were considered
to work under the control and at the behest of the king (Lombard 1967:80),
and blacksmiths' shops, occupying an entire quarter of the capital city, invariably caught the attention of foreign travelers (e.g., Burton 1864 V.I:291;
Forbes 1851:69). Smiths had high status, and even in the early twentieth century Herskovits found they still were among the most honored craftsmen
(1967 V.I:45). The king kept close watch on the production and the rituals
of all smiths in the kingdom. It was the duty of priests of Gu (the Dahomean
counterpart of Ogun) to report to the king's representatives the number of
smiths in each forge and the amount of their production. The king himself
set the date for annual sacrifices to Gu and transmitted it to the blacksmiths,
again, through Gu priests. Since smiths were worshippers of Gu, they were
expected to participate in these rites (Herskovits 1967 V.I:126–27, 181)
in addition to making their daily sacrifices, which, when Skertchly visited
Dahomey c. 1874, consisted of morning offerings to Gu of a water and corn-
flour porridge (1874:387–88).

Interaction

The amount of interaction between peoples of various political and cultural backgrounds during the period discussed here was extensive. Men and women traveled across boundaries by choice and by necessity for economic, political, social, and religious purposes. Despite intermittent hostilities, boundaries were relatively porous and it is likely, as Smith suggests (1976a:47), that ethnic differences simply had a different level of significance than they do today. For one thing, the three kingdoms of Oyo, Dahomey, and Benin all overlapped at one time or another during the 500 years between 1400 and 1900, and this overlap brought their peoples into various types of interaction. For another, the boundaries between the kingdoms, despite being hotly contested in the course of many regional wars, were frontier zones in which there was a great deal of intermixing.

Many eastern Yoruba communities were influenced by both Benin and Oyo. For instance, large areas of Ondo, Owo, Ekiti, Akure, and Otun fell into the orbit of Benin up to the seventeenth century and to lesser degrees to the nineteenth. Benin's influence took many forms, ranging from outright conquest to serving, as it did for Ondo, as a court of appeals in major land and succession disputes (Smith 1976a:193).[7] Its influence on nearby Owo was indirect, but no less effective, for in the reign of Ehengbuda, probably in the late sixteenth century, the heir to Owo's throne was sent to Benin to be trained and raised by the king (Egharevba 1960:33). During the seventeenth and eighteenth centuries, when Oyo reached its peak, much of the same area shifted into its orbit, again, in many ways but largely through military domination.

Similar shifts took place in western and southwestern Yorubaland. The buffer states of Egba, Egbado, and Ketu between Oyo and Dahomey were first part of the Oyo empire, but at the end of the eighteenth and nineteenth centuries they shifted into Dahomey's sphere of influence. Earlier in the seventeenth century the predecessor state to Dahomey, the coastal Kingdom of Allada (Ardra), was subject to the military operations of Oyo. Indeed, the origins of the Fon people were attributed to the intermarrying of Oyo immigrants with people of Allada (Lombard 1967:72). The Fon themselves had a policy of assimilating the ethnic groups under their suzerainty, and were known to intermarry with conquered peoples. Intermarriage, a subject to which we return, was common in the frontier zones, and as a result many people were no doubt able to claim dual identities (Obayemi 1976:235).

All three superpowers of the Guinea Coast also overlapped in the same areas, although at different times. In one case, Benin stretched its empire along the coast westward to Lagos, Badagry, and slightly inland to Ado (in the Egbado region of the extreme southwest of present-day Nigeria) in the sixteenth and early seventeenth centuries. Later, in the eighteenth century,

Oyo and Dahomey both vied for control of Badagry and its surrounding territory, with Dahomey openly attacking Badagry in 1737 (Law 1977:176–77;
Smith 1976a:108). Today some residents of this once-contested area still trace
ancestry to each of the ancient powers. A second case in which the three powers converged was in the southern Yoruba Kingdom of Ijebu. Benin and Oyo
competed for control of the Ijebu in the seventeenth century, and Dahomey
was believed to have attacked this kingdom a century later (Smith
1976a:93).

All three powers colonized their holdings. Whole families were sent by Oyo
into Dahomey and elsewhere (Akinjogbin 1976:397; Law 1977:93). Benin
usually sent its nationals to settle in newly conquered territory, whether it
was annexed or tribute-paying; many of them intermarried, established busi-
nesses in trade or crafts (frequently smithing), and founded subcommunities
that retained an Edo identity for many generations (Akintoye 1971:28–29).
Dahomey, too, sent colonizers into conquered territories. In its holdings in
Yoruba kingdoms, indigenous chiefs remained in office, but Dahomean "doubles" worked with them (Lombard 1967:75).

Military operations necessitated other types of interchange. Mercenaries
sold their services from one kingdom to another (Smith 1976b:83); military
alliances brought about exchanges of personnel; spies were sent to foreign
lands (Akinjogbin 1976:393); and hostages were taken from country to country. A Dahomean prince thus spent many years in Oyo as a hostage (Smith
1976b:56–57). One of the major purposes of warfare, to take slaves, also
brought about the inevitable interaction of people of different backgrounds.
Foreign captives taken into domestic slavery were frequently recruited into
the armies of their Oyo and Dahomean captors (Ajayi and Smith 1964:51–52;
Argyle 1966:86).[8] Female slaves were known to have brought new religious
practices, as for example the Aja woman, Hwanjile, who is said to have introduced the worship of the major deities Mawu, Lisa, and Age into the
Dahomean pantheon (Bay 1983:347; Herskovits 1967 V.II:103–104).

People were included as tribute. Dahomeans gave their Oyo conquerors
40 (some accounts say 41) men and the same number of women per annum.
If this tribute were paid during each of Dahomey's 70 years as a vassal state,
then 5,600 foreign citizens were added to Oyo's population during that period. In addition to his usual payments, the ruler of Oyo demanded and was
given 100 wives in 1779 (Law 1977:165–67).

Trade was a major source of interaction and infusion of new peoples into
one another's territories. Fifteenth-century contacts between Benin and eastern Yoruba kingdoms were mainly for trading purposes and many Edo settled
permanently in trade centers, such as Akure (Akintoye 1971:25–26). Similarly, colonies of Oyo traders are known to have established themselves in
commercial centers, as far north as Kano, in the eighteenth century (Smith
1976a:51). The movement of people for trade also had a western dimension
long before the 1600s when trade routes crossing Oyo territory passed
through what would become Dahomey and extended as far west as Ashanti

country (Morton-Williams 1971:83). Although it is usually believed that most long-distance traders were men, many transnational traders in precolonial eastern Yoruba and Edo areas were women (Akintoye 1971:24).

Ordinary migration from one polity to another, and particularly from outlying areas to prospering towns and kingdoms, appears to have been a common occurrence in the entire Guinea Coast region. Obayemi notes that there was "a period of relatively free interstate movement" before 1600 (1976:254); and oral traditions indicate that migrations were usual throughout the whole precolonial period (e.g., Akinjogbin 1976:377). Dahomean legends recount the migrations of royal princes and princesses outside the kingdom for many purposes (Herskovits and Herskovits 1958:377). In the Kingdom of Ilesha, noted for its migration traditions, two-thirds of the 21 leading chiefs claimed that their ancestors originated in other kingdoms (Obayemi 1976:253). Many migrants were refugees fleeing injustices, dynastic disputes, or civic turmoil, but others were simply seeking independence, wealth, and power in new places.

As indicated, intermarriage was a prime factor in the interaction of peoples of different kingdoms. There were many dynastic intermarriages. The kings of Oyo and Dahomey sent their daughters to one another as wives (Akinjogbin 1976:399; Law 1977:161), and Edo conquerors had a policy of intermarrying with subject peoples (Akintoye 1971:29). Yoruba women who married into aristocratic Fon families were responsible for much of the Yoruba cultural influence in nineteenth-century Dahomey (Bay 1983:347). Kings in the Yoruba and Edo kingdoms sent adulterous wives into exile by placing them under the care of other rulers; and they sent their children (and the children of adulterous wives) to live in the palaces of neighboring kings so as to protect them from jealous rivals (Akintoye 1971:23).

Itineracy also was common. Among the more mobile members of society were hunters, whose occupation dictated their movement (see Ajuwon, Ch. 8 this volume). Hunters in some areas were in charge of protecting roads, and therefore they were in constant contact with other mobile sectors of the population, among whom brass-casters, leather-workers, diviners, herbalists, tattooers, circumcisers, and artists (see H. Drewal, Ch. 10 and 1977:8–9) were prominent. Highly specialized individuals appear to have been in great demand, and oral traditions indicate that mobility for them was as much the rule as the exception. An early ruler of Ilesha, to give only one example, was said to have spent time preceding his ascendance to the throne as a medical expert in Benin (Obayemi 1976:254).

Interaction and Belief

The high level of mobility in the Guinea Coast region no doubt facilitated the sharing of belief systems, and the ideology of Ogun was no exception. If anything, the transmission of Ogun's symbolic complex was enhanced by the extreme mobility of his main devotees: warriors and hunters, as indicated, and also ironworkers.

Blacksmiths were notorious travelers. Many of them left Oyo during its declining years and settled elsewhere. In the city of Ibadan, which became a formidable military power in the mid-nineteenth century, many Oyo smiths attached themselves to military leaders and produced weapons under their protection and patronage (Awẹ 1973:70). Similarly, Edo smiths were well-known settlers throughout the eastern Yoruba kingdoms (e.g., Akintoye 1971:29). Iron-smelters also moved regularly, since ore-bearing sites were frequently depleted (Ojo 1966:97).

Ironworkers were given special treatment throughout West Africa (Barnes 1980:8–13). In some societies, it was a serious crime to kill a smith. In others, they could not be treated as prisoners of war but had to be given privileged care. Indeed, their capture may have been both a fringe benefit and an objective of warfare. Two of the metalworking guilds in Benin, for instance, traced their origins to the north of Benin and claimed they were forcibly brought to the capital of the kingdom during the reign of Esigie, one of the great sixteenth-century warrior kings (Bradbury 1957–61:BS276–77). Smiths, it might be noted, often traveled with armies; and this is believed to be one of the ways ironworking skills and perhaps iron-related rituals and symbols diffused. Smiths and soldiers, in fact, shared the same deity. Not only did ironworkers sacrifice to Ogun, but Edo, Oyo, and Dahomean soldiers all made sacrifices to Ogun and Ogun-related deities before battle (Ben-Amos fieldnotes 1976; Johnson 1969:136; Smith 1976b:49).

Wherever they settled, ironworkers acquired significant ritual status. Their forges and smelters were seen as ritual shrines or sanctuaries for anyone losing a fight or fleeing turbulence. The anvil was widely used for taking oaths and as a sacrificial altar. Moreover, ironworkers (and hunters) were organized into guilds, which served as cult groups organized around the worship of Ogun or Gu. Smelting and smithing were separate occupations, plied by separate professional groups. Yet both groups in Yoruba-speaking communities looked to Ogun as their patron deity and both sacrificed to him. Iron-smelters, who dug for their own ore, made sacrifices in order to find iron ore, to keep shafts from collapsing on them, and to prevent accidents while smelting (Adéníji 1977:9–11).

Clearly, the standardization of a cult system could be accomplished relatively easily with this high level of movement among ritually active devotees. There was, in addition, a conscious attempt to transmit and perpetuate sacred systems across boundaries. Oral traditions of Benin indicate that from the earliest period of the monarchy new deities and religious practices were constantly introduced into the state ritual system. One example was the mother of the late seventeenth-century heir apparent who brought the cult of Orunmila (Ifa divination) into the kingdom to protect her son and ensure his ascension to the throne (Ben-Amos 1983:82).

Cult activities drew people across state boundaries for festivals and ceremonies; many migrants returned on special occasions to their homes or went to well-known cult centers of the deities they worshipped (Morton-Williams 1964:259). This meant, among other things, that cult priests were potentially powerful figures, not only because they controlled supernatural powers but because they also organized and controlled groups of people. The kings of Dahomey were well aware of this power and made it a practice in conquered areas to incorporate foreign deities into the state pantheon and to place their priests under the control of a high priest centered in Abomey (Lombard 1967:76). Needless to say, such centralized control could only aid and abet the standardization of cult practices and beliefs.

Ogun Symbolism

The beliefs surrounding iron, centering on the god Ogun, were found throughout the Guinea Coast. The iron of Ogun was sacrificed to, sworn upon, subjected to stringent taboos, or made into a shrine. Its transformation into a sacred element extended from the least imposing scrap of metal to the most imposing decorative art form. Benin altars to Ogun, found in every forge and maintained by warriors and hunters, were "decorated with all kinds of scrap-iron objects" (Bradbury 1957:53). The same was true among Yoruba peoples; as one contemporary devotee explained, a shrine was called Ogun when two pieces of iron were placed together and a sacrifice performed. "As soon as it is put together it stays Ogun, and will be Ogun forever after" (Barnes 1980:37).

The Fon, Edo, and Yoruba peoples frequently used the warriors' iron weapons as the basis for aesthetic elaboration. In Dahomey, such an emblem was the *gubasa*, a ceremonial sword. According to myth, when the creator came to earth he held Gu in his hand in the form of a *gubasa* and with it he cleared the forest and taught people to build houses and till the soil. The creator then taught humans how to use metal so that they, too, could enjoy the power of Gu—a power that would enable them to secure food, cover their bodies, and protect themselves from the elements (Mercier 1954:233).

Among the more common iron objects that served as insignia of Ogun (Gu) were miniature iron implements (Williams 1973:148–52). They were sometimes hung on iron necklaces and bracelets worn by devotees, or attached to clothing (especially that of hunters and warriors), crowns, or standards—all to signify the power of the iron deity. This tradition may indeed go back 400 to 500 years, as evidenced by the miniature pincers on the belt of the Benin warrior depicted in the fifteenth-sixteenth century brass plaque referred to above (fig. 3.1). When he visited the Kingdom of Dahomey in the late nineteenth century, Skertchly found that emblems of Gu were decorated with miniature hoes, knives, and other tiny iron objects (1874:388); moreover, a life-sized iron statue of Gu, given in 1894 to Musée de l'Homme in Paris as a gift, had miniature sword, pincers, hoe, arrow tip,

FIGURE 3.2. Fon, Republic of Benin (formerly Dahomey). Iron statue of Gu. The deity formerly held a
sword in one hand and a bell in the other. Miniature
iron implements decorate the crown. H. 65″. Musée de
l'Homme, Paris, 94.32.1. Photograph courtesy of the
Musée de l'homme.

knives, and hook hanging from his hat (fig. 3.2). Nearly a century later Verger found in the frontier zone between the former kingdoms of Oyo and Dahomey that miniature iron tools still decorated the standards of Ogun (1957:90). These miniatures included blacksmiths' hammers, tongs, pincers, and pokers; farmers' hoes, cutlasses, or knives; warriors' swords, daggers, spears, or bows and arrows; and other items such as bells, gongs, state swords, scrapers, tattooing knives, and eventually guns. Each miniature carried supernatural force in that it protected and brought good fortune to the wearer or, conversely, harmed his enemies.

The tools of Ogun served as emblems of his various capacities; indeed, they became a kind of shorthand or code that extended into many domains. In Benin, for instance, miniature tools commonly appeared on wrought iron staffs used by herbalists. On the top of these staffs was a bird representing the mystical powers of the herbalist, and below the bird were depictions of hoes, swords, and other iron implements (Ben-Amos 1976:249). In former times an herbalist, taking with him such an iron staff as his means of protection, accompanied soldiers to war to assure success against their enemies. There was, as might be expected, a close relationship between herbalists, who provided war charms and medicines, warriors, who used them, and Ogun, whose supernatural powers were embedded in them. The clothing, and even the bodies, of warriors were heavily laden with medicinal and magical objects. Latoosa, a famous nineteenth-century warrior chief of the Yoruba city of Ibadan, went so far as to insert medicated iron objects in his body to gain added strength (Awẹ 1975:278).

Through their intimate connection with hunting, agriculture, crafts, and even warfare, iron objects served as metaphors for civilization itself. This is vividly portrayed in the patterning of an eighteenth-century Benin royal brass stool now found in the Museum für Völkerkunde in Berlin (fig. 3.3a). The seat of the stool (fig. 3.3b) is divided into three zones. At the top is the cosmos, represented by the sun, the moon, and the cross—a Benin symbol of creation. At the bottom are depictions of the powers of the forest, the untamed wilderness: monkeys with snakes issuing from their nostrils, an image indicating terrifying supernatural powers, and the trunks of elephants grasping leaves, representing the herbal knowledge possessed by creatures of the forest. In the middle zone are symbols of civilization, and these are—not surprisingly—the products of the smith. At the very center is an anvil—the ritual and technological heart of the smithy, the place where the heat of Ogun is tempered and controlled. On either side are the tools of the smith: hammer, knife, pincer, tongs, bellows, and blade. At the peripheries are two iron ceremonial swords, emblems of the social status and powers of the rulers, who control life and death (Ben-Amos 1980:30–31, 37).

Many oral traditions of the Guinea Coast kingdoms captured the essence of the Ogun concept through what we see as the paradoxical themes of aggression and civilization, but which for the cultures in question were united, not contradictory, themes. Thus Ogun was depicted as the aggressive, violent

FIGURE 3.3a and 3.3b. Benin, Nigeria. Royal brass stool. 18th century. H. 15 1/2″.
Museum für Völkerkunde, Berlin, IIIc20295. Photograph courtesy of the Museum
für Völkerunde, Staatliche Museen Preussicher Kulturbesitz, Berlin (West).

warrior whose sword struck swiftly and devastatingly, who "has water at home [civilization] but bathes with blood [aggression]" (Ibigbami 1978:48). In Benin shrines, he was depicted in a war costume, wearing or holding the tools and weapons of his varied occupations. Often his costume and, significantly, his eyes were painted red. To describe someone as having red eyes was a way of indicating his violent temper and capacity for causing harm (Ben-Amos 1980:51). The Yoruba, who also used red eyes for similar symbolic purposes, captured the ferocity of Ogun in the following praise poem:

> Where does one meet him?
> One meets him in the place of battle;
> One meets him in the place of wrangling;
> One meets him in the place where torrents of blood
> Fill with longing, as a cup of water does the thirsty.
> (Idowu 1962:89)

Although the deity was fierce and terrible, he was not evil, for as a civilized being he demanded justice, fair play, and integrity. If appeased, he was tolerant and protective, especially of the poor and dispossessed.

After all, Ogun was responsible for society's most important innovations. His praises were sung by many Yoruba-speaking groups as "Master of the World," the innovative deity who "showed the way" for others; the deity who brought fire; the first hunter; the opener of roads; the clearer of the first fields; the first warrior; the introducer of iron; the founder of dynasties, towns, and kingdoms. Each of these acts was in some way revolutionary. Each was in some way a "first." Indeed, fire was a first principle: it transformed ore into iron, just as it transformed raw food into cooked, and thus, as Lévi-Strauss would put it, nature into culture. Thereafter Ogun brought a new political order through civil war or conquest, a new economy through clearing the fields, a new technology through the introduction of iron, and a new way of life through the founding of towns and cities (Barnes 1980:42ff).

In similar fashion the Fon creator finished his work and then instructed humans to overcome the obstacles of nature, to civilize themselves, by learning to use iron. For Fon, the sword embodied their beginnings. Gu himself was, in some manifestations, perceived as a sword; he was a "force" with no head, only a great tool jutting out of a trunk of stone. From the day of creation onward the sword was given this praise name: *ali-su-gbo-gu-kle*, "the road is closed and Gu opens it." Thanks to Gu, "the earth would not always remain wild bush"; "Gu is the force which helped man adapt himself to the world" (Herskovits and Herskovits 1958:125, 134–35 and 1933:14–15).

The iron sword of Ogun was perhaps his most meaningful symbol, for it condensed the twin meanings of aggression and civilization. It cleared the forest and built the house. More significantly, it vanquished the enemy and crowned the king. The culmination of the coronation ceremony of the Alaafin of Oyo occurred when the Great Sword, the Sword of Justice, was placed in the king's hands. (A sword of this type is included among the weapons, at the far left, on the Benin stool in Plate 3.3b.) Without it he could not wield the supreme power over life and death. Before the King of Oyo could ascend the throne, however, he was required to visit two shrines. The first visit was to the shrine of Oranmiyan—son, father, or brother of Ogun (accounts vary), and grandchild of the creator deity who founded Ife. According to legend, Oranmiyan left the throne of Ife to found a ruling dynasty at Oyo and later to rule at Benin, where his son soon succeeded him. Others of his "offspring" are often said to be (legendary) founders of other Yoruba kingdoms. Certainly, no king was installed at Oyo or Dahomey without the Great Sword, reconsecrated at Ife, being placed in his hands, or, in the case of Benin, without brass coronation objects from the Ooni of Ife.[9] The second visit, following a five-day rest, was to the shrine of Ogun, whereupon, after making sacrifices, the new ruler immediately entered the palace for the first time (Johnson 1969:45).

The relationship of Oyo's Alaafin to the iron deity was complex. Early Alaafin worshipped Erin (Erinlẹ), a hunter deity who was related to Ogun and whose devotees wore iron emblems.[10] Abiodun, who reigned as Alaafin c. 1760–1789 and whose mother was of the Bashorun (head warrior chief) line, adopted Ogun, his mother's deity, and was said to have merged the iron deity with Erin (Abraham 1958:164, 482). Although we may only speculate, it is possibly not accidental that Alaafin Abiodun made his tie to Ogun explicit when Oyo's powers reached their zenith and when, history tells us, he triumphed over his Bashorun in a civil war (Law 1977:54).

The relationship between kingship and the iron deity also was explicit at Ife, the Yoruba kingdom which, as indicated, was believed to have provided the founder, Oranmiyan (Oranyan), of Oyo's ruling house. In Ife, the Ogun Laadin shrine, named for the first mythical blacksmith,[11] was housed within the palace walls and was used by chiefs for debating judicial matters and swearing oaths. The shrine consisted of a large tear-shaped lump of iron called *omoowu*, the blacksmith's hammer, two stone anvils called *okuta Ogun*, Ogun's stones, and, guarding them near the entryway, a stone fish and a crocodile, described as domestic animals to Ogun.[12]

Symbols of Ogun, especially ceremonial swords and the dramatization of warfare, were important features of kingship paraphernalia and ritual throughout the region. The Dahomean King Glele, who reigned in the mid-nineteenth century, adopted the *gubasa* (sword) for his coat of arms (Waterlot 1926:Planche XXI); the blade was pierced with holes whose shape signified Ogun. This identification with Gu was a way of explaining a king's power (Mercier 1952:48, 59).

The sword presented to the king of Dahomey at his coronation provided another avenue by which he could maintain contact with the power of Ogun. Each time he returned from a campaign, the king, dressed in uniform and holding the coronation sword, appeared with his retinue before hunter chiefs and danced and pantomimed the actions of a warrior. The hunters were military reservists[13] who protected the capital city of Abomey during the annual campaigns. At the ceremony, the crowd praised Gu and the king, whereupon the king sent for the *guno*, chief priest of Gu, who took from each hunter a ritual knife, given to him at the start of the ceremony and to which sacrifices had been made, and placed the knives in Guzu (*guzume*), the forest sacred to Gu (Herskovits 1967 V.I:121–22).

The ritual relationship between Gu and the king was reaffirmed when the king ceremonially atoned for his warriors' deeds. In a rite called "washing the hands"[14] warriors were required to bring the heads of their victims to the king, who "purchased" them and then threw them to Guzu, the forest of Gu. The ceremony was intended to protect the king and his soldier "agents" from any supernatural vengeance that might ensue from their campaigns (Herskovits 1967 V.II:95–96).

In many eastern Yoruba kingdoms, such as Ife, Ila,[15] and Ire Ekiti (legendary home of the Yoruba Ogun), the annual Ogun ceremony was presided over by the king, who, holding a sword, joined in a mock battle. At Ife, the Ooni (king) made annual sacrifices during the Ogun festival at several Ogun shrines, one of which consisted of a heap of swords (Bascom 1987). Participants in the Ogun festival's mock battle at Ire Ekiti were believed to have once used machetes, and in accidental cases of overzealousness to have killed one another in an "act of war to remember the battling spirit of Ogun" (Ibigbami 1978:47).

In Benin, the annual Isiokuo ceremony, in honor of Ogun, was said to date to the first dynasty of kings, who ruled perhaps until the thirteenth or fourteenth century.[16] As prelude to the festival, and as it was recorded much later, participants made sacrifices at the shrines of Ogun and Efae (hunters' Ogun), and during the ceremony the king sacrificed to Ogun, praying for success in war. The *oba* and other participants, outfitted with war costumes, iron jewelry, and war weapons, then staged a series of mock battles. One of the highlights of the festival came when the *oba* received medicines from Ine Ogun, a titleholder, who held his ceremonial *ada*, sword, upright while the *oba* held his downward, "to show the power of Ogun."[17]

It is through this intimate relationship with kingship that the power and character of Ogun acquired a profoundly historic dimension. For these kingdoms of the Guinea Coast, Ogun—progenitor of iron and warrior king—summed up a long rise to political supremacy.

Conclusion

Ogun, as one scholar put it, was the symbol, par excellence, of the superior, conquering society (Beier 1959:43). The meanings attached to Ogun were *not* tied to a single place or a single cultural context. They conveyed a widely shared message, an evolutionary statement, perceived as such by these peoples and applied to themselves. Thus, throughout the region, this symbol provided a metaphor through which people reflected on the historical milestones of their development—from first clearing the land to living in a glorious Age of Empire.

NOTES

1. One of the surest dates that can be fixed to the existence of the Ogun cult in the Guinea Coast region is the later part of the eighteenth century. By this time the deity must have existed in Haiti, since the importation of slaves in sufficient numbers to establish Ogun as a local deity had by then ceased. (See Brown, ch. 4 in this volume, for a description of the Ogun cult in Haiti.) Williams suggests that the cult was present in an area that would have included Benin and eastern Yoruba kingdoms c. 1530 (1974:83–86). He bases his estimate on contemporary oral traditions and on the dating of (imported) iron used for ritual objects associated with the Ogun cult. Still another suggestion, as we state below, comes from the oral traditions of Benin that link Ogun to an annual kingship ritual that existed as early as the thirteenth or fourteenth century.

Most of the other Ogun traditions cited in this essay were gathered between the late nineteenth century and the mid-twentieth century. Their repeated references to warfare lead us to believe that these traditions were current among Edo, Oyo, and Fon peoples on the eve of colonial takeover, at the end of the nineteenth century, when warfare was prevalent and when they still lived in independent kingdoms.

2. The authors wish to thank Vincent Pigott and Ellen Sieber for assistance in examining iron technology and production.

3. In recent years it has become apparent that steel of medium to high carbon content was produced in West Africa as long ago as the first millennium B.C. The ancient site of Taruga yielded several steel objects (Tylecote 1975:54–55). The quality of locally produced steel, in the eyes of latter-day smiths, was "vastly superior to imported European hoop iron" (van der Merwe 1980:492–93; see also Bellamy 1904:118). The excellent quality of locally-made iron implements of the late eighteenth century was commented on by the French trader Landolphe who visited Benin (Quesné 1823:49).

4. Trees were said to have been planted to demarcate the boundaries of the two kingdoms (Smith 1976a:47).

5. In Oyo horses were symbols of royalty (Babayemi 1979:34).

6. According to Smith:

Swords were of two main types: the heavier, single-bladed and eccentrically curved *agedengbe*, and the *ida*, usually double-bladed and either with an elongated leaf-shaped blade or approximating to European or Near Eastern types. Other varieties of swords and knives were also used, such as the short *jomo*, the *tanmogayi* (sabre), *ada, ogbo* or *ele* (cutlass), and *obe* (dagger). With the exception of the *obe*, all these were designed primarily for cutting rather than for thrusting or stabbing. (1976a:145)

The ceremonial sword was of the *ida* type.

7. A court of appeals such as this one had considerable importance, since it placed Benin officials in the position of deciding contested chieftaincy or kingship selec-

tions and thereby having a hand in choosing the highest officeholders of a neighboring kingdom.

8. War captives were also used for the well-known annual sacrifices made by the King of Dahomey to ensure the well-being of his kingdom.

9. See Bascom 1969:83; Herskovits 1967 V.I:121; Johnson 1969:7–12; Law 1977:30–31, 122; and Willett 1967:79.

10. The symbolism could be reversed. One emblem of Ogun, therefore, was the tusk or tail of Erinlẹ, who also took the form of an elephant (Idowu 1962:89).

11. For a variation on the meaning of Ogun Laadin see Fabunmi 1969:12.

12. Barnes fieldnotes, 1984. See also Willett 1967:101.

13. In many Yoruba-speaking kingdoms hunters automatically served in the military during wartime.

14. See Armstrong ch. 2 in this volume.

15. See Pemberton ch. 6 in this volume and Bascom 1987.

16. This festival, like those at Ife, Ire Ekiti, and many other communities of the region, continues to be held each year.

17. Ben-Amos fieldnotes, 1976; Bradbury 1957–61:BS559 and 1958–59:OB10; and Egharevba 1949:88.

REFERENCES CITED

Abraham, R. C. 1958. *Dictionary of Modern Yoruba*, London: University of London Press.

Adéníji, D. A. A. 1977. *Iron Mining and Smelting in Yorùbáland*, (translated and edited by R. G. Armstrong), Occasional Publication No. 31, Institute of African Studies, University of Ibadan.

Ajayi, J. F. A., and R. Smith. 1964. *Yoruba Warfare in the Nineteenth Century*, London: Cambridge University Press in association with the Institute of African Studies, University of Ibadan.

Akinjogbin, I. A. 1976. "The Expansion of Oyo and the Rise of Dahomey, 1600–1800," in *History of West Africa*, V. I (2nd ed.), J. F. A. Ajayi and M. Crowder (eds.), New York: Columbia University Press, pp. 373–412.

Akintoye, S. A. 1971. *Revolution and Power Politics in Yorubaland 1840–1893*, New York: Humanities Press.

Argyle, W. J. 1966. *The Fon of Dahomey: A History and Ethnography of the Old Kingdom*, Oxford: Clarendon.

Awẹ, Bọlanle. 1973. "Militarism and Economic Development in Nineteenth Century Yoruba Country: the Ibadan Example," *Journal of African History*, 14(1):65–77.

———. 1975. "Notes on Oríkì and Warfare in Yorubaland," in *Yoruba Oral Tradition*, W. Abimbọla (ed.), Ifẹ: Department of African Languages and Literatures, University of Ifẹ, pp. 267–92.

Babayemi, S. O. 1979. "The Fall and Rise of Oyo c. 1760–1905: A Study in the Traditional Culture of an African Polity," Ph.D. thesis, University of Birmingham.

Barnes, Sandra T. 1980. *Ogun: An Old God for a New Age*, Philadelphia: ISHI.

Bascom, William. 1969. *The Yoruba of Southwestern Nigeria*, New York: Holt, Rinehart and Winston.

———. 1987. "The Olojo Festival at Ife, 1937," in *Time Out of Time,* Alessandro Falassi (ed.), Albuquerque: University of New Mexico Press.

Bay, Edna. 1983. "Servitude and Worldly Success in the Palace of Dahomey," in *Women and Slavery in Africa*, C. C. Robertson and M. A. Klein (eds.), Madison: University of Wisconsin Press, pp. 340–67.

Beier, U. 1959. *A Year of Sacred Festivals in One Yoruba Town*, Lagos: Nigeria Magazine.

Bellamy, C. V. 1904. "A West African Smelting House," *Journal of the Iron and Steel Institute*, 66(2):99–120.

Ben-Amos, Paula. 1976. "Man and Animals in Benin Art," *Man*, N.S. II(2):243–52.

———. 1980. *The Art of Benin*, London: Thames and Hudson.

———. 1983. "In Honor of Queen Mothers," in *The Art of Power/The Power of Art: Studies in Benin Iconography*, P. Ben-Amos and A. Rubin (eds.), Los Angeles: Museum of Culture History, UCLA, pp. 79–83.

Bradbury, R. E. 1957. *The Benin Kingdom*, Ethnographic Survey of Africa, Part 13, London: International African Institute.

———. 1957–61. Benin Scheme Field Notes Series BS. On file at the University of Birmingham Library (England).

———. 1958–59. Benin Scheme Field Notes Series OB. On file at the University of Birmingham Library (England).

———. 1973. *Benin Studies*, London: Oxford University Press for International African Institute.

Burton, R. F. 1864. *A Mission to Gelele, King of Dahome*, Vol. I–II, London: Tinsley Brothers.

Calvocoressi, D., and N. David. 1979. "A New Survey of Radiocarbon and Thermoluminescence Dates for West Africa," *Journal of African History*, 20:1–29.

Connah, Graham. 1975. *The Archaeology of Benin*, Oxford: Clarendon.

———. 1981. *Three Thousand Years in Africa*, Cambridge: Cambridge University Press.

Curtin, P., S. Feierman, L. Thompson, and J. Vansina. 1978. *African History*, Boston: Little Brown.

Davidson, Basil. 1959. *Old Africa Rediscovered*, London: Victor Gollancz.

Drewal, H. J. 1977. *Traditional Art of the Nigerian Peoples*, Washington, D.C.: Museum of African Art.

Duncan, J. 1847. *Travels in Western Africa in 1845 & 1846*, London: Richard Bentley.

Egharevba, J. U. 1949. *Benin Law and Custom*, Port Harcourt: C.M.S. Niger Press.

———. 1960. *A Short History of Benin* (3rd ed.), Ibadan: Ibadan University Press.

Fabunmi, M. A. 1969. *Ifẹ Shrines*, Ile-Ifẹ: University of Ifẹ Press.

Forbes, F. E. 1851. *Dahomey and the Dahomans*, Vol. I, London: Longman.

Goody, J. 1971. *Technology, Tradition, and the State in Africa*, London: Oxford University Press for International African Institute.

Herskovits, M. J. 1967. *Dahomey: An Ancient West African Kingdom*, Vol. I and II, Evanston: Northwestern University Press (first pub. 1938).

Herskovits, M. J., and F. S. Herskovits. 1933. *An Outline of Dahomean Religious Belief*, Memoirs of the American Anthropological Association, No. 41.

———. 1958. *Dahomean Narrative*, Evanston: Northwestern University Press.

Hodgkin, T. (ed.). 1960. *Nigerian Perspectives: An Historical Anthology*, London: Oxford University Press.

Horton, R. 1976. "Stateless Societies in the History of West Africa," in *History of West Africa*, V.I (2nd ed.), J. F. A. Ajayi and M. Crowder (eds.), New York: Columbia University Press, pp. 72–113.

Ibigbami, R. I. 1978. "Ogun Festival in Ire Ekiti," *Nigeria Magazine*, No. 126–27, pp. 44–59.

Idowu, E. Bolaji. 1962. *Olodumare: God in Yoruba Belief*, London: Longmans.

Johnson, Rev. S. 1969. *The History of the Yorubas*, Lagos: C.S.S. Bookshops (first pub. 1921).

Karpinski, Peter. 1984. "A Benin Bronze Horseman at the Merseyside County Museum," *African Arts*, XVII(2), pp. 54–62.

Law, R. C. 1977. *The Oyo Empire c. 1600–c. 1836*, Oxford: Clarendon.

———. 1980. *The Horse in West African History*, Oxford: Oxford University Press for International African Institute.

Lombard, J. 1967. "The Kingdom of Dahomey," in *West African Kingdoms in the Nineteenth Century*, D. Forde and P. M. Kaberry (eds.), London: Oxford University Press for International African Institute, pp. 70–92.

Mabogunje, Akin. 1976. "The Land and Peoples of West Africa," in *History of West Africa*, V. I (2nd ed.), J. F. A. Ajayi and M. Crowder (eds.), New York: Columbia University Press, pp. 1–32.

Mercier, P. 1952. *Les Asé du Musée d'Abomey*, Catalogues VII, Dakar: IFAN.

———. 1954. "The Fon of Dahomey," in *African Worlds*, D. Forde (ed.), London: Oxford University Press for International African Institute, pp. 210–34.

Morton-Williams, P. 1964. "An Outline of the Cosmology and Cult Organization of the Oyo Yoruba," *Africa*, 34(3):243–61.

———. 1967. "The Yoruba Kingdom of Oyo," in *West African Kingdoms in the Nineteenth Century*, D. Forde and P. M. Kaberry (eds.), London: Oxford University Press for International African Institute, pp. 36–69.

———. 1971. "The Influence of Habitat and Trade on the Polities of Oyo and Ashanti," in *Man in Africa*, M. Douglas and P. M. Kaberry (eds.), Garden City, N.Y.: Anchor (first pub. 1969), pp. 80–99.

Obayemi, Ade. 1976. "The Yoruba and Edo-Speaking Peoples and Their Neighbours before 1600," in *History of West Africa*, V.I (2nd ed.), J. F. A. Ajayi and M. Crowder (eds.), New York: Columbia University Press, pp. 196–263.

Ojo, G. J. A. 1966. *Yoruba Culture*, London: University of London Press.

Oliver, R., and B. M. Fagan. 1975. *Africa in the Iron Age*, Cambridge: Cambridge University Press.

Quesné, J. S. (ed.). 1823. *Mémoires du Capitaine Landolphe*, Paris: Bertrand.

Ryder, A. F. C. 1969. *Benin and the Europeans, 1485–1897*, London: Longmans.

Shaw, Thurstan. 1970. *Igbo-Ukwu: An Account of Archaeological Discoveries in Eastern Nigeria*, V.I, Evanston: Northwestern University Press.

———. 1978. *Nigeria: Its Archaeology and Early History*, London: Thames and Hudson.

Skertchly, J. A. 1874. *Dahomey as It Is*, London: Chapman & Hall.

Smith, R. S. 1973. "Yoruba Warfare and Weapons," in *Sources of Yoruba History*, S. O. Biobaku (ed.), Oxford: Clarendon, pp. 224–49.

———. 1976a. *Kingdoms of the Yoruba* (2nd ed.), London: Methuen.

———. 1976b. *Warfare and Diplomacy in Pre-Colonial West Africa*, London: Methuen.

Tylecote, R. F. 1975. "Iron Smelting of Taruga, Nigeria," *Bulletin of the Historical Metallurgy Group*, 9:49–56.

van der Merwe, N. J. 1980. "The Advent of Iron in Africa," in *The Coming of the Age of Iron*, T. A. Wertime and J. D. Muhly (eds.), New Haven: Yale University Press, pp. 463–506.

Verger, P. 1957. *Notes sur le Culte des Orisa et Vodun*, Dakar: IFAN.

Warnier, J.-P., and I. Fowler. 1979. "A Nineteenth-Century Ruhr in Central Africa," *Africa*, 49(4):329–51.

Waterlot, Em. G. 1926. *Les Bas-Reliefs des Bâtiments Royaux d'Abomey*, Paris: Institut d'Ethnologie.
Willett, F. 1967. *Ife in the History of African Sculpture*, London: Thames and Hudson.
Williams, Denis. 1973. "Art in Metal," in *Sources of Yoruba History*, S. O. Biobaku (ed.), Oxford: Clarendon, pp. 140–64.
———. 1974. *Icon and Image: A Study of Sacred and Secular Forms of African Classical Art*, London: Allen Lane.

Karen McCarthy Brown

4

Systematic Remembering, Systematic Forgetting: Ogou in Haiti

O gou is a central figure in Haitian religion. While little known in some areas of rural Haiti, in others he is one of the most important spirits[1] of African origin who are venerated in the Vodou religious system. In cities he has a more prominent role, so that in Port-au-Prince, where no temple neglects him entirely, Ogou frequently is the major spirit of priests and priestesses. Among Haitians who migrate to New York City, those who have Ogou as their *mèt tet,* "master of the head," may well be in the majority.[2]

Ogou in Haiti has his roots in the Gu or the Ogun of the Dahomean or Yoruba peoples, who (along with the Kongo peoples) seem to have contributed the largest concentrations of slaves to Haiti and consequently to have had the strongest influence on its culture. However, he is not simply a reproduction of these African deities. Certainly the Old World played a strong role. Large numbers of slaves were young men whose activities in the African homeland were often centered on the military, hunting, or ironworking—the areas where Ogun was a major patron (Barnes 1980:3, 17, 19–30, and personal communication). It was only natural, then, that this preponderant sector of the incoming population should bring ideas of Gu/Ogun to the New World. In Haiti, however, hunting and smithing were no longer crucial to everyday life, while the soldier took on new guises and added significance. Thus the Haitian Ogou became important to men, and women, of all ages. He also came into contact with Roman Catholicism, the religion of the slaveholders. Indeed, the Catholic saints penetrated the whole world of Vodou— its visual representations, where chromolithographs of the saints came to be used as images for Afro-Haitian spirits, and its naming system, where saint names and Afro-Haitian spirit names came to be used interchangeably. Also central to the development of the Haitian Ogou were several centuries of political and military upheaval, a historical legacy which transformed the African religious cosmos.

It is important to emphasize that any understanding of the centrality of Ogou in present-day urban Haitian Vodou must include an understanding of the history and of the social and political structures of Haiti. Bastide has written that the slave diaspora had the effect of separating "the world of symbols, collective representations, and values from the world of social structures and their morphological bases" (1978:155). In his view, the process by which African religious systems moved into the New World consisted of a search for appropriate social structural "niches" in which symbolic representations could survive.[3] In some cases, such as the match between Ogou and the military in Haiti, such niches were found. In others they were not. When they were found, the fit between cultural image and social structure was never perfect, and therefore the process by which the two came together was one of continuous negotiation, so that, over time, both were changed by virtue of their interaction.

The point I wish to stress about the continuation of African religions in the New World is that elements which are retained as a legacy from the past are subject to systematic and continuous redefinition and restructuring, and that out of this process new cultural forms emerge. The current Haitian Ogou is one such form.

I begin by placing Ogou in relation to the two major pantheons of urban Vodou. I then turn to analyze his various manifestations, mainly through sacred songs. This discussion focuses on military power and its transformations in a variety of political and social contexts. Finally, I will place the Ogou in relation to another group of spirits, the Gède, who occupy a parallel but clearly contrasting place in Vodou cosmology. I conclude that the emphasis given to Ogou in contemporary Haitian Vodou can be attributed to the fact that he is able to mediate between two diametrically opposed forces in Haitian life. These forces, represented by the two major urban pantheons, have gone through many incarnations in the course of Haitian history, but they are perhaps most succinctly named by pairs of contrasting terms such as insiders/outsiders, family members/foreigners, slaves/slaveholders, oppressed/oppressors.

The Rada and the Petro Spirits

The Vodou spirits, or *lwa* as the Haitians call them, were once divided into several *nanchon*, "nations"—Rada, Petro, Kongo, Nago, Ibo, and so on. In most cases, their names clearly indicate their African origins. This pattern is still used in some rural parts of Haiti. However, in and around Port-au-Prince, Haiti's major urban center, two pantheons, the Rada and the Petro, have emerged as dominant, largely by absorbing the other nations into themselves.

The Rada and the Petro groups express contrasting views of the world. One way of capturing this difference would be to say that the Rada pantheon articulates the ethos of insiders and family members, as opposed to the Petro pantheon, which describes that of outsiders and foreigners.[4] One of the most significant changes to take place in African religions as a result of the slave experience was what I call the socialization of the cosmos. For example, natural powers such as those of storm, drought, and disease paled before social powers such as those of the slaveholder. This caused a massive refocusing of the explanatory energies of the African religious systems. This characterization of Rada and Petro as respectively insiders and outsiders is thus in keeping with the general character of African religions in the New World.

The Rada spirits, whose name comes from the town of Allada in ancient Dahomey, are known as *lwa rasin*, "root *lwa*," or by a more general title, *lwa Gine*, "African *lwa*." The Rada are associated with the right hand, with the downward direction, and therefore directly with *Gine*, "Africa," a spiritual home for ancestors and spirits which the Haitians locate in the water under the earth. Hence the Rada pantheon connects the Haitians directly to their African homeland. Indeed, the names and characteristics of most of the spirits grouped in this pantheon have African counterparts.

The Rada *lwa* are intimate spirits who surround one with their protection on a day-to-day basis. Their protective power is of a noncoercive sort and is said to reside mainly in their spiritual knowledge. For example, they are often said to "know leaves," which means they are familiar with herbal healing. Their protective role is further articulated in the fact that they are socially familiar beings who are well known and trusted. They are the elders of the family, and therefore they are sometimes experienced as stern and austere; their fundamental benevolence, however, is never doubted. If a sacrifice is promised to a Rada *lwa* and there is not enough money this year, the spirit can be convinced to wait until next year. The Rada *lwa* thus represent one existential option. Their way of being-in-the-world is defined by family. The central consciousness of this mode of being is group consciousness and its highest value is the preservation of the group.

The origins of the Petro pantheon, and specifically the name itself, are obscure. Some writers have suggested the name can be traced to an eponymous hero, Dom Pedro, who was a Spanish Vodou priest, but there seems to be little historical evidence for this theory.[5] More promising is the suggestion that while few of the specific Petro spirit names indicate Kongo origins, the general ambiance of the group does (Thompson 1983:179–80).

The powers and symbols of the Petro *lwa* stand in marked contrast to those of the Rada group. They are associated with the left hand, with the upward direction, and with leaping flames and heat. In personality, the Petro *lwa* are fierce, severe, and uncompromising. Promises to them must be kept and services rendered with care. One does not break or even bend the rules when dealing with the Petro *lwa*. The ritual vocabulary of the Petro spirits is that of the slaveholders. These *lwa* are served with fire, small explosions of gunpowder, cracking whips, and shrieking police whistles. Some have argued that the Petro spirits represent an expression of rage against enslavement,[6] or an attempt to imitate the slavemasters. I prefer to state it another way: The Petro *lwa* represent an effort to expropriate the power of slaveholding and its contemporary transmutations—oppression, prejudice, economic discrimination— and to use that power against itself.

The Petro *lwa* are the outsiders. Like stereotypic "strangers," the Petro *lwa* tend to look alike and act alike. When they possess their followers, they have personalities that are much less distinguishable from one another than the Rada *lwa*. For example, it is said of the Petro *lwa* that "if you feed one, you feed them all." In spite of this tendency to blend together, the Petro *lwa* are highly individualistic in their mode of being. Likewise, those who seek them out can do so for partisan, even individualistic, purposes. Furthermore, money, notorious for its ability to create social distance, is an area of life where the Petro *lwa* are thought to be particularly effective. The Petro *lwa* thus represent another existential option, a way of being-in-the-world which puts stress on the use of coercive power and the pursuit of self-interest. Because these traits are considered by the Haitians to be too dangerous to become central in the conduct of life, the Petro *lwa* are never given so much emphasis as to displace the Rada *lwa*.

Vodou priests and priestesses in Haiti and in New York are careful to keep their service to the spirits balanced in favor of the right hand, the Rada *lwa*. Yet none is so foolish as to cut himself or herself off completely from the power of the Petro *lwa*.

In urban Vodou, the Ogou are recognized by all to be Nago spirits. This name is the ancient Dahomean title for the Ketu Yoruba (Thompson 1983:17). Nevertheless, these days it is felt that the Ogou should also be classified according to the binary system set up by the Rada and Petro pantheons. The difficulty Haitians currently have in agreeing on how this is to be done points to Ogou's mediating role between the pantheons.

The Rada spirits are associated with water, the Petro with fire. From this perspective, Ogou appears to be clearly Petro. Ogou has a fiery nature: bonfires are lit for him; those who serve him wear red; those who are possessed by him act aggressively. He is also said to fear water, the wisdom of this being captured in the Haitian proverb *Tizo difè di li fou men li pa janm fè nan chemen dlo*, "A firebrand, say it's crazy, but it will never get in the way of water." This otherwise neat picture is complicated by the existence of one Ogou—there are many—who is a water-dwelling spirit. This is Ogou Balendyo, escort of the Rada sea spirit, Agwe. Ogou Balendyo, who also can be identified with Ogou Batala (from the Yoruba Obatala), is known for his herbal knowledge, another Rada domain. For these reasons and because Ogou is clearly a root *lwa* with strong ties to the African homeland, some informants confidently state that the Ogou are Rada spirits. Métraux, who worked in the Port-au-Prince area in the late 1940s, just as confidently assigned at least one of the Ogou (Ogou Yamson) to the Petro pantheon (1972:89). And a Vodou priestess in New York claims that all Ogou are *en dèz o*, "in two waters"; by this she means that the Ogou can manifest themselves equally well in either the Rada or the Petro mode. From this we must conclude that Ogou's ambivalence in relation to the dominant Rada/Petro classification system is a significant dimension of his character.

Ogou's mediating role is further illustrated by the libations offered to the various groups of Vodou spirits. As we might expect, the central element in libations for the Rada *lwa* is water; for the Petro it is fire. Ogou is given libations of rum (fiery water), which are poured on the ground and set on fire, or, mimicking rain, sprayed upward through the air in a fine mist.

The significance of the opposition between Rada and Petro emerges clearly in the ritual rule that the two pantheons cannot be allowed to touch or mix. This principle is articulated in various ways within the Vodou system, including temple architecture, where Rada and Petro altars must be kept separate. Urban Vodou *ounfò*, "temples," consist of a large central space for ritual activities, and *dyevo*, small side-rooms where altars, offerings, and ritual clothing are kept. The number of *dyevo* varies with the financial resources of the temple. Usually the two pantheons are given separate altar rooms; however, even in *ounfò* where only one side-room is available, the Rada and Petro altars are separated by a partition such as a curtain or they are set at right angles to one another. In one temple outside Port-au-Prince where there are several *dyevo*, the separation is further reinforced by the location of an Ogou altar room in between the Rada and Petro chambers.

Ogou's mediating role finds further expression in ritual sequence. Large drumming and dancing ceremonies, of the sort that are common in urban Vodou, begin with an invocation of the Rada spirits in the order of their importance. A similar set of invocations for the Petro spirits follows. The transition from Rada to Petro cannot be accomplished without a shift in the ritual action. Sometimes this is accomplished by a short socializing break in which people eat, drink, and talk with their neighbors. At other times, Ogou will be called between the two pantheons, if only perfunctorily. In each of these examples, we have seen that Ogou mediates between two opposed ways of being represented by the Rada and the Petro pantheons, allowing movement from one to the other.

The urgent work of the various Ogou is to negotiate the social opposition represented in the two major pantheons. The Rada spirits delineate and reinforce familial bonds. They are treated as family and, in turn, treat their devotees with the indulgence and nurturing accorded to family members. The Petro *lwa*, by contrast, embody the individualism, effectivity, and power of foreigners. Petro spirits are not indulgent; they operate according to hard and fast rules that allow no exceptions. The Ogou model a way of being in the world that mediates between family members and foreigners, insiders and outsiders, the home and the larger world outside of it. They are intimate like the Rada spirits, yet powerful like the Petro. But Ogou power, in contrast to that of the Petro spirits, cannot be managed by faithful adherence to rule and principle. Ogou's power is rooted in feeling, specifically in rage, and so it is subject to all the complexities of emotion. As one Haitian put it: "Ogou loves to give people gifts even when he is very angry; he will reward at the same time as he punishes."

The center of Vodou worship, regardless of the classification of the spirits being addressed, is possession-performance. Singing and dancing are said to entice the spirits to possess a devotee. The *lwa* is then said to ride the person like a horse. Once possessed, the *chwal*, "horse," is treated exactly as if he or she were the spirit. Acts of obeisance are performed, gifts are proffered, and the spirit in turn gives advice to individuals and general admonitions to the community. The possession-performance of Ogou, like that of other *lwa*, has certain ritual constants around which the individual *chwal* can improvise. One such constant comes at the beginning of the ceremonial possession, when Ogou does a ritual dance with his sword. First he attacks the imaginary enemy: he rushes wildly about the temple clanging the sword on doorframes and brandishing it in the air. Then he threatens the immediate community: with smaller gestures, he brings the sword's point threateningly close to the bodies of those standing nearby. Finally he turns the sword on himself: lodging the point in his solar plexus, he poses. This performance is to body language what proverbs are to spoken language. In one elegant series of motions, it conveys the message that the same power which liberates also corrupts and inevitably turns on itself.

This exploration of the constructive and destructive uses of power is central to the character of each of the many different Ogou. In the following discussion we will be looking at several of the Ogou through one or more of their songs. It is not possible here to look at the entire range of Ogou symbolism; therefore, a word of caution is necessary. Rather than seeing one Ogou as illustrating a positive use of power and another a negative one, it is more accurate to see each as spinning out another version of the paradox of power expressed in a simple series of movements with the ritual sword.

The Power of Ogou: Against His Enemies

Military imagery is the perfect vehicle to handle the complex social negotiation which is the work of Ogou. Soldiers are given powers beyond those of the ordinary citizen. Ideally they use them to defend the group. Political and military emblems are conspicuously displayed in most Vodou temples. The Haitian coat of arms, with its palm tree, flags, and cannons, appears alongside images of the spirits in temple wall paintings and many temples decorate their ceilings with strings of tiny paper Haitian flags. Until the Duvalier regime fell in February of 1986, pictures of the ruling family often appeared along with the flags. It would be easy to see this as simply politically expedient, but it is not. The political and military imagery penetrates to the heart of Vodou symbolic language about the Ogou. The Ogou are soldiers (Ogou Feray, Sin Jak Majè, Ogou Badagri) or politicians (Ogou Panama, Achade Bokò, Ogou Chango). The military-political complex has provided the primary niche for Ogou in Haiti. It is partly Ogou who, over time, made the Haitian experience of these institutions manageable, and it has been the particular historical con-figuration of these institutions that, in part, gave life and definition to Ogou.

Sin Jak Majè (St. Jacques Majeur) is the senior Ogou. In ceremonies, he is saluted before all other Ogou. Haitians use the Catholic chromolithograph of Santiago, astride his horse crushing the enemy underfoot, to represent Sin Jak. One of the songs used to greet Sin Jak Majè has this refrain: *Sin Jak Majè/ Gason lagè ou ye*, "Sin Jak Majè/ You're a warrior."

Ogou Feray is head of all the soldier Ogou. An especially popular song for him is this one:

1	Seremoni Feray yo premye klas-o
2	Feray Layman, ki chita sou pè-a,
3	l'ap tire kanon. (Repeat)
4	Sa l'a di. Sa l'a fè avek zanfan la-vo.
5	Sa l'a di. Sa l'a fè avek timoun la-vo.

1	Ceremonies for Feray are first class.
2	Feray the Magnet, who sits on the altar,
3	he's firing the cannon. (Repeat)
4	That is what he will say. That is what he will do with his children.
5	That is what he will say. That is what he will do with his little ones.

The language of songs for the *lwa* is cryptic and multivalent. It is never possi-ble to do a full translation or exhaustive exegesis of them. The word *seremoni*, for instance, can refer to healing work done in the name of Feray; to magical work similarly performed (and by implication almost any action done in a Feray manner); to a dancing and drumming feast held for Feray; or to a mili-tary parade, a ritual version of which is performed for Ogou. *Seremoni* also refers to the *vèvè*, abstract drawings which are executed on the floor of Vodou temples to call up the spirits from Africa. The *vèvè* for Ogou Feray is an ab-straction of the Haitian coat of arms. So the reference in this song to the "first class" *seremoni* for Feray can be taken as an allusion to Haiti itself. Such chauvinism is understandable among a people who pride themselves on hav-ing carried out a successful slave revolution and founding the first independ-ent Black republic in the Western Hemisphere.

It should also be said that Vodou military images always include, at some level, a reference to military culture heroes. One is Toussaint L'Ouverture, a brilliant military strategist and canny statesman who emerged as the leader of the revolution soon after it began in 1791. He was considered a saint in his time, and contemporary Haitians continue to venerate him. Subsequent soldier-kings of Haiti have sought to legitimize their rule by imitating Toussaint. Awestruck, unquestioning respect is one layer (among many) in the Haitian attitude toward soldiers, human and divine.

The title Feray the Magnet connects this Ogou to magical and healing powers. Magnets are valued for their ability to find lost objects, particularly pins and needles dropped on the ground. Because of these properties, magnets are often included in healing charms and lucky talismans. Feray Layman is therefore a magician-soldier "who sits on the altar" gathering the lost to himself and waging war in their name. A Vodou altar is the repository of the history of a people. In addition to images of spirits, it contains earthenware pots called *govi* in which reside the protective spirits of the ancestors. In this song, Ogou Feray is thus ensconced at the head of a vast battalion of spirits and ancestors, firing his cannon and launching a revolution on behalf of all his "children." The reference here is clearly to those who follow and serve him, for the Ogou have no children of their own. Through this multivocal symbolism, contemporary Ogou worship in Haiti shows itself to be a fecund marriage of experiences such as the slave revolution with memories of the African Ogun, warrior and forger of weapons. Added to this portrait, through a cryptic reference to Ogou's power to gather in the lost, is a hint at his nurturing or protective side.

The protective power of Ogou is revealed more explicitly in the following verse from a song in which he is called upon to guard the people against police harassment.

1   Aye, Aye.
2   Lapolis a rete mwen.
3   Jij pa kondane mwen.

1   Aye, Aye.
2   The police will arrest me.
3   The judge won't condemn me.

Arrest, often arbitrary, is a frequent fact of life in Haiti: "The police will arrest me"; however, Ogou's protection will suffice in the end: "The judge won't condemn me." Echoes of Ogou's ability to protect those who act in his name could be heard from many sources during the demonstrations and acts of civil disobedience that preceded Haiti's recent change of government.

For example, a fisherman in the northern town of Gonaïves, a center for anti-Duvalier protest, said he was able to stand up to the police only because of special protection given him by Ogou.

The Ogou operate in extreme social situations—in difficult, trying, perilous times—and so the strength they exhibit in themselves and call forth in their devotees is the strength of someone pushed to the limit. The Ogou call on one another and their followers to tap their deepest reserves of energy, as the next song indicates:

1   Ogou Badagri, sa ou ap fè la?
2   Ou sèviye, ou met envèye.

3   M-ta dòmi, Feray, m-envi dòmi-o.
4   M-ta dòmi, Feray, m-pase dòmi-o.
5   Se nan lagè mwen ye!
6   Ou met m-envèye, o Feray o.
7   Gason lagè mwen ye!
8   Yo met m-envèye.

1   Ogou Badagri, what are you doing?
2   You are on guard duty, you must wake up.

3   I would sleep, Feray, I need to sleep.
4   I would sleep, Feray, I am beyond sleep.
5   I am in the war!
6   You must wake me, oh Feray oh.
7   I am a soldier!
8   They must wake me.

In this song Ogou Feray, in his role as leader of all Ogou who are soldiers, calls out to Ogou Badagri, who threatens to fall asleep at his guard post. Badagri responds that he knows it is a situation of war, and even though he badly needs sleep, he is first and foremost a soldier and will stay at his post. The song's message is two-pronged. It first makes a realistic assessment of the situation: This is a situation of war and people are taxed beyond reason. In the second part of the message, it indicates people are up to the challenge. In the New World, in slavery, in the revolution and in the chaotic times that followed it, in the modern experience of political oppression, and for some, as we shall see, in the ghetto life of New York, war becomes the metaphor for life itself.

Ogou is a protective weapon for those who serve him. To wage war daily requires constant watchfulness and herculean energy. It is possible because Ogou taps the deepest source of human energy: anger, the final defiant refu-

sal to admit defeat. Ogou's anger empowers those who serve him, as this song
for Ogou Achade illustrates:

I   Baton pase nan men mwen,
2   Achade pou chè raje mwade mwen. (Repeat)
3   Achade, ki jen m-ap fè sa-ye?
4   Achade, ki jen pou-m fè sa-ye?

I   The club passes into my hand,
2   Achade, for the mad dog bites me. (Repeat)
3   Achade, how am I going to do that?
4   Achade, how am I going to be able to do that?

The same theme is echoed in a song for Ogou Feray which contains the line
Jou m-en kolè enryè pa sa fè mwen, "The day I am angry nothing will happen
to me." In situations of oppression, then, to touch one's anger is to reclaim
one's power, position, and dignity in the world. This is the psychological ma-
neuver at the heart of Ogou's message.

When Ogou is very angry, he can *chante pwen*, "sing a point song."
The point song is another weapon against life's trials. *Pwen* means point,
the point of a story, a comment, a complex human situation, as in, "Do
you get the point?" In short, *pwen* is the condensation of a thing, its
pith. When it is a spirit's power that is condensed, it becomes a talisman.
Within Vodou, *pwen* refers to an object or a series of words or actions
designed to focus the power of a particular *lwa* and thus enable a person
to use that power by internalizing it. *Pwen* can be sung, swallowed, put
under the skin, worn around the neck, or performed over a person. Thus,
when Ogou sings a point song, at the same time that he is sending a pithy
communication to his enemies he is also providing his followers with a
talisman to use when they are angry. One of Ogou's point songs begins
this way:

I   Ankò m-kay mèt-ye.
2   Bef mouri nan men mwen.

I   I am still the master of the house.
2   The bull dies by my hand.

This song evokes an image of rural Haiti where the father is both head of
the household and head priest, controlling the family's access to the spirits

by presiding over their sacrifices. As a point song, it provides a clear and poignant way of reminding those who cross Ogou that he is in charge, while assuring those who serve him that his power will prevail.

The Power of Ogou: Against His Followers

The anger of Ogou vacillates. It is directed outward toward the enemy, but can quickly turn toward his own people when they fail him. Ogou's discipline is severe. To serve Ogou is to be in an army where control of the self makes possible control of the enemy. Ogou's anger and his attacks on his wayward followers are key elements in the possession-performance of Ogou. When the ceremony is large enough and the space sufficient, rituals for Ogou include a kind of military parade, with flags and a sword bearer. After several revolutions around the sacred center pole of the temple, the sword bearer suddenly reverses directions and stages a mock attack on his own retinue. Ogou may even discipline his own *chwal*, "horse," the very person possessed by him. The following is a report of a conversation with a *manbo*, a Vodou priestess who lives in New York, where she has served the spirits for twenty-five years.

> Manbo: When Ogou Feray is really mad, he takes his sword and he (gesture) breaks his own head.
>
> Author: Why do you think he would do something like that?
>
> Manbo: If you do something to make Ogou Feray angry, when he rides you, you suffer. If he is really mad at his *chwal*, when he leaves you have the pain to show for it.

The tendency of Ogou's anger to turn on his own people is captured in another song.

1   Ogou o.

2   Yo di ou ap sonde chwal mwen.
3   Jou m-en kolè m-a vante pwen mwen.

4   Ogou o.

5   Yo di ou ap sonde pwen mwen.
6   Jou m-en kolè enryè pa sa fè mwen.

7   M-di Feray, vre, ou Nago Feray.
8   M-di Feray, ou Nago Feray.

1   Ogou oh.

2   They say you are testing my horse.
3   The day I'm angry, I will boast about my point.

4   Ogou oh.

5   They say you are testing my point.
6   The day I'm angry nothing will happen to me.

7   I say Feray, truly, you are Nago Feray.
8   I say Feray, you are Nago Feray.

In Vodou songs, as in biblical psalms, the spirit is sometimes the speaker and sometimes the one spoken to. In this song, there is an intentional ambiguity about who is speaking. Thus the song communicates simultaneously that Ogou tests those who serve him and gives them protection, a *pwen*, in their time of trial.

Taken a step further, and it often is, Ogou's anger ceases to be about anything as rational as discipline. It becomes blind rage, which, lacking access to the real enemy, destroys whatever is at hand. This is the anger of a child throwing a temper tantrum. One song sung to Ogou with an unusually gay lilting melody captures both aspects of his rage.

1   Ki ki li ki o-ewa.
2   Papa Ogou tou piti kon sa.
3   Papa Ogou enrajè!

1   Cock a-doodle do.
2   Papa Ogou all little children are like that.
3   Papa Ogou enraged!

The song can be read as a caution to Ogou: "Don't be so angry with your followers; all 'children' are that way." Equally, it can be heard as saying, "Ogou throws a tantrum, just like all children."

The vacillation of Ogou's anger, its tendency to switch targets from his enemies to his followers, has historical precedent. This is a facet of his character which is present in the Yoruba tradition,[7] which the slaves no doubt brought to the Island of Hispaniola. It has been amply reinforced by experiences Haitians have had with their own soldiers and politicians. Time and again the Haitians have experienced their leaders turning on them. They are deeply ambivalent about their own military and political history, and that is why Ogou, who moves between constructive and destructive uses of power, has been a natural vehicle for making their history comprehensible.

Three chapters from Haitian history illustrate this point. Jean-Jacques Dessalines was the first Haitian head of state. He gained a place in history by striking the final blow for Haitian independence in 1804. He restored order and brought the economy out of chaos. He also gave the Haitians their revenge by slaughtering all of the whites who remained after the defeat of the French. But he then warned Haitians who resisted his rule of law that they would "merit the fate of ungrateful people" (Leyburn 1966:33). Dessalines built a large army and then began a practice, imitated since, of using it for domestic control. The economic order brought by Dessalines was based on forced labor, and, for the great majority, liberty came to be indistinguishable from slavery. Dessalines outlawed the use of the whip on plantations, but he said nothing when a local vine was used in its place. Laborers, Dessalines said, could "be controlled only by fear of punishment and even death" (Leyburn 1966:41). In spite of this record, some Haitians argue that Dessalines is the most revered of all Haitian heroes. In his own time there were those who felt otherwise. Dessalines was assassinated near Port-au-Prince in 1806.

A second Haitian leader, Guillaume Sam, took office in 1915. Less than a year after his election, and as a result of his execution of 168 political prisoners, Sam was set on by his own people and torn limb from limb. The United States government used this incident as an excuse to invade the country and to deploy its marines to occupy Haiti for nineteen years.

When the third figure, François (Papa Doc) Duvalier, was elected president in 1957, he called on the U.S. Marines to train his army. Like the others, Duvalier used force in pursuit of power.[8] On the one hand, he enjoyed the support of large sectors of the public. He used Vodou networks as a power base and spoke appreciatively of the folk culture of the Haitian people. His popularity was thus built in part on an appeal to Black pride. On the other hand, he established the *tonton makout*, a civilian militia, which exercised an unrestrained brutality toward those who questioned Duvalier's rule. The arrogance, efficiency, and power of the American marines added one more layer of experience to the imagery of Ogou. The Black pride mixed with brutality of the *tonton makout* added another.

Haitians have summed up this aspect of their historical legacy in the following song to Ogou:

1   Sin Jak pa la.
2   Se chè ki la.

1   Sin Jak is not there.
2   It's a dog who's there.[9]

While a previous song (page 74 above) has told us that it is Ogou who puts the club in our hands to deal with mad dogs, this one suggests that the mad dog could be none other than Ogou himself.

The moral, that power is easily abused and that leaders tend to destroy their own people, is stated most succinctly in the spirit known as Ogou Panama. Ogou Panama takes his name from a story told about Florvil Hippolyte, president of Haiti from 1889 to 1896. There were rumblings of political dissent from Jacmel in the South of Haiti, and Hippolyte, it is said, set out on a punitive journey in which he vowed to wipe out the entire town of Jacmel, leaving only one man and one woman to repopulate the area. As he mounted his horse to leave Port-au-Prince, Hippolyte's fashionable Panama hat fell off. The president's son took this as a bad omen and pleaded with him not to go. Hippolyte persisted. He was not yet out of the capital when he fell unconscious from his horse. Shortly thereafter he died. The falling Panama hat not only provided the Haitians with a jaunty refrain for secular songs of political satire (Courlander 1960:150–52), it also provided within Vodou a succinct and appropriately indirect reminder of the dangers of the misuse of political power. One of the songs for Ogou Panama has this refrain:

1	M-di Panama ye,
2	Papa Ogou se neg Panama ye.
3	O Panama ye,
4	Neg Nago se neg Panama ye.

1	I say Panama,
2	Papa Ogou is a Panama man.
3	Oh Panama,
4	The Nago man is a Panama man.

The Power of Ogou: Against Himself

Ogou's anger comes full circle and ultimately is directed against himself. This is the dimension of Ogou's character that reveals itself in the final movement of his ritual sword dance, when he points the weapon at his own body.

Hints of this self-destructive potential are found in Ogou Chango. A brief explanation of the history of this figure is necessary. In Yoruba contexts, Ṣango is the deity of lightning and thunder. As king, Ṣango indulged himself in an arrogant display of power, inadvertently calling down lightning on his own palace and killing his wives and children. In despair he hung himself (Pemberton 1977:20). Likewise, in Yoruba mythology Ogun inadvertently killed his own townspeople and, in despair, committed suicide by falling on his sword (Barnes 1980:28). Ṣango and Ogun, who are quite distinct among the Yoruba, have merged in Haiti.[10] Although Vodou mythology contains no stories about the suicide of Ogou Chango, the "point" of such stories is preserved in his character, as the following song indicates:

1   Kapten Chango, Achade Bokò ye.
2   O Kapten Chango, Achade Bokò ye.
3   Achade li ki ye.
4   Kapten kenmbe, li pa kon lage-ou
5   Kapten Chango, Achade Bokò ye.

1   Kapten Chango. Achade Bokò is.
2   Oh Kapten Chango, Achade Bokò is.
3   Achade is who he is.
4   Kapten holds you, he won't let you go.
5   Kapten Chango, Achade Bokò is.

This song connects Chango to Achade, an Ogou who appears separately in other contexts. Achade is a *bokò*, "sorcerer," and this adds yet another facet to the complex mix of powers which are executed by the Ogou. The powers of the sorcerer, like those of the soldier and politician, are assertive, aggressive ones that are appropriate in confrontational situations. The arena of their action is an eminently social one in which people are divided into two camps: friends/enemies, insiders/outsiders. The inclusion of a sorcerer spirit in the pantheon of the Ogou suggests a situation in which power is unevenly distributed, for sorcery is the weapon of the underdog. Haitians are wary of sorcery. While its effectiveness is accepted, it must be carried out with absolutely correct intentions or it will come back and destroy the one who unleashed its power. The "work of the left hand" is to be avoided because one can easily become trapped in an escalating debt to the powers it calls upon. Finally the only way to pay that debt is with one's own life. The highly ambiguous line in this song, "Kapten holds you, he won't let you go," may speak of care and comfort on the surface, but its sinister meaning lies just below.

Yamson[11] exhibits another dimension of Ogou's penchant for self-destructiveness. Consider the next song:

1   Ogou Yamson sa kap pase?
2   M-ape mande Papa Ogou ki kote ou ye.
3   Lè nou bezwen ou, Ogou Yamson,
4   Nou pa bezwen ou saka tafya.
5   M-ape mande Papa Ogou ki kote ou ye.
6   Kote gildyev ou-a, saka-tafya?

7   Yo ap mande Papa Ogou ki kote ou ye, Ogou Yamson.
8   Lè yo bezwen ou, Ogou Yamson.
9   Yo pa bezwen ou saka tafya.

1   Ogou Yamson, what's happening?
2   I'm asking Papa Ogou where you are.
3   When we need you, Ogou Yamson,
4   We don't need you guzzling rum.
5   I'm asking Papa Ogou where you are.
6   Where is your rum-making apparatus, drunkard?
7   They are asking Papa Ogou where you are, Ogou Yamson.
8   When they need you, Ogou Yamson.
9   They don't need you guzzling rum.

In this song, self-destruction takes the form of degradation.

The degradation of Agèou Hantò,[12] another of the Ogou, comes not through liquor but through other forms of social disintegration, lying and begging.

1   Agèou, ou, o.
2   Agèou, ou hantò!
3   Agèou, ou neg Dahome.

4   Ou mande charite.
5   Ou fè di-set an,
6   T-ap manje youn sèl epi de mai.

1   Agèou, you, oh,
2   Agèou, you liar!
3   Agèou, you Dahomey man.

4   You beg for alms.
5   You passed seventeen years,
6   Eating only one ear of corn.

The direct point of this song speaks of the shame of hunger and the exaggerated stories beggars sometimes tell to move those capable of acts of charity, but the indirect point speaks of the breakdown of the family as the cause of Agèou's plight. In Haiti beggars are reminders not only of the failure of a particular individual to support himself or herself, but also, and more to the point, of the failure of a family to take care of its own. Many times Haitians giving alms will inquire first about the family situation of the beggar and then express more outrage at the absent or irresponsible relatives than at the immediate manifestations of the beggar's destitute condition. The large number of beggars in Port-au-Prince today is a direct reflection of the fracturing of the sustaining family structure that occurs as more and more people are forced to the cities by the soil erosion, drought, and political corruption that are wasting the Haitian countryside.

A poignant song for Ogou Achade captures at once the isolation of the urban migrant cut off from family support, and, reaching back in history, that of the slave cut off from ancestral roots in Africa.

1   Achade o,
2   M-pa genyen mama isit ki pou pale pou mwen.
3   Achade o, zami move o.
4   M-pa genyen fanmi isit ki pou pale pou mwen.

1   Achade oh,
2   I have no mother here who can speak for me.
3   Achade oh, friends are no good.
4   I have no family here who can speak for me.

The songs of Ogou suggest that power is isolating. While the Ogou are said to marry and have lovers from both the Rada and Petro pantheons, they have no children of their own. This biographical detail adds further to our understanding of their power. Theirs is a solitary, individual power, not the collective power of close-knit groups, not the power of the united family. It is true that the soldier is charged with the defense of his people, yet face-to-face with the enemy, he stands alone. Similarly, the politician is isolated in office; the sorcerer works apart and late at night; the city-dweller fends for himself or herself in the world of work; and the immigrant is thrown on his or her own resources. Loneliness is the other side of power.

The loneliness of those who seize Ogou power is thus another form of self-destruction or self-wounding. This kind of chosen isolation causes deep psychic wounds, wounds not easily seen or healed, as is recognized in a song to Sin Jak Majè.

1   Sin Jak o Majè,
2   M-blese, m-pa we san mwen.

1   Sin Jak oh Majè,
2   I'm wounded but I don't see my blood.

Broken families, lost pride, loneliness, alcoholism, indigency, anger without a clear object—these are the wounds of the oppressed and the underside of the self-assertiveness of the Ogou. The following song, which speaks collectively of the Ogou as the Nago *nanchon*, makes this point well. It suggests that while railing against one's fate may not bring success and surely will not bring peace, it provides, quite simply, the last line of defense against suffering. Short of God's miraculous intervention, Ogou-like defiance is the most effective response to hardship. Ogou's tendency to keep fighting in the face of overwhelming odds is thus seen as both an endearing trait and a character flaw.

1   Tout nanchon genyen defo pa-yo.
2   Se pa Nago-a kap pase mizè. (Repeat)

3   Mwen di ye, rele l-a ye.
4   Mwen di ye, rele l-a ye.

5   Kote defans sa-yo? Neg Nago genyen.
6   L-a rele Bondye.

1   All peoples have their flaws.
2   The Nagos don't know how to suffer.

3   I say it is, cry out it will be.
4   I say he is, cry out he will be.

5   Where is their defense? The Nago man has it.
6   He will call on God.

Ogou of the Haitian Diaspora

Haiti is the poorest country in the Western Hemisphere and one of the poorest in the world. The average annual income has been estimated at $260. When this is adjusted to take into account the considerable wealth of the elite, it appears that most people in Haiti get by on less than $100 a year. Eighty percent of the people are illiterate and unemployment in Port-au-Prince hovers around fifty percent.[13] Political repression, poverty, and the diseases associated with malnutrition, including a high rate of infant mortality, are everyday facts of life. Most wealth is controlled by less than ten percent of the population, and the power of this elite group is highly visible and oppressive. Tourism, an important part of the Haitian economy until tourists stopped coming because of the political and social unrest following Duvalier's departure, reinforced the perceived gap between the haves and have-nots of the world. Haiti's moment of glory lies in the past, when her armies and revolutionary heroes stood up to the French and won their independence.

For many Haitians, hope for the future means leaving Haiti. More than a million people, from a total population of 5.5 million, have left the island for the urban centers of North America, principally Montreal, New York, and Miami. Haitians have migrated on and off to the United States since the slave revolution began in 1791, but the present community in greater New York, estimated at 400,000, has been built largely since the late 1950s after François Duvalier came to power. Here the Haitian experience of being on the wrong side of the power balance takes new forms: ghettoization, with all of its attendant problems: racism and degradation at social service agencies; and exploitation on the job market. Those who migrate illegally live in constant fear of being found out and deported. They often work for less than the minimum wage at jobs that are exhausting, and even dangerous. Only a small percentage live with hope for a significantly better future.

Ogou plays a prominent role in the religious life of New York's Haitians. At a small ceremony in Crown Heights, Brooklyn in 1975, some twenty people crowded into the tiny room of a priestess who was carrying out a "headwashing" ritual. The young woman for whom the ceremony was being performed could not find a job and she was plagued by severe and frequent headaches. Her problem was diagnosed as spiritual. She needed to "baptize Ogou in her head" and the headwashing was the first step. When Ogou came to the woman, she had trouble stabilizing the possession. Young and inexperienced devotees sometimes have difficulty making the transition into a trance state. The struggle of this woman was violent and prolonged. When Ogou was finally and firmly in control, a live rooster was brought in. The spirit himself is expected to sacrifice the animal offered to him, but this small and flustered horse of Ogou could not wring its neck. Ogou's anger emerged and, uncharacteristically, it mixed with tears. In this state, Ogou's horse bit through the neck of the chicken.

This was not the only time I have seen Ogou cry in New York. At a much larger and more elaborate ceremony in 1980, Ogou possessed another woman—a strong, no-nonsense person for whom tears in any context would be uncharacteristic. During the course of the possession-performance, the Ogou, in this case Agèou Hantò, spoke with a woman who had lost her oldest child a few months before. The ten-year-old boy was sent back to Haiti to live with family and he died there after being beaten for misconduct. The tears rolled down Agèou's face and the faces of many who listened as he said "You know if I could have helped him, I would have helped him."

The tearful despair of these New York Ogou is a facet of the spirit's character that is difficult to imagine being acted out in Haiti. Perhaps a new dimension of the Haitian Ogou is emerging in the North American setting. Will he one day strut and attack, wave his sword about threatening those near him, turn the point of the weapon against himself, pose defiantly, and then collapse in tears? At the end of the temper tantrum is the exhausted, teary child. It could be said that the majority of Haitian people have always been oppressed, but only in the exile communities do they experience being a minority people on the wrong side of a gross power imbalance. This situation may be bringing out something new in Ogou. Tears could never replace Ogou's aggression, but it may be that immigrant life in New York has revealed another dimension of his anger.

Ogou's way of being-in-the-world provides a cognitive map for Haitians who take up the challenges of contemporary life, whether in Haiti or in New York. As we have seen, Ogou delineates both the possibilities and the potential hazards of doing battle in the modern urban world. This much the Haitian Ogou shares with his contemporary Nigerian counterpart. However, the Haitian Ogou has not taken up the challenge of interpreting modern technology, as he has in Nigeria. To the extent that this latter role has developed at all in Haiti, a country that has experienced much less of modern technology than Nigeria, it has accrued to a different group of spirits, the Gède.

Ogou and Gède

The only other group of spirits that functions in the ritual process as the Ogou do, that is, as mediators between the Rada and Petro pantheons, is the Gède. A Gède possession occuring between the Rada and Petro segments of a ceremony makes a transition possible between these two otherwise antithetical modes. To the extent that ritual process mirrors life process, the Gède and the Ogou can be seen to represent the two major options that the Vodou system provides for handling situations of transition or change.[14]

The Haitian Gède is quite similar to the Dahomean trickster figure Legba and, in some of his aspects, to the Yoruba trickster Eshu (Elegbara). Legba has survived in Haiti but as a venerable old man who has sloughed off his sexuality and, along with it, his tricksterism. For a people so brutally cut off from their ancestral roots, tricksterism may have been unbearable in the spirit responsible for communication between humans and their protective spirits. Legba's tricksterism and his sexuality appear to have been taken on by the Gède. Gède is simultaneously the spirit of the dead, protector of small children, guardian of human sexuality, and irrepressible social satirist. The Gède are licensed to beg, to steal, to tell dirty jokes, and to engage in various other forms of antisocial behavior.

The Gède appear to be the most open and growing group of spirits. Sponge-like, they soak up new roles that appear on the social horizon, many of them having to do with newly introduced professions and technologies. Among the Gède are an automobile mechanic, a dentist, a doctor, and a Protestant missionary. The Gède, the Haitians say, are not a *nanchon* but a *fanmi*, "family." The significance of this will emerge shortly.

As mediators between the opposing forces of Rada and Petro, family members and foreigners, the Ogou and the Gède represent two options for survival in the modern world—a world in which the interaction between insiders and outsiders is increasingly intense, dangerous, and complex. We have seen the option represented by the Ogou. They wage war in the modern world; they face challenges head-on. The devotee of Ogou leaves a starving family to make a living in the city, and ideally to send money home. The Ogou devotee leaves Haiti for New York to do battle with the welfare system and the business world. It is Ogou power that enables the individual to face the isolation inevitably involved in making these moves. It is the distilled wisdom of Ogou's complex personality that keeps an individual from going mad when faced, for example, with the wrenching choice of making progress in the new life or sending money to the family back in Haiti.

The Gède are quite different. Their mediating power comes from a different way of being-in-the-world. The Gède triumph over suffering through humor. Thus a raucous Gède laugh can emerge from a devotee who only an instant before was possessed by a somber, awesome Rada *lwa*. The same quick transition between moods occurs in the marketplace, in the home, and on the job. A tense situation is instantly flipped on its back by a sudden laugh, a quick joke, or a bit of clowning. This is not the confrontational power of Ogou; this is the power of redefinition. And, it always depends on the cooperation of the group.

The Gède are *fanmi*, "family," par excellence. As spirits of death and sexuality, they connect Haitians to their macro-family extending backward through time to the ancestors and forward in time to descendants yet unborn. They are the spirits to whom one can bring the smallest of life's problems. They are gossips who process neighborhood events and invoke in-group norms. Their powers are distilled homely wisdom and satiric humor that dissipate fear and level pretense.

Here lies the complementary centrality of Ogou and Gède. Life presents many problems, not the least of which are oppression, deprivation, and isolation. The social cul-de-sac represented by situations of extreme oppression does not necessarily lead to surrender. There are two possible human responses: rage or humor, Ogou power or Gède power.

Summary and Conclusion

For slaves in the New World, social conflict pushed issues that were traditionally emphasized in African religious systems into the background. The powers of nature paled in relation to the powers that some human beings exercised over others. The religious heritage of the African homeland shifted and blended in response to a need for emphasis on social problems. In Haiti Ogou emerged as central and important because he was effective in this perilous social negotiation.

Ogou's importance in urban Haitian Vodou is clearly demonstrated in his mediating role between the Rada and Petro pantheons. His position as a mediator is reinforced when we compare the Ogou to the parallel, but contrasting, Gède. The opposition between Rada and Petro is seen as an opposition between different ways of being-in-the-world. Familial modes of action appropriate to in-group situations are opposed to the partisan and coercive ways of the foreigner or outsider. Ogou's personality and his mode of action, imagery, song, and possession-performance provide a model for negotiating between these otherwise irreconcilable ways of being.

In Haiti, Ogou's central theme is power. Ogou the revolutionary hero frees his people and puts weapons in their hands for self-protection. He intervenes on their behalf before the civil authorities. He gathers his followers to him like precious lost objects. But he also exacts strict discipline and punishes those who tire or waver. Sometimes his anger turns to blind rage, irrationally attacking those close to him or even himself. His penchant for self-destruction is acted out in sorcery, alcoholism, and indigency. Ogou thus articulates the possibilities and the dangers of power as it is found in contemporary life. He shows the way to the self-assertion and self-respect necessary for success in the modern world. Yet each of his manifestations keeps the negative side of claiming power clearly in view.

Ogou in Haiti provides an accurate description of the social conditions of an oppressed people. In psychological terms, he presents an almost clinical diagnosis of what happens when people internalize anger. However, it would be naive to assume that the Vodou spirits simply mirror the Haitian people. All religions have a moral dimension that makes the transformation of human lives possible (Brown 1987). The transformative potential of Haitian Vodou does not reside in the capacity of the spirits to model morally appropriate behavior, but rather in their capacity to keep the full range of possibilities latent in any way of being-in-the-world before the eyes of the believers. The assumption is that people will choose a right way to behave (there may be many right ways) in a given situation when they have sufficient insight into that situation. Haitian military history yields rich moral lessons when filtered through Ogou. The metaphoric extension of military power to civil power, and beyond to all situations of willfulness and assertion, allows Ogou to give guidance in many troublesome areas of life.

Just as Ogou has interpreted the history and social structure of the Haitian people, so have those realities shaped him. The hunting and iron-smithing connections of the Old World Ogun have not survived in Haiti, because these occupations are no longer central to Haitian life.[15] Neither has the Haitian Ogou taken up the challenge of dealing with modern technology. The central conflict in Haitian life is social conflict. The defining imagery of the Haitian Ogou is military imagery. The Haitian Ogou's anger, alternately turning outward toward the enemy and inward toward his own people and even himself, has parallels in the African Ogun. However, these Ogou traits have been reshaped through interaction with Haitian history. Ogou therefore has new personae (Ogou Panama) and new dimensions of character (in New York, Ogou cries).

Any attempt to account for the changes that African religious systems underwent in the New World must be sensitive to the complex interactions between memory and the material conditions of life in that new place. Through the Middle Passage, into the life of slavery and on into the life of minority peoples, African culture searched for niches in the New World order. Some aspects of African culture found these niches; others did not and were forgotten; those that did were changed in the process. The point is to see these rememberings and forgettings, as well as the apparently new creations, as systematic. African religions did not survive in happenstance fragments in the New World. They blended, shifted, and took on new forms in response to new social conditions, and they continue to do so today.

NOTES

1. Haitians refer to the Vodou *lwa* (a Fon word) as *sin yo*, "the saints," and as *espri yo*, "the spirits," but never as gods or divinities. God, Bondye, is the one and only god and the *lwa* are his servants or messengers. I respect this distinction and follow their language in this paper.

2. Every Vodou initiate has a *mèt tet*, "master of the head." This is the Vodou spirit with whom that person is most closely related. To some extent, there is a mirroring between the personality of the spirit and that of the devotee.

3. "Niche" is the term Bastide uses to describe those parts of the New World social structure that were receptive to African cultural interpretations.

4. This particular formulation of the contrast between the Rada and Petro pantheons is my own. See my Ph.D. dissertation (1976:80–112) for a more detailed analysis of this point. Such precise and abstract language is not characteristic of the way Vodou is discussed among Haitians.

5. The earliest reference to this theory of the origin of the Petro name occurs in Louis Elie Moreau de Saint-Méry 1797–98: v.l, pp. 210–11. Moreau de Saint-Méry is questioned on this point, however, by Alfred Métraux (1972:38–39).

6. Maya Deren believes that the origins of Petro worship are found in "rage against the evil fate which the African suffered . . . to protest against it" (1970:62).

7. "There are stories of Ogun's intoxication with the taste of blood in battle. Such is his thirst that on occasion he kills his own followers as well as the enemy." See Pemberton 1977:17.

It is interesting that Pemberton, who uses the structural method of analysis in this article, also found Ogun to be a mediating figure between two major groups of Yoruba deities. He describes the opposition between these two groups as that between life and death, or culture and nature.

8. "The readiness of Duvalieristes to use force probably exceeds that of any Haitian government in more than a century." Sidney W. Mintz, "Introduction to the Second Edition" of Leyburn 1966: xvi.

9. Dogs are not sacrificed in urban Haitian Vodou, but the dog is a traditional sacrifice among the Yoruba for Ogun. See Barnes 1980:39 and Pemberton 1977.

Pemberton quotes an *oriki*, "praise name," for Ṣango which states: "The dog stays in the house of its master/but it does not know his intentions" (pp. 19–20).

10. The appropriateness of a union between Ogun and Ṣango is instinctively understood by the contemporary Yoruba poet Wole Soyinka. Their coming together, he says, would be "the ideal fusion . . . to preserve the original uniqueness and yet absorb another essence" (1967:86).

11. The name of the spirit Ogou Yamson is possibly derived from that of Oya Yansan, who among the Yoruba was a consort of both Ogun and Ṣango. However, the Vodou Ogou Yamson is male; there are no female Ogou in Haiti.

12. Agèou Hantò is an Ogou whose relationship to a Cuban spirit is instructive. In Cuban Santeria, Agaju is associated with the fire of dormant volcanoes. This fire connection provides one link to the Haitian Ogou. Another can be seen in the relation between the drought imagery in the song for Agèou Hantò (seventeen years and only one ear of corn to eat) and the barren and blighted landscape around volcanoes. Such a correspondence between Cuban and Haitian imagery could suggest an original African source for this spirit's connection to dry, uninhabitable terrain. Another name for the Cuban Agaju is Agaju Solo, the solitary one. In keeping with the strong social emphasis of Haitian Vodou, the image of natural desolation and solitude has been replaced with a social one. Agèou's solitary state arises from social ostracism; he is a beggar. Personal communication, Judith Gleason.

13. Such figures from Haiti are not precise since there are no accurate census data. However, most people who know the country would agree about the general accuracy of these figures taken from an article by Gilbert Lewthwaite in *The Baltimore Sun*, November 1981.

14. The link between Ogou and Gède is expressed in many places in the Vodou system. One such place is the initiation ritual. Each person is initiated "on the point" of their *mèt tet,* their major or controlling spirit. This means, among other things, that initiates literally lie down on the emblem of that spirit. When a person's *mèt tet* is a Gède, special measures have to be taken because the death and sexuality connections of the Gède forbid their presence in the initiation chamber. In those cases, it is Ogou who stands in for Gède.

Furthermore, in the chromolithograph of Santiago that is used for Sin Jak Majè, the knight behind Santiago is commonly understood to be Gède. His full armor, including helmet and visor, is said to make him resemble a skeleton.

15. While it is true that the iron-smithing connections largely have been lost to Ogou in Haiti, they survive in details of Ogou symbolism such as the name of Ogou Feray (*feraille*), "scrap iron," and the Nago shrine that is maintained at most urban Vodou temples. This shrine is a simple clearing on the earth near the temple entrance where bonfires are lit for Ogou. The fire is built around an iron rod thrust into the earth. Métraux notes that this rod is called Ogou's forge (1972:109).

REFERENCES CITED

Barnes, Sandra T. 1980. *Ogun: An Old God for a New Age*, Philadelphia: ISHI.

Bastide, Roger. 1978. *The African Religions of Brazil: Toward a Sociology of the Interpenetration of Civilizations*, Baltimore: The Johns Hopkins University Press.

Brown, Karen McCarthy. 1976. "The *Vèvè* of Haitian Vodou: A Structural Analysis of Visual Imagery," Ph.D. dissertation, Temple University.

————. 1987. "Alourdes: A Case Study of Moral Leadership in Haitian Vodou," in

Saints and Virtues, John S. Hawley (ed.), Berkeley: University of California Press.

Courlander, Harold. 1960. *The Drum and the Hoe: Life and Lore of the Haitian People*, Berkeley: University of California Press.

Deren, Maya. 1970. *Divine Horsemen: The Voodoo Gods of Haiti*, New York: Delta.

Leyburn, James G. 1966. *The Haitian People*, with an introduction by Sidney W. Mintz, New Haven: Yale University Press.

Métraux, Alfred. 1972. *Voodoo in Haiti*, New York: Schocken.

Moreau de Saint-Méry, Louie Elie. 1797–98. *Déscription topographique, physique, civile, politique et historique de la partie française de l'isle de Saint-Dominique*, 2 vols., Philadelphia.

Pemberton, John III. 1977. "A Cluster of Sacred Symbols: Orişa Worship Among the Igbomina Yoruba of Ila-Orangun," *History of Religions*, vol. 17, no. 1, pp. 1–28.

Soyinka, Wole. 1967. *Indanre and Other Poems*, London: Methuen.

Thompson, Robert Farris. 1983. *Flash of the Spirit: African and Afro-American Art and Philosophy*, New York: Random House.

Renato Ortiz

5

Ogum and the Umbandista Religion

To understand the role of Ogum in the Umbanda religion it is necessary to be familiar with the structure of the Umbandista universe as a whole and, above all, its meaning within Brazilian society. Umbanda is not an Afro-Brazilian religion; unlike Candomblé, the religion with which it will be compared here, Umbanda roots are neither black nor African. This does not mean that the African contribution has been unimportant to the formation of Umbandista religion. Quite the contrary, it is fundamental to the development of this new type of possession cult. However, the histories and the scope of influence of the two religions differ. Umbanda is a national religion; Candomblé is one cultural group's religion. Consequently, Ogum differs in each of them. The Ogum of Candomblé is one god among many; he is an unpredictable but accessible member of the spirit world. By contrast, the Ogum of Umbanda has been elevated to an inaccessible position in the cosmos, where he controls unpredictable spiritual forces; indeed, this Ogum has been elevated in some sectors of Brazilian society to the extent that he is a symbol of national identity.

Candomblé is a celebration of the collective African memory on Brazilian soil (Halbwachs 1968; Bastide 1971). The myths and the rites of Candomblé resurrect the gods and the mythic histories originating in Africa. I do not mean that this memory is faithfully reproduced in Brazil; it does suffer from gaps and lapses of memory, and it takes on new elements which are introduced through the process of syncretism. Meanwhile, even when syncretism occurs, the pole of reference continues to be the African continent. For example, even though he has been syncretized with Saint George, Ogum does not lose his original characteristics. Orixá (deity) Ogum possesses traits analogous to the Catholic saint: both are warriors and they combat their enemies.

But the analogy can only be taken so far; Ogum possesses a mythic history which in the minds of Candomblé acolytes cannot be confused with the Catholic hagiography. Syncretism is a form of *bricolage* that treats the Brazilian Catholic influences starting with a system of anterior classification, the collective memory (Bastide 1970). The changes which occur in the religious universe are filtered through the African system of classifying the world. Candomblé is a black religion, even when it is celebrated by mestizos and whites.

Umbanda, on the other hand, is a synthetic and not a syncretic religion. It makes use of the African element but it is not defined by it. Umbanda is a Brazilian religion in that it integrates various religious movements: Candomblé, Catholicism, and Spiritism (as introduced by Allan Kardec). It is a blend of many cultural elements, and for that reason I have referred to it as a synthesis. Without doubt, the African contribution is of fundamental importance, but the black element can be understood only when it is considered from the point of view of all Brazilian society. Umbanda is a national religion, even when practiced by mestizos, blacks, or whites.[1]

It is not easy to describe the history of Umbanda, for studies on this topic are few. There is agreement, however, that the religion emerged and was consolidated around the 1930s. One of the first *terreiros* (cult houses) of which we hear, the *Tenda Espírita Mirim*, was founded in 1924 in Rio de Janeiro. In this period many other cult houses appeared: *Cabana Espírita Senhor do Bonfim, Tenda Espírita Fé e Humanidade, Cabana Pai Joaquim de Luanda, Centro Espírita Religioso São João Baptista, Tenda Africana São Sebastião*, all in Rio (Bandeira 1970; 1961).[2] In 1926, the *Centro Espírita de São Jorge* was founded in Porto Alegre. Little by little, the *terreiros* were united as confederations, and in 1939, the first *Federation Espírita Umbandista* was formed in Rio de Janeiro: it subsequently served as a model for other federations in the rest of the country. In 1941, the First Umbandista Congress took place, with the sole purpose of systematizing the religion and codifying its rituals.

The emergence of the religion also can be documented through the change in meaning of the term *Umbanda*. Francisco Valente showed that the word *Umbanda* (of Kimbundo origin, an Angolan language) was initially used to describe both religious objects and the Kimbanda (an expert in spiritual matters), but was not used to identify a systematized religion that somehow differed from the rest (Valente 1970; Quintão n.d.). Brazilian historians, writing at the beginning of this century, also gave no indication that such an identification had occurred. The Afro-Brazilian syncretism, later Candomblé, was known by the names of *macumba* or *baixo espiritismo* (lower-level spiritism) (Rio 1976). Umbanda was not used in a more generic form until the 1930s, when it slowly became associated with the notion of a religious system. The eyewitness account of a participant in the First Umbandista Congress is very telling on this point. He writes:

A name was necessary to baptize the religious modality which, even before
forming its own personality, was proposed with so much prestige. Umbanda
was chosen. But who chose it? No one can answer that. It is now known that
it began to be used here in the Federal District and in the State of Rio de
Janeiro. Much later, it was popularized, and spread to Bahia where it was incorporated by northern Candomblés and Xangôs. (Bandeira 1961:81)

The emergence of Umbanda in the 1930s is not fortuitous. To understand
the importance of this timing, we must return to Brazilian history. Great social changes took place at the end of the nineteenth century: slavery was abol-
ished (1888) and free work was substituted for slave labor; the Republic was
proclaimed (1889); incentives for European immigration were established;
and urbanization and industrialization processes began to intensify. These
changes had an effect on the whole society, and particularly on the black segment of the population, which began to migrate from the countryside to the
city and, in the process, to occupy a marginal position at the very time a new
social order was being constructed.[3] One consequence was that, faced with
marginalization, Candomblé could survive only as a closed community opposed to the wider society. This did not happen with those practices of African origin which were disseminated into the wider population. Thus, on one
hand cults of African origin became more atomized, while on the other there
was a disintegration and dispersal of other aspects of the collective African
memory.

During this same period, Allan Kardec's Spiritism spread among the
poorer classes. Kardecism, which had a French origin, began to develop in
Brazil in 1865 in the middle class. From the very beginning, spiritualism in
Brazil was religious in form and distanced itself in a way from the rationalism
of Kardec. The first (1873) organized spiritualist movement, *Sociedade de
Estudos Espíritas do Grupo Confúcio*, the Society of Confucian Spiritual
Studies, of Rio de Janeiro, had the motto "true spirits do not exist without
charity," and it advocated the practices of homeopathy and faith healing. The
therapeutic orientation of the movement increased over time until it became
a focus of the religion. Consequently a schism developed between the "mys-
tics" and the rationalists. The latter remained close to the French tradition
of Kardecism, while the former moved away by considering the medium as
principally a healer. Spiritualism was disseminated among the popular
classes, especially blacks and immigrants, in this modified, therapeutic form.
Little by little, whites introduced it to the lower classes, mainly immigrants
and blacks. The interjection of this white element into popular religious
culture reinforced the process of separating black elements that existed
outside the closed Afro-Brazilian communities from the collective African
memory.

The role of "intellectuals" in forming the new Umbandist religion in the
1930s was crucial. The term *intellectual* is used here to designate individuals
who seek to systematize the religious universe. In this respect, Gramsci's con-

cept of the "organic intellectual," as it applies to the religious, not political, realm, is germane. The organic intellectual gave form to Umbanda, just as Weber's intellectual-priest systematized a world religion.[4] The new Umbanda religion emerged, therefore, as the *bricolage* of intellectuals, who "pieced" together elements of the past, including elements of Afro-Brazilian origin. As these elements were reinterpreted within the new religious future, they broke away from the collective memory of the past.

The 1930s, then, possessed a special meaning in the history of Brazil. A period of social disintegration which began at the close of the nineteenth century was followed by a period of consolidation and modernization out of which, by the 1930s, an urban, industrial society emerged. The rise of Umbanda, a new religious cult, taking place as it did in urban centers, thus paralleled the rise of a new socioeconomic order.

The Umbandista Intelligentsia

The role of the middle class in the formation of Umbanda is emphasized by several authors (Brown 1977; Ortiz 1975b). The intellectuals, who almost always come from that social class, are fundamental to its development. Intellectuals write books, establish Umbandista federations, hold congresses, and, above all, seek to systematize the religious beliefs. To a certain extent they act as "theologians" seeking to justify different aspects of their "doctrine." The explanations of the intellectuals retain a mystical quality, but at the same time contain an element of rationality that is characteristic, in the Weberian sense, of global traditions. Several examples illustrate the point.

In treating the principle of reincarnation, as regulated by the spiritual world, an Umbanda manual states:

> Reincarnation is a divine precept of the Father, through which he rewards or punishes, according to each one's merit, since reincarnation has the following as its predetermined ends: to rescue the individual from error and sins committed in previous lives; to furnish spiritual development for the individual; and to impose on each new arrival certain missions of great importance which must be fulfilled while on Earth. (Candido 1965)

As can be seen, this explanation provides a rationale to Umbanda followers for the ongoing intervention of the spiritual world in their lives. The influence of Kardec's Spiritism was a strong element in formulating this rationale. In his widely influential work, *Livro dos Espíritos* (*Book of the Spirits*), Kardec attempted to give the faithful principles by which they might understand the world and to justify the kind of ethical action that would make the salvation of souls possible (Kardec 1857 and 1870).

A second example concerns the justification of magic in Umbanda. A manual states:

All treatises on magic make reference to *pontas de aço* (*objetos com pontas*
or steel points) which are the most effective means of dissolving certain ag-
glomerations of larva, evil fluids, and miasmas. The ancients used swords and
steel points in their magical operations, just as today steel points, particularly
daggers, are used in Umbanda possession rites. The function of the steel point,
i.e. sword and dagger, in possession is like a lightning rod in the thunderstorm.
The principle is found in physics, and therefore it is a scientific function.
(Magno 1952)

In this instance the scientific justification for magic is directed toward both
an internal and an external public: the goal is to demonstrate that the religion
is not a bundle of superstitions, as is frequently assumed by certain "culti-
vated" sectors of the population, but that the values of the modern scientific
world are applicable to the values of Umbanda.

Similarly, the theology of Umbanda also functions to associate the new religion, as a whole, with modern (e.g., scientific) values. This permits Umbanda
to define itself as a system of beliefs rather than of superstitions, and to attribute the latter to the Afro-Brazilian cults. The concept of science is used to
justify the modernity of the Umbandista cult, which opposes, in principle,
the traditionalism of Candomblé and what are considered to be its "backward" practices, that is, those which are said to pertain to an inferior stage
in the development of civilization. Some examples will illustrate the point I
wish to highlight. In referring to the Candomblé offerings that are made to
the spirits of the river and the sea, one writer states:

It is common to see shallow bowls, bottles, ribbons, pig tails, bloody meat, and
even pure blood from slain animals at offering sites. This is pure ignorance,
pure cruelty. It exhibits a lack of knowledge of sacred, spiritual values. The
Divine Umbanda does not accept such barbaric rituals which unfortunately display the backwardness of many creatures. (Oliveira 1971:46–50)

Referring to Candomblé sacrifices (*despachos*) associated with Exu, another
writes:

Sacrifices placed in the middle of crossroads containing bottles or other materials which harm traffic and offer danger to children, aside from bringing scandal
to the Afro-Brazilian cult, are hereby forbidden. (Freitas 1969:98)

Referring to the behavior of spirits at *terreiro* rituals, a third writes:

We call attention to the leaders of the *terreiros* in case possessed spirits use
obscenities. This behavior makes them unworthy of our trust—*pretos-velhos*
and *caboclos* become unworthy of trust—and lose the confidence of laymen.
(Anonymous 1972:11)

Many warnings such as these are directed, above all, to the *terreiros* of the
popular classes, where the practices of Afro-Brazilian origin are more evident
than in the *terreiros* of the middle class. There is still a cleavage between "offi-

cial" Umbanda precepts and their actual acceptance by the leaders of some cults. Just as there are two types of Catholicism—one of the priests and the other of the people—in Umbanda one can discern a distinction between the religiosity of the intellectuals and that of ordinary followers.

The thing which attracts attention in Umbandist discourse is the preoccupation with integrating new values which resemble a religion of the modern world and primarily the idea of "civilization." In the battle to legitimate their religion, Umbandists use moral values and scientific values to elevate their position. In using moral values, their attempts are not unlike those of Mary Douglas, who uses concepts such as purity and pollution to categorize various aspects of a society's value system. For Umbandists, the assignment of positive and negative values provides them with a way to differentiate themselves from the so-called backward practices of Candomblé. Thus the principle of reincarnation carries out an important cognitive function, for it allows adherents to assign Afro-Brazilian cults to an earlier stage of civilization and to place Umbanda at a more elevated position in the spiritual hierarchy.[5]

The Spirits, Good and Evil

Umbanda provides a religious "language" for the integration of human concerns with spiritual force. It is a cult of possession, and in this aspect it is similar to the variety of possession cults which exist in Africa or in Latin America. Communication between the sacred and the profane world comes about through trance during which a medium is "mounted" by a spirit which descends from beyond. The possessed devotee is the "horse of the saint"— the saddle in which spiritual entities ride to manifest their presence on Earth. All Umbanda sessions consist of invocations to the spirits, during which the spirits descend in order to understand and resolve the problems which afflict devotees. The problems include illness, unhappiness in love, or financial failure. The close of each session comes only after the spirits listen attentively to the problems of devotees and bestow charity on them. At this point, they return to the Kingdom of Aruanda.

The spiritual beings of Umbanda differ fundamentally from those of Candomblé. The Umbandist pantheon is, in principle, made up of four types of spirits, grouped into two categories: a) spirits of light: *caboclos, pretos-velhos, crianças*; and b) spirits of darkness: *exus*. The *caboclos* are spirits of Brazil's Indian ancestors, and they represent energy and vitality. They are vigorous spirits, who beat their chests strongly with their fists to offer greetings; they like cigars and smoke heavily during religious sessions. The *pretos-velhos* are spirits of old slaves who represent humility. When they descend, the bodies of the mediums curve, twisting as if they were old men or women overwhelmed with the weight of age. They speak with hoarse voices, but gently and affectionately, thereby transmitting a sensation of trust and familiarity to those who consult them. The *crianças* come in part from the notion of *erê* (spirits of deceased children), which is well-known in the world of Candomblé.[6] Compared to the *caboclos* and the *pretos-velhos*, the *crianças* have an evocative, rather than therapeutic, dimension. They represent the idea of purity and innocence and bring happiness to the cult in the form of folk games. When the children descend, the mediums adopt a childlike attitude; some, who do not know how to walk, crawl on the floor on all fours; others suck their thumbs; and still others speak in an infantile language.

The spirits of light are arranged in a hierarchy. According to Umbandistas there are seven *linhas* (sacred zones) in which the saints are grouped: Oxalá, Iemanjá, Xangô, Ogum, Oxossi, Crianças, and Pretos-Velhos. Each *linha*, headed by an *orixá* (the term is derived from the Yoruba, *orişa/orisha*, meaning god or goddess), is subdivided into successive spiritual divisions. Hence Orixá Ogum is the commander of a sector of the spiritual world in which there are a limitless number of *caboclos*. *Caboclo Ubiratã, caboclo Ubirajara,* and *caboclo Rompe-Mato* are Indian ancestor spirits who belong to the Ogum *linha*. Put in the language of Umbanda, Ogum is the chief of a phalanx of *caboclos*. In Umbanda, unlike Candomblé, the *orixá* does not descend; rather, the spirits who are his messengers come to Earth to listen to human problems.

The Umbandista universe is more extensive than Candomblé, in that the number of spirits is greater than the number of *orixás*. But, in logical terms, what the Umbanda system earns in extension, it loses in comprehension. Ogum is an *orixá* and therefore he does not make himself manifest in a "trance." His spirit messenger is present, but he is not. Consequently, the myths that envelop Ogum (and other spirits) tend to disappear. This allows a greater level of ambiguity to surround the interpretations and behaviors of the *caboclo*. In Umbanda the spiritual personality has a somewhat empty, indeterminate quality. For example, who are *caboclo Ubiratã, Ubirajara,* or *Rompe-Mato*? They simply represent an anonymous mass of Indians who played a generic role in the foundation of Brazilian society. The indeterminacy of the identity of each *caboclo* provides the adept with personal freedom in expressing what he feels the spirit's personality to be. The result is that a personality of a specific *caboclo* is, above all, an expression of the personality in whom it is incarnate, and not a personality taken from myth, as in Candomblé. Even if two *caboclos* possess the same name they never have the same attitudes, or behaviors, because they do not participate as part of the same mythic plot. Behind the *caboclo* stereotype the anonymity of history can be found.

The great difference between Umbanda and Candomblé is the division of the religious universe into compartments of good and evil. Candomblé does not separate the two, whereas Umbandistas define them as the conflict between Umbanda proper (good) and Quimbanda (evil). Ogum is a spirit of light and in this sense he radically opposes backward spirits who inhabit the Kingdom of Darkness. Yet it means that part of the religious world is outside the influence of Ogum's *caboclos*. For example, death and sex are two fundamental elements which exist on the side of darkness; the adept, who may by chance have a nocturnal desire, must seek out an *exu*—never a *caboclo*—in order to realize that desire. Any request to physically eliminate someone, or to realize a sexual desire for another person, can be accomplished only by *exus*. The *caboclos* are specialists in the Kingdom of Good, in other words, in healing illness or alleviating misfortunes, domestic problems, and so on. This does not mean that they do not possess the strength necessary to carry out requests connoted as deviant; it is simply that *caboclos* are considered "advanced" spirits, and undertaking such requests is incompatible with their position.

Among the African *orixás*, there is a special relationship in Umbanda between Ogum and the *exus*. The "point song" below helps to illustrate this relationship:

1	Que cavaleiro é aquele
2	Que vem cavalgando pelo céu azul
3	Ele é São Jorge Guerreiro
4	Que vem comandando a falange de Ogum
5	Traz um escudo no braço
6	Sua espada na cinta
7	E uma lança na mão
8	Ele é São Jorge Guerreiro
9	Que é defensor do cruzeiro do Sul
10	Ele é Ogum matinata
11	Que vem defender o cruzeiro do espaço
12	Em seu cavalo branco
13	Sempre montado
14	É um vencedor de demandas
15	Que na sua gira vem saravar.

1	That gentleman is the one
2	Who comes riding through the blue sky.
3	He is Saint George the Warrior
4	Who commands Ogum's phalanx.
5	He carries a shield on his arm,
6	His sword on his belt,
7	And a spear in his hand.
8	He is Saint George the Warrior
9	Who is defender of the Southern Cross.
10	He is Ogum, the early riser
11	Who defends the crossing place,
12	On his white horse,
13	Always mounted.

14   He is the conqueror of quarrels
15   Who salutes us in trance.

The idea of conquering quarrels (disputes or cases arising over illegitimate requests) is associated with the warrior spirit Ogum, who, like Saint George, combats his enemies. The requests in this case are evil and are only achieved through the help of spirits of darkness. Like the *exus*, the spirits of darkness are strong entities who work with the dangerous dimension of nighttime. Only a stronger spirit can conquer them. Ogum has this superior energy, and at the last moment defends the order of goodness, the Kingdom of Umbanda, against interference from the order of evil, the Kingdom of Quimbanda.

Ogum's control over the Kingdom of Darkness is better understood after one, first, apprehends certain facts concerning the dynamics of the religious universe and, then, analyzes ritual sessions in which *exu* appears. The division of the world into two compartments creates problems for Umbandistas, since they are obliged to relate to the dangerous parts of the universe—albeit in an ambiguous way.[7] The problem that arises for adepts is to deal with the manifestations of *exu* without threatening the spiritual order of the Kingdom of Light. Umbandists solve the problem by establishing a separation between two types of *exu*: pagan and baptized. The religious literature and the practices in the *terreiro* (in this matter there is no cleavage between the intellectuals and ordinary devotees) are clear. The separation is explained as follows:

> The different situations of the two *exus* are defined by their names. The pagan *exu* exists at the margin of spirituality—without light, without knowledge of spiritual development—working on evil magic in the full Kingdom of Quimbanda. The baptized *exu*—characteristically defined as human soul—has been made sensitive to good by working on the "road of spiritual development." The baptized *exu*, as it is said, works for good within the Kingdom of Quimbanda; he is obliged to live in his environment and serves as a policeman operating in a den of marginal characters. (Bandeira 1970:138)[8]

Accepting the concept of baptized *exu* allows Umbandists to incorporate into their religious universe a moral dimension which is fundamental to any notion of completeness. The ambiguity of *exu* allows him to be characterized sometimes as pagan and at other times as baptized. The behavior of the adept in the *terreiro* reveals either one or the other characteristic. In the *terreiro*, all spirits must abide by principles of religious morality, for example, they must not use foul language. During possessions in which *exu* is present there is a constant uncertainty and tension. Will the pagan *exu* explode at any moment? Will the expectations consistent with the Kingdom of Light be met? To achieve the latter, Umbanda sessions must be carefully prepared and the *exus* controlled. A "point song" about Ogum reveals this preoccupation with uncertainty:

1   O sino da capelinha faz belem, blem, blom
2   É meia-noite o galo já cantou
3   Seu Tranca Ruas [exu] que é dono da gira
4   O dono que Ogum mandou.

1   The chapel bell goes ding, dong, ding.
2   It is midnight and the rooster did sing.
3   Mister Tranca-Rua [an *exu*] is the owner of the trance,
4   The owner that Ogum did send.

This point song, a fairly familiar hymn in the *terreiros*, is sung as part of the opening of *exu* rituals. Each ceremony begins with an invocation to Ogum, the *orixá* who is well known for his dominating strength over the *exus*. He represents the separation between good and evil, and provides a symbolic expression of the fact that an inferior spiritual principle must give way to a superior principle. Through their song, adepts seek a diminished margin of ambiguity in the performance of ritual: the spirits that descend are baptized *exu*, they act under Ogum's control, and thus they adhere to the principles of Umbanda.

Umbanda and Brazilian Culture

Umbanda and Ogum play a particularly meaningful role in contemporary Brazilian culture. As I tried to make clear at the beginning of this essay, Umbanda is a national religion developed in Brazil at a particular point in its history. The main spirits, *caboclos* and *pretos-velhos*, are national historical legacies who are transformed into supernatural agents exclusively by Umbanda. The adepts of Umbanda are aware of these distinctive elements in their belief system. In fact, when seeking to enhance the qualities of their faith, many adepts unhesitatingly affirm that Umbanda is the only authentically national religion, in contrast to "imported" beliefs, such as Catholicism, Protestantism, Kardec's Spiritism, and even Candomblé.[9]

The theme of Brazilianness can also be encountered at other levels of the religious universe. One of these is the use of the *caboclo* as a representative of the Brazilian Indian. If we ask about the real influence of the indigenous Indian culture in Umbanda, we observe that it is secondary because the religion was formed in the great urban centers, where the presence of the Indian has been virtually nonexistent. The idealized model of the Indian adopted by Umbanda corresponds to the stereotypic vision which Brazilian society has of the Indian. Edison Carneiro is correct when he states that it was Romanticism which spread an image of the good, courageous Indian and stripped him of all traces of primitiveness (1964). The Romantic movement developed in mid-nineteenth century just as Brazil set itself free from the colonial Portuguese yoke. To establish ideological roots as a fledgling nation and to contrast itself with foreign countries, the movement's intellectuals tried to establish a symbolic model of nationhood. They were faced with unanswered questions. Who were the Brazilians? What was their identity, their race of origin? The answers were furnished by Romantic authors who transformed the Indian into a model of *brasilianismo*. There could be no other solution, since the two other dominant populations evoked images of the Portuguese colonizer or the African slave. Promoted to the rank of founder of the Brazilian people, therefore, was the Indian—however despoiled of his true features— whose resistance to the Portuguese colonizer was interpreted as being a catalyst for independence. In this way, *caboclo* spirits affirm the notion of Brazilianness inside Umbanda.

The issue of national identity goes beyond the frontiers of the Umbandist religious world, however. There is a long tradition of writers, journalists, academicians, and politicians dealing with the notion of Brazilianness. One of the influential mediums through which identity is defined and reinforced is the motion picture. For several film directors, the Afro-Brazilian Orixá Ogum, as represented in Umbanda, is a symbol of Brazilian nationality. Two films, *Antonio das Mortes: The Dragon of Evilness vs. the Warrior Saint* by Glauber Rocha, and *Amulet of Ogum* by Nelson Pereira dos Santos, center on Ogum. The first film tells the story of the battle between the poor and the rich and ends with the death of a large estate owner from the northeast (representing the dragon of evilness) who is eliminated by a black (Ogum) mounted on the white horse of Saint George. The second film tells a tale of crime and love, having as its center the world of Umbanda, but not, it should be stressed, Candomblé. In this film the hero, who has been dedicated to Ogum, is involved in the underworld, where, so long as he wears his deity's amulet, he can protect the innocent and eliminate dangerous gangsters. Ogum's role in both films is consistent with his role in Umbanda: in the war between the forces of evil and good, he defends those in need, rights social wrongs, and upholds the value system when it is threatened.

What must be underlined is that both films make political and social statements in an idiom consistent with Brazilian culture. In the 1960s, these two directors were part of the "New Cinema," whose mission was to create a national art form which projected an authentic Brazilian culture onto the screen, in contrast to the alien culture that was imported from outside. It is in this sense interesting to follow the destiny of Ogum, whose adventures and misadventures on Brazilian soil led him to be considered a medium for expressing the characteristics of national identity.

NOTES

1. For a more detailed study of the differences between Umbanda and Candomblé see Ortiz 1975a.

2. Brown considers the Umbandista religion was born in Rio de Janeiro during the middle 1930s. Her thesis seems questionable to me since the available historical data are insufficient to support it. There is no doubt that the Umbandista movement in Rio de Janeiro developed faster than in other states. However, it should not be forgotten that in Porto Alegre we know that *terreiros* have existed since 1926. See Brown 1985.

3. For further elaboration on the social changes that affected the black population in Brazil see Fernandes 1966; Fernandes and Bastide 1971; and Pinto 1953.

4. See Gramsci 1968 and Weber 1971. For a comparison between Gramsci and Weber on the topic of religion see Ortiz 1980.

5. Unfortunately, it is not possible in this article to cover the relationship between the intellectuals and the Umbandistas of the *terreiros* more thoroughly. It should be stated that the values considered legitimate by the global society have a greater penetration in the *terreiros* of the middle class than in the *terreiros* of the popular classes. This creates an internal conflict for the religion which has the characteristics of a battle over religious power.

6. On the role of the *erê* in Candomblé see Bastide 1958 and Cossard 1970.

7. For a more detailed study of the division between good and evil in Umbanda see Ortiz 1979.

8. See also Fontenelle 1952 and Scliar 1971.

9. See the series of articles edited by Pessoa 1960.

REFERENCES CITED

Anonymous. 1972. "Exu," in *Revista Mironga*, agosto-setembro.

Bandeira, Cavalcanti. 1961. *Umbanda evolução histórico-religosa*, Rio de Janeiro: Apostila apresentada, no. 11, Congresso Umbandista.

———. 1970. *O que é a Umbanda*, Rio de Janeiro: Editora Eco.

Bastide, Roger. 1958. *Les Candomblé de Bahia*, Paris: Mouton.

———. 1970. "Mémoire collective et sociologie du bricolage," *L'Année Sociologique*.

———. 1971. *As Religiões Africanas no Brazil* (2 vols.), São Paulo: Editora Universidade São Paulo.

Brown, Diana. 1977. "O papel de classe média na formação da Umbanda," *Religião e Sociedade*, no. 1.

———. 1985. "Uma história da umbanda no Rio," *Cadernos do ISER*, no. 18.

Candido, Felix. 1965. *A Cartilha da Umbanda*, Rio de Janeiro: Editora Eco.

Carneiro, Edison. 1964. *Ladinos e Crioulos*, Rio de Janeiro: Civilização Brasileira.

Cossard, Binon. 1970. *Contribution à l'étude des candomblés au Brésil*, Ph.D. thesis, Ecole Pratique des Hautes Etudes, Paris.

Fernandes, Florestan. 1966. *Integração do negro na Sociedade de Classe*, São Paulo: Universidade São Paulo.

Fernandes, Florestan, and Roger Bastide. 1971. *Brancos e Pretos em São Paulo,* São Paulo: Editora Nacional.

Fontenelle, Aluisio. 1952. *O Espiritismo no conceito das religiões e a Lei da Umbanda*, Rio de Janeiro: Editora Espiritualista.

Freitas, Byron T. 1969. *Os Orixas e a Lei da Umbanda*, Rio de Janeiro: Editora Eco.

Gramsci, Antonio. 1968. *Os intelectuais e a Organização da Cultura*, Rio de Janeiro: Civilização Brasileira.

Halbwachs, Maurice. 1968. *La Mémoire Collective*, Paris: Presses Universitaires de France.

Kardec, Allan. 1857. *Le Livre des Esprits*, Paris: Librairie Spirite.

———. 1870. *Caractères de la Révélation Spirite*, Paris: Librairie Spirite.

Magno, Oliveira. 1952. *Umbanda e Ocultismo*, Rio de Janeiro: Editora Espiritualista.

Oliveira, Jorge de. 1971. *Umbanda Transcendental*, Rio de Janeiro: Editora Eco.

Ortiz, Renato. 1975a. "Du syncrétisme à la synthèse: Umbanda une religion brésilienne," *Archives des Sciences Sociales des Religions*, no. 40.

——— 1975b. *La Mort Blanche du Sorcier Noir*, Ph.D. thesis, Ecole Pratique des Hautes Etudes, Paris (published in Portuguese, Editora Vozes, 1978).

———. 1979. "Umbanda magie blanche, Quimbanda magie noire," *Archives des Sciences Sociales des Religions*, no. 47/1.

———. 1980. *A Consciência Fragmentada*, Rio de Janeiro: Brasiliense.

Pessoa, J. A. 1960. *Umbanda: religião do Brasil*, São Paulo: Editora Obelisco.

Pinto, L. A. Costa. 1953. *O Negro no Rio de Janeiro*, São Paulo: Editora Nacional.

Quintão, José. n.d. *Gramática de Quimbundo*, Museu de Luanda.

Rio, João do. 1976. *As Religiões no Rio*, Rio de Janeiro: Nova Aguilar.

Scliar, Marcos. 1971. *Umbanda Magia Branca*, Rio de Janeiro: Editora Eco.

Valente, Francisco. 1970. "Feiticeiro ou Quimbanda," *Ultramar*, ano 10, no. 39.

Weber, Max. 1971. *Economie et Société*, Paris: Plon.

This essay was translated from the Portuguese with the assistance of Maria Elena Viera Branco, Wilson Trajano Filho, and Charlene Flanagan.

PART TWO

The Meaning of Ogun in Ritual, Myth, and Art

6

The Dreadful God and the Divine King

1   Atótó! Arére!
2   Kéléjì ó má fò, kigbárája ó má lura ra wọn.
3   Àwa dé, ègbodò ilé kò gbọdò ṣọdọ poro.
4   Ìlògì kò gbọdò ṣọlo ṣúkúṣúkú.
5   Ọmọ kékeré ilé kò gbọdò sọkún kí ngbó.
6   Kí ọlómú ó fi ọmú bọ ọmọ rè lénu.
7   Ọjó Ògún tòkè bọ aṣọ iná ló fi bora, èwù èjè lówò.
8   Ọpò olókó ló fi òkò rẹ dáná;
9   Ọpò olóbò ló l'àbò rè dáná.
10 Ẹdun olú irin, àwọnyè òrìṣà tíí bura rè sán wọnyìnwọnyìn.
11 Ifèèfèè lolè lebu, panlawọ, olùjèkà, má bù mí jẹ.
12 A mu sí Póngà; ó ba Póngà jé.
13 A mu sí Àkò-Ire, o là kò dànù.
14 A mú Ògún wọdò Ògún sì là omi lógbọgba.
15 Èrù jèjè tíí ba ará àdúgbo.
16 Ògún Ọgbórọ ló ni ajá; òun lapa já fún.
17 Ògún Onírè ló lèjè; Mọlàmọlà ló ni èkuru.
18 To ní gbàjámo, irun ló njẹ.
19 Ti òkọlà níí jẹ ìgbín.
20 Ògún gbénàgbénà igi lónjẹ.
21 Suminiwa, Ajọkẹopo.
22 Èrù Ògún mà ḿbà mí o.
23 Abi-ọwó-gbọgbọgbọ tii yọ ọmọ rè nínú òfin.
24 Yọ mí.

1   Silence! Silence!
2   Let no one talk: let no household utensil touch another.

3   We are here. Let no one pound any new yam.
4   Let no one grind anything.
5   Do not allow me to hear children crying.
6   Let every woman breastfeed her child.
7   On the day Ogun arrived from the hilltop, he wore a bright red
     dress, a cloth of blood.
8   He caused many a man to burn his penis;
9   He caused many a woman to slash open her vagina.
10   The owner of iron; the enraged òrìṣà who bites himself.
11   The fire that drives thieves away, that changes the color of iron and
     devours the wicked; do not harm me.
12   He was taken to Pọ́ngà; he ruined Pọ́ngà.
13   He was taken to Àkọ̀-Ire; he ruined Àkọ̀-Ire.
14   We took Ogun to the river, he divided the river in half.
15   The terrible one who strikes terror in men's minds.
16   Ogun of Ọ̀gbọ́rọ́ eats dogs and we give him dogs.
17   Ogun of Onírè needs blood; Ogun Mọlàmọlà eats mashed beans.
18   Ogun, who controls razors, feeds on hair.
19   Ogun, who controls those who circumcise, feeds on snails.
20   Ogun, who controls carvers, feeds on wood.
21   Suminiwa, Ajọkẹopo.
22   Oh! I am afraid of Ogun.
23   Ogun, whose long hands can save his children from the abyss.
24   Save me.[1]

Among the 20 million Yoruba people of southwestern Nigeria, Ogun is one of the principal deities in the pantheon of òrìṣà (gods). The regional variation in the person and number of the gods is so great that the Yoruba say that there are 401 òrìṣà. In this vast and complex religious system, only Ifa, the deity of divination, and Eṣu, the deity who carries offerings and sacrifices to the gods and to other spirit powers, are as widely known and worshipped as Ogun; and in many communities only ancestral festivals rival in importance that for Ogun in the annual liturgical calendar.

In the northern Yoruba town of Ila-Ọrangun[2] there are two civic festivals in which Ogun is prominent. The one, Ọdun Ogun, is held for seven days in early June.[3] The other, Ọdun Oro, also referred to as Ọdun Ọba (festival of the king), is held for thirteen days in early September. In this essay I describe segments of the two festivals, but concentrate on the ritual segment, which in the festival for Ogun is called "Iwa Ogun" and in the festival for the king is called "Iwa Aṣọ." It is a rite of considerable complexity and dramatic action. Its importance in Ila is indicated by the fact that it is performed three times in the annual liturgical calendar, once in the festival for Ogun and twice in the festival for the king.

In many respects rituals and, by extension, festivals are like myths in that they may be "read" as textual statements and interpreted in terms of the images, motifs, and structural patterns of which they are composed. They may also be understood as religious metaphors as Fernandez has argued, and, following Geertz, as "enactments, materializations, realizations" of a particular religious perspective "that moves beyond the realities of everyday life to wider ones which correct and complete them" (Fernandez 1977:100–131; Geertz 1973:112). My reading of the ritual of Iwa Ogun, and of the material representations and oral traditions associated with it, suggests that Ogun symbolizes the reality and ambiguity of violence in human experience, a violence that creates through acts of destruction, but which can also destroy what it has created. The rites of Odun Ogun require the Yoruba to recognize the irony of cultural existence: death is essential to life. Yet these same rites reveal that if humans are to achieve social and political accord, then they must submit to a cultural power which can appease, even transcend the dreadful power of Ogun. That is what is acknowledged in the festival of Odun Ogun and affirmed in Odun Oro.

Odun Ogun: The Festival for Ogun

Odun Ogun is a community-wide celebration. The principal participants are associated with three distinct aspects of Ila society: kingship, chiefship, and occupation. The participants representing kingship include the *oba* (king, also called Orangun), the *olorì* (king's wives), the *omoba* (members of the royal family), the *omodégbélé* and *emèsè* (palace servants and messengers), the Baale Onilu (chief drummer), and the palace drummers. The chiefly participants are town, warrior, and lineage chiefs, who ordinarily inherit their titles through their kin groups. These chiefly groups are the *afóbaje* (seven senior chiefs, who are known as the kingmakers), an unspecified number of junior chiefs,[4] the Balogun and Ologun (warrior chieftaincy groups),[5] the Ikegbe (ritual chiefs who are associated with installing and burying the king), and the Ojuwa (heads of lineages who are affiliated with Chief Elemona, an *afóbaje* chief, who is the messenger between the senior chiefs and the king). The representatives of occupational groups include the Oloode (chief of hunters), the Oloriawo Onifa (leader of the divination priests), and the Oloriawo Onisegun (leader of the herbalist priests). Blacksmiths conduct essentially private rituals at their stalls during the festival. They do not participate in the public spectacles.

Days 1 through 6

In 1977, when I first witnessed Odun Ogun, the festival began with a ritual reenactment of the founding of the town of Ila-Orangun. On the morning of the first day, the six senior Ologun warrior chiefs, led by Chief Elekehan, paraded to the site of the ancient and abandoned town of Ila-Yara, which lies about five miles to the south of Ila-Ǫrangun; according to palace tradition, Ǫrangun Igbonnibi in 1460 led the members of the Arutu family from Ila-Yara to the site of the present Ila-Ǫrangun.[6] Each warrior chief carried an *ògbó* or an *òdùrǫ* (a cutlass or an iron cudgel) to which *màrìwò* (fresh palm fronds) had been tied. At the site of the abandoned town the chiefs tied *màrìwò* around an *àràbà* (white silk cotton) tree, and there they worshipped Ogun by sacrificing a dog and praying for peace. Just before sunset the warrior chiefs returned to Ila-Ǫrangun, bringing with them a rock, which was added to several hundred other rocks constituting the Ogun Ǫja (one of the town's Ogun shrines) located in the Ǫba Ǫja (the King's Market). Four kolanuts were placed on the rock by Chief Ẹlẹkẹhan as he praised Ogun and prayed for peace. Word was sent to the *ǫba* that the rock from Ila-Yara had arrived and the Ogun festival had begun.

On the following day, the blacksmiths hung *màrìwò* at the entrance to their stalls and sacrificed dogs to Ogun at their smithy shrines (fig. 6.1). Together, with all others who work with metal instruments—carvers, carpenters, barbers, circumcisers, facial scarifiers—they smeared their tools with sacrificed blood and offered praises and prayers to Ogun. Each dog's head was added to a collection of skulls, bits of metal, palm fronds, and *oògùn* (packets of medicine) suspended above the large rock or cement mound that is Ogun's shrine.

On the third day, the *ǫba* joined the warrior chiefs in making three sacrifices to Ogun. The rite, called Iṣagun, was performed once in the morning and twice in the afternoon. On each occasion the king, dressed in the robes and wearing the beads of a chief, left the palace to meet the senior warrior chiefs at the Ogun shrine opposite the palace gates. The Balogun warriors were represented by their chiefs, Otun Balogun and Osi Balogun, and the Ologun warriors by their chiefs, Ẹlẹkẹhan, Oloyin, and Sagiku. The king was accompanied by Chief Ẹlẹmǫna, the Ojuwa chiefs, and the *ẹmẹsẹ̀*.[7]

The king and warrior leader briefly confronted each other before making their sacrifice. As the king approached the Ogun shrine, he and Chief Ẹlẹkẹhan rushed toward each other with raised cutlasses, but they stopped short of a conflict as each touched his cutlass to the ground three times. Ẹlẹkẹhan greeted the *ǫba* and invited him to the shrine. The Ogun shrine was at the base of what was once an enormous *àràbà* tree, around which *màrìwò* was tied.[8] Here the *ǫba* and Chief Ẹlẹkẹhan joined in offering kolanuts and the following prayer:

1   Ògún! Obí re re o.
2   Fún wa ní àláafià.
3   Ma da wahale silu.

1   Ogun! We give you kola.

FIGURE 6.1. A blacksmith's Ogun shrine. A devotee sits before the great stone for Ogun. From the rafters hang *màrìwò*, a dog's head, and other sacrificial items and sacred emblems.

2   Give us peace.
3   Do not make trouble in our town.

In the past, a dog was brought to the shrine by the king's servants and the warrior leader offered a second prayer:

1   Ògún, eran rẹ re o.
2   Ma pa wa o.
3   Gbà wá lówó ikú.
4   Ma jẹ́ k'ọ́mọ dé rí ewu ọkọ̀.
5   Ma jẹ́ k'ágbà rí aìsàǹ.
6   Ma jẹ́ káboyún sọ oyún nù.
7   Ma jẹ́ k'óde rí àgbàkó.
8   Jẹ́ ká ní àláafìà.

1   Ogun, here is your festival dog.
2   Do us no harm.
3   Keep us safe from death.
4   Do not let the young have accidents.
5   Do not let the elderly suffer disease.
6   Do not let pregnant women have miscarriages.
7   Do not let the hunter be killed.
8   Let us have peace.[9]

With a swift, deft swing of his cutlass, Chief Ẹlẹkẹhan severed the dog's head from its body. The head was tied among the palm fronds on the tree trunk so that the blood dripped on the stone of Ogun. (Although the sacrifice of the dog is omitted today, kolanuts are offered to Ogun and the participants carry out the other parts of the rite.)

Chief Ẹlẹkẹhan moved to the palace *gbẹ̀du* drums, on which the *ọmọ-dégbélé* (king's messengers) were beating the rhythms for Ogun, touched his cutlass to the ground three times, saying, "Ogun, we come to beg for peace!" and danced a few steps. The king and each of the warrior chiefs honored Ogun in the same fashion. Then to the multiple rhythms of the *gbẹ̀du*, *bàtá*, and *dùndún* drums, the *ọba*, and his entourage, led by the Ologun and Balogun chiefs and followed by the Ẹlẹmọna, the Ojuwa chiefs, the *olorì*, and the *ẹmẹsẹ̀*, paraded around the shrine. On the seventh time around, the rhythms quickened and the participants circled the shrine at a run. Before returning to the palace, the *ọba*, sword in hand, danced at length to the drum rhythms for Ogun (fig. 6.2).

Later in the evening of Iṣagun, the chiefs joined the king in the palace for a feast. They arrived in order of their seniority, knelt before the king,

FIGURE 6.2. The *ǫba* dancing to the *gbèdu* drum at the Ogun shrine during the rite of Iṣagun.

and saluted him three times: "*Kábíyèsí. Ẹ kú Ọdún.*" ("Your Highness. Festival greetings.") The *ọba* replied, "*Àṣẹ.*" ("Let it come to pass.") Then the representatives of the Ikẹgbẹ chiefs, followed by the Balogun and Ologun chiefs, arrived, each saluting the *ọba* by touching his cutlass or cudgel to the ground three times and repeating the festival greetings. The king then led the chiefs to a banquet in the palace, but he did not eat with them. Throughout the next four days the Ologun chiefs feasted one another in accordance with their rank.

On the afternoon of the fourth day, Ila's hunters became active in the festival. The Ọlọọdẹ of Ore's compound, one of seven hunter chiefs for whom Ogun is the patron *òrìṣà*, came to the palace to greet the *ọba* on behalf of Ila's hunters. Accompanied by members of his family, hunters, dancers, and drummers, the Ọlọọdẹ escorted two *egúngún láyẹwú* (masquerades for deceased hunters) into the outer courtyard of the palace. One of the masquerades, called *aláàrù láyẹwú*, was entirely covered by a large, conical, tent-like construction made of antelope skins with four antelope horns protruding from the top. It was removed before the dancers approached the *ọba* and the Ojuwa chiefs, who were seated on the porch of the palace reception hall. The dancers were dressed in close-fitting cloth costumes designed to resemble a forest cat. A braided hairpiece of a type worn by hunters hung down the left side of the head. The hunter's flywhisk was carried on the left shoulder and leather pouches of protective medicine, similar to those worn by hunters, were tied about the waist and neck (fig. 6.3). The masquerades danced before the *ọba* and chanted *ìjálá*, (poetry associated with Ogun of the hunters). They sang the praises, not only of Ogun and the *ọba*, but also the *oríkì* (praise names), of the hunter chief and of the lineage and house from which the masquerades came. The king presented kola and money to the masquerades and asked that they convey his greetings to all of Ila's hunters.[10] That evening Ila's hunters gathered at the Ọlọọdẹ's house to feast and sacrifice a dog to Ogun.

There was now a two-day respite from the bloody sacrifices to Ogun before the festival was concluded.

Iwa Ogun (Day 7)

The final rite of Ọdun Ogun, a rite called Iwa Ogun, began in the afternoon on the seventh day. The king's servants prepared the veranda at the front of the palace, placing a rug, the king's throne, and a hassock before three elaborately carved panels at the center of the veranda wall. The panels frame a doorway which leads to a small chamber and, beyond it, the palace courtyard. A few townspeople moved slowly along the three roads which meet at the front of the palace.

Simultaneously, the chiefs assembled near the palace. The seven senior chiefs and representatives of the junior chiefs gathered on the veranda of the house of Chief Ọbale (the second-ranking senior chief and the head of the

FIGURE 6.3. The hunter's masquerades, *egúngún láyè̩wú,* chanting *ijalá* at the palace.

palace servants). The leaders of the Balogun and Ologun warrior chiefs and of the Ikẹgbẹ ritual chiefs assembled at the Ogun shrine, which was near Ẹlẹmọna's compound and halfway between the palace and Chief Ọbale's compound (see fig. 6.4). *Gbẹ̀du* drums were beaten at the Ogun shrine and at Chief Ọbale's veranda. They did not compete in volume or complexity of rhythm, however, with the *gbẹ̀du* and *dùndún* drums played in the palace courtyard.

The Ewe Ogun also took their place at the Ogun shrine. They are daughters of the Igbonnibi ruling house, whose son now occupies the throne.[11] The *ọmọba* (princes) and other members of the ruling house joined the townspeople in front of the palace veranda. The crowd had become quite large and the passage of traffic was brought to a halt.

The king's arrival was announced by the drums. Although royal umbrellas were raised above his head, he was dressed as a chief, in an embroidered red gown. After paying homage at an unmarked burial site of his predecessor, Ọrangun Igbonnibi,[12] the *ọba* left the palace courtyard and moved to the veranda with his servants and drummers, who sounded the rhythms reserved for the *ọba*. The king's wives and children sat on his right; beyond them sat the *ọba*. The *ẹmẹsẹ̀* and the *ọmọdégbélé*, armed with whips, stopped all traffic.[13] No one must cross the area between the palace and Ọbale's house, on pain of becoming a servant or wife of the *ọba*. Twenty minutes passed. The townspeople grew restless and the *ọba* impatient, and all looked in the direction of Ọbale's compound.

After long delays, the Ikẹgbẹ chiefs, Ọbasinkin and Ọdọọde, accompanied by a drummer, moved across the road from the Ogun shrine to Chief Ọbale's veranda.[14] They greeted Chief Ọbale and then, to the sharp, staccato rhythms of the *bàtá* drum, danced before the assembled senior and junior chiefs. In response to the Ikẹgbẹ dance, the chiefs left Ọbale's veranda and moved to the edge of his compound, where they sat facing the distant *ọba*. At the same time, the *ọba*'s chief drummer, Baale Onilu, left the palace veranda and moved in the direction of Chief Ẹlẹmọna's house, which is just beyond the Ogun shrine. He "called" Ẹlẹmọna by drumming his name, inviting him to join the *ọba*. The Ẹlẹmọna responded by leading the Ojuwa chiefs to the king.

The Ojuwa chiefs greeted the king with extreme deference. As they approached the *ọba*, they removed their hats, placed their fans on the ground, and rolled up the flowing sleeves of their gowns, knotting them behind their necks. They knelt, rubbed the palms of their hands together, and Ẹlẹmọna saluted the *ọba*:

1   Ẹ kú Ọdún.
2   Kábíyèsí, ẹbọ á fín.
3   Èrù á dà!

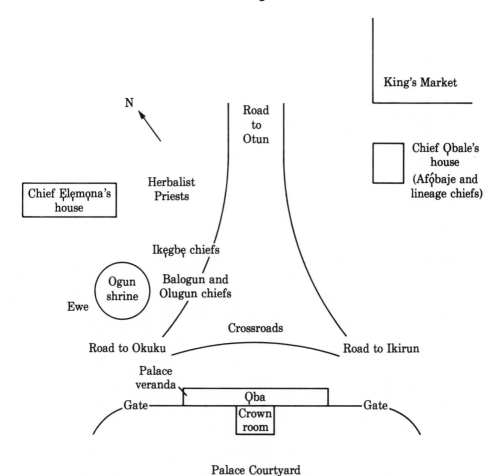

FIGURE 6.4. Iwa Ogun: Ritual Space and Participants

4   Agbèrù o gba ebo!
5   Alásekà o bá ọ sé!
6   Ilú á rójú.
7   Ilú á tòrò.
8   Ògún ò rí wòlú.
9   Ikú ọmọ wẹ́wẹ́ kòrí wọlú.
10   Èmí tí o se ọdún ní ni yóò se ẹẹmi.
11   Ìgbà yín á tù wá lára.
12   Ẹyin lao ṣà lẹ́ẹ̀mîi.
13   Kábíyèsí.

1   Festival greetings.
2   Your highness, may the sacrifice be accomplished.
3   It will happen!
4   Your predecessors will make it successful!
5   The ancestors will assist you.
6   May there be no disturbance in the town.
7   May there be peace in the town.
8   May war not come.
9   May death not take little children.
10   May you be able to perform this (rite) next year.
11   May your reign be peaceful for us.
12   May we be able to greet you again next year.
13   Your highness.[15]

Then the Ojuwa chiefs prostrated themselves before the king. In response the *ọba* rolled his flywhisk between the palms of his hands, touched it to the hands of the senior palace messenger, and instructed him to touch the up-raised palms of the hands of Chief Ẹlẹmọna and the other chiefs, to present them with kola, and to beckon them to the throne. When Ẹlẹmọna presented himself to the king, the king instructed him to go to the chiefs at Ọbale's veranda and invite them to the palace front in order that the festival for Ogun might be concluded.[16]

When Ẹlẹmọna conveyed the king's request, the senior and junior chiefs remained aloof. In an effort to bring the chiefs into the proceedings, Baale Onilu drummed Ẹlẹmọna's name and again led him and the Ojuwa chiefs to Ọbale's compound. As before, Ẹlẹmọna greeted the senior and junior chiefs and invited them to the palace. They refused and the emissaries returned to the palace veranda, where they again saluted the king. With tension mounting, the emissaries returned a third time to the chiefs. This time, however, Baale Onilu stood in front of the Ẹlẹmọna and drummed with such power that he required Chief Ẹlẹmọna and the Ojuwa chiefs to dance the distance separating the *ọba* from the recalcitrant chiefs. Once again Ẹlẹmọna greeted the chiefs, but this time, as he stretched forth his hands, he pleaded: "This is the hand of the Ọrangun. He asks you to come nearer to him. There is no conflict between you and him." The Ẹlẹmọna then touched the hands of each chief. At last the emissaries persuaded the chiefs to accompany them as far as the center of the road, where they took seats in a line adjacent to the Ogun shrine.

At the moment the chiefs responded to the Ẹlẹmọna, the king left his throne. He entered the small chamber behind the carved panels of the veranda and changed from the clothes of a chief to royal robes and the conical beaded crown with veil called Ologun Ade (The Crown of the Warrior Chief). When Ẹlẹmọna and the Ojuwa chiefs returned from their success-ful mission, the *ọba* reappeared in his royal person (fig. 6.5). The king moved

FIGURE 6.5. The Ọrangun-Ila wearing the Ologun crown and greeting Ila's chiefs during Iwa Ogun.

rapidly to the Ogun shrine, where he was greeted by the Ologun warrior chiefs and where he offered kola to Ogun. Chief Ẹlẹkẹhan placed the offering on the shrine and, on behalf of the king, prayed:

I	Ògún, obì ọba re o.
2	O ńtoro àláafiá.
3	Ma pá o.
4	Jẹ́ kó s'àmódún kó mú.
5	Obì ẹ wá lẹ́ẹmi.

I	Ogun, here are the *ọba*'s kolanuts for you.
2	He asks for peace.
3	Do not harm him.
4	Let him live that he may return again to offer
5	you kolanuts next year.

The *ọba* then proceeded to the center of the road, where he stood silently before the seated senior and junior chiefs.

The climax was reached when a mock battle broke out between the palace servants and the warrior chiefs led by Ẹlẹkẹhan. The skirmish took place in the space between the king and the other seated chiefs. The antagonists clashed, striking one another with branches and making threatening gestures with cudgels and swords (fig. 6.6). Finally, at a signal from Chief Ọbale, the fighting stopped.[17] As the Ojuwa chiefs had done earlier, the senior and junior chiefs rolled up the sleeves of their gowns, placed their fans on the ground, and prostrated themselves before the Ọrangun (fig. 6.7). The *ọba* again rolled his flywhisk between his hands and touched the hands of Chief Ẹlẹmọna who in turn touched the hands of each chief, raising him up. When all were standing, the palace drummers began their rapid rhythms and the *ọba* danced along the line of chiefs before returning to the palace veranda. Once the Ọrangun was on his throne, the chiefs of Ila moved in a phalanx toward the king. They knelt and greeted him with the salutation: "Ẹ kú Ọ-dún. Kábíyèsí. Ọba aláàṣẹ èkejì òrìṣà." ("Festival greetings, your highness! The king's power is like that of the gods.") The *afọ́baje* sat to the left of the king, opposite the Ojuwa chiefs, thereby creating an open stage between the palace and the Ogun shrine.

The chiefs and priests were then honored before the king. The chief drummer looked in the direction of the Ogun shrine, sounded the praise names of the various chiefs, who in sequence bowed, touched their cutlasses and cudgels to the ground, and danced before the king (fig. 6.8). Then the drum called the diviner and the herbalist priests. They too touched their staffs of office to the ground three times and danced before the king. Finally, the princesses left the Ogun shrine, chanting the king's praises as they approached

FIGURE 6.6. The mock battle enacted by the palace servants and the Ologun chiefs during the rite of Iwa Ogun.

FIGURE 6.7. The *afóbaje* and lineage chiefs greeting the *ọba* at the palace in the rite of Iwa Ogun.

their kinsman; they knelt before the throne, and a servant gave each one a kolanut and a coin, as he had done to all others.

Finally, the king was honored before the chiefs. The palace drummers marched to the crossroads in front of the palace and the crowd fell silent. Baale Onilu faced the king and drummed the names and *oríkì* of the twenty-three kings of Ila from the time of Ọrangun Ajagun-nla, son of Oduduwa, to the present reigning *ọba*, Ọrangun William Adetona Ayeni, Ariwajoye I. The virtuoso solo performance, called *Ẹ̀kà kékà*, took fifteen minutes. As he completed the praises of the *ọba*, the crowd shouted: "*Kábíyèsí! Kábíyèsí! Kábíyèsí!*" and his highness left the throne to dance before the chiefs, in order of their seniority, and the townspeople. To the cheers of the crowd, the king, alone, entered the palace by way of the carved veranda door.

The public *ètùtù* (an obligatory ritual action) for Ogun had been performed. There was now a final, secret rite called Ikate (The Rolling Up of the Carpet) or Ikawa (The End of Iwa).

The *ẹmẹsẹ̀* cleared the entire area in front of the palace as far as the entrance to the king's market to the east and to the bends in the roads from the north and the south that converge at the palace front. No one was permitted to look upon the palace veranda or enter the outer courtyard as long as the palace *gbẹ̀du* drums were beaten by the *ọmọdégbélé*. While the senior *olorì* carefully rolled up the carpet and the palace servants removed the throne, hassock, and umbrellas, the *ọba* received Chiefs Ọbala, Ọbale, Ọbasinkin, and Ọbajoko in the chamber behind the veranda panels.[18] Each chief, stripped to the waist, wore a dark, strip-woven cloth (*aṣọ aláàro*) that was knotted on the left hip. Kneeling before the seated *ọba*, they greeted their king with the traditional salutation. The king gave the chiefs a calabash of palm wine, from which they pretended to drink. Observing that they did not drink the wine, the king chided them and asked why they refused to accept his hospitality. The chiefs' only response was to say "*Kábíyèsí*." Each chief received a kolanut and was dismissed.

When the crown was removed from the king's head, he left the chamber and entered the outer courtyard and proceeded to the unmarked shrine of Igbonnibi. There he offered a prayer to the ancient Ọrangun, stepping upon the ground three times with his left foot. This festival for the *òrìṣà* of iron was now over.

Iwa Ogun: Analyzing the Ritual Action

Every ritual entails a use of space and has an axis along which the movement of the participants takes place and by which their movements are controlled. In Iwa Ogun, the axis is clearly the line of action between the veranda of the palace and the veranda of Chief Ọbale's compound. It passes through the point at which the three principal roads of Ila meet, and its midpoint passes the shrine of Ogun. Only the chief drummer and the people he calls

FIGURE 6.8. The *ọba* wears the crown *Ològún adé* as he sits on his throne. A woman chief dances before him.

and leads may walk along or cross the axis with impunity. It is a dangerous space, for it is charged by the tension of competing centers of power and, passing so close to Ogun, it is vulnerable to the eruption of violence.

The Ọbale's Veranda: Gathering Place of the Chiefs

Chief Ọbale is second in rank among the seven senior town chiefs of Ila. The title, Ọbale, is a contraction of *ọba ilé* (the one who is king in his own house). It refers specifically to the fact that the senior chiefs meet on Chief Ọbale's veranda each week, and whenever else necessary, to discuss the affairs of the town. From the veranda they may observe the movement of persons to and from the palace, at the crossroads, and in the marketplace. Here the town's senior chiefs talk with representatives of the junior chiefs and shape community policy. Hence, as the gathering place of the chiefs, Ọbale's veranda reflects the fact that Ila, like other Yoruba towns, is essentially an aggregate of descent groups. Senior and junior chieftaincy titles are hereditary among the lineages, which thereby become the basic representative units of the political system.[19]

At the outset of Iwa Ogun, the *ọba* must suffer the ritual affront of waiting for Ila's chiefs, who have assembled at Chief Ọbale's house. In this way, the king is made acutely aware of the fact that the people over whom he reigns have another allegiance, another locus of political identity than that which is expressed in his royal person. This is the primordial bond of kinship. Furthermore, as the king watches the chiefs gather on Ọbale's veranda, he is reminded of his own enforced residence of three months in Ọbale's compound prior to being crowned Ọrangun-Ila.[20] In those three months the king's person undergoes what might appropriately be called a substantive change.

The senior *afọ́baje* chiefs are kingmakers. At the death of a king, they consult the senior divination priests and select a new *ọba* from among candidates presented by the royal house whose turn it is to provide a king.[21] When the name of the *ọba*-elect is announced, the candidate "flees" and "hides" until he can be found by the palace servants. He is then taken to Chief Ọbale's house, stripped of his clothes, examined for physical deformities, and ritually washed and dressed in a new white cloth. For three months he remains in Ọbale's house, receiving visitors on the veranda, but never leaving the compound. During this period, the *ọba*-elect is instructed by the senior chiefs in his political and ritual responsibilities.

Among the many rites of enthronement, these are acts which set the king-elect apart from his own kin group and enable him to establish a new line of kinship relationships. In the past, one of these rites required the new *ọba* to eat the heart and drink maize gruel from the skull of the deceased Ọrangun, and to offer prayers to the *orí* (head or personal destiny) of his predecessor.[22] This ceremony signals a separation; the new *ọba* is indicating that his destiny is now defined through a new line of descent. This is a line of sacred kings—a line that has its origins in Oduduwa, the divine mythical king of all Yoruba. The ritual of eating the predecessor's heart and worshipping his *orí*, whose destiny can affect the success of his rule, is analogous to sacrificing to one's parents' *orí*, whose personal destiny can affect the course of a child's life. The man who is king may still sacrifice to the *orí* of his parent, but not as the king. Officially he belongs to a unique kind of descent group— that of the Orangun-Ila. This is a line of consanguineally-related sovereigns whose genealogy consists only of those who have held the office of king. The descent group is not of the same order as the lineages of the chiefs or the ruling house lineages, both of whose genealogies are reckoned according to a consanguineal parent-to-child relationship. Rather, the Orangun-Ila descent group is a separate line which—while being carved out of the ruling house lineages—has a separate, corporate life of its own.[23] Kingship may be analogous to chieftaincy in that it connotes high political office, but it must be clearly differentiated from chieftaincy because kingship, as we shall see, possesses an authority that transcends that of lineage chieftaincy.

The Palace Veranda: Images of Power

The Oba's Crown

A transformation takes place on the veranda of the palace at the moment in the ritual when the chiefs move from Obale's veranda to the center of the road near the Ogun shrine. The king enters a small chamber, called Ori Ojopo, behind the veranda door. There he removes the clothes of a chief (i.e., a lineage head), dons the beaded crown and royal robes of his office, and returns to the palace veranda as Orangun-Ila. In this manner, the authority and power of kingship are graphically presented to the chiefs and the townspeople.

The *oba*'s crown is the principal symbol of royalty. All kings who wear the crown trace their descent from Oduduwa. One tradition states that Oduduwa gave a beaded crown to each of his sixteen sons, the youngest of whom was Orangun, and each of them established his own kingdom.[24] Thus, the present Orangun has observed that the faces that decorate the conical portion of his crown "represent the face of Oduduwa and the sons of Oduduwa."[25] That is to say, the faces represent male power. But what about the large bird perched atop his crown, and the cluster of birds attached on the sides of the crown? Henry Drewal has noted that "bird imagery in many Yoruba art forms refers directly to the vital force possessed by females (living, ancestral, deified), collectively known as 'our mothers.'" He suggests, correctly, I believe, that the "birds surrounding the top of the crown signify that the king rules only with the protection of the mothers" (Drewal 1977:4). Thus, with reference to the great bird on the crowns of Ila's kings, the Orangun observed that it "represents the *oba*'s *àṣẹ* (king's power)."[26]

The meaning of *àṣẹ* is extraordinarily complex. It is used in a variety of contexts, only one of which is kingship. Verger translates *àṣẹ* as "the vital power, the energy, the great strength of all things" (Verger 1966:35).[27] It also refers to a divine energy manifest in the process of procreation. *Àṣẹ* does not entail any particular signification, and yet it invests all things, exists everywhere, and, as the warrant for all creative activity, opposes chaos and the loss of meaning in human experience. Nevertheless, *àṣẹ* may be used for destructive ends. Its presence appears to vary throughout the universe. It is more manifest in the *òrìṣà* than in people, but it can be accumulated by humans.

The significance of *àṣẹ* is revealed in the Yoruba creation myth. One version states that when Olodumare, the High God, decided that the world should exist, he commissioned *òrìṣà* Ọbatala to take a calabash of sand and a five-toed cock, and, with the aid of a chain, to lower himself to the surface of the primeval waters.[28] Having poured the sand upon the waters, Ọbatala was to place the cock on the sand. As the cock scratched, sending the sand flying in various directions, the continents of the earth would take form. On his way to fulfilling his commission, Ọbatala passed a gathering of *òrìṣà* who were drinking palm wine. Accepting their invitation to join them, Ọbatala drank excessively and fell asleep. Oduduwa knew of the High God's commission, and, seeing the sleeping Ọbatala, he took the calabash of sand, the cock, the chain, and fulfilled Olodumare's wishes. The place of creation was the town of Ile-Ifẹ (spiritual center of the Yoruba). When Ọbatala awoke and saw what Oduduwa had done and heard his claim that he had authority over the earth, Ọbatala was enraged and a great struggle between the two *òrìṣà* ensued. At length Olodumare intervened. He gave Ọbatala the power to shape the bodies of the human beings who would populate the earth, and bestowed on Oduduwa the power and privilege of being the first king and founder of the Yoruba people.

The myth clearly distinguishes two types of creative power. There is biological power, which shapes the individual's physical existence for good or ill; Ọbatala is said to create albinos and hunchbacks, as well as beautiful and well-formed people. And there is political power, which shapes people as social and moral beings. In keeping with the creation myth, the present Ọrangun-Ila identified one of the faces on his crown as the son of Oduduwa who established the line of Ila kings. The crown and, hence, the Ọrangun himself are linked to both the powers of Ọbatala, which are also associated with "the mothers," and the powers of Oduduwa—the power of procreating and the power of establishing and preserving the body politic. The latter is identified with the distinctive urban life-style and political centralization of Yoruba peoples, apart from which, as the Ọrangun observed, "life would be like life in the bush."[29]

Other features of the crown suggest that royal power exceeds the powers expressed in the iconographic references to Oduduwa. The feet of the large bird on the peak of the crown are tied to the hidden *oògùn àṣẹ* (powerful medicines) which the chief herbalist placed in the crown when it was made. "It is the *oògùn àṣẹ* which gives me power. It makes the *ọba* powerful over all kinds of spirits, even over witches."[30] The ọba may look at the bird perched on the crown, but he must never look inside the crown. He must never see the hidden medicinal powers. To do so would risk blindness. Thus, when the crown is worn, it is placed on the ọba's head by the senior wife standing behind him, by one who possesses the àṣẹ of "the mothers."

The crown is a visual metaphor of the authority and power of the ọba. In its structure and iconography it refers to a power that relies upon and transcends the contrastive powers of male and female. It links, bridges, relates opposites. The crown is "looked on as an òrìṣà."[31] But the crown is "looked on" only in the performance of a ritual such as that of Iwa Ogun. It is in the ritual context that the Yoruba see and know the supernatural power of the crown.

The Carved Panels

The carvings on the panels at the rear of the palace veranda repeat the symbolism found in the crown. The carvings, it will be recalled, frame the doorway which leads to Ori Ojopọ, the chamber where the original crowns of the kings of Ila are kept. The carvings merit close attention (fig. 6.9).[32] They tell us and the people of Ila about the roles and the powers of the ọba in Igbomina society. The three panels, each 9½ feet high and 2½ feet wide, contain 79 human figures engaged in a variety of domestic and ritual activities. Animals such as snakes, lizards, dogs, or birds are used decoratively to subdivide the panels or as part of the activities portrayed.

The king dominates the central panel in size and position. The lower two-thirds of the central panel constitutes the door which leads to the chamber of the original crown. The upper portion of the door depicts a seated ọba wearing a crown and holding a royal staff and flywhisk. He is surrounded by wives and servants, all of whom look to him as they engage in various acts of service. Above his crowned head is an inverted U-shaped, serrated design, probably representing the royal umbrella.[33] The remainder of the door-panel is divided into three groups of figures. Immediately below the ọba is a warrior on horseback, accompanied by male servants who bear arms or blow flutes and horns, and women who kneel and lift up their breasts. The next band of figures portrays, at the left, an Ifa priest holding a divination chain and a woman holding a divining tray. In the center a couple engage in sexual intercourse. To their right a palm wine tapper is shown at work, while a man with a palm wine calabash and a woman holding her breasts wait below him. The third panel, containing hunters with captured animals and birds, decorates the lower portion of the door.

The panel immediately above the door is divided into two sections. Two couples, engaged in sexual intercourse, and the figure of a child form the upper section. The lower section contains figures of Aworo-ose, a priest of òrìṣà Ọbatala and òrìṣà Oṣoosi, dancing before the igbìn drums of Ọbatala and holding the bow and arrow of Oṣoosi. Other devotees carry libations for the two òrìṣà.[34]

FIGURE 6.9. The carved panels on the palace veranda. The door leads to
Orí Ojópọ̀.

The panel to the left of the doorway concentrates on the emblems and devotees of various òrìṣà. Five equal sections depict Oṣun, deity of healing waters; Osanyin, deity of medicinal herbs; Ṣango, deified king of ancient Ọyọ;
Ogun, deity of war and of iron; and Osumare, the deity whose emblems are
the rainbow and the python.

The panel to the right is varied. The center section includes worshippers
of òrìṣà Oko, god of the farm, and, once again, Ogun, whose devotees hold
a sacrificial dog. Separated by joined snakes and lizards is the top cluster of
figures in which an armed servant stands watch over two slave women who
pound yam and a man who holds a rope tied to the waist of another female
slave. The lower portion of the right panel is dominated by a man balanced
at the top of a long bamboo pole, while musicians and acrobats, as well as
a man holding his erect penis in one hand and a large staff in the other, perform to the left and below him. Another cluster of figures to the right includes
a Muslim holding his prayer beads and Koranic slate and a man leading his
son by the arm and shaking his cane in the direction of the circus performers.
Finally, at the bottom of the panel two men lead a hobbled antelope.

The ọba of the veranda carvings is surrounded by images of generative
or marginal activity and by figures whose status or activity of the moment
places them on the margin of society: òrìṣà worshippers, warriors, hunters,
couples engaged in sexual intercourse, palm wine tappers, slave women preparing food, diviners, drummers, captives, and acrobats. If we pursue the
meanings conveyed by the carvings about the àṣẹ of the ọba, then we see
that the palace is something more than the converging point of political activity. As in all Yoruba towns, the palace of the Ọrangun is located in the center
of the town. The compounds of the senior chiefs are located in four of the
five quarters into which Ila is divided; their houses more or less surround at
varying distances the palace grounds.[35] Yet the carvings do not depict an ọba
surrounded by chiefs, but an ọba at the center of a far more complex nexus
of people and activities.

The palace is important in the ritual life of all people of Ila. There are
shrines for many of the òrìṣà within the palace grounds; also, with one exception, every festival for an òrìṣà includes a time when the devotees come to
the palace to dance before the Ọrangun, offer prayers to the òrìṣà for the
king's well-being, and receive from the king offerings for the òrìṣà and gifts
for the worshippers. The exception is the festival for Ṣoponna, the òrìṣà of
smallpox and other dread diseases. The devotees of this fearsome god do not
visit the palace or the marketplace; but they do receive offerings and gifts
from the king, which are carried to them by one of the palace servants. At
a distance, they too make prayers and offerings for the king's health and
safety. It is not surprising, therefore, that the veranda panels should depict
the Ọrangun surrounded on three sides by òrìṣà worshippers.

The fecundity of the community also is linked to kingship. It is no accident,
the Ọrangun indicates, that the carving of the ọba is below that of the
Ọbatala priest. Recall that in the creation myth, Ọbatala is given the power

to shape the human body. He "changes blood into a child, and causes deformity in children when he is angry."[36] Hence on the veranda panel above the dancing Ọbatala priest, couples engage in sexual intercourse and a child lies at their side. Still, the same panel portrays the ọba's ability to deny life. Immediately below the king is a warrior on horseback. Like the warrior or hunter, the ọba wields power which can kill in order to sustain life, and he must do so for the sake of his people. In this role, too, the ọba is like the òrìṣà, who take the sacrifices offered by humans so that the gift of life may be given to them.

Drummers and acrobats are marginal people in Yoruba society. Like the priests of the òrìṣà, they are privileged, for they are thought to be possessed of unusual powers. Performers such as these violate conventional behavior by moving, and enabling others to move, in their action and their imagination, across the social boundaries which separate people or which define socially acceptable activities. Nevertheless, they are granted privileged status in the society and are often brought within the palace. The palace is an anomalous realm and its chief resident also is a marginal person. The presence of performers, therefore, reinforces and reflects the uniqueness of the place.

The intertwined snakes and lizards which separate the human scenes on the panels are more than decorative details. They symbolize the essential activity of the universe: the activity of generation and regeneration. The logic of existence is that there is an interlocking interdependence of all things in the continuous struggle of life and death. This logic is at work in both the details and the larger scenes portrayed on the veranda panels, as well as in the rituals of Ila's festivals.

If I have read the iconography of the panels correctly, then the message they convey is that the person of the crowned ọba embodies a vital power. The extraordinariness of this power is such that it plays a salient role in shaping peoples' perceptions of reality. According to the Ọrangun, when a man passes through the veranda doorway, enters the room behind the carved panels, and receives the ancient crown of Ila on his head, "the orí [the destiny] of the crown and the orí of the ọba are brought together. The àṣẹ of the crown is bound to the head of the man. He becomes Ọrangun-Ila. Two heads, two destinies, come together. That is what Ori Ojopọ means."[37] Ordinary people must not look on the face of the king who possesses such power, just as an ọba must not look at the oògùn àṣẹ hidden within the crown. For this reason, a veil of beads conceals the ọba's face, that is, the face of the man, William Adetona Ayeni. As with all masks, concealment is designed to disclose a power, a reality, not otherwise observable. It is the cluster of faces and birds on the crown that are seen and that reveal the sacred power of the ọba's orí (king's head). As the chiefs affirm in their salutation to the king: *Ọba aláàṣẹ èkejì òrìṣà!* (The king's power is like that of the gods).[38]

Dressed in the regalia of office, it is a formidable figure who leaves the palace veranda and approaches the chiefs who are gathered in the road near the Ogun shrine.

The Shrine for Ogun: The Owner of All Iron

The Ogun shrine is the place where the powers of the chiefs and the king are brought into opposition. In the meeting of the chiefs and Qrangun, midway between the veranda of Qbale's compound and the veranda of the palace, the Qrangun's first act is to offer kolanuts and a prayer for peace at the Ogun shrine. He then faces Ila's seated chiefs. The failure of the chiefs to rise and pay respect to the king is an affront that can only lead to conflict.

The centrality of Ogun in this dramatic confrontation is consistent with the deity's importance in Ila traditions. The praise name, "Ogun, god of war and god of iron," indicates two of the realms in which Ogun's power is experienced by the community. As a warrior-god, Ogun brought the followers of Qrangun Igbonnibi to Ila. Later, his power aided other qbas in defending the town, sometimes at a terrible price, when Ogun seemed to turn against his own. Consequently, his oríkì are filled with fearful lament:

1	Ojọ́ Ògún,
2	Ṣí lo, ṣí lo, ṣiló, ní má sẹ aiyé.
3	Dùgbè dùgbè a gba óde oòrun kẹ̀kẹ̀.
4	Ipé ńpé jú a si kùn fé kún.
5	Òtòpàkó a ṣí kùn fẹ jẹ̀.
6	Paranganda ní dà fọ́mọ ódó.
7	Abiri, abihun à ṣimu òrìṣà.
8	Mo rí fàájì rẹ.

1	On the days when Ogun is angered,
2	There is always disaster in the world.
3	The world is full of dead people going to heaven.
4	The eyelashes are full of water.
5	Tears stream down the face.
6	A bludgeoning by Ogun causes a man's downfall.
7	I see and hear, I fear and respect my òrìṣà.
8	I have seen your (bloody) merriment.[39]

In the sacrifices and prayers offered to Ogun by the warrior chiefs and the king on the first and third days of the festival, and again in the rite of Iwa Ogun, there is an acknowledgment of remembered violence which drank the blood of men.

As the "owner of all iron," Ogun provides the tools which are essential to the community. In truth, Ogun's contributions to cultural existence are many. The praise poem which introduces this essay indicates that Ogun is the circumciser, scarifier, hair-cutter, or carver. Elsewhere he is known as "The possessor of two machetes: with one he prepares the farm, and with the other he clears the road" (Idowu 1962:86). By way of recognizing these vital contributions, blacksmiths and hunters sacrifice dogs to Ogun on the second and fourth days of the festival and bathe their iron tools in the blood of the animal. This sacrifice to Ogun emphasizes his dual nature. The dog is offered only to Ogun. All other òrìṣà who receive animal sacrifices taste only the blood of goats or rams, that is, the blood of herbivorous animals. The carnivorous beast belongs to Ogun. But the dog also is a carnivorous animal which can be domesticated. Thus Ogun receives what he is; he is the deity who eats flesh and drinks blood, yet his destructive work is culturally legitimated.

Cultural existence has its costs. It requires acts of violence, not only against the person who is the enemy but also against oneself and one's children, and against the forest, the land, and the animal. Circumcision or scarification, to name only two, are acts of violence—self-inflicted wounds which serve as marks of cultural and social differentiation.

Here, then, is revealed the irony of human existence: death is essential to life. This is the reality, the truth about themselves, with which Ogun confronts humans. But if death is essential to life, what kinds of death are necessary? What power justifies and limits acts of violence upon others, as well as upon one's own person? What saves one from the intoxicating power of blood and the beguiling self-justification that arises out of death's specter? The pathos of the Ogun worshipper is that neither the devotee nor Ogun can answer these questions, as the following praise song from another Yoruba community makes clear:

1   The light shining on Ogun's face is not easy to behold.
2   Ogun, let me not see the red of your eye . . .
3   Ogun is a crazy òrìṣà who still asks questions after 780 years!
4   Whether I can reply, or whether I cannot reply,
5   Ogun please don't ask me anything.[40]

If Ogun cannot resolve the question which his dilemma imposes upon people, then how are people to live with it? This, I believe, is what the rite of Iwa Ogun seeks to address, when it is celebrated after the respite of two days from the bloody sacrifice of dogs offered during the opening days of the Ogun festival.

The rite of Iwa Ogun is fraught with tension. Initially, the king faces the chiefs as a peer, dressed in the gown and beads of a chief. Later, he approaches the chiefs in a royal robe, wearing the great crown. At the Ogun shrine, and appropriately so, the tension provided by this shift in the king's persona produces conflict. Each side is saying to the other: "I shall make you come!"[41]

The ritual erupts into a reenactment of civil war when the two centers of power are pitted against each other. The senior and junior chiefs represent Ila as an aggregate of descent groups with their individual histories and myths of origin. Kinship is a centrifugal force in Ila's political life, which the chiefs represent. On the other side, the Ọrangun transcends ordinary blood ties and compound boundaries. He represents a centripetal force, the unity of Ila as a town. According to Chief Ọdọọde, it is important that the Ọrangun make the first move to resolve the conflict. When the Ọrangun leaves the palace veranda to stand before the chiefs, he is saying: "You chiefs have power (àṣẹ). You install the Ọrangun." This acknowledgment of chiefly power or authority by the ọba enables Chief Ọbale to respond by leading the chiefs to the ọba. Only when the chiefs collectively perform the nonviolent self-sacrificial act of homage to the king can peace be known and corporate life affirmed. Again, according to Chief Ọdọọde, the chiefs are saying: "You, Ọrangun, have power (àṣẹ). We no longer have authority over you. Your power and our power are different."[42]

The Palace Veranda: The Power of the Crown Acknowledged

Iwa Ogun concludes when the king returns to the palace veranda and receives representatives from various sectors of the community: chiefs, priests, royalty, performers. The movement of all of these groups, with the exception of the palace drummers, from the Ogun shrine to the ọba, stands as a collective appeal to a power which transcends, rather than thrives on, conflict. Iwa Ogun means "the essential character of Ogun." The rite extends the dimensions of the problem of violence and culture, the focus of the first four days of the festival, into the political realm. The problem of violence has been narrowed to civil conflict when society is defined solely in terms of lineage groups living in an urban setting. In such a context the problem of the locus of political authority becomes acute. While Ogun can create the implements of culture, Ogun's iwà, his essential character, does not let him control the destruction entailed in his creative power. That, as we have seen, is the pathos of Ogun: he cannot provide political order. Another power that transcends that of Ogun is necessary if there is to be community among the patrilineages. That power is to be found in the authority (àṣẹ) of the Ọrangun-Ila.

When the Ọrangun-Ila leaves his throne and dances before his people, he does so as one in whom there is a concentration of power. He dances not to a single drum, but to the multiple rhythms of all the drums of Ila and to the chanting of his praise names by the assembled crowd. Unlike the diversities and oppositions that lead to conflict in ordinary human experience, the sacred power of the *ọba* holds these oppositions in an awesome alliance. It would appear that the power of the crown is its capacity to bring the diverse and conflicting destinies of men together into a relatively peaceful accord. The Ọrangun's crown is the symbolic center and warrant for Ila's corporate life.

Once his power is publicly affirmed, the *ọba* retires to the palace. Before he places the ancient crown of Ila in the chamber where "destinies meet," the four chiefs who have accompanied the king into the chamber remind him of the essential mistrust of kingship by the lineage chiefs in the insulting obviousness with which they pretend to drink the palm wine and refuse to accept the king's hospitality. In Iwa Ogun the power which brings unity and peace is acknowledged as being possessed by the Ọrangun, but not quite. A more decisive affirmation waits for the festival called Oro.

Ọdun Oro: The Festival for the King

The rite of Iwa Ogun is performed again three months after Ọdun Ogun as part of Ọdun Oro, a thirteen-day festival also known as Ẹbọra Ila. On this occasion the rite, which is performed twice, is known as Iwa Aṣọ or Iwa Oro. Ọdun Oro is Ila's new year festival, since it marks the beginning of the new liturgical calendar.[43] The underlying concern shaping this festival which was expressed in the ritual of Iwa Ogun is whether political authority resides with the lineage chiefs or the king. For the people of Ila this is the essential question in terms of which the problem of violence and culture must be resolved.

A thirteen-day festival involves large numbers of people in many diverse activities. On some occasions the rites are collectively shared, on others they occur in private places and at random moments. Rather than attempt a full description of Ọdun Oro, I concentrate on the sequence of rituals, which reveals the structure, logic, and meaning in which participants share.

Rites of Preparation

Divination prefaced the Ọdun Oro festival. Six days prior to the actual rites, the senior priests of Ila gathered at the house of their chief priest to prepare for an all-night divination vigil to be held the following evening. The vigil, known as Ọdun Idafa or Ifa Ajọbọ (the communal worship of Ifa), was the longest and most carefully performed divination rite in Ila.[44] When I observed it, the rite took place in the presence of Chiefs Ọbale, Ẹlẹmọna, and Ọdọọde at the palace in the assembly hall of the chiefs. The purpose of the rite was to ascertain the sacrifices to be made by the king and the chiefs during the festival in order to assure the peace and well-being of the town in the year to come. When completed, in the early morning hours, the sounds of the hunters' gun shots rang out from the palace grounds. They signaled to the townspeople that every house must prepare sacrifices for Ọdun Oro.

The day following the vigil was known as Ọjọ Aguntankojeja (The Day on which Sheep do not go to the Market to Eat), for the markets are closed and the fate of sheep was now linked to rites of sacrifice. Later in the day, the chiefs assembled at Chief Ọbale's house to watch the procession of Ifa priests, as they returned the divination tray from the palace to the house of Oloriawo Onifa, the leader of the Ifa priests.

During the next four days, at four o'clock in the morning and again at seven in the evening, Ila's drummers assembled in front of the palace to hear Baale Onilu perform *Èkà Kékà*. The fourth day of drumming marks the first festival day. The repeated drumming of the names and praises of the twenty-three Ọranguns-Ila establishes kingship as one of the two major foci of the coming festival and indicates why it also is known as Ọdun Ọba, the King's Festival.

Isunsunlefa (Day 2)

There are seven important moments in the thirteen days of Ọdun Oro. The first is called Isunsunlefa and actually occurs on the second day of the festival. The leaders of Ila's divination priests went to the palace to roast three new yams, portions of which were offered to *òrìṣà* Ọbatala, Ọsoosi, Osanyin, Ọṣun, Oko, Ṣango, Ogun, and Eṣu, and to sacrifice a goat to Orunmila, the god of wisdom, in order that the festival might be celebrated successfully.[45] In the past, similar rites were performed in many compounds. It is a day for remembering the lineage forefathers in stories told by elders and fathers to the children, in lamentation and praise songs sung by the wives and daughters of the house, and in the offering of kola and foodstuffs at the grave sites of the deceased.

Iwa Iyan (Day 3)

The following day, Iwa Iyan, is also known as Ọjọ Awejewemu (The Day for Eating and Drinking). The senior and junior chiefs proceeded to the palace, where they paid homage to the king and, according to rank, offered prayers for his well-being. As in the opening rites of the Ogun festival, the king was dressed in the simple regalia of a chief. As the chiefs knelt before him, the king touched his flywhisk to the hands of his servant, who in turn touched the hands of each chief. Having received the chiefs, the king invited them to a feast, which, as in the Ogun festival, he did not attend. The palace rite began a series of feasts that stressed lineage chieftaincy. In the days that followed, the seven senior chiefs feasted one another and the junior chiefs, according to rank.

Iwa Aṣọ (Day 7)

The third important moment was the rite of Iwa Aṣọ, which occurred on the seventh day of the festival. It began a sequence of rituals that more or less constituted a unit. Iwa Aṣọ is in every respect a repetition of the rite of Iwa Ogun, which concluded the Ogun festival, and I return to it below.

Isule (Days 8 through 10)

During the next three days, that is, from the eighth through the tenth days of the festival, the rite of Isule took place in every compound except those of the royal houses. "Isule" means the worship (*ìsu*) of the home (*ilé*). It offers an opportunity to petition the lineage ancestors through salutations and sacrifices for help with individual problems. Some pray to the deceased for children, others for a safe delivery, and still others for prosperity or protection from the power of witches. Families that have produced twins use this occasion to place offerings before their altar carvings for deceased twins and petition their favor.[46]

On the morning of the eighth day, the king, with his senior wives, went to his family compound, the House of Olutojokun. The king sacrificed a ram at his father's grave and requested the blessing of his genitor upon him and his family. He was feasted and honored by members of his family and for a brief time was once again a son in his father's house. It was a moment of utmost importance; for in the king's act of homage to his lineage ancestors he affirmed, along with the townspeople, the importance of the descent group in defining personal and social identity.

In the afternoon the king went with his wives to Ọbalumọ's compound to honor the first settler of Ila and also to sacrifice a cock at the grave of the mother of Ọrangun Igbonnibi. (All such rites are performed on the king's behalf by Chief Ẹlẹmọna and the palace servants.) Ila tradition recalls that when Ọrangun Igbonnibi arrived at the present site of Ila he found the house of Timo, a hunter. Timo welcomed the king and invited him to establish his palace opposite his house. In return Igbonnibi conferred the title of Chief Ọbalumọ on Timo on the condition that Timo would acknowledge Igbonnibi's authority and in recognition of the hunter's claim to have descended from a royal line in a distant town.[47] The rite, therefore, introduces political history into the festival, a "history" that may well preserve information about the past, but that also serves to establish a "character" for present relationships, legitimating the authority of the king and the status of the Ọbalumọ chieftaincy.[48] The rite thus purports to refer to a time when the political order shifted from one in which a lineage head was the highest authority to one in which a king became the central authority of the community's several lineages, that is, "a tribally structured kingdom."[49] Acknowledging the mother of Ila's founding king—for the ritual is called

Imuarugbo, "To Honor the Elderly Women"—acknowledges the dependence of royal (masculine) authority upon the procreative power of women.

Later in the afternoon the princes of the Igbonnibi and Arutu royal houses brought rams and male goats to the palace to be sacrificed at the shrine of Orangun Igbonnibi by the palace servants in the presence of the king. Two days later the princes from the Okomo royal house did the same.

Iwa Aṣọ (Day 11)

On the eleventh day, the rite of Iwa Aṣọ was performed again. There is no variation in the performance from Iwa Aṣọ of four days earlier, or from the concluding Iwa Ogun rite of the Odun Ogun festival. But why is it performed a second time in the Oro festival? And why is the ritual referred to as Iwa Aṣọ rather than Iwa Ogun?

The two performances of Iwa Aṣọ, coming before and after the many rituals of Isule held throughout the town in the compounds of the lineages and at the palace by the princes of the royal houses, are public actions that ritually enclose the numerous private rites of Isule. Recall that the festival began with divination rites performed in every compound to honor the ancestors and to determine the sacrifices to be offered later in the rites of Isule. On both occasions the ritual emphasis was on the lineages and their primary significance for defining the social identity of the participants. But in Iwa Aṣọ, as in Iwa Ogun, an alternative referent for defining Yoruba social identity—namely, the king—is acknowledged; and a deeply rooted conflict in Yoruba social experience is disclosed regarding the relationship between kinship and kingship in defining the basic moral allegiance in Yoruba society. Hence, the conflict and the possibility of its resolution are enacted in Iwa Aṣọ. It is that reality which ritually encloses the celebrations of Isule performed by the lineages. Even during the period of Isule the conflict is implicit as the royal houses gather at the palace, not in their family compounds, to perform the sacrificial rites to their royal ancestors.

The change of the name from Iwa Ogun to Iwa Aṣọ already indicates a significant shift in the focus of the Oro festival as compared with the Ogun festival. Aṣọ means "cloth." Hence, Iwa Aṣọ means "the character or essential quality of cloth." For the Yoruba, cloth is one of the principal modes of cultural expression. For one thing, it expresses wealth and status. It is perfectly appropriate to admire the cloth a person is wearing by congratulating him/her on the enormous amount of money spent for it. And it is often the case that considerable sums disproportionate to other expenditures are spent to purchase a man's handwoven, elaborately embroidered robe, or a woman's wrapper and head-tie. Furthermore, cloth is rivaled only by oratory as the principal means by which people reveal in a social frame of reference the "positive" qualities of their individuality, that is, their character. At the ceremonies discussed here, the king and chiefs dress uniquely and sumptuously to honor the community and thereby reveal their respect for its members. Hence, the shift in the ritual's title to Iwa Aṣọ represents a change in meaning away from violence and the uncertainty of cultural existence.[50]

Sakungbengbe (Day 12)

On the twelfth day of the festival the *olorì* (queens) of Ila, including the wives of former Ọranguns, as well as the older wives of the present king, process from the palace to Chief Ọdọọde's compound. The ritual is called Sakungbengbe. Chief Ọdọọde is one of three chiefs closely related to the palace. Specifically he supervises the ritual responsibilities of the queens. His position—along with that of Chief Ọbale, who is responsible for the palace servants, and Chief Ẹlẹmọna, who is the messenger between the king and the senior chiefs and who has access to the palace at all times—indicates that little can happen within the palace that is not known by the town's chiefs.

When the queens arrived at Ọdọọde's house, the chief greeted them dressed in the garments of a woman. Following the refreshment of palm wine, the queens led Chief Ọdọọde to the King's Market to dance and pay honor at the shrine of Amotagesi, the second Ọrangun. According to Chief Ọdọọde, Amotagesi possessed powerful herbal "medicines" (*oògùn*) and once transformed himself into a beautiful woman in order to marry the Olowu, another "strong man in medicines," who had repeatedly waged war on Amotagesi. After seventeen years, Amotagesi, having learned Olowu's secrets, transformed himself into a man and returned, only to find that his son had usurped the throne. With the help of several chiefs and a mask called Egunsanyin, which was endowed with magical medicines, Amotagesi regained his throne.[51] The ritual of Sakungbengbe thus introduces another aspect of Ila history. It recalls a situation in which the king's physical power to defend the town was inadequate and required the acquisition of hidden or covert power, a power analogous to that which women possess. Thus, Chief Ọdọọde, dressed as Amotagesi, yet carrying his sword of office as an Ikẹgbẹ chief, goes with the senior queens to the market shrine of Ila's second Ọrangun to honor him. The action also prepares for the concluding rite of the festival in Chief Ọdọọde's compound.

Isinro (Day 13)

The final ritual, called Isinro, which means "burial" or "completion of Oro," began in the afternoon when the king processed from the palace to the house of Chief Ọdọọde, a distance of just under a mile. The king was preceded by drummers and surrounded by his palace servants and wives. Chief Oloyin, representing the Ologun warriors, ran back and forth across the road in front of the *ọba* to warn people to clear the way. As the Ọrangun proceeded along the road to Ọdọọde's house, he paused before the house of Chief Ẹlẹmọna and the house of Chief Ọbale and performed *ètùtù* by touching his beaded staff to the ground three times and offered prayers for the chiefs and their families.[52]

The ceremonies were composed of elaborate displays of courtly etiquette. The king was dressed in a magnificent robe and appeared in public wearing a small beaded crown. He was seated in the courtyard on a large, circular dais. Attendees included town chiefs, the women of Ọdọọde's and of Olutojokun's house, and representatives of important groups, for example, the herbalists and the warrior chiefs. Chief Ọdọọde again appeared in women's clothes, carrying the Ikẹgbẹ cutlass. He invited the king to enter his house for refreshments. Once inside, the chief placed his cutlass on the ground between himself and the king as a sign of peaceful greeting. In a gesture of recognition of Ọdọọde's authority within his own house, the king picked up the cutlass and presented it to the chief with prayers for the house of Ọdọọde.

When the king reappeared in public, he wore the great conical, veiled crown called Ilawa (*Ìlá Ìwà*), the crown, as the Ọrangun-Ila described it, which reveals "the beauty of the Ọrangun-Ila, his character."[53] Ila's lineage chiefs took turns dancing before the *ọba*. The last to dance were the Ikẹgbẹ chiefs, who have a special role to play in the coronation and funeral rites of Ila's kings, and Chief Ọdọọde. The chief drummer repeated the *Èkà* recital, naming past kings, and the *ọba* concluded the event by dancing before the cheering chiefs and townspeople.

Interpretation

The ritual action of Ọdun Oro is twofold. On the one hand, the locus of ritual activity moves from many separate, private celebrations to a corporate, public ritual celebrated by all of the community. The logic of the movement is to be noted in the sequence of locations of ritual activity. From the perspective of the public, the movement from diverse places of ritual activity in the compounds to the single, shared space is essentially a shift in sacrificial attention from the family ancestors and descent groups to the king and the town.

On the other hand, the *ọba* moves from his seclusion in the circumscribed space of the palace into the public realm. Here, too, the ritual is governed by an underlying logic. The progression of rituals over the thirteen days moves the king out of the palace into the midst of the town, and in the process the role and authority of the king are affirmed. Recall that on the third day of the festival the chiefs gathered at the palace to pay their respects to Ila's paramount chief, for the king is dressed in the robes of a chief. They are feasted by the king, just as they feast one another in the days that follow. By contrast, in the celebration of Isinro, the king wears the richly embroidered robes and the beaded crowns of the Ọrangun. Throughout Isinro the chiefs treat him as one possessing a higher power, the sacred authority of the wearer of the crown.

Before the transfer of political authority to the king can take place, the struggle between kingship and kinship must be articulated and mediated. That is accomplished in the rituals of Iwa Aṣọ on the seventh and eleventh days. Both rituals begin with a mock battle near the shrine of Ogun and change course by concluding with the lineage chiefs' affirming the divine power of kingship. The fear that civil strife can erupt among the lineages requires that there be the recognition of another moral bond—a loyalty that unites persons and groups without denying their diversity and difference.[54]

Conclusion

As we have seen, festivals, as well as the rituals of which they are composed, have a structure and a logic that shape their meaning. The symbolism of the rituals expresses a shift from one source of political authority to another, and in the ritual process, deeply felt contradictions regarding culture and violence, political order and disorder, are acted out and, for the moment, resolved.

The logic of Ogun ritual in the Ila case is deeply intertwined with the realities of political history. In the study of the political structure of six eighteenth- and nineteenth-century Yoruba kingdoms, Lloyd argues that an inherent conflict of interest between kings and chiefs characterizes Yoruba political systems. He contrasts two types of political systems to make the point. Tribally structured kingdoms vest authority with a council of chiefs and the king acts as an arbiter, whereas strong centralized monarchies vest ultimate authority in the king and the chiefs act as advisors. Yoruba kingdoms are neither. None of them achieved full centralization, and therefore what shapes the Yoruba vision of history is a perpetual struggle for power (Lloyd 1971:1–8).[55]

Accordingly, the contest for political power dominates the ritual action of Iwa Ogun and Iwa Aṣọ. The rites reveal that from the point of view of society defined in terms of descent groups, kingship is alien to the sentiments, obligations, and allegiances of kinship. Furthermore, the centralization of power in a king poses the threat of tyranny and the denial of social differentiation through blood ties.[56]

Yet, without a king there is the threat of discord among the descent groups and the specter of death which accompanies civil strife. As Thomas Hobbes observed, ". . . during the time men live without a common power to keep them all in awe, they are in that condition which is called war; and such a war, as is of every man, against every other man" (1947:81–82).

Human conflict is therefore resolved with nonhuman power. In both festivals, the locus of the power is the crown. It is the gift of the first (divine) ancestor to his "sons"; it is bestowed on the wearer by the most powerful members of the community—the senior chiefs; it contains mystical power in the form of medicines prepared by priests; and on ritual occasions it is placed on the king's head by his senior wife, who possesses the covert power of "the mothers." Thus, when chiefs kneel before the king, they salute the fact that his power is "next to the gods." When townspeople look on the crown during ritual performances, they see the awesome power of sacred kingship, and they return to their compounds in peace.

The achievement of solidarity asks a price. Sacrifices, as well as prayers, must be made to the ancestors by the full community, and sacrifices must be made to the civic deities by the chiefs and king. In this pursuit, one deity stands out above all others. Repeatedly in the ritual cycle, the community's most prominent citizen appears at the shrine of Ogun, dancing for the òrìṣà of iron and war, honoring him, and asking for peace. In this way, and on behalf of his subjects, the king turns the powerful deity who can divide and destroy into a force upon whom they can rely to perpetuate their society.

NOTES

1. My translation of this *oríkì* (praise song) is based on Yoruba and English texts collected in the city of Ibadan and published by Simpson (1965:319; 1980:31–32). I am grateful to Jacob Olupọna of the Department of Religious Studies, University of Ọbafemi Awolowo, Ile-Ifẹ, Nigeria for his assistance with questions of translation and orthography of Yoruba passages throughout the essay.

2. Research on the Ogun festival was made possible from June to August 1977 by a summer stipend from the National Endowment for the Humanities. Previous research trips to Ila-Ọrangun in 1972 and 1974, which laid the groundwork for this study, were supported by grants from the Ford Foundation and the Social Science Research Council. Subsequent research in 1981 and 1982, the latter made possible by a basic research grant from the National Endowment for the Humanities (RO-20072–81–2184) shared with Henry J. Drewal, permitted further inquiry and the checking of earlier observations, notations, and interpretations. The research on Ọdun Oro in 1984 was supported by a National Endowment for the Humanities summer stipend and a grant from the Committee for Research and Exploration of the National Geographic Society. I am grateful to *National Geographic Research* for permission to use the data on the Oro festival previously published in their Scientific Journal (Spring 1986), Vol. 2, No. 2, pp. 216–233 in my essay on "Festivals and Sacred Kingship Among the Igbomina Yoruba."

I am indebted to His Highness, William Adetona Ayeni, Ariwajoye I, Ọrangun-Ila, for his support of my research in Ila in granting me permission to photograph the festivals and engaging with me in extended conversations regarding the festivals, the rituals of which they are composed, and the history of the royal houses of Ila. Lamidi Fakẹyẹ, master carver of Ila, introduced me to his hometown in 1971. His lively and sustained interest in my inquiries made access to the ritual life of the people of Ila, both in the privacy of their compounds and in public festivals, possible in a way that only the trust of family and friend could provide. I am also grateful to Sunday Adewumi and D. G. Taiwo for their invaluable and sensitive research assistance in Ila.

3. Although it is said that Ọdun Ogun is the oldest festival or the first festival in Ila, the dates for all festivals are determined in relationship to the concluding date of the new year festival, Ọdun Oro, and then in relationship to one another in an

established sequence. The liturgical calendar is the responsibility of Chief Lowa, who consults with the king and with various chieftaincy and cult groups. Chief Lowa is a descendant of Ọrangun Amotagesi, who was the junior brother of Ọrangun Ajagun-nla, son of Oduduwa. Ọrangun Amotagesi reigned in Ila-Yara and was father of Igbonnibi, who later led the people of Ila to their present town site. Chief Lowa: personal communication, *ilé* (house or compound) Lowa, August 12, 1982.

On Ogun festivals in the ritual life of Yoruba towns see Bascom (1987) on the Ogun festival in Ifẹ; Beier (1959) on the Ogun festival in Ilobu; Beier (1956); Ogunba (1977) for reference to the Ogun festival in Ondo; Ojo (1966:171) for a map of Yoruba towns where Ogun is the main civic deity; Peel (1983) for references to the Ogun festival in Ilesha; and Ben-Amos and Barnes ch. 3 on Ogun worship in Oyo.

4. The seven senior chiefs inherit named titles which reside in a specific lineage. The junior chiefs are simply lineage representatives.

5. Ila's warrior chiefs are divided into two groups, the Balogun and the Ologun. In the past, the Ologun chiefs were the defenders of the town. The Balogun chiefs fought beyond the town walls in expeditions of conquest or reprisal, or in alliance with the chiefs and kings of other towns.

6. The history of Ila-Yara appears to have been filled with strife between lineage groups, as well as among the royal houses over succession. Prince Arutu, having failed to gain the throne, left Ila-Yara in 1452 with his junior brother, Prince Igbonnibi, and his followers and settled in Ila-Magbon, where he was declared Ọrangun. Just before his death, Arutu gave the beaded crown of the Ọrangun to Igbonnibi and instructed him to lead the people of Ila to the place where Igbonnibi would "touch the ground with the Orere Staff." It would be known as Ila-Ọrangun (Adetoyi 1974:10–11).

7. Chief Ẹlẹmọna is one of the seven senior chiefs known as *afọ́baje* (kingmakers). Ẹlẹmọna is the first person in the morning and the last person in the evening from outside the palace to see the king. He may enter any part of the palace at any time. He is also the traditional head of the *ọmọdégbélé*, the palace slaves and servants. The Ojuwa chiefs are lineage chiefs associated with the Ẹlẹmọna who assist him in carrying out his official responsibilities.

The *ẹmẹsẹ̀* are messengers of the Ọrangun who come from the town's lineage groups other than the royal houses or Chief Ọbale's house, since he is the traditional head of the *ẹmẹsẹ̀*.

8. The tree was cut down in 1975 at the request of the chiefs because it was believed to be the gathering place of the witches, and it was feared that witches were preventing the prosperity known in other parts of Nigeria from coming to Ila. In 1976 electric power arrived in Ila, followed by a medical clinic, new markets, and in 1980 a teacher training college. In 1981 a large young *àràbà* tree was planted at the site of the Ogun shrine to serve as the appropriate focus of public rituals for the *òrìṣà*.

9. Chief Ẹlẹkẹhan: personal communication, *ilé* Ẹlẹkẹhan, June 7, 1977. According to Chiefs Ẹlẹkẹhan and Oloyin, a dog was sacrificed each time Iṣagun was performed. But protests from the Muslim and Christian communities in Ila regarding the public sacrifice became so strong, with threats of disrupting the ritual, that the practice was ended in 1973.

10. Ila's hunter chiefs, listed in the order in which their *egúngún láyẹ̀wú* appear in the Ogun festivals, are Chief Odebiyi of *ilé* Lodo, Chief Ogundipẹ of *ilé* Osoo, Chief Ogundele of *ilé* Iyalode, Chief Babtunde of *ilé* Ore, Chief Raji Oladoyin of *ilé* Olode, Chief Ajide of *ilé* Ẹlẹkẹhan, and Chief Taiwo of *ilé* Alapo.

11. According to palace historians, there was one ruling house of Igbonnibi when Ila was founded. Over the years two others were recognized, the house of Arutu, which traces its line to Ọrangun Arutu, an older brother of Igbonnibi, and the house of Okomọ, which descends from Ọrangun Okomọ, a son of Igbonnibi. The kings of

Ila are alternately chosen from the lineage segments that make up each ruling house.

12. There are no marked grave sites for Ila's former kings. When an ọba dies, it is said that his body is escorted from the palace by the Ikẹgbẹ chiefs; but it is not known where the body is taken. Before this last rite, the deceased ọba's heart and skull are used in rituals of installation of the ọba-elect. Then they are buried at unmarked locations in the palace grounds. It is to these places that the king pays homage when he leaves and returns to the palace during the rituals of the Ogun, Oro, and Egungun festivals.

13. The ọmọdégbélé (palace servants) were slaves taken in intertribal wars by the warriors of the ọba or given by kings of neighboring towns to the royal family on the occasion of the death of an ọba. The slaves carried the clothes and other gifts to the family of the deceased and then remained as palace servants of the new Ọrangun and messengers to the courts from which they came. The kings most closely associated with the Ọrangun through the palace servants appear to have been the Owa of Ilẹṣa, the Alaafin of Ọyọ, the Ooni of Ifẹ, the Ajero of Ijero, and the Alara of Aramoko (Adetoyi 1974:24).

14. The Ikẹgbẹ chiefs are known as Irọnṣẹ ọmọ Odùdúwà (messengers of the son of Oduduwa). Their cutlasses are said to have been given to them by Oduduwa to clear the way to the town that the Ọrangun, son of Oduduwa, established. The Ikẹgbẹ chiefs escort the new Ọrangun from his installation in Ọbale's compound to the palace and accompany the remains of a deceased ọba from the palace to the burial ground. Chief Ọdọọde: personal communication, ilé Ọdọọde, July 11, 1977.

15. The prayers and salutations in the ritual were given by Chief Ẹlẹmọna: personal communication, ilé Ẹlẹmọna, March 12, 1981 and August 7, 1982.

16. As the salutation suggests, the ọba's person is sacred and therefore no one must touch him. Physical contact is made by the king placing his flywhisk in the hands of the senior palace servant (ẹmẹsẹ̀), who in turn touches the upraised hands of Chief Ẹlẹmọna and the other chiefs.

17. Chief Ọbale does not actually "signal" the end of the conflict, but simply "leads" the chiefs in the appropriate action. Chief Ọdọọde: personal communication, March 10, 1981. Ordinarily Chief Ọbala, a more senior chief, leads this part of the rite, but he was ill in 1977.

18. Chiefs Ọbala and Ọbale rank first and second among the senior chiefs, the kingmakers. Chief Ọbasinkin is the leader of the Ikẹgbẹ chiefs. Chief Ọbajoko ranks first among the junior lineage chiefs.

19. For discussions of Yoruba social and political structures see Eades (1980); Fadipe (1970); Law (1977); Lloyd (1962, 1971, 1973); and Peel (1979, 1983).

20. Ọrangun-Ila: personal communication, July 20, 1977.

21. The selection of candidates for ọba is overseen by Chief Alasan, second in rank among the twelve lineage segments of the Igbonnibi ruling house and leader of the ọmọba (princess of all three ruling houses). The Alasan presents the name(s) of the candidate(s) to the afóbaje. According to palace historians, Ọrangun Amotagesi appointed Ila's kingmakers and assigned their functions (Adetoyi 1974:22).

22. When I inquired of the Ọrangun about this tradition, he answered: "There are some things about which I may not speak freely" (personal communication, June 28, 1974). When the question was put to the late Chief Ọbale, he answered: "No. That is no longer done in Ila. We have our own rites" (personal communication, July 3, 1974). It would have been difficult to have performed some of the rites other than in a token way at the 1967 installation of the present Ọrangun, since the conflict over a successor to the throne took seven years to resolve.

The acts of eating the deceased King's heart and drinking maize gruel from his predecessor's skull in the installation rites of an ọba are reported by Lloyd (1954:336–84), Morton-Williams (1960:354), and Ojo (1966:77). It is not clear whether Lloyd's inquiry is the sole source of information for the others or whether they have their own independent sources.

It should be noted that the Yoruba word _orí_ may be translated either as "head," referring to one's skull, or as "personal destiny," depending on the context of use.

23. Ila kingship was once inherited according to rules of primogeniture. It now rotates among member-candidates put forward, in turn, by their royal houses (lineage segments).

24. Among Yoruba people, the right to wear a beaded crown is associated with the establishment of an independent kingdom (Agiri 1975:169–70). There has been a long history of challenges and conflicts over the claims of rulers and communities to wear or hold a beaded crown (Asiwaju 1976). Ila's claim to being an _ilú aladé_ (crowned town) is an unchallenged tradition.

25. Ọrangun-Ila: personal communication, July 20, 1977.

26. Ọrangun-Ila: personal communication, July 20, 1977.

27. See also M. Drewal's discussion of _àṣẹ_, ch. 9.

28. For discussions of the cosmological and political variants of Yoruba creation and establishment myths see Agiri (1975), Bascom (1969), Idowu (1962), and Johnson (1969).

29. Ọrangun-Ila: personal communication, July 20, 1977.

30. Ọrangun-Ila: personal communication, July 20, 1977.

31. Ọrangun-Ila: personal communication, July 20, 1977.

32. The panels were carved during the reign of Ọrangun Oyinlola Arojojoye (1924–1936). Ogundeji (1870–1962), master carver of Aga's compound and the Baale of Ila's carvers, supervised the project. He assigned Akobiogun Fakẹyẹ (1878–1946) and his son, Adeosun, of Inurin's compound to carve the central panel, which includes the door to the chamber called Orí Oj́ópọ̀. The panels on either side of the door were carved by Ogunwuyi (c. 1890–1965) of Ore's compound and Oje (c. 1875–1960) of Aga's compound.

33. Henry Drewal suggests that the serrated design depicts the royal umbrella, since it always covers the _ọba_ when he wears a beaded crown. Personal communication, January 15, 1979.

34. In Ila, the Aworo-ose is the chief priest of Ọbatala and also the chief priest of Oṣoosi, a hunter deity. Combining priestly roles for different deities is not unusual in Ila. Iya Oṣun, the chief priestess for Oṣun, is also the leader of the worshippers of _òrìṣà_ Ọbalufon. The dual responsibilities reflect the history of a particular lineage group, which "brought the _òrìṣà_ to Ila," but also suggest the complementarity of the gods in the ritual symbolism of _òrìṣà_ worship. See Pemberton 1977:1–28.

35. Ila-Ọrangun is divided into five quarters: Isedo, Iperin, Eyindi, Okejigbo, and Oke-Ẹdẹ. The seven senior chiefs and the lineages composing the three royal houses are all located in the first four quarters, which surround the palace. The Oke-Ẹdẹ quarter lies to the south, its northern portion separated from the palace grounds by a narrow band of compounds included in the Okejigbo quarter. Oke-Ẹdẹ is famous for its herbalist priests. According to local tradition, no person from Oke-Ẹdẹ was ever taken into slavery or captivity during the slave raids and wars in the nineteenth century. It is also the quarter in which the _igbó egúngún_ (forest of the ancestors) is located.

36. Ọbatala Priest Oyewole Akande: personal communication, _ilé_ Aworoose, July 30, 1974. It is generally believed that the mingling of woman's menstrual blood with man's semen creates a child.

37. Ọrangun-Ila: personal communication, July 20, 1977. Henry Drewal notes that the literal meaning of the term _orí ojópọ̀_ is "the collection or gathering together of heads" (personal communication, January 15, 1978).

38. The translation of *èkejì* in the salutation to the king poses an interesting problem. Abraham (1970:152) translates *èkejì* as "the second," but also as "companion," as in *èkejìimi* ("my companion"). In conversations with the Orangun-Ila and Chief Obala, as well as colleagues at the University of Ife, it appeared that in the salutation to the Orangun-Ila *èkejì* may be translated as "like," "like unto," or "similar to," meaning that the power of the *òrìṣà* is employed as a simile for the power of the king. *Èkejì* may also be translated as "next to" or "second to," suggesting that the king's power is not simply like, but is of the same substance or nature as, that of the gods, although of a diminished order. Both translations and their distinctive connotations are, I believe, appropriate. While a king reigns, his *àṣẹ* (power or authority) and the sacredness of his royal person are dependent upon the crown, which "is (has the power of) an *òrìṣà*," as the Orangun-Ila observed. But when a king dies (although it is repeatedly affirmed that "kings do not die"), it is understood that the king becomes an *òrìṣà*. A king's death, therefore, is viewed as the movement from a wordly existence, in which his power is derived, to life in the fullness of *òrìṣà* power. For a king it is the transition from likeness to the identity of being as an *òrìṣà*. The salutation functions as an *oríkì* (a praise name or attributive name). It predicates to the king a power from a realm to which he, as a human, does not belong and within which he does not legitimately act. In the context of the ritual performance of Iwa Ogun, the metaphoric attribution of *òrìṣà* power to designate the power of the king is the culmination of a sequence of actions in which the person and authority of the king are distinguished from those of the chiefs.

39. Ade Anike: personal communication, *ilé* Iyalode, July 23, 1977.

40. Beier and Gbadamosi note that this praise poem was collected in "the area between Ẹdẹ, Ilobu and Oshogbo," which is 45 miles southwest of Ila-Orangun (1959:13, 21–22).

41. Chief Odoode: personal communication, *ilè* Odoode, March 12, 1981. Prince Adetoyi suggests that the mock battle might be a historical reference to a conflict between Orangun Adeyemi Okusu and the chiefs of Ila in the late sixteenth century. Orangun Okusu treated Ila's chiefs and elders with disdain and forced the people of Ila to dig fortification trenches around Ila. On hearing of a plot by the chiefs and townspeople to overthrow him, the king fled to his mother's home in Ipe, where he died (personal communication, August 7, 1982). See also Adetoyi 1974:13.

42. Chief Odoode: personal communication, *ilé* Odoode, March 12, 1981.

43. As Prince Adetoyi makes clear, the "celebration of Oro festival in Ila . . . is quite different from how it is being celebrated in other Yoruba towns," where Oro refers to a society through which the community's ancestors control and punish criminals and whose presence is known in the sound of the bull-roarer. Rather, "Oro festival at Ila is regarded as the time of Character Celebrations, the time for remembering the first Orangun of Ila, the other past *obas* of Ila, the important chiefs and our beloved fathers and mothers . . . who had passed away to eternity" (1974:27). Thus, as the Orangun-Ila explained, the festival's name, Ẹbọra Ila, is a conflation of *ẹbọ* (sacrifice) and *igboro* (town center), which means "sacrifice for the whole town" (personal communication, July 20, 1977).

44. I am grateful to the Oloriawo Onifa, leader of the Ifa priests, for permission to witness the rites of Odun Ifa and to Chief Odoode for conversations about these rites.

45. Just seventeen days earlier, when Odun Idafa began, the Obatala festival had come to an end, marking the day on which new yams could be sold in the king's market.

46. Johnson refers to "a festival [in Oyọ] called Isule customarily held in the month of July, [when] all the members of the royal family gorgeously dressed go in procession

to a certain place to worship the spirits of their dead ancestors" (1969:213–14). For a discussion of the rites for deceased twins see Pemberton 1988.

47. In March, at the conclusion of the rite of Itadogun, when an announcement is made that a festival for the ancestors will begin in 17 days, a masquerade called Onise Timo, the Messenger of Timo, appears at Ọbalumọ's compound to instruct its chief and elders to prepare for the forthcoming festival. This rite reinforces the centrality of Timo in Ila tradition.

48. On history as "charter" and Yoruba historiography see Law (1973:25–40 and 1977:12–25), Lloyd (1973:205–23), Ogunba (1973:87–110), and Peel (1979: 110–11).

49. The phrase is used by Lloyd in his discussion of Yoruba kingdoms in the eighteenth and nineteenth centuries (1971:1–8).

50. Another way in which cloth is displayed socially is called *aṣọ ẹbí*, "family cloth." *Aṣọ ẹbí* is identical cloth, usually expensive, worn by family members (or other social groups) at public gatherings to express their solidarity and support of one another. On the occasion of Isinro, the women from Olutojokun's compound, the lineage "house" of the reigning king, wore *aṣọ ẹbí*, as did the women of Chief Ọdọọde's compound, where the rite of Isinro was performed.

51. Chief Ọdọọde: personal communication, *ilé* Ọdọọde, September 5, 1984.

52. Myths, rituals, and political responsibilities link Chiefs Ọbale, Ẹlẹmọna, and Ọdọọde. While Ọbale and Ẹlẹmọna are senior chiefs, Ọdọọde represents all of Ila's chiefs at rituals of divination performed on behalf of the king, the chiefs, or the town. Each of the chiefs has an ancestral masquerade called Olọbaloro, which includes as part of the costume a carved headdress depicting a leopard surrounded by human and animal heads. A story tells how each was a messenger to the mother of the *ọbas* of Aro-Ekiti, Ijero, and Ila. Only the Ọrangun-Ila was grateful for the small gift of a bead in a pot that the messengers brought with them from Ifẹ. When it was discovered that the pots were filled with beads, the Ọrangun-Ila showed his gratitude by establishing the chieftaincies of Ọbale, Ẹlẹmọna, and Ọdọọde and performing a ceremony in which he declared that the Ọrangun's prosperity would always be closely linked to their presence. Yet this presence denies privacy to the king and circumscribes his independent movement. (Chief Ọdọọde: personal communication, *ilé* Ọdọọde, March 12, 1981.)

53. Ọrangun-Ila: personal communication, March 14, 1981.

54. In his analysis of the sequence of dances in "the festival of the king," Ọdun Osu, in Owu-Ijẹbu, Ogunba observes that the festival begins with a series of "loosely connected events lasting for a few days, all in an atmosphere of general merriment. Then, there is a central event of a historical and military nature which is usually mimed. Then, the king may conclude the ceremony by dancing in full pomp and pageantry for the whole community." Ogunba believes that the Osu Festival is "typical . . . of the African 'royal drama' . . . [and] can serve as a paradigm for kings' festivals" throughout Yorubaland and West Africa (1977:368).

55. Yoruba kingdoms cannot be compared with the highly centralized Benin kingdom of the Edo to the southeast of the Yoruba (Bradbury 1957) or the Fon of Dahomey, which developed when Dahomey was a tributary state of Ọyọ (Akinjogbin 1967; Argyle 1966).

56. This is clearly the message conveyed in Ọdun Egungun, the festival for the ancestors, by the severely limited role of the king throughout the festival and by the ritual remembrance of Ọrangun Ijimogodo, who had the secret of the ancestral masquerades brought to Ila, but who was put to death by the chiefs in the forest of the ancestral masks for having betrayed the secret to his wife (Pemberton 1978, 1986). According to Wande Abimbọla, a similar story is told about Olufimo Adodo, a former

king of Akoko-Ekiti, in Ifa verses (personal communication, February 19, 1981). This ancient story is the basis for A. Isola's play, *Aye ye montan.*

REFERENCES CITED

Abraham, R. C. 1970. *Dictionary of Modern Yoruba*, London: University of London Press.

Adetoyi, A. 1974. *A Short History of Ila-Qrangun*, Ila-Qrangun, Nigeria: Iwaniyi Press.

Agiri, B. A. 1975. "Yoruba Oral Tradition with Special Reference to the Early History of the Qyǫ Kingdom," in W. Abimbǫla (ed.), *Yoruba Oral Tradition*, Ile-Ifę, Nigeria: Department of African Languages and Literatures, University of Ifę, pp. 157–97.

Akinjogbin, I. A. 1967. *Dahomey and Its Neighbors*, Cambridge: Cambridge University Press.

Argyle, W. J. 1966. *The Fon of Dahomey*, London: Oxford University Press.

Asiwaju, I. 1976. "Political Motivations and Oral Historical Traditions in Africa: the Case of the Yoruba Crowns, 1900–1960," *Africa* 46(2):113–27.

Bascom, W. 1969. *The Yoruba of Southwestern Nigeria*, New York: Holt, Rinehart & Winston.

———. 1987. "The Olojo Festival at Ife, 1937," in *Time Out of Time: Essays on the Festival*, Alessandro Falassi (ed.), Albuquerque: University of New Mexico Press, pp. 62–73.

Beier, H. U. 1956. "God of Iron," *Nigeria* 49:118–37.

———. 1959. "A Year of Sacred Festivals in One Yoruba Town," Lagos, Nigeria: A Special Issue of *Nigeria Magazine*.

Beier, H. U., and Gbadamosi, B. 1959. *Yoruba Poetry*, Ibadan, Nigeria: A Special publication of *Black Orpheus*. General Publications Section, Ministry of Education, Nigeria.

Bradbury, R. E. 1957. *The Benin Kingdom and the Edo-speaking Peoples of Southwestern Nigeria,* London: Ethnographic Survey of Africa, West Africa, No. 13. International African Institute.

Drewal, H. J. 1977. *Traditional Art of the Nigerian Peoples,* Washington, D.C.: Museum of African Art.

Eades, J. S. 1980. *The Yoruba Today*, New York: Cambridge University Press.

Fadipe, N. A. 1970. *The Sociology of the Yoruba*, Ibadan, Nigeria: Ibadan University Press.

Fernandez, J. 1977. "The Performance of Ritual Metaphors," in J.D. Sapir and J.C. Crocker (eds.), *The Social Use of Metaphors*, Philadelphia: University of Pennsylvania Press, pp. 100–131.

Geertz, C. 1973. *The Interpretation of Cultures*, New York: Basic Books.

Hobbes, T. 1947. *Leviathan*. New York: Oxford University Press.

Idowu, E. B. 1962. *Olodumare: God in Yoruba Belief*, London: Longmans.

Johnson, S. 1969. *The History of the Yorubas*. London: Routledge.

Law, R. 1973. "Traditional History," in S. O. Biobaku (ed.), *Sources of Yoruba History*, Oxford: Clarendon Press, pp. 9–24.

———. 1977. *The Qyǫ Empire c. 1600-c. 1836*, Oxford: Clarendon Press.

Lloyd, P. C. 1954. "The Traditional Political System of the Yoruba," in *Southwestern Journal of Anthropology* 10(4):336–84.

————. 1962. *Yoruba Land Law*, London: Oxford University Press.

————. 1971. *The Political Development of Yoruba Kingdoms in the Eighteenth and Nineteenth Centuries* (Royal Anthropological Institute Occasional Paper No. 31), London: Royal Anthropological Institute of Great Britain and Ireland.

————. 1973. "Political and Social Structure," S. O. Biobaku (ed.), *Sources of Yoruba History*, Oxford: Clarendon Press, pp. 205–223.

Morton-Williams, P. 1960. "The Yoruba Ogboni Cult in Ọyọ," *Africa* 30(4):362–74.

Ogunba, O. 1973. "Ceremonies," in S. O. Biobaku (ed.), *Sources of Yoruba History*, Oxford: Clarendon Press, pp. 87–100.

————. 1977. "Traditional African Festival Drama," in O. O. Oyelaran (ed.), *Seminar Series* Number I (1976–77), Part II, Ile-Ifẹ, Nigeria: Department of African Languages and Literatures, University of Ifẹ, pp. 354–83.

Ojo, G. J. A. 1966. *Yoruba Culture: A Geographical Analysis*, London: University of London Press.

Peel, J. D. Y. 1979. "Kings, titles and quarters: a conjectural history of Ilesha. Part I, the traditions reviewed," *History in Africa* 6:109–35.

————. 1983. *Ijeshas and Nigerians*, New York: Cambridge University Press.

Pemberton, J. 1977. "A Cluster of Sacred Symbols: Orisha Worship Among the Igbomina Yoruba of Ila-Orangun," *History of Religions* 7(3):1–28.

————. 1978. "Egungun Masquerades of the Igbomina Yoruba," *African Arts* 11(3):40–47, 99–100.

————. 1986. "Festivals and Sacred Kingship Among the Igbomina Yoruba," *National Geographic Research: a Scientific Journal* 2(2):216–33.

————. 1988. "Yoruba Carvers of Ila-Ọrangun," in C. D. Roy (ed.), *Iowa Studies in African Art*, Vol. III.

Simpson, G. E. 1965. "Selected Yoruba Rituals: 1964," *Nigerian Journal of Economic and Social Studies* 7(3):311–24.

————. 1980. *Yoruba Religion and Medicine in Ibadan*. Ibadan, Nigeria: Ibadan University Press.

Verger, P. 1966. "The Yoruba High God," *Odu* 2(2):19–40.

Adeboye Babalọla

7

A Portrait of Ògún as Reflected in Ìjálá Chants

*Ì*jálá are Yoruba poetic chants used in entertaining and saluting Ògún. As those who are familiar with the Ògún tradition very well know, the *oríkì Ògún* (verbal salutes to Ògún) within *ìjálá* reveal, little by little, the nature of the deity. One of the most striking revelations of the *ìjálá* is the contradictions found in them. This paper addresses these contradictions and argues that Ògún symbolizes a universal contradiction: humans are strong and, at the same time, they are frail. The constant oppositions in the texts of *ìjálá* artists are therefore a necessary and explainable part of this poetic tradition.

The contradictions, and in some cases the variations, found in Ògún traditions as they are rendered by *ìjálá* chanters are of three kinds. First, the figure of Ògún displays opposing personality traits (e.g., he is fiery and cool) or symbolic traits (e.g., he represents death and healing). Second, the literary construction of the chants opposes metaphors and images thereby reinforcing, through structure, contradictions that occur in content and meaning. Third, the devotees of Ògún place him in a bewildering variety of contradictory mythical traditions. Ògún founds many towns, conquers many people, and pursues several occupations. The wide variation in traditions raises questions as to the authenticity or correctness of any of them. But this problem is resolved in the *ìjálá* verbal salutes to Ògún. As one *ìjálá* artist declares: "*Ògún méje l'Ògún-ùn mi*" (The Ògún that I know are seven in number). Thus, many forms are attributed to the god Ògún. But what is important is the total picture that the many contradictions and variations eventually create. It is the sum of the parts that provides insight into what Ògún actually represents to the Yoruba.

Ìjálá-chanting[1] is a tradition found primarily among the Ǫyǫ Yoruba, though pockets of *ìjálá* artists exist among the hunters in some of the communities adjacent to the Ǫyǫ-Yoruba.

One of the Yoruba legends accounting for the origin of *ìjálá* well illustrates the contradictions found in this tradition. In the book *The Content and Form of Yoruba Ìjálá*, I reproduce in English four legends that claim *ìjálá*-chanting was originated by Ògún during his lifetime (Babalǫla 1966:4–7). There is no need to repeat them here. Instead, I have a recently collected legend on the same theme, a legend that attributes the origin of *ìjálá* not to Ògún but to Erinlè, a hunter deity who also has a place in the Yoruba pantheon.[2] This variation seems remarkable in that the informant is a well-known devotee of Ògún,[3] yet he gives to another god the credit for originating *ìjálá*-chanting, which is traditionally referred to as *aré Ògún* (Ògún's entertainment). To Ògún he ascribes only the popularizing of *ìjálá*-chanting. The legend, told with some commentary, runs thus in English translation:

Erinlè[4] was the very originator of *ìjálá*-chanting. He was a hunter who used to go on frequent hunting expeditions from his hometown, Àjàgbùsì, to the forests within a day's journey on foot. As he had no wife he decided one day to make his abode in the forest. So he built a hut with stakes for walls and leaf-thatch for roof under a mighty *gbìngbin*[5] tree near the bank of a river. The monkeys in the forest were his favorite game and he used to sell their carcasses, fresh or roasted, in Àjàgbùsì on market days.

To amuse himself during his lonely sojourn in the forest he began to chant utterances in Yoruba in a peculiar style featuring a nasal twang. Whenever he was in the market he also used to invite prospective buyers of his bush meat, with sentences chanted likewise. Thus he drew special attention to himself, until one day some stalwart medicine men followed him from the market to his forest abode to ascertain where he came from. Erinlè welcomed his guests with utterances in his peculiar chanting style and bade them wait for him in his hut while he went into the forest to get some fresh bush meat for them to take home. He made good his promise before the visitors departed.

This was how Erinlè's fame quickly spread in Àjàgbùsì town. The people regarded him as an uncanny man who had befriended the spirits living in the forest.

Soon, some men decided to make farms near Erinlè's hut. They got his permission not only for this but also for making their own dormitory huts near his. Soon, a village developed. Erinlè taught the people his special style of chanting and they gave it the name *ìjálá* from the notion that the chanting style was best described as *"ohun tí à ń já tí a sì ń lá"* (that which is chanted on and on protractedly and is also licked up or relished with gusto).

One day Ògún, a blacksmith, farmer, and hunter born and bred in

Sakí, came to Àjàgbùsì in the course of his wanderings and met Erinlẹ̀ in the marketplace. It was Erinlẹ̀'s chanting that attracted Ògún, and Ògún went with him to his village in the forest. Thus began their friendship, which deepened on account of their common occupation, hunting.

Ògún's favorite pastime then was drumming and dancing. In the course of his friendship with Erinlẹ̀, Ògún taught Erinlẹ̀ how to make drums, how to produce lively drum music, and how to dance to the music. On the other hand Erinlẹ̀ taught Ògún how to chant *ìjálá* and Ògún really took a fancy to it, mastering it, and excelling in it.

As Ògún was an itinerant hero, he quickly spread the knowledge and love of *ìjálá* all over Yorubaland, so much so that people thought he was the originator of *ìjálá*-chanting with singing, drumming, and dancing at intervals, and started to describe it as *aré Ògún* (Ògún's entertainment).

After Erinlẹ̀'s death by accidental drowning in the river that flowed past his forest village, his corpse was never recovered and this led to his being deified. His first worshippers were people closely associated with him in his lifetime. They therefore commenced a tradition of profuse chanting about historical events, interspersed with drumming and dancing, during their acts of worship. Until this day the Erinlẹ̀ devotees are recognizable by iron or brass neck chains that they wear along with matching bracelets. When they dance, the initial rhythm of the drumbeat tallies with the following words if uttered repeatedly with increasing speed:

> *Pinkún! Pinkún!*
> *Àjànbìtì!*[6]

When these drumbeats reach their fastest point, the drumming switches over to that of the hunters (Ògún devotees) and so does the dancing. This is a reflection of the friendship between Erinlẹ̀ and Ògún during their earthly lives.

The tradition that Erinlẹ̀ can also be considered a legitimate originator of *ìjálá*-chanting and not contradict the legends which attribute this task to Ògún, or *vice versa*, is explained by the close relationship of the two deities. Both Erinlẹ̀ and Ògún are hunters, as are most *ìjálá* artists. Erinlẹ̀ is a solitary figure who, at the beginning of the legend, lives alone in the forest. Later his fame draws others to join him, and he becomes the founder of a new settlement. Some of the *ìjálá* texts reproduced in the following pages reveal that Ògún, too, is a solitary figure who not only lives and travels alone but also founds new settlements. In other respects, devotees of the two deities share similar attributes: both use iron as a symbolic emblem, and both draw on the same drum rhythms and dance steps in their rituals. The attributes of the two figures are interchangeable in several dimensions, and this then justifies the liberties taken in the legends that, on the one hand, attribute the origin of *ìjálá* to Erinlẹ̀ and, on the other, to Ògún. In short, they are separate deities who in significant respects occupy a large overlapping segment of the same cosmological domain.

Before turning to some excerpts from texts of *ìjálá* performances, it is important to point out that an *ìjálá* artist, like every Ògún devotee, is expected to keep faithful to the transmitted texts of verbal salutes which he has learned in the course of both his training and his practice. He is forbidden to make improvisations on the verbal salutes to Ògún, or to incorporate counterfeit topics of his own creation into his performance. Ògún is a god whose symbol, iron, is used voluntarily in law courts in Yorubaland for the taking of oaths by witnesses to affirm that the truth will be told. Therefore, only the truth about Ògún is to be told in the *ìjálá*. Although an artist sometimes resorts to euphemisms in the presentation of Ògún's fiery temper, there are no skeletons hidden away in Ògún's cupboard.

In the following exchange, the many-sided character of Ògún is reflected. Two *oníjalá* (*ìjálá* artists)[7] make use of stark contrasts as a way of building a general picture of the deity and the ideology that supports his cult. Ògún is given what, at a glance, seem to be contradictory attributes but which, on further consideration, are reconcilable as two sides of the same coin. Since the Creator made the world, both good and evil are now noticeable in it; therefore, the recognition of the opposing personality traits in Ògún's character is regarded not as an abnormal thing but just as a thing in consonance with humankind's lot.

Ìjálá Excerpt 1

(Gbàdàmọ́ṣí)

1	Ìbà oooo ni ng ó f'ọjọ́ òní jú ooo.
2	Lákáayé, mo wáà d'ójú-òòde.
3	Pàá mo wáà dé fúnrà\u00e0mi Àkàndá—
4	Abójòsúpọ̀ arẹmọbíeji.
5	Aká mulukú-yígi-dí-'nà-ẹgàn.
6	Èmi Aríbùkí Gbàdàmọ́ṣí mo dé tìkálárà\u00e0mi.
7	Gbàdàmọ́ṣí ọdẹ̀ẹ̀'lú Òfàààr.
8	Ògún mo ríbàà, k'íbàa mi k'ó mọ́ọ ṣẹ.
9	Ońlé-owó ọlọ́ọ̀dẹẹ-'mọ̀.
10	Awónúwóto ìjà náà kankan re.
11	Ọ̀kárá f'idà hayín.
12	Labalábá kan'mí akọ ẹtà, ó tú gììrì.
13	Ṣòóńlé-Ìwó ọkọ Adéọlá, olúwaa'yáà mi.
14	Asínrín aboojulẹ́nu.
15	Ọ̀gẹ̀dẹ̀ àgbagbà tí í s'ọmọ 'ẹ̀ kọ́ dẹ̀ngbẹ̀rẹ̀.
16	A-bùn-ún-ni-má-gbà-á.

17 Ogunlabí tí í wín ni í kún t'ọwọ́ ẹni.
18 Òrìṣà tí í gbà lọ́wọ́ ọlọ́rọ̀ tí í fi í fún òtòṣì.
19 Ògún ó f'owóo'lé ọlọ́rọ̀ ṣ'ọ́ọ̀dẹẹ gbogbo wa.
20 Ikin adádéjọba.
21 Àwàlàwúlú òrìṣà tí í jẹ'gba ekòló mọ́ bì.
22 Òrìṣà t'ọ́ bá sọ pé tÒgún ò sí, Lákáayé.
23 Òrìṣà náà ní'ó f'eyín araa rẹ̀ hóò'po iṣu jẹ ni.
24 Abẹ́rẹ́ mú tojútimú.
25 Ẹjẹ o t'ibi ire wọ̀run.
26 Ẹgun òṣùṣú tí i kọ'ra'ẹ̀ lébè.
27 Ọkùnrin yalayala ní'gbó enígbó.
28 Ọkùnrin yàlàyàlà ní'jù ọlọ̀tẹ̀.
29 Ọkùnrin gìdìgbà n'ígbóò 'Jẹ̀bú.
30 Atóónàlórógùn ọdẹ atàpárìnyẹ́nkú.
31 Alá-ta-pa, afòkúsàmìọ̀nà.
32 Gbáláuntàwi iná gbá'lẹ̀ẹ 'jù gẹrẹrẹ.
33 Ògún nì ng kéé sí, bẹ̀ẹ ni ng ò p'Óbòkun.
34 Ògún nì ng kéé sí, bẹ̀ẹ ni ng ò p'óògùn.
35 Ìbà ni ng ó f'ojọ́ òní jú.
36 K'áí t'òní lóórin délẹ̀,
37 Áá tó'jọ́ méje.
38 Fágbèmí ìbà lọ́wọ́ọ̀ rẹ oooò.
39 Àjànàkú, ìbàà lọ́'ọ̀ rẹẹẹẹ.
40 Àràbà ni bàbá,
41 Ẹni a bá l'abà náà ni baba ẹni.
42 Ọmọ Lágúnádé, mo ríbà.
43 K'íbàà mi k'ó mọ́ọ ṣe.
44 Ọmọ Lágunárèe t'Àmàdú,
45 T'Alùtótó t'Ègbẹ̀di Òwu t'ọba Arọ́wáyan.
46 Arọ́wáyan lọ́tùn-ún a-bàálè-èyí-lósì.
47 Òkàn kunkun tí wọn ń fi méjì í pààrọ̀.
48 Ọmọ ọba ọ̀rọ̀ tíí bẹ́ṣin lọ́nà múgùn.
49 Ọba dimudimu lórí ẹṣin.
50 Ọmọ Ìtándógún.
51 Ọmọọ Táa-o-rẹ́fọ̀n.
52 Ọmọ Ògúnróunbí.
53 Ọmọ Ìtándógún.
54 Ọmọọ Ta-á-o-rẹ́fọ̀n.
55 K'ágbàà'wo Ọya lórí ẹran.

1   It is in homage, homage profuse that I intend to render all my chants
        today.
2   Lákáayé,[8] I have now arrived at the open-air social gathering.
3   I have come fully prepared, I Àkàndá[9]—
4   A man laden like rain clouds with forthcoming precipitation.

A man who drenches people like rain.

5   A man as big as a barn, who one day pushed a log
Across the footpath leading to the distant farm.

6   I, Aríbùkí Gbàdàmọ́ṣi, have arrived in top form.

7   Gbàdàmọ́ṣi a hunter who hails from Ọ̀fà Town.

8   Ògún, I pay you homage.
May my homage prove beneficial to me.

9   Your house is full of wealth though its roof is thatch.

10   Destroyer of the human-frame who thereby causes an uproar.
An uproar involving accusation and counter-accusation.

11   A bellicose man who scrapes his teeth with a sword.

12   A butterfly chances upon a civet-cat's excrement
And flies away very fast.[10]
Such is the dread in which Ògún is held.

13   Ṣòónlé-Ìwó,[11] husband of Adéọlá,[12] my mother's divinity.

14   A veritable *asín*[13] rat whose mouth is defaced with a nasty ulcer.

15   You are a plantain tree,[14] keeping its fruits aloft in safe custody.

16   When you give out gifts you give them for good.

17   You are Ogunlabí,[15] who gives one loans to supplement one's
resources.

18   You are the divinity who takes from the rich to give to the poor.

19   Ògún shall guard the dwelling place of each one of us
With money from the rich people's homes.

20   Ikin,[16] who became a king and wore a crown.

21   Rugged and rough divinity who eats two hundred earthworms
Without feeling sick at all.[17]

22   Any divinity who scoffs at Ògún Lákáayé

23   Will use his teeth in place of a knife for peeling boilt yam pieces
Before eating the yam.

24   A needle is sharp at both ends.

25   When blood comes out to gaze at the sky,
It does not issue from a good incident.

26   You are the *òṣùṣú*[18] thorny plant which casts itself in a series of
heaps.

27   You are the swift warrior moving to battle in the enemy's bush tract.

28   You are the waddling fighter cautiously advancing in enemy forest
territory.

29   You are the stalwart assailant confronting the enemy in Ìjẹ̀bú[19] woodland.

30   Hefty hunter who walks haltingly.

31   Hunter who shoots at game and kills hunted animals galore,
Thus marking his way with animals' carcasses.

32   The forest fire that completely destroys the undergrowth
Together with the mass of shed leaves on the ground.

33	I am addressing Ògún, mark you, it's not Obòkun.

33   I am addressing Ògún, mark you, it's not Obòkun.
34   I am addressing Ògún, mark you, it's not óògùn.[20]
35   I will devote all my chants to homage-paying today.
36   Starting to chant from my repertoire today,
37   I can go on for a full week.
38   I pay homage to you, Fágbèmí.[21]
39   I pay homage to you, Àjànàkú.[22]
40   You, Àràbà,[23] are our father,
41   Just as the man who precedes one in settling in a farmstead
        Virtually becomes one's father.
42   Offspring of Lágúnádé,[24] I pay homage to you.
43   May my homage prove beneficial to me.
44   Offspring of Lágunárè of Àmàdú,[25]
45   Of Alùtótó,[26] of Ègbèdi Òwu,[27] of king Aròwáyán,[28]
46   Whose palace had two parts, the right-hand one which he used for pub-
        lic affairs,
        The other on the left-hand side, which he reserved for his private life.
47   Whenever a valuable object of his was lost by someone,
        Two such objects were to be provided in replacement.
48   Offspring of a king who used to mount any horse
        That he found on his way.
49   A king who used to appear heavily clad on a horse.
50   Person associated with firing a gun twenty times.
51   Person associated with the tradition of hunting buffaloes.
52   Offspring of Ògúnróunbí.[29]
53   Person associated with firing a gun twenty times.
54   Person associated with the tradition of hunting buffaloes.
55   With a view to procuring her favorite horns for the goddess Qya.[30]

Ìjálá Excerpt 2

(Qmọ Kowéè)

56   Ìbàa bàbá, ìbàa yèyé.
57   Qlójọ́-òní mo júbà orin ìn mí ki ng tóó máa lọ.
58   Ojó ọrún ìbà.
59   K'íbàà mi ó máa sẹ ní olele ní olele.
60   Mo ríbà mo ríbàa bàbáà mi.
61   Fajúfúwọlé Ògún babaà mi káre.
62   Sùsùká-rù'pá-Ògún-kèdukèdu.
63   K'á múra oko jàgàjígí Ajíté-pẹpẹ-Ògún-gbèngèdè.
64   Ò-gb'órí-ègún-rán wọn-níyò-lójà-gágá.
65   A-gb'óri-igi-sò'kòò-'jàá'lè.

66   Ọkọ Ọ̀gbẹ̀gún, Alóṣòópọ̀bọ.
67   A-d'orí-orókè-má-kọ̀'-rọ̀ọ̀-jà.
68   Òun náà l'ó kọ́ mi lórin.
69   Bẹ́ẹ̀ ni kì í kuku kọ ìpa orin wò.
70   Tí a bí ni mọ́ o leè hun ni.
71   Kò ní í hun mí.
72   Èkúkúú'ṣu kì í kúkúú họ̀bẹ̀.
73   Mo ríbá mo ríbàa bàbáà mi.
74   Ìbàa bàbá ìbàa yèyé.
75   Àràbà ni bàbá.
76   Ẹni a bá lábà náà ni baba ẹni.
77   Ọba Akọ́dá, mo júbà orin-in mi ng tóó máa lọ.
78   Aṣẹ̀dá mo júbà orin-in mi.
79   Kódẹ̀ǹlẹ̀gẹ́, mojúbà orin-in mi ng tóó máa lọ.
80   Akọ́dá ní í dá tiẹ̀ ní eréwé.
81   Aṣẹ̀dá ní í dá tirẹ̀ ní'lẹ̀ pẹ̀pẹ̀.
82   Kódẹ̀ǹlẹ̀gẹ́ náà ní í dá tirẹ̀ ni òfuru jágá dọba.
83   Kódẹ̀ǹlẹ̀gẹ́ ọba Àkórì, ọbayíga a-kẹ̀-bí-àlà.
84   Ọlálọmí ọ gbà á l'ẹ́nu mi ọ lọọ tọ́jú orin.

56   Homage to my fathers, homage to my mothers.
57   O Creator of this day, I pay you my homage before proceeding with
          my chant.
58   O four-day week, I pay my homage to you.
59   May my homage prove beneficial to me resoundingly.
60   I dutifully pay homage to my father.
       I stylishly pay homage to my father.
61   My father who used to carry with him a handbag
       Whenever he was going into the Ògún shrine; I salute him.
62   He who used to carry with a pad on his head,
       The parcel containing a deceased hunter's hunting gear
       And walk becomingly with it to where it should be deposited.
63   Who used to wear from the house to the farm
       A tunic bedecked with sheathed knives, medicinal charms, and a mini-
          ature gun.[31]
       Who daily prepared a low framework for roasting animals' carcasses
          to glorify Ògún.
64   He who used to hand down instruction from his hunter's platform
       High up among a tree's leafy branches—
       Instruction that someone should go and buy salt from the marketplace
          in town.
65   He who used to throw down, from high up on the tree,
       Stones of combat.
66   Husband of Ọ̀gbẹ̀gún,[32] he who used to kill monkeys

With his gun fired from a squatting position.
67 He who dared to engage in combat while on a hillock.
68 'Twas he who taught me the *ìjálá*-chanting technique.
69 He never, even as a joke, chanted hostile words.
70 What one has inherited from one's parents does not harm one.
71 *Ìjálá*-chanting will not harm me.
72 For a partly rot-infected yam tuber
Does not harm the knife used in cutting off the rotten part.
73 I dutifully pay homage to my father.
74 Homage to fathers, homage to mothers.
75 The Àràbà is our father.
76 Just as the man who precedes one in settling on a farmstead
Virtually becomes one's father.
77 Priest Akódá,[33] I pay you my homage before proceeding with my chant.
78 Priest Aṣèdá,[34] I pay due homage to you in respect of my chant.
79 Priest Kódèńlègé,[35] I pay you my homage before proceeding with my chant.
80 'Twas Akódá who used to do his work of divination on the leafy boughs.
81 'Twas Aṣèdá who used to do his work of divination on the earth.
82 And 'tis Kódèńlègé who usually does his own work of divination in the air.
83 Kódèńlègé, King Almighty, Highest King attired in radiant white.
84 Olálọmí,[36] do take over from me now and sing a song.

After introductions, the first *ìjálá*-chanter turns to Ògún, calling attention to his nurturing qualities and then to his destructive qualities. He has a house "full of wealth," i.e., general prosperity, which he shares with those who need his help, while at the same time he is a hot-tempered, belligerent deity who is capable of destroying "the human frame." One of the most intriguing aspects in this juxtaposition of qualities is Ògún's zeal in protecting the oppressed. He is an Aeneas or a Robin Hood-like figure, who is good to the poor and needy, using the abundance of the rich to help those in want, and thus acting as a crusader against injustice. One canon of good conduct that is strongly held by the Yoruba is that the rich should help the poor. The wealth of a rich person is believed to be basically the result of a good *orí*[37] (predestined lot), though it is also partly due to self-application. A Yoruba adult who is really an *ọmọlúàbí*, a person of good character and conduct, habitually uses money unselfishly, caring for the family and helping people in need. In Yoruba society, sharing is an important virtue and Ògún stands ready to see that justice, in terms of rectifying imbalances in wealth, is carried out. Indeed Ògún is a stickler for justice. He is looked to as a protector who will promptly respond to the appeals of the oppressed in their encounter with an unjust fate. In this respect, Ògún is a warrior against injustice within his own society, just as he is a warrior in battles against outside enemies or in forests against animals unwilling to be killed for human food.

The protective and nurturing aspects of Ògún's nature are also strong themes in the *ijálá* chanted by the second artist. This is demonstrated by the homage paid to Ògún. The homage calls attention to, and establishes, a dependent relationship. In return for homage, Ògún, like a father, elder, ancestor, or founder, is expected to protect his faithful dependants. The *oníjalá* is explicit in his exhortation: "May my homage prove beneficial to me." Just as a good parent responds justly to a dutiful child, a deity is expected to respond justly to a supplicant who properly performs his duty to the deity.

Ògún's relationship to justice is also revealed in a keen sensitivity to deceit. As a result, his devotees call on him for oath-taking (see *Ìjálá* excerpt 3). Upon a sword, a piece of iron, or a measure of earth[38] (any of which signals the deity's presence), no devotee of Ògún dares swear falsely. If one breaks an oath, one may be castigated with "*Ògún l'áá ję' rí ę*" ("Ògún shall afflict you with a fatal accident").

Ògún's hot temper makes him a dreaded figure. Yet it is this very characteristic which renders him powerful enough to protect and defend the outcasts of society with whom he in fact identifies. Ògún, therefore, wields a double-edged sword: "The needle is sharp at both ends." While protecting some, for example the honest, the innocent poor, or the victims of military attack, Ògún inevitably inflicts pain on others—the deceitful, the miserly rich, or one's enemies in warfare. The paradoxical nature of this beneficent/destructive deity is contained, without contradiction or condemnation, in the symbolic emblems associated with his cult. The cutlass, to name but one, is a useful implement that serves humans by cutting paths, felling trees, or clearing new farm plots. Yet, accidentally or on purpose, the cutlass causes wounds that can "destroy the human frame."

The same paradox is revealed in Ògún's actions. In an attempt to mete out justice, Ògún is sometimes unwittingly unjust. The dilemma is well illustrated in a famous legend in which the people of Ìrè refuse to answer Ògún's call for palm wine (Babalǫla 1966:5). Annoyed with what is interpreted as a deceitful response, Ògún slaughters many of the townspeople, only to learn later that they are observing a traditional taboo that enjoins them to refrain from speaking on a particular festival day. Ògún's response, while varied in the oral traditions, usually makes use of the double-pointed needle theme. Filled with remorse for perpetrating injustice, Ògún either falls on his sword and kills himself (see *Ìjálá* excerpt 3) or in a nonviolent gesture retreats to a remote hilltop (see *Ìjálá* excerpt 6) to lead a solitary life, brooding in isolation from society.

The incident at Ìrè which causes Ògún to make "his own blood flow" is recalled in the following *ijálá* excerpt.

Ìjálá Excerpt 3

(From a performance by Aláwodè Ògúnòwe at the
Òwe Sector of Abẹokuta town)

1   Ògún ni ng ó sìn, ng ò s'n Eégún.
2   Ògún ni ng ó sìn, ng ò sìn-ìn'ṣà.
3   Ògún ni ng ó sìn, ng ò s'n ẹbọrakẹbọra.
4   Ògún jèéwó tán
5   Ògún yó ṣubúlulẹ̀
6   L'ágbẹ̀dẹ.
7   Wọ́n l'"Ògún-ùn,"
8   Wọ́n ní, "Kín ní ṣe ọ́
9   T'ọọ yó ṣubúlulẹ̀
10 L'ágbẹ̀dẹ?"
11 Ó l'éwòó tí òún jẹ
12 L'òun yó ṣubúu'rẹ̀ l'ágbẹ̀dẹ.
13 Òdínu òòṣà
14 Tí í bu'ra 'ẹ̀ ṣán wọ̀n-ìn-wọ̀n-ìn,
15 Yánkan-n'Írè.
16 Ọm'AAdìgbòlẹ̀gbọ̀.
17 Ọ́ já ń'nú okó pamọ́.
18 Ó bù ń'nú òbò sọfà.
19 Wọ̀lọ̀wọ́lọ́
20 Ùn-un ní í ta dúndùn mọ́bẹ̀.
    Orin:
21 *Lílé:*   Òrìṣà l'Ògún, ẹ má dalẹ̀.
22   Ẹní bá mÒgún, e má dalẹ̀.
23 *Ẹ̀gbè:*   Òrìṣà l'Ògún.

1   I will always worship Ògún, I won't worship Eégún.[39]
2   I will always worship Ògún, I won't worship any other divinity.
3   I will always worship Ògún, I won't worship any of the embodied spirits.[40]
4   After eating a meal of *èéwó*[41]
5   Ògún slowly fell off his seat to the floor
6   In his smithy.
7   People present asked him,
8   "What went wrong with you
9   And caused your slowly falling off your seat to the floor
10 In your smithy?"
11 Ògún in reply said that 'twas the *èéwó* eaten
12 That he celebrated by slowly falling off his seat.[42]

13   A reticent divinity
14   Who bites off and noisily munches parts of his own body,
15   Thus making his own blood flow at Ìrè.[43]
16   Offspring of Adìgbòlẹ̀gbọ̀.[44]
17   He cuts off and keeps part of the penis.
18   He breaks off and gives away part of the vagina.
19   'Tis snippets of meat
20   That contribute most to the flavor of a nice stew.
      Song:
21   *Lead*:   Ògún is a divinity, so don't break your oath.
22   Whoever knows Ògún, don't break your oath.
23   *Refrain*:   Ògún is a divinity.

The next *ìjálá* excerpt continues to reveal the many facets of Ògún that his Yoruba devotees are aware of.

Ìjálá Excerpt 4

(From a performance by Àjàní Ògúnkànmí Jóògún of Ẹdẹ town)

1   Ǹlẹ́ oo !
2   Ògún Eníràn, o le o.
3   Ògún Oníré ní í jajá.
4   T'Enirèè ní í jàgbó.
5   Ògún-ùn kọ̀làà òun ní í jẹgbín-ín.
6   Ògún onígbàjámọ̀ irun orí ní í jẹẹ.
7   T'Àgalamọ̀sà a jẹ ọ̀ tọ̀ tọ̀ èèyàn.
8   T'odè wọn a si jẹ ahun.
9   Ògún-un mi, ǹlẹ́ !
10   'Tó' bí ẹní b'aró méjì, asọ̀nbọ̀ọkò.
11   Apòòsàmá-pÒgún ara'ẹ̀ l'ó tanjẹ,
12   Ọ́ dá m'lójú gbangba.
13   Èmi ọmọ Mọnílọ́lá mo ti mọ̀ bẹ́ẹ̀.
14   Ògún tó mi í sìn ní tèmi, Ajugudunírin.
15   Ògún mo fi ọ́ bọ párá, ọ la párá.
16   Ògún mo fi ọ́ bàkọ̀, ọ làkọ̀ pèrẹ̀.
17   Ògún l'ó pọkọ 'ójúu'ná.
18   Ògún payà s'éyìn à-àrò.
19   Ògún palárinà s'íta gbangba.
20   Ó dá m'lójú mo ti gbà báàun.
      Orin:
21   *Lílé*:   Ògún jọ̀ọ́ bá m'gbéjò dí i mọ́lé.
22   Ògún jọ̀ọ́ bá m'gbéjò dí i mọ́lé.

23		Ẹni s'ọ̀rọ̀ mi tí ò jẹ́ kí ng gbọ́.
24	Ègbè:	Ògún bá m'gbéjò di i mọ́lé.
25		Ògún-ùn mi ǹlẹ́ o !
26		Ó tó ná onílù orin-ìn mi.
27		Àrìpọ̀ l'à á rì'Gún àjọbọ.
28		Ẹni inú ń bí o ri tirẹ̀ lọ́tọ̀.

1　I greet warmly!

2　Ògún Eníràn,[45] you are stern.

3　King Oníré's Ògún eats dog meat with relish.

4　That of king Enirè[46] fancies ram meat.

5　The circumcisers' Ògún eats snail meat.

6　The barbers' Ògún eats human hair.

7　That of Rebels eats full-bodied human beings.

8　That of rivers eats tortoise flesh.

9　I greet you, my Ògún!

10　In reverence for you, I say "Tó," which sounds like the dripping of indigo dye.

　　You are the owner of a mighty, lidded straw basket.

11　Anyone who, while shouting praises to the divinities,

　　Omits praises to the god Ògún,

12　Is certainly wallowing in self-deceit.

　　I am very sure of this.

13　I, a son of Mọnílọ́lá,[47] know that for a fact.

14　Ògún, possessor of a massive stock of iron, suffices me as a divinity to give worship to.

15　Ògún, when I placed you in the roof's interior, you made a gash in it.

16　Ògún, when I put you in a scabbard you split the scabbard in a jiffy.

17　'Twas Ògún who once killed the bridegroom on the fire.

18　Then Ògún killed the bride behind the fireplace.

19　Finally Ògún killed the go-between in the courtyard of the compound.

20　I am sure of this, this is what I believe.

　　Song:

21　*Lead:*　Ògún, please send a snake to confine him to his room.

22　　　　Ògún, please send a snake to confine him to his room.

23　　　　The man who speaks ill of me

　　　　While I am not present.

24　*Refrain*:　Ògún, please send a snake to confine him to his room.

25　　　　My god Ògún, I greet you!

26　　　　That will do for now, dear drummer to my song.

27　　　　We customarily come together to set up Ògún emblems

　　　　To represent our communal Ògún.

28　　　　Whoever does not like this should set up his own Ògún.

The *ìjálá* artist begins with a greeting to Ògún and quickly switches to a full-blown verbal salute addressed to the deity. This verbal salute expands our knowledge of the diverse spheres in which Ògún is the appropriate supernatural figure. Thus authority figures, the king of Ìrèé (Oníré) and the king of Ìrè (Onírè), worship Ògún by offering a dog or a ram to him in sacrifice. Ògún's favorite sacrifice is believed to be a dog but the artist mentions a ram as a play on the idea that Ògún actually "eats"[48] more than a single thing. The barber's razor made of steel is Ògún who eats hair. The axe-wielding logger and the sculptor using an axe and chisel use instruments made of steel, which represent Ògún eating the sap of trees. The rebel's or warrior's sword wielded in battle is Ògún eating humans.

Ògún is also the patron deity of circumcisers, who rely on iron implements in pursuit of their trade. The phrase "the circumciser's Ògún" refers to "the circumciser's knife." Ògún becomes the knife. Hence it is Ògún who cuts the foreskin of the penis or part of the clitoris from a person. "The circumciser's Ògún eats snail meat" because usually the snails whose fluid has been used on the circumcision wound are buried in the ground as an offering to Ògún. The snail's clear, light grey liquid also has masculine associations and symbolic connotations of peace and coolness. The snail liquid is used medicinally to heal the wound caused by the circumciser's knife, and therefore Ògún is said to "drink the liquid from the snail."

For each of these occupational groups, Ògún is a special, patron deity, since their livelihood is dependent on iron technology. In the case of kings, Ògún's patronage is highly valued because the general welfare and safety of their subjects is their responsibility. Because they share common symbols, the various groups of Ògún devotees can all come together as a single ritual body, or they can form separate cult societies wherein each makes use of a slight variation on the overall Ògún theme. This freedom of association for worshippers of Ògún is made clear in the last line of *Ìjálá* Excerpt 4: "Whoever does not like this should set up his own Ògún."

The verbal salute is concluded with utterances extolling the power of Ògún and calling attention to the accidents such power can cause. In this respect it returns to the double-pointed needle theme. The *oníjálá* describes iron implements and then notes that they can make a gash in the grass roof, split a scabbard, or kill bride, bridegroom, and the matchmaker.[49] The song with which the artist rounds off his performance returns to the theme of Ògún as a crusader against injustice. The song is presented as being sung by a morally injured party. Someone is backbiting against him; he therefore invokes Ògún, in the form of a poisonous snake, to attack the backbiter in his home.

In the next *ìjálá* excerpt, the chanter laments the ignorance of those people who underestimate the power of Ògún that can be unleashed when the occasion calls for it.

Ìjálá Excerpt 5

(From a performance by Rááji Ògúndìran Àlàó on a
ritual occasion in his hometown, Ẹripa)

I	Ó wáá tó oooo:
2	Ògún l'èmi í sìn ìn, igi lásán l'ará-oko ń bọ.
3	MÒgún l'à bá k'Ìrè.
4	Mogbe l'á bá k'ará Ìlákùkọ.
5	Àwọn tí ò gbọ́n,
6	Àwọn tí ò dà,
7	Wọn a ní k'Ógùn-ún ó l'áwọn l'ọ́nà-odò.
8	Ẹní bá sọ bẹ́ẹ,
9	Ma l'áwọn ògìnnìjọ̀ginnìjọ nù un.
10	Àwọn gọ̀ngọ̀gọ́ñgọ àwọn ràwìnnìrawinni.
11	Àwọn tí ò gbọ́n tí ò dà.
12	Ni 'ọ́n-ọ́n p'Ógùn-ún ọ́ l'áwọn l'ọ́nà-odò.
13	Ògún mọ́ lèé mi n'íbìkọ́ọ̀kan.
14	Ní 'jọ́ Ògún gba'lé Ìlógbò lọ ariwo ẹkún wáá gbẹnu.
15	Orí ọmọdé rí bí èdá odó.
16	Orí aagbalagbà rí bí èso àfọ̀n.
17	Èbẹ̀ l'à ń b'Ògún k'ọ́ mọ́ sọọ'léè 'Lógbò dahoro.
18	Ògún mọ́ bínúu 'jọ́kan n'íléè mi.
19	Ẹ ẹ́ gberin àb'ẹ̀ẹ gberin?
20	(Orin tẹ́lùúkú bá dá l'ọmọọ rẹ̀ẹ́ gbè.)
	Orin:
21	*Lílé*: Àrà l'èmi ń f'Ògún-ún dá.
22	Àrà nì ń f'Ògún-ún dá.
23	Gbogbo ìṣòwò ibi mo b'ọdẹ dé rèé o.
24	*Ègbè*: Àrà nì ń f'Ògún-ún dá.

I	It is now high time indeed for me to say as follows:
2	It is the god Ògún that I worship,
	But the country bumpkins worship mere trees.
3	MÒgún[50] would be a fitting epithet for Ìrè.
4	Mogbe[51] would be a fitting epithet for Ìlákùkọ[52] citizens.
5	Those who are not wise,
6	Those whose mental development was arrested in childhood,
7	Say they want Ògún to drive them back on their way to the river.
8	Whenever some people say this,
9	I comment, drawing attention to them as foolish people.
10	Absolute nincompoops they are.
11	Complete morons, thorough simpletons.

12   Only unwise people whose development stopped in childhood
      Request Ògún to drive them back on their way to the river.
13   Ògún, please don't drive me from anywhere.
14   On the day Ògún passed through Ìlógbò[53] town,
      The inhabitants were thrown into wailing.
15   Children's heads lay scattered on the ground like broken pestles.
16   Adults' heads lay scattered about, like African bread-fruits.
17   We started appealing to Ògún, begging him not to ruin Ìlógbò town.
18   Ògún, please don't grow angry in my home any day.
19   Will you now sing the refrain to my song?
20   [Whatever song the Èlúkú[54] starts, his followers sing its refrain.]
      Song:
21   *Lead:*   Innovations are my stock-in-trade with my Ògún.
22   Innovations are my stock-in-trade with my Ògún.
23   All you fellow-hunters, this is how far I have come with hunting.
24   *Refrain:* Innovations are my stock-in-trade with my Ògún.

The *ìjálá* artist first declares the superiority of Ògún—whose emblems are
iron implements or slabs of rock—over the trees that are worshipped by rus-
tics when they are on the farm.[55] He then pokes fun at "unwise people" who
unwittingly invite Ògún's wrath by asking him to "drive them back on their
way to the river." Little do they know of the destruction Ògún can cause.
To illustrate this the chanter describes the terrible holocaust that occurred
when "Ògún passed through Ìlógbò town."

The *ìjálá* concludes on two notes. The first is a prayer that Ògún in the
form of violent strife may never visit one's own home. The second, at a tan-
gent to the destructive Ògún, is an assertion that the *ìjálá* artist's devotion
to Ògún led him to giving innovative performances of Ògún's entertainment.

The unfolding of Ògún's character is continued in the next *ìjálá* excerpt,
where solitariness is a prominent theme.

Ìjálá Excerpt 6

(From a performance by Olókòtó-ìbọn, an *oníjalá*
from Ile Olu Ọdẹ in Oṣogbo town)

1   Ìbà l'á ó f'òní jú, aré Ògún dọ̀la o.
2   Ìbà Ògún Lákáayé, ọsìn imọlẹ̀.
3   Ògún aládàáméji t'ó mú bí iná.
4   B'ó ti ń f'ìkan ṣánko.
5   Bẹ́ẹ̀ l'ó ń f'ìkan yẹnà.
6   Ní'jó Ògún ń t'orí òkèé bọ̀ mo m'aṣọ t'ó mú bora.

7   Aṣọ iná l'ó mú bora, ẹ̀wù ẹ̀jẹ̀ l'ó wọ.
8   Mọ̀rìwò l'aṣọ Ògún.
9   Aṣọ t'Ógùn-ún ní l'ó fi fún'galà.
10   At'ijọ́ náà àt'ìjọ̀ nàà o,
11   Tí wọ́n bá pàgalà wọn a l'Ogùn-ún,
12   L'ó t'òde wáá gbaṣọ l'áraa rẹ̀.
13   Ògún oníléowó, ọlọ́nàọlà.
14   Ògún onílékańgunkàngun-ọ̀run.
15   Ògún t'ó pọnmi silé tán t'ó wáá fẹ̀jẹ̀-wẹ̀.
16   Ògún awọ́nlẹ́yinjú.
17   Ègbè lẹ́yìn ọmọ òrukàn.
18   Ògún méje l'Oogún-ùn mi !
19   Ògún Alárá ní í gb'ajá ńlá.
20   Ògún Onírè a gb'àgbò gàgàrà.
21   Ògún Ìkọ̀lé a gbàgbín.
22   Ògún Ẹlẹ́mọnà ní í gb'ẹsun-un'ṣu.
23   Ògún Akìrun a gbà'wo-àgbò.
24   Ògún-un gbẹ́nàgbẹ́nà oje igi ní í mu.
25   Ògún olóólà ní í jẹjẹ̀.
26   Njẹ́ níbo l'a ti pàdé Ògún ?
27   A pàdé Ògún n'íbi-ìjà.
28   A pàdé Ògún n'íbi-ìta.
29   A pàdee rẹ̀ n'íbi-àgbàrá ẹ̀jẹ̀.
30   Àgbàrá ẹ̀jẹ̀ tí í de ni lọ́rùn bí omi Ago.
31   Òrìṣa t'ó ni t'Ògún ò tó ǹkan rárá,
32   Òrìṣà náà yóò f'ọwọ́ hó'ṣu rẹ̀ jẹ ni.
33   Bàbáa mi Ògún Onírè ọkọ Àjíkẹ́.
34   Agbórí-igi-sọ̀kòìjà-sílẹ̀.
     Orin:
     Lílé: Òrìṣà l'Ògún.
              Òrìṣà l'Ògún.
              Ẹní bá mÒgún k'ó ma fÒgún ṣiré o.
     Ègbè: Òrìsà l'Ògún.

1   We shall devote all our chants today to homage-paying.
2   Ògún's entertainment will commence tomorrow.
3   I pay homage to Ògún Lákáayé, a divinity worthy of worship.
4   Ògún who had two very sharp cutlasses, sharp as fire.
5   He used one for clearing an area for making a farm in the forest.
6   The other he used for cutting a path in the forest from one place to
        another.
7   The type of clothing that Ògún wore,
     On the day he made his descent from the hill to the plain,
     I know very well.
8   He wore a flame-red coverlet over a blood-red tunic.

Fresh palm fronds were also part of Ògún's clothing.

9   These he passed on to Mr. Bush-Buck, *Ìgalà*,[56] one day.

10 Since that day until today,

11 When a bush-buck is killed in a hunting raid,

12 The hunters say Ògún has called on it and forcefully recovered his clothes.

13 Ògún has plenty of money in his house.
    Ògún acquires plenty of wealth on the road.

14 Ògún's dwelling is a polyhedral house in heaven.

15 'Twas Ògún who, after storing water in abundance in his house,
    Then proceeded to have a bath of blood.

16 Ògún whose eyeballs are of a rare type.

17 Supporter and provider for any orphaned youngster.

18 The Ògún that I know are seven in number!

19 King Alárá's[57] Ògún demands and is given a big dog.

20 King Onírè's[58] Ògún demands and is given a huge ram.

21 The Ògún at Ìkọlé[59] is appeased with snails.

22 The Ẹlẹ́mọnà's[60] Ògún demands and is given roasted yam tubers.

23 King Akìrun's[61] Ògún fancies rams' horns which he is given.

24 The wood carvers' Ògún enjoys drinking the vital juice from trees.

25 The circumcisers' Ògún feeds on blood.

26 I now ask: "Where is Ògún to be found ?"

27 Ògún is found where there is a fight.

28 Ògún is found where there is vituperation.

29 Ògún is found where there are torrents of blood.

30 Torrents of blood, the sight of which nearly strangles one,
    Like the water of River Ago[62] in flood.

31 Any divinity who belittles Ògún outright,

32 Will use his teeth in place of a knife for peeling boilt yam pieces.

33 My sire, Ògún, lord of Ìrè, Àjíkẹ́'s[63] husband.

34 He who used to throw down, from high up on the tree,
    Stones of combat from his gun.

Song:

Lead: Ògún is a divinity.
          Ògún is a divinity.
          Whoever knows Ògún should not mock Ògún.

Refrain: Ògún is a divinity.

The solitariness of Ògún is a prominent theme in this and other *ìjálá* texts. He is presented as a traveler whose wealth gained on the road is used, as mentioned earlier in other *ìjálá* excerpts, to help those in want. Specifically mentioned here are orphans, who, like himself, are alone in the world and who, because they are without the usual social supports, are categorized as antisocial or asocial. The theme is reinforced in the image of Ògún, who descends, from his home on a hilltop where he lives alone, to the plain below. In another legend, Ògún lives in solitude on a hilltop near Ìrè, also called Ìlú Iná, Town of Fire (Babalola 1966:5). While such antisocial behavior is no doubt recognized as unnatural by the *ìjálá* artists, they do not condemn it. Rather, they and their communities accept it as part of the extraordinary quality that a supernatural figure is expected and allowed to display.

Ògún's clothing provides further insight into his character. The robes are blood-red or fire-red, signaling his fiery, belligerent comportment and furious temperament. As in Western culture, red is a color indicative of danger. However, Ògún's clothing also includes an overlay of *màrìwò*, fresh palm fronds, worn round the waist over the red garments. The significance of this *màrìwò* may be discerned from the contemporary survival of its connotation in Yoruba society. *Màrìwò* is used along footpaths as a signal that a shrine is nearby; it serves as a special decoration on sacred trees at the time of annual worship; some *egúngún* have their costume draped with *màrìwò* and on a motor vehicle fresh palm fronds signify either that a corpse is being conveyed in the vehicle or that the driver of the vehicle is proclaiming his loyalty and homage to Ògún at the time of the annual Ògún festival. In each case *màrìwò* has supernatural associations and indicates to passersby that they are close to a divinity. There is no doubt that the fresh palm fronds inject a pacific image into the picture of Ògún drawn by the verbal salutes addressed to him. On the other hand, the fiery red clothing renders him a dreaded, supernatural personage.

Ògún's face also reflects his character. His eyes are fiery and "of a rare type"; they are radiant, resplendent, and so penetrating that Ògún is capable of reading the inmost thoughts of a person he meets by chance. And he mostly meets people "where there is a fight . . . where there is vituperation."

Like the other *ìjálá* excerpts already used in this essay, this text also turns to the theme of the many-sided Ògún. He has seven manifestations, just as his dwelling is seven-sided. Most of the aspects recounted here have been previously discussed. However, one addition to the occupational catalogue for Ògún is agriculture. Ògún uses his cutlass for farming and for cutting out a path in the forest. He also provides the iron from which blacksmiths forge agricultural implements (hoes, cutlasses, or knives) for farmers to use.

In the final *ìjálá* excerpt, Ògún is praised as a universal deity.

Ìjálá Excerpt 7

(From a performance by Adédìran Ògúnmólá of Ondo,
who learned the art while living in Oyo)

1   Àgbàrá-òjò l'Ògún.
2   Ibi gbogbo ní í gbéé rìn.

3   Ògún l'ó l'ǫdę ǫdę l'ó ni'igbó.
4   Ògún l'ó l'Òrìṣà-Oko.
5   Ògún Lákáayé.
6   Ògún aládé, aládé-Ifę̀.
7   Òkérè-ǫmǫ.
8   Ògún Onírè tí ò jehoro,
9   T'ó j'éhoro ó yan ka'nú-oko.
10 Ògún Oníre tí ò ję kǫ̀nkǫ̀,
11 T'ó ję́ kǫ̀nkǫ̀ ó máa j'ǫlá abiyamǫ l'ómi.
12 Ajá l' ońję Ògún.
13 Ǫ̀kǫ́ l'Ògún fę́ràn jù, ó dájú gbangba.
    Orin:
14 *Lílé*:   A ì í jǫ̀kǫ́ǫ́ gbélé.
15   A ì í jǫ̀kǫ́ǫ́ gbélé.
16   B'ę́ę bá j'ajá Ògún tán,
17   Ę kálǫ s'íjù.
18 *Ègbè*:   A ì í jǫ̀kǫ́ǫ́ gbélé.

1   Ògún is a torrent of rainwater.
2   He goes everywhere.
3   Ògún is the hunter's lord and master.
    The hunter is the forest's lord and master.
4   Ògún is Òrìṣà-Oko's[64] lord and master.
5   Ògún Lákáayé.
6   Ògún, a crowned king, wearing an Ifę̀[65] crown.
7   King who enjoyed his offspring's offerings.
8   Ògún, king of Ìrè, who, not fancying the hare,[66]
9   Allowed the hare to swagger about among the crops on a farm.
10 Ògún, king of Ìrè, who, not fancying the bullfrog,[67]
11 Allowed the bullfrog to enjoy a mother's privileges in the pond.
12 Ògún's special food is dog meat.
13 'Tis dog meat that Ògún fancies, this is very sure.
    Song:
14 *Lead*:   'Tis forbidden to stay at home after eating dog meat.
15   'Tis forbidden to stay at home after eating dog meat.
16   As soon as you've finished eating Ògún's dog,[68]
17   Do come along to the high grass parkland.[69]
18 *Refrain*: 'Tis forbidden to stay at home after eating dog meat.

Far from being worshipped in a single town, Ògún is worshipped through-out Yorubaland. And just as "a torrent of rainwater" flows everywhere, so too does Ògún impinge upon the lives of all Yoruba.[70] *Ògún Lákáayé* is the praise name that proclaims: "Ògún's fame is worldwide." The same theme is developed in a slightly different way when the *oníjálá* declares that Ògún is not simply the lord and master of a single sector of society but that he is important in the lives of many people: hunters, farmers, and even kings. All in all he is a universal, well-traveled personality.

The association between Ògún and kingship is stressed in this and other *ìjálá* chants. Ògún is the king of Ìrè who relishes the fact that in his veins flowed Oduduwa's blood from Ifè, the legendary cradle-city of all Yoruba. As a crowned king of Ifè origin, Ògún is a legitimate ruler in the eyes of the Yoruba.

There is an important connection between kingship and beginnings. This takes the form of Ògún's involvement with royal dynasties. This association also extends to the divine world. The legend which opens this essay likens Ògún to another deity, Erinlè, who founded a village in the forest. Other legends state that Ògún was the first deity to descend to the earth from heaven. He led the way with his cutlass, clearing a path for the other gods as they followed him into the world.

Linking Ògún with kingship, and particularly the first king of a dynasty, is one of the many ways communities make symbolic use of this figure. There is a marked tendency to link a settlement's ancestry and historical events to Ògún. This is especially apparent if, in towns such as Ìrè, the ruling dynasties are in power through military conquest or civil war. Elsewhere the association can be related to the blacksmith status of Ògún and the fact that the introduction of ironmaking is associated with or under the patronage of the ruling lineage, since itinerant smiths (or even iron traders) needed the protection of authority figures to work safely in a new place. Finally, if hunting was significant in a place, Ògún also could be associated with its beginnings. While each settlement builds its own Ògún traditions, there is a preference for the ancestral tie between the ruler and Ògún because, as a blood relative, it connotes the greatest degree of social proximity. A blood relationship gives credence to a story. If a royal lineage has Ògún as an ancestor or offspring, and this can be traced to the founding period of the settlement, this will boost the prestige of the town. No one will speak lightly of the place. Ògún brings honor and fame to a place. If iron is an important part of the economy, Ògún's presence gives that endeavor blessings which result in prosperity. Ògún's presence gives historical depth to a town, and deep roots are more highly valued than shallow roots.

The important point is that people are talking about their origins and the involvement of the divinity in the process. Often there is a parallel legend, accompanying the cosmological legend, that involves a historical human figure. So the origins are explained on two levels: the supernatural and the human. Hence, there are founding legends and oral traditions that may credit both Ògún and a named king with founding the same town. The two types of traditions—mythological and historical—can collapse the two figures into a single founder, such as *Ògún Oníré*, Ògún and the first king of Ìrè. The human founder also brings prestige, authenticity, and legitimacy to a community, adding to the fact that there are deep roots. The supernatural figure brings protection, peace, and prosperity. It should be stressed that this use of a supernatural founder does not mean that other divinities will not be worshipped both in civic ritual and in separate cult groups. Rather, crediting a deity such as Ògún with founding a place means that this patron deity will be given preeminence. The people of a town use whatever divinity (or divinities) fits their way of life and history.

When people account for their origins or explain their view of the world, they tend to use the most appropriate symbolism to achieve these ends. Symbols, of which Ògún is exemplary, have many meanings and interpretations. All symbolic forms the deity takes are correct forms; all variations in founding legends are correct variations; and all of the personality traits or characteristics are correct, despite their seeming oppositions. Ògún is neither good nor bad. There is no moral evaluation of the deity's many characteristics in terms of right and wrong. As a larger-than-life figure he is expected to reflect the contradictions of human nature. A deity such as Ògún condenses a broad range of human experience into a single figure and serves as a means by which contradictions in that experience can be resolved.

It is inconsequential that Ògún is the founder-king of several places, the founder-blacksmith of others, or the founder-hunter of still others. What is consequential is the composite picture each of these tales provides: Ògún is a legitimator of beginnings, foundings, and innovations, and each *oríkì Ògún* is a folk etymology, relevant to the specific place in which it is performed. Together the etymologies delineate a symbolic "space" over which Ògún "presides." When human events or circumstances fall into this space, Ògún serves as a metaphor for the experience being related. When events fall outside that space, another deity may be the more appropriate metaphor or symbolic figure.

The overall picture, presented by the *ìjálá* artists' *oríkì Ògún*, depicts an Ògún that is linked to beginnings, especially those in which iron technology or hunting is prominent. He is a heroic figure, who is strong enough and violent enough to bring dread into the hearts of people, yet protective enough to render them grateful for the benefits that are a product of his strength. He is just and unjust at the same time, not because he is capricious but because the two are inseparable. In the world of humans, actions must be given values, whereas in the world of the gods these values can be withheld. This is why the picture of Ògún presents an ambivalent deity. The verbal salutes to Ògún in *ìjálá* chants remind us that in highly-placed men strength and frailty are often inseparable, and they recognize that this dilemma brings loneliness and solitude. This, then, is one of the fundamental aspects of the human condition that the *ìjálá oríkì Ògún* texts collectively portray, and as the *oníjàlá* tell us, this condition, like a torrent of rainwater, is universal.

NOTES

1. For detailed and systematic literary analysis of *ìjálá*, see Babalọla 1966, 1968, and 1975.

2. Erinlẹ̀ is one of the beneficent water divinities. He is believed to be on earth in the River Erinlẹ̀, whose source is close to a small town called Ìlobùú near Oṣogbo. However, Erinlẹ̀ has devotees spread all over Yorubaland; some worship Erinlẹ̀ as a goddess.

3. His name is Gbàdàmọ́ṣí Aríbùkí, whilst his praise name is *Ọlọ́ọ́dẹ Ìlú Ọ̀fà*. He hails from the famous northern Ọyọ Yoruba town of Ọ̀fa, but now lives at Ebutemẹta, Lagos.

4. *Erinlẹ̀* is a name whose etymology, like that of Ògún, is lost in antiquity. However, Erinlẹ̀ is a name given to a male child whose umbilical cord at birth was found to be twined round an arm.

5. *Gbìngbin*: a tree (resembling the chestnut tree) with dense evergreen foliage that provides good shade.

6. *Pinkún* and *Àjànbìtì* are onomatopoeic words, imitating the sounds of the drum beats.

7. One of the artists is Gbàdàmọ́ṣí Aríbùkí, who told me the Erinlẹ̀ legend given in this paper. He performed the *ìjálá* with a junior companion, Ọmọ Kowéè, at a monthly social gathering of a society in Ebutemẹta on July 27, 1962.

8. *Lákáayé* is a praise name for Ògún, meaning "He whose fame is worldwide."

9. *Àkàndá* is a personal praise name given by the father to this *ìjálá* artist when an infant. The name means "One uniquely created."

10. The image here is based on the belief that the odor emanating from a civet-cat's excrement is obnoxious to a butterfly. It is used to convey the Ògún devotee's belief that Ògún's anger is offensive and dreadful, not to be contemplated.

11. *Sòónlé-Ìwó*: "Straight-bound for Ìwó Town." This is an allusion to the fact that iron (Ògún's symbol) is mined in the environs of Ìwó, in a village called Ìsundúnrin.

12. Husband of Adéọlá: Adéọlá is the personal name of the *ìjálá* artist's mother. Ògún is referred to as the woman's husband because the word 'ọkọ' in Yoruba, meaning "male partner in marriage," implies also "lord and master." Ògún is the woman's divinity, and therefore her lord and master.

13. *Asín* is a type of rat having a foul smell and a pointed mouth. Ògún is called a veritable *asín* rat because some of the things offered in sacrifice on his emblems (iron prongs or granite slabs) become rotten and give off a foul odor.

14. A plantain tree: This is a metaphorical picture of Ògún used when many tiny gourds, containing magical medicine, are fastened to his tunic across the breast.

15. *Ogunlabí* is a nickname for Ògún; it means "We've given birth to war." It is a way of calling Ògún "War Personified" on account of his bellicose nature.

16. *Ikin*: This term is used metaphorically here, whereas it literally refers to the collection of sixteen sacred palmnuts of Ifá divination invariably kept by an Ifá priest in an ornamented, lidded bowl made of wood. The *ìjálá* chanter likens Ògún to *ikin*; Ògún's eminence as a king in his lifetime is compared to the eminence of *ikin* in Ifá divination, and Ògún's crown is compared to that of the *ikin* represented by its ornamented lid.

17. Line 21 alludes to iron in the form of a hoe-blade. Since Ògún's primary emblem is iron, therefore, as a farmer tills the soil with a hoe and the hoe digs up or cuts many earthworms in the process, Ògún eats "two hundred earthworms without feeling sick at all."

18. *Òṣùṣú*: a thorny, trailing plant which forms dense thickets here described as "heaps." Ògún is metaphorically called *òṣùṣú* because of his roughness and dangerousness—qualities possessed by *òṣùṣú*.

19. Ìjẹ̀bú woodland is mentioned simply as an example of a war theater. Ìjẹ̀bú is an area of Yorubaland that is close to the coast. It was often invaded by the Ibadan warriors in the nineteenth century. As each warrior carried a gun made of iron, the warrior represented Ògún.

20. Ògún . . . not *oògùn*: This is a play on words for humorous effect. The *ijálá* artist thus emphasizes the identity of the personage to whom his verbal salute is addressed. *Oògùn* means "medicinal charm"; the artist chooses to mention this because its consonants and vowels are identical with those in Ògún, whereas the tones on both words are dissimilar, and there is a difference of meaning.

21. Fágbèmí is the personal name of the Head Priest of the Ifá cult in Lagos Municipality who was present on the occasion of the *ijálá* artist's performance and to whom the homage was paid.

22. Àjànàkú is the Head Priest's surname.

23. Àràbà is the traditional title for the Head Priest of the Ifá cult in a particular area.

24. "Offspring of *Lágúnádé*": This is a quotation from the verbal salute to the *Olówu* lineage to which the Àràbà belonged.

25. 26, 27, 28. *Àmàdú, Alùtótó, Ẹ̀gbẹ̀di Òwu*, and *Arọ́wáyán* are the names of some of the royal ancestors (*Olówu* lineage) of the Head Priest previously named.

29. *Ògúnróunbí*: The name of another ancestor of the same *Olówu* lineage.

30. Two naked swords and two horns of a buffalo represent the goddess Ọya in her temple. The connection between Ọya and the buffalo is that Ọya is the goddess of the River Niger and buffaloes, in herds, frequent the River Niger along the savannah section of its course.

31. The phonaesthetic word *jàgàjígí* in the Yoruba text captures the visual impact of the various items with which the hunter bedecked his tunic.

32. *Ọ̀gbẹ̀gún* is the pet name of the hunter's wife; it means one who has a full body and is robust and beautiful.

33. *Akọ́dá*: The fourth in order of precedence among the major Ifá priests in Ọ̀yọ́ Area.

34. *Aṣẹ̀dá*: The fifth in order of precedence among the major Ifá priests in Ọyọ Area.

35. *Kódẹ̀nlẹ̀gẹ́*: A rare Yoruba name for Almighty God. Its etymology is unclear.

36. *Ọlálọmí*: Using metonymy, the artist names the principal lineage ancestor of his partner, whose Muslim name is Gbàdàmọ́ṣí.

37. *Orí* is each individual's personal divinity when conceived as an object of worship. In terms of the individual's experience, it represents the person's predestined lot in life.

38. Ògún worshippers believe that since iron ore is mined from the earth, swearing by the earth is as sacred and effective as swearing by Ògún himself.

39. *Eégún*: Ancestral spirits, as an object of worship, represented by masqueraders.

40. Embodied spirits: demons, nymphs, dryads, and so on.

41. *Èéwó*: mashed, boilt yam pieces mixed with palm oil.

42. Ògún *deliberately* fell off his seat slowly.

43. This is the reference to the incident at Ìrè. In remorse, Ògún is here said to have cut off pieces of his own flesh and munched them. It is *not* connected with the incident at the smithy.

44. *Adìgbòlẹ̀gbọ̀*: The nickname of one of Ògún's ancestors; the name means "He who dashed himself against *ẹ̀gbọ̀*" (a certain useful plant).

45. *Eníràn* is a term used by the *ijálá* artist to describe Ògún as a "Trouble-Lover"; the word is a dialect rendering of 'oní + ọ̀ràn' ("one who has trouble" literally).

46. *Enirè* is a dialect rendering of Onírè (Lord or king of Ìrè).

47. *Mọnílọ́lá* is the personal name of the *ìjálá* artist's father; it means "This child has a share of honor."

48. Of course this is anthropomorphic. In reality the tradition holds that Ọ̀gún accepts a sacrifice: "*Ọ̀gún gbà.*"

49. Should an affray somehow occur at a wedding celebration, this kind of multiple death can result from the use of knives and daggers.

50. *MỌ̀gún* = *imu Ọ̀gún* = Ọ̀gún's place. Since the inhabitants of Ìrè annually hold a grand Ọ̀gún Festival (*Ọdún Ọ̀gún*) in memory of Ọ̀gún's exploits in the town during his lifetime, Ìrè may rightly be described as "Ọ̀gún's place."

51, 52. *Mogbe* = *imu ogbe* = a place where cocks' combs abound. *Ìlákùkọ́* is the name of a village; it means "Where the people have cocks." Therefore, the village may rightly be called "a place where cocks' combs abound."

53. Ílógbò town is 13 kilometers from Ìnísà in Ọ̀ṣun area. "Ọ̀gún passed through Ílógbò" is another figurative way of saying "An internecine strife burst out in Ílógbò."

54. Line 20 was said in the voice of ordinary speech by the *ìjálá* artist's pupils, in reply to his question in line 19. This reply is an ornamented "Yes." The ornamentation lies in the use of a proverb which alludes to the *Ẹ̀lúkú*, which is a type of ancestral spirit (represented by a masquerader) in the Ìjẹ̀bú area of Yorubaland. The masquerader is very friendly with children and he gets them to sing, giving the lead by first singing the main melody.

55. Farmers on distant farms where they are resident for a few months before coming home (to their town) for a festival find solace in worshipping trees traditionally held sacred, for example, *Ìrókò, Àràbà, Akòko, Àyàn*, and others.

56. *Ìgalà*, bushbuck: The bushbuck's coat has several vertical stripes down its sides. These stripes are like the stripes formed by palm fronds around Ọ̀gún's waist.

57. *Alárá* is the title of the king of Ará, a town now known as Arámọkọ in Ondo State of Nigeria.

58. *Onírè* is the title of the king of Ìrè; the huge ram is presented as an extra after the traditional dog has been offered in sacrifice to Ọ̀gún.

59. Ìkọlé is a town now in Ekiti Yoruba territory. The snails offered to Ọ̀gún are additional to the dog.

60. *Ẹlẹ́mọnà* is said to be the title of the king of Imọnà, a town now extinct in the Ekiti Yoruba area.

61. *Akìrun* is the title of the king of Ikirun, a town in the Odò Ọtin District north of Oṣogbo.

62. River Ago is a local river near the *ìjálá* artist's hometown, Oṣogbo.

63. *Àjíkẹ́*: Tradition holds that this is the *oríkì* name of Ọ̀gún's favorite wife.

64. *Òrìṣà-oko*: the goddess of agriculture. Ọ̀gún is her lord and master because a variety of iron implements (Ọ̀gún) is a *sine qua non* for the farmer's work that she is to bless.

65. See legends 1 and 2 in Babalọla (1966). An inference is drawn that Ọ̀gún once reigned briefly at Ile Ifẹ̀.

66, 67. The point being made is that for a sacrifice to be offered to Ọ̀gún, his devotees harass neither the hare nor the bullfrog (both having dainty meat) but rather the dog, whose meat is Ọ̀gún's favorite delicacy.

68, 69. The song urges the hunters to remember to participate in the hunting trip in the high-grass parkland in the evening of the Ọ̀gún Festival day after they have eaten the meat of the dog offered in sacrifice to Ọ̀gún.

70. There are famous Ọ̀gún shrines and festivals in Ìrè and Ibadan (Ọyọ State); also in Ondo and Ikarẹ (Ondo State).

REFERENCES CITED

Babalǫla, S. A. 1966. *The Content and Form of Yoruba Ìjálá*, Oxford: Oxford University Press.

———. 1968. *Ìjálá*, Lagos: Federal Ministry of Information.

———. 1975. "The Delights of Ìjálá," in *Yoruba Oral Tradition*, Wande Abimbǫla (ed.), Ile Ifè: University of Ifè.

'Bade Ajuwọn

8

Ògún's Ìrèmòjé: A Philosophy of Living and Dying

Oral traditions maintain that the god Ogun led four hundred and one Yoruba divinities when they descended to earth at Ifẹ-Oodaye, the exact location of which we are, today, not sure. These traditions also state that Ogun helped the divinities to survive in their initial settlement on earth and to effect harmony among themselves as they struggled with new and unforeseen circumstances. Ogun's ability to direct the various activities of the other divinities emanated from his philosophy that one must display courage and heroism in living and in dying while serving one's fellow men. For Ogun, the only means of achieving honor in life was to live up to this philosophy. The leadership ideals associated with Ogun have been preserved in ritual and oral traditions associated with hunting and warfare, both of which Ogun enjoined his followers to know and to perform. Today, one of the best sources for examining them, and the one on which this essay concentrates, is *Ìrèmòjé*, a corpus of poetic chants sung at funeral ceremonies, also known as *Ìrèmòjé*,[1] held for deceased hunters.

Of the various traditional rites of passage for the dead which are still observed in West Africa, ceremonies attached to the Yoruba hunter's guild appear to be among the more widespread. Other death rites are performed by religious groups such as those devoted to Ṣango (the god of lightning and thunder) or Ifa (the divination oracle) of Nigeria; by the Ẹlẹgbara worshippers of the People's Republic of Benin; or by occupational guilds, including the Yoruba and Hausa calabash carvers of Nigeria or the Ewe cloth weavers of Ghana. The funerals for deceased members of each of these groups are the sole concern of members. By contrast, the death rites for Yoruba hunters are a full community affair. Nearly everyone in a traditional Yoruba community is in one way or another connected to Ogun and likes to have a hand in a ceremony which honors the deity who gave to the world its first divine model-performance for a leader.

The communities from which the data in this study come are Ọyọ, former capital of the Yoruba-speaking peoples' largest precolonial empire, and towns surrounding it. At its peak, c. 1780, the Ọyọ Empire stretched from the Niger River in the north to the sea in the south and from Dahomey in the west to the Benin border in the east. It is thought that hunters' guilds were spread throughout this area, and that they welcomed and protected fellow hunters in their travels. That being the case, the traditions associated with the guilds were no doubt widely circulated and understood. In fact, knowing the traditions was possibly a "password" for gaining acceptance in a strange place. Today, the geographical core of the old empire is preserved as Ọyọ state, one of twenty-one states in Nigeria. It embraces one of at least a dozen Yoruba-speaking subgroups, each of which has its own dialect and historical traditions. Part of the reason that we may speak of them collectively as Yoruba is that some common traditions were disseminated across subgroup boundaries by such travelers as the hunters.

The *Ìrèmọ̀jé* Tradition

Oral traditions concerning the origin of hunters' death rites state that when Ogun was on earth he taught men the art of hunting and warfare. He organized and trained hunters in occupational guilds and then established rules and regulations to guide them in all facets of their professional, religious, and social activities. For the entertainment of himself and his followers, he also established two sets of poetic chants, one called *Ìjálá*, to be performed on various occasions, particularly Ogun festivals,[2] and the other *Ìrèmọ̀jé*.

During the latter part of Ogun's life on earth he was greatly concerned that the hunting profession and its traditions be preserved after his departure. He feared the loss of his cherished hunting charms, and, more importantly, the *Ìrèmọ̀jé* chants, which preserved the philosophy which was central to him and to his way of life. Consequently, Ogun consulted the Ifa oracle, who counseled him to order the hunters to perform the *Ìrèmọ̀jé* at the final funeral rites for their departed colleagues. It was Ifa, it might be noted, who christened the chants as *Ìrèmọ̀jé*, the etymology of which is unclear. Thus Ogun directed guild members to perform the chants henceforth, warning them that this final observance was to be taken as a sacred religious duty. Failure to perform this duty would place a deceased hunter in a state of peril in which he would not be able to find his proper place among the ancestors. It is this injunction to which the chanters of *Ìrèmọ̀jé* refer when they say:

1   Ọdẹ yòówù o ku,[3]
2   Tá a bá ṣèrèmọ̀jé ẹ̀,
3   Ọ̀dọ̀ Olúmọkin ló ń lọ.
4   Ọdẹ yòówu tó ṣídẹ lọ,
5   Tá à bá ṣèrèmọ̀jé ẹ̀,
6   Tòun tegbére ni ọ́ jọ máa jẹ.

1   A hunter who dies,
2   For whom *Ìrèmọ̀jé* is performed,
3   Shall join *Olúmọkin*[4] in heaven.
4   A hunter who dies,
5   For whom *Ìrèmọ̀jé* is denied,
6   Shall join the company of demons.

The effect of the message is such that the children of deceased hunters often double their pace in arranging *Ìrèmọ̀jé* performances for deceased parents. This, then, is the way the *Ìrèmọ̀jé* ritual performance became an intimate part of the Yoruba hunters' way of life.

While the observance of *Ìrèmọ̀jé* has divine justifications and sanctions, it also has a number of important social functions. For one thing, when word is spread that an *Ìrèmọ̀jé* is to be performed, members of Yoruba hunters guilds gather from far and near, from villages and towns, to commune, socialize, and renew their ties to one another as well as to renew their loyalty to the hunters' traditions and ethics. For another, the *Ìrèmọ̀jé* ritual performance provides guild members with an opportunity to mourn collectively their loss and, as Van Gennep showed to be the case in death rites throughout the world, to reintegrate the remaining members of the society with one another. The *Ìrèmọ̀jé* marks the termination of the deceased's membership in his earthly occupation, and thus the performance signals to the public that he has ceased hunting— an important step, since it is a bad omen for the living and the dead to "hunt," that is, to consort, together. As a way of marking the separation of the living from the dead, *Ìrèmọ̀jé* chanters sing:

1   Ìgbà mîi,
2   Ìgbà mîi,
3   Ká má tùún jọ règbẹ́ pọ̀ mọ́.

1   In future,

2   In future,
3   Stop going a-hunting with us.

It is believed that this chant represents Ogun's own order to the deceased to refrain from ever hunting again with his living colleagues and, instead, to take up his earthly profession in heaven. There he will be exposed to superior hunting skills, as imparted to him by Ogun.

Finally, despite the closure that the funeral ceremony puts to the social relationship between the survivors and the deceased, the actual performance is believed to bring the living into the company of the deceased hunter for one final tribute, and into the company of Ogun himself.

The *Ìrèmọ̀jé* Performance

The *Ìrèmọ̀jé* ritual performance is usually held in an open space outside the house of the deceased. It begins at about 10 p.m. and continues until dawn. The general audience—including farmers, blacksmiths, barbers, drivers, and other users of iron implements—ordinarily is seated in a large circle, with the hunters separating themselves from the others by taking their places on woven mats spread on the ground. The hunters' drummers sit at one corner of the circle so that they can easily be seen by the *Ìrèmọ̀jé* chanters (fig. 8.1) at the opposite corner, and by the audience. The members of the deceased's family sit at their left. The seating arrangement enables the drummers to salute each set of participants as a group.

The focal point of the assembly, at the center of the ring, is the hunter's paraphernalia, arranged on a forked post so as to represent the deceased himself (fig. 8.2). The paraphernalia includes his hunting clothes and personal equipment, such as a dane gun, flint, powder, cutlass, and knife. The effigy is intended to be an impersonation of the deceased. It has been reported that in other cases a living impersonator briefly appears and calls farewell to the assembled group.[5] Whichever is the case, the impersonation is the means chosen by the living to bring the deceased into their company for a farewell meeting.

An assortment of items is tied to the hunter's effigy. It symbolically represents the earthly role of the hunter and, simultaneously, the distinctive qualities of his deity, Ogun. Many of these items come from the kit which is taken to the forest where the hunter expects to spend long periods in solitary pursuit of game. One set of items consists of foodstuffs. The most prominent are roast beans, Ogun's favorite food (perhaps because they can be preserved for several days and eaten cold); red palm oil, the color by which he is, incidentally, known; ground pepper (evidence of the hunter's vitality); guinea pepper (an important item in hunter's charms); and salt (to preserve the hunter's catch). A second set of items represents forest products: fresh palm

FIGURE 8.1. *Ìrèmòjé* chanters.

FIGURE 8.2. The deceased hunter's paraphernalia is displayed as the centerpiece of the *ìrèmòjé* performance.

kernels and fresh palm fronds (*màrìwò*). The palm is a special tree in the Ogun tradition. It provides food (its oil) and wine (Ogun's favorite beverage). It provides fuel (the palm kernels) for the smithy. And it provides the "clothes" (i.e., the *màrìwò*) of Ogun—clothes which he wore when he emerged from the forest and which signaled his role in bringing civilization— the Iron Age—to humankind. The clothes of Ogun are used to decorate his shrines, or as a sign along a path that indicates it leads to the shrine of another divinity. A third set of items consists of the iron tools of the hunter and other, random, pieces of iron. They represent more explicitly the fact that Ogun was the deity who introduced metal and metallurgy. A fourth set includes an assortment of magical charms which ensure the hunter's survival when he encounters dangerous situations in the forest and which aid him in tracking and killing game. Ogun is believed to be the divinity who controlled the mysteries of hunting charms and who gave them to the hunters. Finally, there is a set of items which represent other professions, but which the hunter must employ when he lives alone in the forest. The significance of these items is explained when we examine the *Ìrèmòjé* chants themselves.

The ceremony is presided over by the commander-in-chief of the hunters' guild, the Aṣipadẹ. When Ogun was on earth he appointed the Aṣipadẹ as the senior member of his titled chiefs, conveying to him his powers and instructing him to act as his personal representative. The Aṣipadẹ is, therefore, entitled to tell his colleagues when to go hunting, to war, or to the farm, and, indeed, when to carry out a number of outdoor activities in which guild members are collectively engaged. One of them is the *Ìrèmòjé* ceremony, and in this context the Aṣipadẹ directs the seating arrangement, the chanting of dirges, and the accompaniment of drummers. During the *Ìrèmòjé* performance, the Aṣipadẹ is thought to become Ogun himself and, therefore, he is offered respect and deference which exceed the normal amount given him at other times. Anyone who disregards the Aṣipadẹ's orders at funeral ceremonies, in effect, disregards Ogun himself. Even the drummers, who normally are an uncooperative group of people, readily obey the guild leader in this ritual context.

The personality exhibited by the Aṣipadẹ ideally mirrors the personality of Ogun. This is in keeping with a widespread belief that devotees' personalities should resemble the personalities of the deities they follow. Ogun is fierce, his eyes fiery, and his mannerisms harsh. The Aṣipadẹ is expected to reveal the same qualities. Similarly, the devotee is expected to exhibit Ogun's character traits: bravery in war, skill in hunting, and virtue in morals. Only a man who displays these traits is eligible to hold the title of Aṣipadẹ. The following *Ìjálá* chant sets forth some of these expectations:

1   Ẹni tí ò gbónágbònàgbóná,[6]
2   Kò le è jAṣipadẹ.
3   Bẹ́ẹ̀ lẹ ni tí ò lógùngùn bí àrònì,

4   Kò leè jAṣípadẹ.
5   Ẹni tí ò láyàa yìnbọnjẹ,
6   Mo ní kò leè jAṣípadẹ wa.
7   Èmi láyàa yìnbọnjẹ.
8   Mo lè kerin lójú.
9   Mo lè pẹfọn níjà.
10   Mo lè jAṣípadẹ.

1   A person who is not ferocious,
2   Cannot be installed Aṣípadẹ.
3   A person who does not possess charms like àrọ̀nì,[7]
4   Cannot be installed Aṣípadẹ.
5   A person who cannot commit suicide by the gun,
6   I say, cannot be installed Aṣípadẹ.
7   I am brave to the point of committing suicide by the gun.
8   I can challenge an elephant.
9   I can challenge a bushcow.
10   I can be made Aṣípadẹ.

Ìrèmòjé performances restate these expectations to inspire the assembled crowd and to instruct youthful hunters who aspire to hold the Aṣípadẹ chieftaincy title and to follow the lead of Ogun himself.

Ìrèmòjé Themes

The themes of *Ìrèmòjé* can be placed under two divisions: those which focus on life, and the ideal way to live it, and those which focus on death and its inevitability. Several themes are elaborated upon within each division, and they convey the Ogun philosophy. I now turn to those themes.

Ogun did for humans what he did for the divinities: he showed them the way to live on earth. This role is emphasized in the following praises sung to Ogun by the *Ìrèmòjé* artists:

1   Ògún Lákáayé.
2   Oṣìn Mọlẹ̀.
3   Òòsà tó sọgbó dilé,
4   Òòṣà tó sògbẹ́ dìgboro,
5   Òòṣà tó sàkìtàn dọjà.

1   Ògún, Chief Lákáayé.[8]
2   Chief Ọṣìn Mọlẹ̀.[9]
3   The deity who made the forest his home,

4   The deity who made the forest-heart into a township,
5   The deity who made a refuse pit into a market.

As the praises suggest, Ogun was an innovator, a founder, and a leader, each role demanding self-reliance.

Ogun's life in the forest, the life which is stressed in the *Ìrèmọ̀jé*, is the kind of life which brings out the need for self-sufficiency. It should be pointed out, however, that Ogun was a marginal divinity who lived half of his life in the wild and disorderly state of nature (the forest) and the other half in the orderly state of human existence (the township). Of these two kinds of life, Ogun best loved that in the forest and wished to instill in his followers the qualities which would produce that same devotion as well as the self-assurance and versatility expected of a leader.

Before going to the forest, Ogun gathered all of the materials he would need to sustain himself for long periods of time. These materials, then, form the bulk of the items which are usually attached to the hunter's effigy at the center of the funeral ceremony. The gear includes items representing the many professions hunters are required to know if they are to sustain themselves when they are alone. During the *Ìrèmọ̀jé* performance an item representing a profession is taken separately from the effigy, displayed to the audience, saluted by the living hunters, and praised by the chanters. For example, a tool represents Ogun as the carpenter who builds his hunting lodge; medicine represents Ogun as the physician who heals his wounds; a pot represents Ogun as the cook who prepares his meals; and preservatives represent Ogun as the chemist who cures his meat.

The kinds of tributes given to the hunter's equipment are illustrated by the following two excerpts taken from *Ìrèmọ̀jé* chants. The first is sung as a needle is held up to public view; the second accompanies the display of the hunter's mending thread:

A.
1   Ògúnjìnmí ọwọ́ọ̀ rẹ́ tajáa bàbáà rẹ.[10]
2   Abẹ́rẹ́ wọnú ọ̀fin ó ráá poo.
3   Abẹ́rẹ́ ò ní balẹ̀ ó ró gbọ̀ngbọ̀n.
4   Abẹ́rẹ́ ọdẹ,
5   Tí fi í lẹsọ nínúu 'gbó rèé oo.
6   Àrà mọ̀ jí èlèè.
7   Òwú dúdú ọdẹ náà rèé o o,
8   Àrà mọ̀ jí èlèè.

1   Ògúnjìnmí,[11] you have caught your father's dog.[12]
2   A needle that falls into a pit is lost forever.

3   A fallen needle will never give a loud sound.
4   Here is the hunter's needle,
5   With which he mends his clothes in the forest.
6   Attending hunters awake.
7   Here is the hunter's black thread,
8   Attending hunters awake.

B.
1   Ṣòkòtò ni mo bọ̀,[13]
2   N ò bọ dígòóò mi.
3   N jọ́ọ mo bá bọ dígbóò mi,
4   Ìyọnu ni í ṣe.
5   Ojú pọ́ndẹ ńjù a firàwé dáńá.
6   Gbogbo ẹ̀ ò dùn mí, bí i dígòó mi tóya.
7   Kẹ̀kẹ́ ta dídùn aṣọ lèdidì èèyàn.
8   Dìgòó ọdẹ náà rèé oo,
9   Àrà mọ̀ jí èlèè.
10 Atare ọdẹ náà rèé oo,
11 Àrà mọ̀ jí èlèé.

1   I wear a pair of trousers,
2   I do not wear my hunting outfit.
3   Whenever I wear my hunting outfit,[14]
4   This signifies trouble.
5   In the forest, a poor hunter will make fire with dry leaves.
6   While I least regret other losses, I feel the most my torn hunting outfit.
7   A thread well-spun makes clothes that make humans handsome.
8   Here is the hunter's outfit,
9   Attending hunters awake.
10 Here is the hunter's guinea pepper,
11 Attending hunters awake.

The needle (lines 2–4 of A) and the thread (line 7 of B) indicate that the hunter must master the skills of the tailor so that he can mend his torn clothing and protect himself from cold weather and the discomforts of insect bites while he is alone in the forest. Such instruments, however small, contribute to a hunter's comfort and the ease of his forest life. This is why the needle is praised as a thing which appears so insignificant that "it can be lost forever" (line 2 of A) but which, in truth, has great value, i.e., "hunters awake."

A more important consideration is that a hunter's outfit plays a significant role in the actual chase (lines 2–6 of B). The hunters wear special clothing during trying moments—when there is danger in the forest or when an important attack is about to be mounted. The hunter relies on his outfit to conquer magically the game he stalks and to ensure his own survival and success. Parts of the hunter's special outfit can be seen in the sculpture of a Yoruba hunter (fig. 8.3). The hat is the most prominent item the artist has portrayed here; it contains magical materials in the long pouch (hanging down the hunter's back) which protect the wearer and ensure his survival in the next world. Special charms also are tied to the hunter's dog and hung around the hunter's waist and neck. Should the hunter's outfit become torn, it cannot serve him adequately. But the hunter cannot turn back. The *Ìrèmọ̀jé* makes this point with considerable emphasis:

1   Kò pa, kò walé,
2   Ọkọ Àkútè.

1   He who catches not, dares not return home,
2   Husband of Àkútè.[15]

As we see, even if the hunter is unable to repair his clothing (if the needle and thread are lost), he must persevere with courage, for he dare not return home without catching a respectable amount of game.

All in all, the performance which accompanies the presentation of hunter's gear is designed to convey several messages to the audience. One is that the hunter is a versatile member of the community. Another is that the lonely, self-reliant life of the hunter is a sacrifice made by him for the well-being of others.

A second theme in the *Ìrèmọ̀jé* performance which concentrates on the exemplary life focuses on manliness and three virtues which an ideal male member of society is expected to exhibit during his lifetime: heroism, courage, and bravery. The following are examples of heroic praises, known as *oríkì*, sung at *Ìrèmọ̀jé* performances:

1   Kìnìún igbó kìjikìji
1   Lion of the thick forest.

2   Ajẹ́ ogun Jalumi
2   Witch of the Jalumi war.

3   Iku Ogun
3   Death of war.

4   Elégbèje Àdó
4   One who owns a thousand and four hundred gourds of charms.

FIGURE 8.3. A Yoruba hunter and his hunting dog. Charms are tied to the dog's neck. The hunter wears charms around his waist, neck, and arm. The hat has materials inside to ensure the hunter's survival in the forest. (Wood sculpture, University of Ife Museum.)

The chanters devote a large portion of their presentation to describing the heroic exploits of the deceased person in terms such as these. The praises refer directly to the hunter who is being honored, to hunters and warriors in general, and to Ogun himself.

So that he may deserve public salutes such as these after his death, it is believed that each hunter strives to challenge and kill courageously the fiercest forest animals: lions, leopards, and bushcows. Part of his honor also comes from being able to face game with skill, perseverence, and patience.

Traditionally a hunter automatically became a warrior—usually a scout—in time of conflict. Hence he also strove to face and to fight wars bravely. The hunter who sought honor and fame in warfare was a man who quickly took up his arms and went to battle with speed and vigor. The following saying describes some of the qualities expected in a hunter-warrior:

1   "Gbà mí, gbà mí," kò yeégún,
2   "Ibi ogún lé mi dé rèé; kò yọdẹ."
3   "Gbà mí, gbà mí," kò yóọsà,
4   "Ibi ẹrán lé mi dé rèé," kò yọdẹ.

1   It is a paradox for masqueraders to call for help from humans,
2   For a hunter to say, "This is how far war drove me," is unbefitting.
3   It is a paradox for a deity to call for help from humans,
4   For a hunter to say, "This is how far game drove me," is unbefitting.

In this saying, the hunter-warrior is compared to the divinities, for neither man nor god can call upon his inferiors for help in the face of danger.

Manliness is not simply a matter of *emulating* the divinities, manliness also is linked to *using* divine power. The following chant tells us that the hunter who has noble goals is the hunter who owns charms:

1   Ògúndíyà Akítíẹpẹ,[16]
2   Ìkà ògàn tíí bo 'ra rẹ́ẹ́ mọ́lẹ̀.
3   Báwí, bàwì, báwí,
4   Mo ní ẹ ma ṣe b'Ogùúndíyà wí.
5   Ìran ọdẹ ní ti í lápó.
6   Ọdẹ tí ò lápó,
7   Ọdẹ tí ò lájàbò,
8   Kò leè sọdẹ erin.
9   A tóńtórí ọdẹ ẹfòn lájàdì.
10   Odẹ tí ò lájàbò lóọ́ọ́,
11   Tòun tobìnrin ni wọ́n jọ ṣọgba.
12   Èmí légbé.

13   Èmí sì lájàbò.
14   Mo láfèèèrí pèlú.
15   Mo láyèta ọdẹ.
16   Ode tí ò ní wọnyí, oo,
17   Láwujọ obìnrin ló gbé ń sọdẹ.

1   Ògúndíyà Akítíẹpẹ,[17]
2   A wicked thorn that buries itself.
3   Reprimand, reprimand, reprimand,
4   I warn you not to reprimand Ògúndíyà.
5   It is the hunters' tradition to own apó.[18]
6   The hunter who does not possess apó,
7   The hunter who does not possess àjàbò,[19]
8   Can hardly be a hunter of elephants.
9   Neither can he be a hunter of bushcows at Àjàdì.[20]
10   The hunter who does not possess àjàbò,
11   Is like a woman.
12   I have egbé.[21]
13   I have àjàbò.
14   I have àfèèrí.[22]
15   I also have the hunter's ayẹta.[23]
16   The hunter who does not own these,
17   Is a hunter in the midst of women.

One secret behind the hunter or warrior's professional success in life is related, then, to his ability to use charms to his own advantage. Such supernatural aids represent another theme in the Ìrèmòjé chants and, as indicated, are part of the gear which is displayed at the funeral.

When Ogun was on earth, he, too, possessed many charms; he used them to control humans and to perform miraculous deeds. He used his charms to hold an enemy to ransom, render a lion and other wild animals feeble, heal the sick with immediate effect, make himself invisible in the face of a charging animal, float on water, or become immune from attacks made by enemies wielding cutlasses or knives. His most powerful charms consisted of special iron armlets which could divert the course of bullets away from himself and toward another direction. Figure 8.4 is a brass sculpture of a hunter going to war with an iron armlet on his right arm. This armlet and the other charms of Ogun were marks of high status and authority—a signal of manliness, without which, as the Ìrèmòjé remind us, the hunter is powerless, like a woman.

The belief that charms are essential to success remains strong today in situations of confrontation despite the introduction of modern weaponry and its efficacy. An excellent example of the continued relevance of this belief comes from the Ibadan area (part of the precolonial Ọyọ Empire), where in

FIGURE 8.4. A Yoruba hunter going to war, riding a horse and armed with a dane gun. He wears a metal armlet. (Brass sculpture, University of Ife Museum.)

1968–1969 a large number of relatively low-income groups of people, mainly farmers, joined to protest government tax levies and other unpopular policies which the common people felt were unfair. The protest became known as the Àgbékòya Uprising, that is to say, "farmers rebel against oppression and punishment."

One of the leaders of the uprising was the Olu Ode, head of the senior members of the hunters' guild of a community under the jurisdiction of municipal Ibadan; another was the Jagun Ode, head of the junior members of another nearby guild. Under the leadership of their professional hunters, large numbers of very low-income farmers, hunters, and laborers were organized and communications channels were established for staging a series of demonstrations designed to harass police and military forces which had been deployed by the government to control the situation.

The significant point about the Àgbékòya Uprising in this context is that the hunters were armed not only with weapons (certainly less plentiful or efficient than military weapons), but more important, in the public view, with charms and iron armlets. Up to 3,000 protestors, led by the hunters, staged demonstrations in the city of Ibadan, singing war songs and incantations. As was later written:

> Many stories were told by terrified policemen and soldiers of, for example, 'the ground rising and falling in waves' when patrols were ambushed, and of men being deformed or injured without being touched by bullets or matchets.[24]

In the armed confrontations which took place during the Ibadan demonstrations, between eight and eleven government officials, military, and police were killed; and up to forty rebels and some thirty-five unidentified civilians were killed. Elsewhere in Yoruba divisions, where the protest had spread, there were some seventy-five deaths, mainly among civilians.[25] In the end, local leaders were called upon to restore peace and, in so doing, they effected a settlement in which the tax levy was lowered significantly. Throughout Ibadan, the hunters were credited with bringing victory to the Àgbékòya rebels—a victory which, it was believed, was won with the powers of Ogun and the charms he had left to his followers.

The theme of living an exemplary life next finds specific expression in the lifetime achievements of the deceased hunter whose funeral is being held. The following Ìrèmòjé is addressed to the deceased hunter:

1   Baálé iléè mi,[26]
2   Arálágbe má sàá,
3   Olóbèé tèmi nìkan.

1   The head of my family,
2   One who never runs away on sighting a beggar,
3   My breadwinner alone.

In this case, the chanter—a woman—secured information about the deceased—his kindness to the down-trodden and his concern for the well-being of his family—from his wife, and then composed a chant based on it. *Ìrèmòjé* chanters strive to present the virtues of the deceased to the assembled audience.

But all is not praise at the *Ìrèmòjé* performance. While the close relatives of the departed hunter are eager to assuage their sorrow in verbal compliments, Ogun instructed his followers to objectively assess the deceased's achievements. *Ìrèmòjé* artists are able to interject balance in their praises because they are not closely related to the deceased. One of the conventions they use in describing the failings of the deceased is to do so with humor. A light touch relieves emotional tensions while it injects a note of realism. The following chant illustrates the kind of humor which is used:

I   'Mọdé ìí gbẹ́nu lọ́wọ́.[27]
2   Ẹnuù rẹ́ rún ju tiwa lọ.
3   Àbọ́ ọ̀ mọ'hun tí ń be?
4   Àbọ́ ọ̀ mọ'hun tí ń be?
5   Jawajawa léti bí àgbà 'sọ̀nà.
6   A birun ń 'mú bí òbò 'sàlẹ̀.
7   A bikun ń 'mú bí òkùnrùn àgùtàn.
8   Ìbà ńlẹ̀ n tóó máa lọ.
9   Lóòótó nikú já wa lódòdò àwa lọ.
10 Ọ̀ràn náà jọ bí ẹrín lójúù mi.

I   Boy, would you shut up your mouth.
2   Your mouth stinks worse than ours.
3   Are you not aware of what is happening?
4   Are you not aware of what is happening?
5   See the stripes at his ears are like those of an old carver.
6   See the whiskers by his nose are like those of a vagina.
7   The mucous in his nose is like that of an ailing sheep.
8   I salute you before I proceed.
9   Indeed, death deprived us of our flower.
10 In my view, the occasion is one for laughter.

The chanters make vulgar remarks as a way of entertaining the audience and assuaging the grief of the bereaved. Hence the chanters mock one another and hurl insults—neither of which is taken seriously. In fact, the chanters carry on a friendly verbal duel which extends from one occasion to another and from time to time in the same performance. Finally, tension is relieved through dancing on and off throughout the night.

All things considered, the greatest test of human courage and the most important consideration in evaluating the personal lives of deceased hunters is to determine how well they react to difficulty. The magnitude of one's misfortunes or losses, or their frequency, is not important when compared with one's reaction to them. The overall message of the Ìrèmọ̀jé with respect to the exemplary life is that manliness rests on one's capacity to bear the vicissitudes of bad events without dismay.

Our second division in the Ìrèmọ̀jé themes concentrates on the inevitability of death. These chants are intended to instruct the living in the way they should face death and what they should expect after it.

To begin, the chants state that death is cruel. It nips in the bud lives that are flowering and not just lives that have begun to fade. Untimely death is treated in the Ìrèmọ̀jé by a recurrent use of flower symbolism, as in the Ìrèmọ̀jé immediately above, and as in the following chant:

1 Irókòó lọọọ,[28]
2 Àkànbí loo.
3 A à rÁKànbí mọ́.
4 Ọmọ Adéyẹmọ.
5 Ikú já wa lódòdó àwa lọ.
6 Lóko-lódò a ò rónílé,
7 A ò mọ 'bi onílé filé 'lẹ̀ lọ.

1 Irókò is deceased,
2 Àkànbí[29] is deceased.
3 We no longer see Àkànbí any more.
4 Offspring of Adéyẹmọ.[30]
5 Death has cut off our flower.
6 Here and there, we no longer see the house-owner,
7 We do not know where the house-owner went.

A cruel death is one which unexpectedly deprives the community of a valued member. The flower quite naturally stands for man's mortality; the suddeness of death is likened to cutting a flower (or a tree) in bloom.

The sense of deprivation and cruelty of death also is expressed in house symbolism. In addition to the above allusion to the empty house (lines 6 and 7), the following Ìrèmọ̀jé also relies on an empty house theme:

1 Mo kílé òò.[31]
2 Ilé ọ̀ jẹ́ oo.
3 Háà! mo sàgò sílé,
4 Ilé ọ̀ fọhùn.
5 Mo wọ́lé bẹ́ẹ̀ n ò bérò mọ́.

6   Ń bo lonílé ìí wà?
7   Ibo lọ́ a lọ òoo?
8   Ilé tó ti kún tẹ́lẹ̀ ń kọ́,
9   Ilé ti sọ̀gangan ọ̀nà tákéé sọ férò,
10   Ilé ìí gbẹ̀kan ò ooo.

1   I salute the house.
2   There is no answer.
3   Alas! I greet the house,
4   There is no answer.
5   I enter the house to find no more people.
6   Where is the house-owner?
7   Where has he gone?
8   A house that was once full of people,
9   That was a point of direct call for many,
10   Has become desolate and unhappy.

When death takes away a member of the community, the house may be full of inhabitants, but the absence of one resident creates an emptiness among those who remain. Death therefore is equated to "pulling down" the house—that is, the binding structure which holds the community, the hunters' guild, or the family together.

Death is more cruel when it is a "bad death." Not even the most potent charms can ward off a bad death, as the *Ìrèmọ̀jé* warn:

1   Àjùwòn Àkànbí,[32]
2   Ọdẹ n bó o légbéé.
3   Kì í sẹ pọ́dẹ ò légbé.
4   Ọdẹ n bó o lájàbòò.
5   Kì í ṣe pọ́dẹ ò lájàbò.
6   Egbé lọdẹ́ẹ́ fi í sọkọ erin nínúu 'gbó.
7   Àjàbò lọdẹ́ sìí fí sọkọ ẹfọ̀n níjù.
8   Ṣùgbọ́n bíkú bá dé,
9   Ikú wọn ò megbòo 'gi.
10   Mè gbẹbọ.
11   Mè gbòògùn.
12   Kò sí 'gbà tá ò ní kú.
13   Ikú ẹléyà nìkàn ni ọ̀ dáa.

1   Àjùwọ̀n Àkànbí,[33]
2   Hunter, I thought you had *egbé* magic.
3   It is true you have.

4   Hunter, I thought you had a *àjàbò* magic.
5   It is true you have.
6   Egbé is used by hunters to capture elephants in the game-forest.
7   *Àjàbò* is used by hunters to conquer lions in the game-forest.
8   But when Death comes,
9   Magic cannot serve as an antidote.
10   Sacrifice cannot ward off Death.
11   Magic cannot ward off Death.
12   Death is the inevitable end of man.
13   Bad Death alone is what we pray against.

Just as a warrior must defend himself against the enemy, the living must battle to avoid a bad death and the forerunners of a bad death. This battle is waged on many fronts, as it were, and is vividly portrayed in the following chant:

1   Ikú kọ̀ dá pa,[34]
2   Bẹ́ẹ̀ ni kò dá jà.
3   Ọmọ Ogun rẹpẹtẹ ló kó loojú Ogun.
4   Ó rán kọ̀ rán,
5   Ó rán mẹ́tàdín lójúù mi gbangba.
6   Àrùn lọ rán saájú.
7   Ẹ̀gbà ló rán tẹ̀lé e.
8   Ó rófò.
9   Ó répè.
10   Ó rẹ́wọ̀n lójúù mi gbangba ló ṣe.
11   Ni Baba ọdẹ́ wá domi akọ̀kọ́ nùùù,
12   Omi atan ni wọ́n ń mu.

1   Death does not kill alone,
2   Nor does he fight singly.
3   He goes to war with plenty of warriors.
4   To count the forerunners he sends to war,
5   He sends about seventeen in my presence.
6   He sends *Disease* first.
7   He sends *Paralysis* next.
8   He sends *Loss*.
9   He sends *Curses*.
10   He sends *Imprisonment* in my presence.
11   Death finally comes to kill the hunter's father,
12   Who now drinks of heavenly water.

Man is the lone warrior who is pitted against death's team of warriors. The warrior team, collectively known as *ajogun*, consists of "malevolent supernatural powers" or supernatural "war lords."[35] Death himself is one of the *ajogun*. Together with the others, he polices the world and protects it from human beings who violate the ethics and mores of society—the values which Ogun espoused and which we already have examined.

At the same time a bad death is to be avoided, death itself is inevitable. The *Ìrèmọ̀jé* are explicit in this regard:

1   Kọ̀ sẹ́ni tíkú ò leè pa.[36]
2   Ẹ má bìínú ọmọ̀ọ̀ 'Rókò.
3   Kọ̀ sẹ́ni tíkú ò leè pa.
4   Bí ó ti pẹ́ tó,
5   Bí ó ti yá tó,
6   La ò tíì mọ̀.
7   Ọ́ dá mi lójú,
8   Ẹ kúù 'fojú ní pẹ̀kun ẹ kú ewu.

1   Death has full control over human life.
2   Be consoled, offspring of 'Rókò.[37]
3   Death has full control over human life.
4   How late,
5   Or how soon,
6   Is what we know not.
7   I am sure,
8   To everyone, birth and death salutes will be paid.

It is with these comforts in mind that death can be taken as a normal occurrence. As such it must be faced courageously. The following *Ìrèmọ̀jé* instructs the bereaved in how best to face the death of a valued member of their community:

1   Bọ́dẹ bá kú,[38]
2   Ọdẹ kì í sunkún.
3   Ọdẹ kì í sẹ̀jẹ̀,
4   Ìrèmọ̀jé Ògún lọdẹ fi í ṣàárò ara wọn,
5   Kẹ́ní ọ́ gbón róhun mú dira.

1   When a hunter dies,
2   His colleagues never weep.
3   They never shed bloody tears,

4   They chant Ogun's *Ìrèmòjé* to mourn his death,
5   And the wise will draw inspiration therefrom.

This chant also infers that the "wise will draw inspiration" by learning how to face their own death. Manliness and courage are thus displayed not only in the manner in which one faces the death of others but also in the preparations one makes for one's own death.

Humans are subject to an inevitable, controlled cycle of life and death. They may take succor in the fact that on completing the cycle they will be honored in death as they were honored in life. Honor, however, cannot be found in material acquisitions. The *Ìrèmòjé* make this clear:

1   Ebi kì í jé á pawó àná mó òò,[39]
2   Àlàdé omo Obíèsan.
3   Mo fé kó o máa gbó dáadáa.
4   Odún nìí màá raso.
5   Èmíì màá rèwù.
6   Odúń méta òní ma dágbádáa sányán.
7   Lóríi kílàkílò ni 'kú bá ni.
8   Ògúndélé, òrun dèdèèdè bi ohùn arò.

1   One cannot make savings in the face of hunger,
2   Àlàdé, offspring of Obíèsan.
3   Listen to me attentively.
4   This year, I will buy one type of clothing.
5   Next year, I will buy another type of clothing.
6   Year after next, I will buy still another type of clothing.
7   As man continues his relentless struggle, Death will catch up with him.
8   Ògúndélé, rest in peace.

Whether or not man can save, or buy many types of clothing, death does not allow him to take earthly acquisitions into the next world. Rather, life must be spent enjoying its pleasures, not in hoarding them: "One should not be a miser to one's stomach." This philosophy is contained in the next *Ìrèmòjé*:

1   Ńjó e rí kéré,[40]
2   E je kéré.
3   Ògúnjìnmí, a-lé-ràá-wègi lo,
4   A-lé-toolo já lumi,

5   Ńjọ́ ẹ rí họ̀mù,
6   Ẹ jẹ họ̀mù.
7   Ọjọ kan ń bẹ
8   A á sùn a ò ní jí mọ́.
9   Eyín ìjòbì a deyín ìjawùsá.
10   Eyíin jẹranjẹran a deyíin fọ́ọgunfọ́ọgun.

1   When you have little,
2   Eat little.
3   Ògúnjìnmí,[41] who chases 'Ràá[42] into the thick forest,
4   Who chases Toolo[43] until it drops into the river,
5   When you have plenty,
6   Eat plenty.
7   A day will come
8   When we will sleep never to wake again.
9   Teeth that hitherto chewed kolanut will grind walnut.
10   Teeth that hitherto chewed meat will break bones.

Man must, in many ways, be an opportunist and, as the *Ìrèmọ̀jé* instruct, make the most of each day, each morsel, each small reward. A proverb is quite explicit in this regard:

1   Ibi táyé bá gbé bá ni là á jẹ ẹ́.
2   Bí òjò ń pa ọ́, máa tọ̀ sí ara.

1   Whenever you have the abundance of life, don't miss it.
2   As rain drenches you, empty your bladder as you go along.

In the final analysis, honor in life comes from living it to its fullest and taking advantage of each opportunity.

Death cannot be considered as a finality, however. It is a gateway to another kind of life: the life of an ancestor. The *Ìrèmọ̀jé* thus move from the solemnity of death to the joy of another kind of existence. The following excerpt from the *Ìrèmọ̀jé* instructs the living concerning immortality:

1   Mọ pọsẹsẹ-pọsẹsẹ,[44]
2   Ọwọ́ọ̀ mi ò bÁkànbí mọ́.
3   Babaá wá diná òrun kò tiẹ̀ kú mọ́.
4   Babaá wá sí tiẹ̀ dòòrùn,
5   Eyí ta ó fi sásọ gbẹ kalẹ́.
6   Àkànbí ire lálẹ̀dé òrun.

1   I trotted and trotted,
2   I couldn't reach Àkànbí any more.
3   Our father has been transformed into a heavenly light which never
     dies.
4   Our father has even been transformed into a sun,
5   Whose rays shall dry our clothes.
6   Àkànbí, rest in peace.

Deceased hunters who become ancestors are thus a source of light; they permit no obscurity. The "sun" refers to all of those souls who have displayed sufficient energy while on earth that they may thereafter illuminate the spirit world.

The deceased who become ancestors are also likened to trees:

1   Baba àwá ti dìmùlè.[45]
2   Wọn ti digi àlóyè,
3   Èyí tí ò leè kú mó,
4   Èso wẹẹrẹ ni wọn ń so.

1   Our father is now an ancestor in whom to confide.
2   He is a transplanted tree that thrives,
3   A tree that no longer dies,
4   But bears countless fruits.

An ancestor is like a "transplanted tree" in that he has demonstrated an ability to "take root" in a new setting. He "thrives" in that he has been resurrected in the countless descendants who have been left on earth to reproduce in the generations yet to come. In Yoruba belief, children who resemble their deceased forebears, usually grandparents or parents, are a reincarnation of their souls, which have been reborn in them. This belief is symbolically represented by the effigy of the dead hunter, which is, as we have seen, the central figure at the ceremony. The ancestral role of the deceased members of society is shown in an ability to live on in the spirit world and to direct, influence, and even control human activities from afar. It is this belief, then, which enables the deceased hunter to return to his colleagues for a final farewell.

Conclusion

The philosophy of Ogun, as conveyed to us by the Ìrèmòjé, contains three important tenets with respect to the model existence. The first is that humans are essentially alone. The solitary existence of Ogun and his hunter-followers is, in many ways, a metaphorical solitude. Humans must be self-reliant. The good life, the honorable life, the exemplary life is one in which the individual can meet his own material needs. This attribute is economically summed up with the presentation of the seemingly insignificant needle and thread. The ideal life is, all in all, one in which the individual faces his ordeals—be they ordeals of living or of dying—through his own inner strength.

The second tenet is that the ideal individual takes a leadership role. In this respect the warrior motif comes to the fore in the *Ìrèmòjé*, for it is through this theme that leadership is most clearly portrayed. The role played by the Aṣipadẹ in the funeral ceremony is a living reminder of the leadership role expected of the Ogun follower. The Aṣipadẹ looks out for the participants, seeing to their needs and guiding them through the ritual. Charms, moreover, also are symbolic representations of leadership in the form of manly valor, and they remind the assembled witnesses that the ultimate source of that valor lies in the power which comes from supernatural forces. By using the charms, the hunter-warrior is better able to protect, defend, guide, and provide for others, especially the members of his community and his family. The charms contain the message that the leader who defends his own people is a person who knows how to control himself and his foes.

The third tenet is that man will be judged by his own achievements. The accomplishments which carry the greatest weight are those which are won in the service of others. Each individual, say the *Ìrèmòjé*, is responsible for his own success. The amount of courage and heroism one is able to bring to the complex problems and confrontations of life must be mixed with a certain amount of opportunism, vigor, and lust for life. Each of these ingredients contributes toward the individual's achieving his own kind of greatness and his own kind of honor. His immortality lies, then, in his heirs' memories of his achievements.

In Yoruba society, the death of a hunter is an occasion for reinforcing the values associated with an honorable life. The hunter's funeral communicates these values through the oral traditions which are contained in the *Ìrèmòjé* funeral dirges, through the ritual performance enacted by the Aṣipadẹ, and through the many symbolic representations placed at the center of the gathering. By means of each of these elements the members of a community periodically renew their acquaintance with, and reaffirm their commitment to, the philosophy of Ogun. As we have seen, it is a philosophy designed to embrace the ideals associated with a "good life."

NOTES

1. They are also known as Ìpà. See also Simpson 1980:33.
2. See chapter 7 for an examination of the *Ìjálá*.

3. Chanted by Làmídí Abónìkaba at an Ìrèmòjé performance at Ọyọ in 1975.
4. Olúmọkin: another name for Ògún.
5. See also Simpson 1980:36–37.
6. Chanted by Làmídí Ògúndíyà at an Ìrèmòjé performance at Apinni, Ọyọ.
7. Àrònì: An imaginary elf, believed to possess immense charms, who can become invisible at will.
8. Lákáayé: Ògún's cognomen, meaning "the deity whose influence spreads around the world."
9. Ọ̀ṣìn Mọlẹ̀: Ògún's chieftaincy title, the meaning of which is now obscure.
10. Chanted by Làmídí Abónìkaba at Ọyọ in 1975.
11. Ògúnjìnmí: A hunter's name, meaning "the god Ògún blesses or favors me."
12. This means that the hunter is like a dog in that he is very clever and stealthy.
13. Chanted by Adebayọ at Akeètàn, Ọyọ, in 1972.
14. Dígòó is the hunting outfit. It consists of short trousers equipped with charms and worn by hunters specifically to attack and magically gain victory over any charging game animals.
15. Àkútè: The wife of a one-time heroic hunter.
16. Chanted by Adebayọ at Akeètàn, Ọyọ, in 1972.
17. Ògúndíyà: Personal name. Akítíẹpẹ: A nickname describing a tough, hardy person.
18. Apó: Quiver for arrows.
19. Àjàbò: Charm to render a challenger weak and unable to fight with vigor.
20. Àjàdì: A high, bushy hill in the Ọyọ area.
21. Egbé: A charm which enables the holder to fly away from danger.
22. Àféèrí: A charm which makes the holder invisible.
23. Ayẹta: A charm which diverts bullets away from the human target.
24. Beer 1976:194–95.
25. See Beer 1976:162, 190, 194, 245–52.
26. Chanted by Ògúnyóyin at Ọyọ in 1976.
27. Chanted by Lániyàn Àwuùbẹ́ at an Ìrèmòjé performance at Àpínni, Ọyọ.
28. Chanted by Àjàlá Adebayọ for Pa Ìrókò at Akeètàn, Ọyọ, in April 1972.
29. Àkànbí: The offspring of Adéyẹmọ.
30. Adéyẹmọ: A previously deceased heroic hunter.
31. Taken from dirges chanted by Olókòtó for Ògúndélé at Akeètàn, Ọyọ, in 1976.
32. Taken from dirges chanted for Pa Ògúnọle by Atóyèbí at Àpínni, Ọyọ, in 1975.
33. Àjùwòn Àkànbí: Another deceased hunter.
34. Taken from dirges chanted by Lamidi for Ògúndélé at Akeètàn, Ọyọ, in 1976.
35. See Abimbọla 1973:50.
36. Taken from dirges chanted for Pa Ògúndáre by Atóyèbí at Agúnpopo, Ọyọ, in 1975.
37. Rókò: A previously deceased hunter.
38. Taken from dirges chanted by Lániyan for Pa Ìrókò at Akeètàn, Ọyọ, in April, 1972.
39. Chanted by Atóyèbí while performing Ìrèmòjé for Pa Ògúndélé at Akeètàn, Ọyọ, in 1975.
40. Taken from dirges chanted by Adebayọ for Pa Ìrókò at Akeètàn, Ọyọ, in 1972.
41. Ògúnjìnmí: A previously deceased heroic hunter.
42. 'Ràá: A shortened name of Ìrákúnnúgbá, a very aggressive game-animal; the Western Hartebeeste (*Bubalis Major*).
43. Toolo: A fast-moving but easily charging game-animal; a member of the deer family (unidentified).

44. Taken from dirges chanted for Pa Ògúndípẹ̀ by Olokoto at Àpáàrà, Ọyọ, in 1976.
45. Taken from dirges chanted by Lamidi for Pa Ògúndípẹ̀ at Àpáàrà, Ọyọ, in 1976.

REFERENCES CITED

Abimbọla, Wande. 1978. "Yoruba Traditional Religion," in *Contemplation and Action in World Religions*, Yusuf Ibish and Ileana Marculescu (eds.), Seattle and London: University of Washington Press, pp. 218–42.

Beer, Christopher E. F. 1976. *The Politics of Peasant Groups in Western Nigeria*, Ibadan: Ibadan University Press.

Simpson, George E. 1980. *Yoruba Religion and Medicine in Ibadan*, Ibadan: Ibadan University Press.

Margaret Thompson Drewal

9

Dancing for Ògún in Yorubaland and in Brazil

D ance is an integral part of African ritual.[1] Addressing metaphysical beings or powers, it is a poetic, non-verbal expression continually created and re-created by countless performer/interpreters over generations. In its formulations of time, space, and dynamics, dance transmits a people's philosophy and values; it is thought embodied in human action. A primary vehicle for communicating with the spirit realm, it is at the same time perceived to be an instrument of the gods through which they communicate with the phenomenal world. As such, ritual dance is an unspoken essay on the nature and quality of metaphysical power. Indeed, for the Yoruba, dance—in certain contexts—is metaphysical force actualized in the phenomenal world.[2]

In western Yorubaland this is dramatically illustrated in ritual dances associated with Ògún, the deity whose quick, aggressive actions may bring violent death and destruction or, by contrast, may bring the birth of children. It is also evident in dances of Candomblé in Bahia, Brazil, where during the early nineteenth-century Yoruba captives were sold into slavery (Pierson 1942:35) and where, as a result, the influence of Yoruba culture, and of Ògún, is strong (Bastide 1978:66, 205–206, and 253–55). To place these ideas about dance into a broader Yoruba philosophical context, the following discussion considers the Yoruba concept of metaphysical power and its more well known relation to utterances.

The power of utterances has been widely documented in Africa (cf. Ray 1973; Peek 1981) and in Yorubaland (Prince 1960; Beier 1970:49; H. Drewal 1974; Verger 1976–77; and Ayoade 1979:51). Prince observes, for example,

that among the Yoruba "to utter the name of something may draw that something into actual existence . . . not only within the mind and body of he who
utters and he who hears the word, but also in the physical world as well"
(1960:66). And Ayoade points out, "to the initiated the sound of the words
is the audible manifestation of its innate force" (1979:51). In certain contexts,
voicing action verbs literally activates dynamic forces. Thus Verger reveals
that, in Yoruba incantations (*ọfọ̀*) chanted during the preparation or application of medicines (*òògùn*) to invoke the dynamic essences of all their ingredients, a monosyllabic action verb drawn from each ingredient's name is pronounced following that name to set the ingredient into action. For
example:

1 ewé ọ̀ọ́yọ́ àjẹ́ bá wa yọ àrùn kúrò n'ìhà
2 ewé awùsá sà àrùn ìhà
3 ìyẹ́ agbe gbé àrùn ìhà kúrò
4 ìyẹ́ àlukò kó arun ìhà kúrò

1 *ọ̀ọ́yó àjẹ́* leaf chase away (*yọ*) the disease of the flank for us
2 *awùsá* leaf heal *(sà)* the flank disease so it may go away
3 *agbe* feather carry *(gbé)* the flank disease outside
4 *àlukò* feather pick *(kó)* the disease out of the flank (Verger 1976–
   77:254)

Verger suggests further that appellations are attributed to ingredients based
upon particular actions described by verbs used in formulating them. It is thus
the action or, more accurately, the *acting* verbs inherent in names and incantations which, when voiced, enable them to mobilize the inner essence of a
spirit or force. Beyond this, however, it is the sound qualities of the acting
verbs which make them dynamic.

The sound qualities of verbs, nouns, adjectives, and adverbs in Yoruba incantations often correspond to the dynamic qualities of actions in the natural
environment. In the following invocation, utterances simulate actions in
evoking the way an Egúngún spirit called Àgàn becomes manifest.[3] Serving
as a formula for bringing the Egúngún festival into the world (*ayé*)
(H. Drewal and M. Drewal 1983:2–4), this invocation uses an analogy to rainfall, playing upon its dynamic qualities—not just one quality, but a whole repertoire of qualities—to convey the spirit's elusiveness. Like rain, the spirit
Àgàn comes to the world qualitatively in a myriad of ways:

1 Mo dé wẹ́rẹ́wẹ́rẹ́ bi eji orì alẹ́
2 Màrìwòoo! Àgànóoo!

3 Mo dé kùtùkùtù bí ejí òwúrọ̀
4 Màrìwòoo! Àgànóoo!
5 Mo dé pápàpá bi ejí ìyálẹ̀ta
6 Màrìwòoo! Àgànóoo!
7 Ojú aláàbẹ̀dẹ kò tó'lẹ́ arọ́
8 Màrìwòoo! Àgànóoo!
9 Ojú amọ̀kòkò kò tó'lẹ̀ amọ̀
10 Màrìwòoo! Àgànóoo!
11 Mẹ̀mẹ̀mẹ̀ nigbe ewúrẹ́
12 Màrìwòoo! Àgànóoo!
13 Bọ̀bọ̀ nigbe àgùtàn
14 Màrìwòoo! Àgànóoo!
15 Mojí lóòrọ̀ kùtùkùtù
16 Mogbé inini ọrun w'aiyé
17 Mo wọ̀ rùrùrùrùrù
18 Màrìwòoo! Àgànóoo!
19 Mo dé t'ogbó t'ọ̀gọ t'àkọ̀ t'idà
20 Màrìwòoo! Àgànóoo!
21 Gbámù! Òfo!
22 Gbámù! Òfo!
23 Gbámù! Òfo!
24 Amamamamamamama!
25 Ẹ má a wá!
26 Ẹ má a wá!
27 Ẹ má a wá! (Recorded in Ilaro, 1977)

1 I come *wẹ́rẹ́wẹ̀rẹ́* [small, quick, and light, i.e., drizzling] like the early
   night rain
2 *Màrìwòoo! Àgànóoo!*
3 I come *kùtùkùtù* [forceful and quick, i.e., pouring] like the early morning rain[4]
4 *Màrìwòoo! Àgànóoo!*
5 I come *pápàpá* [large, heavy, slow sporadic drops] like the rain at sun-
   rise
6 *Màrìwòoo! Àgànóoo!*
7 The eyes of the blacksmith cannot see underneath the ground of his
   shed
8 *Màrìwòoo! Àgànóoo!*
9 The eyes of the potter cannot see the inside of clay
10 *Màrìwòoo! Àgànóoo!*
11 *Mẹ̀mẹ̀mẹ̀* cries the female goat
12 *Màrìwòoo! Àgànóoo!*
13 *Bọ̀bọ̀* cries the female sheep
14 *Màrìwòoo! Àgànóoo!*

15   I get up early in the morning
16   I bring dew from the otherworld to earth
17   I become *rùrùrùrùrù* [all pervasive, literally the sound of walking over
         dewy grasses]
18   *Màrìwòoo! Àgànóoo!*
19   I come with cudgels, a sheath, a sword
20   *Màrìwòoo! Àgànóoo!*
21   Grasp it! Nothing's there!
22   Grasp it! Nothing!
23   Grasp it! Nothing!
24   Amamamamamamama!
25   Be looking! We are looking!
26   Be looking! We are looking!
27   Be looking! We are looking!

That Yoruba acknowledge a relationship between the dynamics of speech and the dynamics of action is evident in their verbal characterizations of dance, particularly in the use of evocative words, or what Babalọla (1966:67–68) calls word-pictures, words which by their very sound and intensity evoke mental pictures or images. Hence, a dance for the ancient female deity *Oòduà*, perceived to be cool, patient, and calm, is described by Ọ̀họ̀rì Yoruba as gentle (*ijó jẹ́jẹ́*). In addition to its definition—gentle—the sound *jẹ́jẹ́* is evocative. Its oral dynamics in this context evoke light, moderately and evenly paced, effortless motion. In contrast, a dance associated with the god of thunder and lightning is described by an Ègbádò priestess as being very powerful (*ijó kíkan kíkan tó l'abgára*), literally "a dance performed *kíkan kíkan* with forcefulness." *Kíkan* connotes a forceful release of energy as if under pressure (personal communication, Rowland Abíọ́dún, 1981). Like *jẹ́jẹ́*, the phrase *kíkan* simulates verbally the effort quality of the dance, that is, one in which a dominant motif is raising (*kí*) and percussively dropping (*kàn*) the shoulders repetitively, i.e., *kíkan kíkan*. *Kí* is quick, sharp, and high (or up) in tone; *kan* is forceful, full, and heavy, dropping in tone. The dance further evokes, in its speed and thrust, the dynamics of lightning and thunder—in that order—associated with Ṣàngó. In fact, from this perspective, the image of lightning and thunder can be seen, like the analogy to rainfall illustrated above, to derive meaning from its actual dynamic qualities, qualities which in turn reflect the nature of Ṣàngó's own power.

In Yoruba thought, there is a direct correlation between the dynamic qualities of both dance and oral performance and power known as *àṣẹ*. According to Beier (1970:49), "Yoruba believe strongly in the power of the word, or rather in a mysterious force called ashe . . . that quality in a man's personality which makes his words—once uttered—come true." One Yoruba singer alluded to this concept of voiced *àṣẹ* in referring to certain songs he performs which have efficacy because, when voiced, they operate as "wind (èfúùfù) combatting wind"; that is, the force exerted in voicing a song *acts upon* other forces permeating the world that are believed to be creating a particular situation (cf. H. Drewal 1974). Going a step further, Verger (1964:16) states that *àṣẹ* is "the principle of all that lives or acts or moves . . . everything which exhibits power, whether in action or in the winds and drifting clouds, or in passive resistance like that of the boulders lying by the wayside."[5]

In its broadest sense, *àṣẹ* is metaphysical power. It has been translated as "authority" or "command" (Abraham 1958:71), "a coming to pass . . . effect; imprecation" (Crowther 1852:47).[6] However, when Yoruba speak of an individual with *àṣẹ, aláṣẹ,* a person with authority, they usually mean one with innate metaphysical power who by virtue of this power maintains complete and awesome control over spiritual realms and, by extension, over social ones. In and of itself, *àṣẹ* has no moral connotations; it is neither good nor bad, positive nor negative (Verger 1964:16). It is the principle of realization (dos Santos 1976:71). It is absolute power and potential, present not only in utterances, but in all things—rocks, hills, streams, mountains, leaves, animals, sculpture, ancestors, gods, and actions. It is through voiced power, or *àṣẹ,* that devotees of Ògún call him and seek his advice. It is also with voiced *àṣẹ* that they bring him into the phenomenal world.

For the Yoruba, evidence of the presence of *àṣẹ* in the various things of the natural and supernatural realms is displayed in their qualitative aspects. Thus Yoruba define and classify plants used in medicines by taking into account their odors, their colors, their textures, their responses when touched, and their effects upon those who touch them (Verger 1976–77:249). According to Warren et al. (1973:ii), "If one asks herbalists why they select certain ingredients [for their medicines] one learns that it is because they are bitter or sweet, red or black, hard or slimy, or that they possess some other quality." The qualities of inanimate objects, such as leaves, rocks, ores, or other natural elements, as Warren and Verger indicate, are inherent in their tastes, textures, shapes, and colors. Animated beings such as humans and animals express innate power in their behavior, that is, in their everyday actions and utterances.[7] In performative phenomena, such as in ritual utterances and dance, these qualities are expressed dynamically through patterned time. To a great extent, utterances and actions carry this power precisely because they are intrinsically dynamic.

If oral recitations possessing *àṣẹ* invoke supernatural forces, bring them into existence, and set them into action, then dance represents more literally the materialization of those forces in the world. It is through dance, through what Langer (1953:187) refers to as "a play of powers made visible," that metaphysical forces become manifest. Nowhere is this relationship between words and actions more explicit than in the verbal and kinetic exertions associated with the deity Ògún, the hot, vengeful warrior who kills with quickness and directness.

The Dynamics of Ògún

The *àṣẹ* personified by Ògún is driving force—that which thrusts into new realms, breaks new ground, and achieves the ordinarily unachievable. Ògún represents accomplishment, exploration, and innovation (Barnes 1980:7, 28–29). He penetrates the frontiers of the unknown—the forest, the battleground, and the fringes of society. He both benefits mankind and on occasion destroys parts of it, and in his quests he is insatiable, tenacious, and unyielding. His path is often fraught with unexpected hazards. It is Ògún's nature to be quick, direct, and strong. Whether creative or destructive, his dynamic can be characterized as explosive.

Many of Ògún's symbols, such as the *àgbaadù* snake, represent his *àṣẹ*. Small and black, with a red stripe on its neck, the *àgbaadú* or *òṣúùró* snake reportedly is very quick, vicious, and deadly and, because of its small size, is able to attack people completely by surprise.[8] Iron also embodies Ògún's *àṣẹ* (cf. H. Drewal, chapter 10). Consistent with the nature of his power, iron implements when used by people to perform work demand actions of quickness, forcefulness, directness, and an explosive release. Like Ògún's acts, these acts can be creative, but they can also be destructive, whether by intent or by accident. Working with iron, man thus partakes of Ògún's dynamic force. Hence, human action can be seen to derive ultimately from metaphysical force, or *àṣẹ*. Indeed, this relationship between human action and metaphysical force to a large extent accounts for the need of people who use iron implements to sacrifice to Ògún. Individuals revitalize Ògún through sacrifice so that they may partake of that vitality and manage it safely.

Ògún's *àṣẹ* can, therefore, be heard and observed. It is expressed physically and audibly in the dynamics of dance and oral performance. Both dance and utterances are physical exertions which express attitudes toward time, space, weight, and flow (Bartenieff 1980:51).[9] Some combination of quickness, forcefulness, and directness expressed in an explosive release of energy recurs frequently in Ògún's performative imagery; these same qualities are also alluded to in the physical and behavioral properties of the many objects and beings, like iron and the *àgbaadú* snake, which make up his symbolic complex. The following analysis of the dynamic qualities of oral texts and dances specific to Ògún demonstrates how they display the *àṣẹ* of Ògún.

One of Ògún's dominant images is that of destruction. Barnes, in fact, views Ògún as "a metaphor for the dangerous and destructive powers of mankind" (1980:28). An oral praise poem reinforces the destructive image:

1   O p(a) ọkọ s(i) oju ina
2   O p(a) aya s(i) madiro
3   O p(a) wọn wẹrẹwẹrẹ sa l(i) (o)de
4   Ogun ni ẹjẹrengun ile alaigbọran

5   O gbe ori olori sawisa
6   O wo (o)ko oloko rojo rojo
7   O pọn (o)mi si (i)le fi ẹjẹ wẹ
8   Ogun l(i) ọn jẹ agbe (i)rin omo pa omo
9   Sare m(u) omi wa o pa meje
10   Ọkunrin giri bi ẹni ṣi lẹkun
11   O pa s(i) otun o ba otun jẹ
12   O pa s(i) osi o ba osi jẹ

1   He kills the husband before the fire,
2   He kills the wife in the foyer,
3   He kills little ones as they flee outside.
4   Ogun is the ẹjẹregun leaf in the house of the proud, fierce man.
5   He seizes the head of another freely,
6   He stares at the penis of men.
7   With water in the house he washes with blood.
8   Ogun who makes the child kill himself with the iron he plays with;
9   While carrying water he kills seven (people).
10   Man trembles like someone who opens the door.
11   He (Ogun) kills on the right and destroys on the right,
12   He kills on the left and destroys on the left. (Verger 1957:176, my
     translation)

The action verb *pa*, to kill, is common in praise poetry and invocations
for Ògún, and its dynamic in oral performance is analogous to the visible dynamics of movement. Hence the oral expression can be subjected to the same
analytic treatment that is given to physical effort.[10] The verb *pa* pronounced
in oral texts conveys a blow which is spatially direct, sudden, and powerful,
executed with an explosive release. In this volume (chapter 2), Armstrong
uses the spelling *kpa* to underscore the vocal force of the Yoruba "p" sound.[11]
Its repetition, *"Ó pa ọkọ. . . . Ó pa aya. . . . Ó pa wọn wẹrẹwẹrẹ"* (lines 1–3)
and so on, conjures up an image of Ògún with cutlass in hand slashing out
at those around him. Indeed, one of his most widely known praises is, "He
killed them with one blow (instantly)" (*Ó p'awọn bere kojo*). This verbal
image is enacted physically in Ilaro, where, on certain occasions, a hunter
possessed by Ògún rushes through the town, cutlass in hand, and decapitates
any dog in his path with one stroke of his iron blade. Another invocation for
Ògún declares:

1   Ó pa oko síbi iná
2   Ó pa aya si bálùwẹ̀
3   Ó pa omo pa ìya
4   Adamolore kège kège

5   Kùtùkùtù l'òguń ba
6   Àiyí gǫlǫtǫ s'oko oloko
7   Ekun oko eke wo

1   He kills the husband near the fire,
2   He kills the wife in the bath house,
3   He kills the child, kills the mother.
4   Sword-cuts-off-heads *kège kège.*
5   Early in the morning, Òguń met them;
6   They were found stone-dead in the farm of another farmer.
7   Ogun will punish those who don't fear him. (Olúpǫnà 1975)

The phrases above play upon harsh *p* and *k* sounds pronounced with explosive energy. They possess a dynamic that is unleashed in the act of pronouncing them, and convey force through the effective patterns of stress placed on consonants, words, or phrases, that is, the combination of tone, speed of syllables, vocal force, and flow—all of which combine to simulate physical effort. Again, the word *pa* (kill) is direct, quick, and explosive. In another phrase containing a word-picture, "Sword-cuts-off-heads *kège kège*," the image of heads rolling is conveyed. The sound *kège* has a heavy, sluggish quality and, when repeated, suggests continuous motion. The syllable *kè* interrupted by the sound of *ge* followed by a short pause and repetition sets up a rhythm which evokes an image at once horrific and humorous, that of a heavy, irregularly shaped sphere—the head—rolling after the quick, powerful thrust of Òguń's cutlass. It is evident from these examples that Yoruba have a great sensitivity to dynamic qualities and that they use them quite deliberately in verbal performance—and, as we shall see, in dance—to evoke, and thus ultimately to invoke, the vital force of Òguń.

Throughout Yorubaland there are many different Òguń dance styles. For the purposes of this paper, however, one distinct style and its context will be discussed: Òguń possession trance dance associated with a ritual festival for the gods in western Yorubaland. A comparison then will be made with Òguń possession trance dance in the Yoruba-derived Candomblé houses of Bahia, Brazil.[12] These examples provide us with insight into the role of dance and the significance of its dynamic qualities in ritual. Using the body as an expressive instrument, the Òguń dancer evokes, and thus invokes, the actual dynamic qualities which constitute the essence of the god and accomplishes this by manipulating and controlling time, space, energy, and flow in accordance with traditional precedent.

Possession Trance in Western Yorubaland

Invocations, praise poetry, music, and dance are essential to nearly all Yoruba ritual in which spiritual forces are actualized. Invocations and drumming performed before the onset of possession trance both in Yorubaland and in Brazil serve to bring Ògún into contact with devotees. Through dance, spiritual forces materialize in the phenomenal world. The god is said to mount (*gùn*) the devotee (*eléégún*, literally, "one who is mounted") and, for a time, that devotee becomes the god. Temporarily, then, the animating spirit of the deity (*èmí òrìṣà*) displaces that of the individual being mounted (Oṣitola 1982). Whatever the priest does from the moment he enters the trance state is thought to represent the god's own actions. Among the Yoruba, possession trance states are expressed through the medium of dance. To my knowledge, there is no instance of possession trance among the Yoruba which does not occur as dance or in association with dance.

Spirit mediumship is the most significant role of a priest. The uniting of devotee and deity into one image often causes some confusion for researchers who, for example, try to establish the identity of figures represented in Yoruba sculpture. Sculpture represents the union of the priest and deity in the depiction of the former with the costumes, hairstyles, and paraphernalia identified with the latter (M. Drewal 1986). Likewise, these identical fashions are observable in ritual dance. It is through dance, however, that the priest brings the active deity (not a symbolic representation) into the phenomenal world for the community. To become possessed by the gods is, therefore, the primary role of the medium.

As in all initiations into priesthoods throughout Ègbádò and Òhòrí areas, Ògún devotees go through extensive training, which in large part is devoted to preparing them for spirit mediumship. They metaphorically die and are reborn. According to Verger:

> An initiation always begins with a symbolic death and resurrection which marks the novice's break with his past and shows his birth into a new life consecrated to the deity. . . . During the period which separates the day of resurrection from that on which the novice receives a new name, . . . [the novice] seems to lose all reason, he is plunged into a dazed state of mental paralysis; he has forgotten everything, no longer knows how to speak and talks only in unintelligible sounds. The novice in this state is called *Omotun*, new child (1954:337).

Mediums become differentiated in the particular dances, music, and songs attributed to their personal deities and in their performance styles. Throughout Egbado and Òhòri areas, however, there is consistency in the practice, initiation, and training of mediums, as well as in the broad style of entering trance. The novices' clothes are taken away, their heads are shaved, and they are secluded in a dark shrine, where they must remain quiet and still for some weeks. During this period, the head is bathed regularly in the *àṣẹ* of the deity, made up of an amalgam of leaves, blood of animals, and pulverized minerals (Verger 1954:324 and 1969:n.2, p. 65). Furthermore, the *àṣẹ* of Ògún is rubbed into incisions made in the shaven head. This is thought to fix the power of the deity in the head of the devotee and to stimulate possession trance. The initiate is now known as *adóṣù*, one who has received the medicine, or *òṣù*, of the god. Later, special hairdos are worn by the newly initiated to identify them with their particular god and to show that this is a head endowed with power. Finally, the devotee receives a special new name which suggests Ògún's hold or claim on the initiate, such as Opelajumiedebo, "The-one-who-kept-late-and-came-speaking-a-new-language," or Omulel'okiti, "The-one-whose deity-carried-her-to-Omolu's-mound (shrine)." Both names refer to possession trance; the first refers to a ritual language spoken during trance which reflects the dialect of the Ọhọrí Yoruba subgroup from which this particular Ògún practice spread, and the second refers to the notion that Ògún took charge of or claimed a devotee by carrying her to Omolu's shrine. The verb here implies that she was "carried" via a trance state.

In possession trance performance, the left side is stressed to symbolize the spirit realm. Ògún mediums in Yorubaland carry iron implements in their hands, often in their left hands.[13] Likewise, the priest of Ẹlẹ́gba, the divine messenger, carries a cudgel in the left, and the priest of Ṣàngó also carries in the left a staff representing a neolithic axe of paired thundercelts (M. Drewal 1986). The left in Yoruba society is used in many other ritual contexts: inside the Ògbóni lodge on special meeting days, Ògbóni members greet each other and guests with the left hand;[14] when *òjẹ* don the Egúngún masquerade they step into the cloth with the left foot;[15] and deities greet the community with the left hand, that is, the possessed priest, whose head has been mounted by the deity, greets the community with the left, as illustrated in figure 9.1, in which Ògún shakes left hands with a kneeling female.

These contexts of lefthandedness have a common purpose. In every case they involve spiritual communication. As one devotee put it, "The right is used by men; the left is used by the gods." Hence, when one enters the Egúngún cloth to make the Egúngún spirit manifest, one must step in with the left foot, and when offering a gift or sacrifice to deities one presents it with the left hand.

The prevalent interpretation in the literature on the Yoruba of the unclean, antisocial left hand is misleading in that it does not allow us to perceive the importance of the left for spiritual communication in a ritual context. The left is reserved for ritual and must not, therefore, be used in ordinary social discourse. In this way the sacred is kept separate from the profane to protect the integrity of both worlds at once (Hertz 1973:7); as Yoruba would put it, the world (*ayé*)—a domain where people reside only temporarily—is ritually separated from the otherworld (*òrun*), a metaphysical realm of permanent existence. Seen from this perspective, it is then possible to understand why the social use of the left is unacceptable and even considered to be deviant behavior.

Hand-held objects particular to Ògún and carried in the left hand inevitably signal a possession trance context, when the deity mounts the head of his priests. The priest literally becomes Ògún, and whatever the possessed priest

FIGURE 9.1. Draped in *mariwo*, a priestess possessed by Ògún shakes the left hand of a kneeling woman. Igbogila, Nigeria, 1978.

says and does is taken to be Ògún's own words and actions. In the left hand, possessed priests carry objects symbolic of the god's powers, the iron blades of Ògún, the cudgel of Ẹlẹ́gba, the bow and arrow of Ọ̀ṣọ́ọ̀sì, or the thundercelts of Ṣàngó. These power symbols in the left hand signal a visitation from the spirit realm, but at the same time they assert the authority and the responsibility of the medium to be the god's conduit in this world.

In any ritual where iron or iron implements are required, particularly in blood sacrifices performed with iron blades, Ògún must be dealt with first, for iron itself is Ògún. It represents Ògún's vital power, his capacity for quick, forceful, overt action concretized in iron tools and implements of all varieties (cf. H. Drewal, chapter 10). Iron implements are a symbol of Ògún's worldly accomplishments, whether those accomplishments are destructive or productive, whether they involve the iron cutlasses, arrows, and guns of warfare, automobiles and motorcycles, the blades of circumcision, the hoes of farming, or the adzes and knives of carving. Iron implements and Ògún get things done quickly and forcefully. That is the nature of their power. Thus, while iron implements carried by the mediums symbolize Ògún's nature and his dynamic potential, the left hand which wields them speaks of his ability to penetrate the phenomenal world allowing devotees to tap his force.

In western Yorubaland, a religious group whose principal deity is Omolu, an earth deity in charge of contagious diseases, especially smallpox, believes that all deities, including Omolu, have their own Ògún and their own Ẹlẹ́gba (also known as Èṣù, the trickster). Ẹlẹ́gba is the divine mediator who must receive the first invocations and sacrifices; he is the "god of the crossroads" who makes initial contact with other gods on man's behalf. He personifies the intersection of the world and the otherworld. Ògún, on the other hand, represents the path itself. He facilitates Ẹlẹ́gba by "clearing the way." Therefore, ceremonies which involve Ògún often place him first in the ritual order together with Ẹlẹ́gba, the divine mediator.[16] Ẹlẹ́gba and Ògún work hand in hand. Informants explain that, as the god of iron, Ògún is first to enter and clear the bush where the shrines of all the other deities are installed (*Ògún ló ṣàlè f'òrìṣà dó*)—a way of saying that without Ògún no other deities can be worshipped on earth. He is in front, unyielding and "courageous like the road" (*Anaya pátá bí ọ̀nà*). As an ambitious, courageous warrior he is determined to go first. This is communicated explicitly when, during a procession to the bush, the site of Omolu's shrine on the outskirts of town, the female medium possessed by Ògún Igbó, "Ògún of the Bush"—shown in figure 9.1 wearing palm frond vestments—charges to the front of the line intent upon commandeering the group. Consistent with his perceived personality, Ògún acts quickly, directly, and forcefully. His inclination to rush forth quickens the pace of the entire group. Because Ògún's courage and tenacity can place the female medium, who is mortal, in great physical danger, attendants continually restrain her from fully asserting Ògún's prerogatives.

Dancing for Ògúń in Western Yorubaland

In Igbogila, an Ẹ̀gbádò community northeast of Ilaro toward Nigeria's western border, a religious group that combines many olórìṣà, literally "owners of deities," performs rituals for those deities every five days (every four days by a Western count).[17] These are essentially danced rituals, the primary object of which is possession trance. Deities represented among the olórìṣà cluster around and symbolize the realm of the bush. In order of their ritual performance, they are Ògúń, Eyinlẹ, Ìrokò, Ondo, Omolu, and Ẹlẹ́gba.[18] Eyinlẹ̀ (Erinlẹ̀) is a deity associated with streams and hunting; Ìrokò is a bush deity associated with the African teak tree of the same name. Omolu appears to be the dominant deity in this group; he is the god of contagious diseases, particularly smallpox. Not specifically identified with the bush, however, is Ondo, the deified founding forefather of the town of Pobẹ in Benin (R.P.B.).[19]

In the shade of a large tree, the group sets up chairs for its own members and for spectators. The mediums, with shoulders bare and chests bound with cloth, stand side by side to open the ceremony and invoke Ẹlẹ́gba, by placing their left feet forward (fig. 9.2). Attention is focussed on the spiritual (left) side, since what is to follow is direct communication with the spirit realm. The mediums slowly and repetitively place their left feet forward, returning each time to their starting position with both feet side by side. Turning to face the opposite direction, they repeat the exercise. With this formulaic opening, they then form a circle, dance counterclockwise, invoke each deity in the aforementioned order, and sing his praises (fig. 9.3). The songs, the dances, and the drum rhythms are particular to each god or set of gods. The song determines what the drums play and how the devotees dance.

After a process of honoring and invoking each deity in song and dance, beginning with Ògúń, the mediums break out of the circle, and the drums again invoke Ògúń. Ògúń's mediums gaze downward; their dance movements diminish. A change in attitude occurs, from outgoing and playful to concentrated, serious, and inwardly focussed. As if bound to the spot, the mediums stop moving their feet (fig. 9.4); upper torsos veer to the side; heads drop; and left knees quiver, causing their bodies to tremble. The priests in this state are called "horses of the gods" (ẹṣin òrìṣà). Attendants rush to straighten their cloths and bind their waists and breasts tightly (fig. 9.5), in much the same way a rider saddles a horse, pulling the straps tightly to secure the saddle in place, for Ògúń must "mount" (gùn) and ride his medium. At this point, the mediums are fully transformed into the deity. They repeatedly lick their lips in an agitated fashion. Their upper torsos drop, the heads roll back, and eyes roll upward (fig. 9.6). Attendants quickly close the mediums' eyelids and bring their heads forward. The final sign that Ògúń is present is signaled when the medium emits a deep guttural yell. It is said that when the god mounts

FIGURE 9.2. With bare shoulders, the mediums stand side by side to open the ceremony, invoking Ẹlẹ́gba by placing their left feet forward. Igbogila, Nigeria, 1978.

FIGURE 9.3. Dancing counterclockwise in a circle, the mediums invoke each deity one by one. Igbogila, Nigeria, 1978.

FIGURE 9.4. As if bound to the spot, the possessed medium entering trance stops moving her feet, and her upper torso and head veer to the side and drop forward. Igbogila, Nigeria, 1978.

FIGURE 9.5. Attendants rush to straighten the cloth of the newly possessed medium and bind it tightly to her waist and breast much in the same way that a rider saddles a horse. Igbogila, Nigeria, 1978.

FIGURE 9.6.   Four mediums become possessed by Ògúń simultaneously. The one on the far left is prepared to dance, awaiting a cue from the musicians. Initially their upper torsos drop slightly forward, and their heads often roll back as their eyes roll upward into the sockets (third medium left). An attendant closes the eyelids of the medium second from the left, bringing her head forward.

FIGURE 9.7.   With hands placed on her hips, an iron pincer in her left, a medium possessed by Ògúń takes a giant step, leading with the whole left side of her body, as she makes her way to the gathered crowd. Igbogila, Nigeria, 1978.

FIGURE 9.8. A possessed medium greets members of the audience with
"Ẹ kú o!" Igbogila, Nigeria, 1978.

the medium's head he roots the medium's feet to the earth; thus, attendants release the possessed mediums by slapping or stepping on the tops of their feet. The possessed mediums then take giant steps, leading with the whole left side of their bodies, and make their way to the gathered crowd (fig. 9.7). Hands are placed on the hips, and knees and feet are lifted and extended forward. After greeting the entire assemblage with *"Ẹ kú o!"* (fig. 9.8), the mediums sing, dance, and pray. Ògún in this way directs the drummers.

During the performance, spectators give money to Ògún and the drummers. The amount ranges from several cents to one dollar with an average of about twenty cents. By "spending money" (*nínà'wó*) for Ògún, spectators receive special recognition and blessing from him. In a sense they invest in his dynamic power, and in return they receive the benefit of that power.

More than one Ògún priest may be possessed simultaneously (fig. 9.6), but only one comes forth at any given time to sing. An Ògún may step forward to sing, for example:

1   I am afraid of everybody.
2   But if anybody claims to be higher than Ògún,
3   I shall lower him down (Verger 1969:60).

A ceremony's progression is spontaneous in that the mediums decide on the spur of the moment which song to sing, and this in turn determines what the drums play and what dance is performed. Likewise, the mediums determine at what point they will stop a dance and begin a new one.

The Ògún mediums perform several dances, which are rhythmically and visually distinct, and these can be in any order as long as they are appropriate to Ògún. In none of the dances are the mediums' orientations in the dance space predetermined; rather, they tend to scatter themselves and face any direction. Further, they do not relate to each other physically. They dance simultaneously, yet independently.

As noted above, Ògún mediums carry various instruments in their hands to identify the power of their deity. Iron blades of various descriptions evoke Ògún's role as hunter and warrior; miniature flintlock guns suggest similar ideas; miniature iron pincers evoke the work of the blacksmith. In figures 9.9 and 9.10, for example, Ògún mediums (Olóògún) each carry an iron spade in the left hand. In this context, the mediums usually carry a combination of implements in both hands, which are held rather statically, moving only in response to active shoulders. Whatever the particular combination of instruments, one is usually iron. Ògún's presence then is implicit even before the onset of possession trance. The implements speak of Ògún's acts; the dance on the other hand evokes the dynamics required for those acts.

Ògún's dances express the nature of his vital force. In all of them, the head is calm; in contrast, the shoulders are active, especially the shoulder blades or scapulae, which are repetitively raised and lowered, a special characteristic of Òhòrí style dancing.[20] Known as èjìká, a term which refers both to the shoulders and the movement associated with the shoulder blades, these gestures have an amazing range of dynamic possibilities, from gentle and subtle to forceful and exaggerated, and from fluid and smooth to sharp and angular (fig. 9.9). As performed by Ògún, however, they are distinctly forceful, quick, sharp, and exaggerated, in keeping with his explosive manner. The èjìká of the thundergod Şàngó is performed similarly to convey similar attributes of power (M. Drewal 1986). Knees are flexed, and torsos are pitched forward from the hips at approximately a 45 degree angle. From this position, and with active shoulders, a number of different stepping patterns and rhythms are performed. These patterns are fairly short, often in counts of four, and repetitive.

Ògún's dances range from extremely rapid to moderately paced. The most moderate of them conveys a stalking dynamic. Its overall quality can be characterized as cautious, that is, a combination of hesitancy and determination. The movement bursts forth with a quick, strong step, and is then held back, restrained for an instant before it bursts forth again; a third step exhibits an even more sustained movement with a final large burst of energy that ends in a crouching position, again held (fig. 9.10). The medium steps on one foot and places the other slightly to the back side in a wide stance, pausing for an instant in a very deliberate fashion. Stepping then on the other side, she repeats the pattern. On the third step, instead of placing the foot, she slides it past the other; it skims the ground, then goes out and around so that the medium changes direction toward the sliding foot. The slide is suspended and, at the last possible moment, in time to the music, the medium lunges forward in a slight crouch onto the other foot. This position is held again in a long pause to give it emphasis. Thus the medium steps: &1 hold, &2 hold, &3_slide 4 hold, and so on. The implements carried by the mediums are held motionless in front of the torso. While there is a clear emphasis on pauses and sustained movements, these are interspersed with strong bursts of energy which are sudden and emphatic that ultimately evoke an overall dynamic of stalking.

Another of Ògún's dances uses similar elements to produce slightly different qualities and rhythm. It, too, has a stalking dynamic. But this time the medium takes three long, low strides at a pressing pace and then with a catch step either continues in the same path or changes direction; thus, stepping 1 2 3&4; 1 2 3&4. With each step, the scapulae jump forcefully outward and upward and then plunge emphatically in again, thus double-timing the feet. The forcefulness and directness of this dance give it a feeling of determination. No matter which way Ògún travels, he does so with a sense of pressing urgency and self-confidence.

In both dances, Ògún is forceful. In the first, restraint combined with bursts of energy evokes both force and quietude and conveys a sense of caution.

FIGURE 9.9. Back view of a medium possessed by Ògún, carrying an iron blade in her left hand. Her shoulder blades pop out forcefully in rhythm to the lead drum. Igbogila, Nigeria, 1978.

FIGURE 9.10. Carrying iron blades in the left and a carved miniature dane gun in the right, "Ògún" (foreground) bursts forth in a crouching position—held for an instant in a very deliberate fashion—in a step that evokes stalking. Igbogila, Nigeria, 1978.

In the second, he is the epitome of Ògún as a driving force. Pursuing a direct path quickly with long, low strides, he is "courageous like the road," as his praise name recalls.

A third and final dance, the àgèrè, can be performed both for Ògún and for Eyinlè, who is also found widely throughout Yorubaland.[21] The name refers at once to the dance and to a traditional hunter's drum (Abraham 1958:30), even though any one of a number of different drums can play the àgèrè rhythm and accompany the dance. Àgèrè can be performed anytime either Ògún or Eyinlè is honored. For example, it can be performed by the hunter/warrior association during rituals at the shrine of Ògún Ilu, also known as Ògún Àjobo, that is, the Ògún for the Town, or the Ògún Everybody Worships Together;[22] by priests of other deities, like Şàngó, during rituals in which Eyinlè is invoked; and by certain masquerades known as Eléyinlè (Owners of Eyinlè), who dance during Egúngún "performances of miracles" (ap'idán) (cf. Drewal and Drewal 1978:34–35, pl. 15). While the first two dances are fairly localized within western Yoruba groups influenced by the Ọhọri, the àgèrè Ògún appears to be more widespread, often associated with Ọyọ-derived institutions, although this may be the result of a historical melding of traditions from different regions.

The àgèrè has a quality distinct from the others. Its rhythm is rolling: one foot essentially remains in place while alternately the other foot shifts backward and forward and backward and forward—each time assuming full body weight. After the second forward step, the moving leg then becomes the stationary one so that the sequence is repeated on the other side. If the dance progresses at all, it does not travel far. This dance in different contexts is performed with varying degrees of energy. Female caretakers of Eyinlè shrines, who are not necessarily mediums, dance it very gently with small, easy steps, whereas Ògún mediums in possession trance perform it powerfully with large leg gestures so that, instead of a rolling feeling, it jumps. Quickness and forcefulness in combination once again speak of Ògún's innate power.

As mediums begin to tire from being "ridden" by Ògún, an attendant stretches out their arms over their heads (fig. 9.11). When Ògún finally leaves the female medium's head, he withdraws suddenly. Her body tenses all over (fig. 9.12) and, if near a spectator, she grabs hold tightly. Attendants must be ready to catch the medium and help her to the sidelines to be seated, or the medium will have a difficult time coming out of the trance state. With the attendants' aid, the medium leaves the performance space, and a number of measures are taken to clear her head and return her to normalcy. Attendants pour gin over the medium's head and rub it in to revive and alert the inner head; they blow into the ears and onto the top of the head (fig. 9.13), press the base of the neck, press their foreheads against the medium's forehead, stretch the medium's arms upward and then place them on the knees, and pull the legs forward by the big toes, all the while calling the medium's special name bestowed at initiation.

The medium revives as if from a deep sleep and sits quietly gazing into space.

Dancing for Ògún in Bahia[23]

In Bahia, initiates of Candomblé go through a ritual death and rebirth (Herskovits and Herskovits 1942a:10 and 1942b:273). They are secluded for three to twelve months; their clothes are taken away, never to be worn again, and their heads are shaved (Pierson 1942:286–87); they are innoculated on their heads with sacred cuts to infuse them with the vital force of their deity (Herskovits 1943:501); the head is further washed regularly in a solution of leaves and other natural ingredients to attract and stimulate the vital force of the deity (Verger 1955); and the initiates are given new names (Herskovits 1943:501; Verger 1954:337). During this time, the devotees learn, among other things, the songs and dances of their particular deity. This spiritual retreat serves to dedicate the devotees to their deities and to prepare them for receiving the vital force of their god through possession trance (Omari 1984:23) (fig. 9.14).

Among the Ketu and Nago Candomblé houses, danced ceremonies known as *obrigação* begin publicly as the "daughters of the gods" enter the *barração*, the ceremonial house, accompanied musically by the drummers.[24] Holding their two fists together in a manner in which one holds a horse's reigns while riding, the daughters enter single file to a rapid cadence with small cantorlike steps, the *mae de santo* (literally, "mother of the saint," the female head of Candomblé) in the lead.[25] The entrance is said to represent a horse and to serve the purpose of dispatching Exu, god of the crossroads, for Exu is "a messenger boy" (*menino de recado*) between men and the gods. The horse is a symbol of mediation, a symbol which recurs in possession trance when the mediums are said to be literally the "horses" of the gods.

With tiny, quick steps, the devotees circle counterclockwise and, as the *mae de santo* reaches the spot closest to the front door, she raises her arms toward it and, crossing her two index fingers at a right angle, makes the sign of the crossroads, the metaphorical intersection between the world and the spirit realm. Twice more, she steps back, whirls around quickly, and gestures toward the door, crossing her index fingers to open the ritual, that is, to mark the time and place to begin spiritual communication.

When the devotees have formed their circle, they invoke the gods with three chants each, beginning with Ogun. This segment of the ritual is known as a *xire*, the same as the Yoruba word *şiré*, indicating "a play" or "an entertainment" for the gods, for it is the purpose of this portion of the ceremony to coax the gods from their otherworldly domain into the phenomenal world. The *mae de santo* sings in Yoruba, *A xire Ogun o! A xire Ogun!* "We play for Ogun oh! We play for Ogun!" The devotees join in the chant and dance. Led by the *mae de santo* and accompanied by the drums, the devotees honor

FIGURE 9.11. As a medium begins to tire from being "ridden" by Ògún, an attendant stretches her arms and torso. The medium carries iron pincers. Woman in background, left, carries iron gongs and Ògún sword. Ẹgua, Nigeria, 1978.

FIGURE 9.12. When Ògún finally leaves the head of the medium, he withdraws suddenly. Her body tenses all over as attendants hold her tightly. Igbogila, Nigeria, 1978.

FIGURE 9.13. A man leans over to blow on top of an Ògún medium's head to clear it as attendants support her. Igbogila, Nigeria, 1978.

FIGURE 9.14. The "coming out" (*saida*) of a newly initiated medium. Ipitanga, Bahia, Brazil, 1974.

and invoke the gods one by one.[26] After Ogun comes Oxossi, god of the hunt; Osanyin, god of herbalism; Omolu, god of disease; Nana, goddess of deep water; Oxumare, goddess of the rainbow; Yewa, goddess of water; Yemanja, goddess of the salt water; Oxun, goddess of fresh surface water; Yansan, goddess of wind and war; Xango, god of thunder and lightning; and Oxala, god of creativity.

When the devotees have finished invoking the gods, the *mae de santo* starts again and this time the devotees begin to fall into a trance. They kick off their shoes, and they begin to quiver. Their upper torsos and heads drop forward, and their chests rock back and forth rapidly in short, sharp motions. Sometimes a devotee may become instantly possessed, as if suddenly struck with the full force of the deity. This is visibly communicated by an unexpected burst of energy from the devotee which seems to thrust her out into space, body rigid, and which sends attendants scrambling to keep her from falling or landing on other participants. Attendants adjust the possessed's cloth by tying it tightly around her breasts, in the case of female deities like Yansan, Oxun, and Yemanja, or, in the case of males, either over the left shoulder or over both shoulders, crisscrossing on the chest (Omari 1984:22); they also assist the "horses" until they have regained control and are transformed into the deity. Fully possessed, the mediums prostrate themselves before the drummers and the *mae de santo* and, as the manifestation of the deity, greet the spectators. In trance the possessed mediums stand with hands either on their hips or folded behind their backs. After dancing to a song associated with the deity, the possessed mediums are led out of the dance enclosure. The particular god honored at any given ceremony determines which other gods will "visit"; thus, if Xango is honored, his wives—Oxun and Yansan— are likely to visit and, if Omolu is honored, chances are his mother, Nana, will make an appearance.[27]

A break in the ceremony occurs while attendants prepare the mediums in the clothes of the deities. When ready, the deities form a single line led by the *mae de santo*. In the ceremonies in which Ogun visits, he always comes first. A slow processional song is played by the drummers as the *mae de santo* sings,

> *Ago, ago l'ona.*
>
> Make way, clear the way.

The line of deities enters slowly. As the Herskovits's (1942b:277) recall, "First comes the god of war, in green, wearing as a male deity, lace-edged pantalettes, a short wide skirt over them, dagger in hand, a sash about the waist tied in a wide bow, a brilliant cap as of a prince in an Arabian Nights tale."

The dances which characterize Ogun, in contrast to those performed in western Yorubaland, are mimetic. They act out in a stylized way Ogun fighting with his cutlass. Crucial to this mime, however, are the dynamics of

Ogun's actions, and indeed this is what seems to capture the imagination of observers. Thus:

> The outward manifestations of the ecstasy of the children of Ogun, god of war, are much more forceful than those of the children of Oxun, goddess of fresh water. The former have something of the brutality of armies in battle, some of the hardness of steel, while the latter have a liquid, amorous quality— the fascinating sensuality of lazy rivers or still lakes sprinkled with sunlight. (Bastide 1978:377)

Whether or not Ogun carries a scythe or a sword:

> He brandishes it with eyes closed, slashing about wildly on all sides in his dancing. Sometimes, in a thrilling mock duel, he will fence with an agile devotee who has nothing but her bare arms to use as weapons. Such a brave daughter will be rescued from him, just in time to prevent injury, by being drawn away from the fray by several alert *ekedes* [assistants]. (Leahy 1955:9)

This dance, reflecting the nature of Ogun's vital power, is quick and direct with an explosive thrust.[28] As Ogun, the medium slashes, but does not do so "wildly on all sides." Inclining his body toward a diagonal, he takes two large steps, closes his feet to change to the opposite diagonal, and repeats the pattern in the opposite direction. While his stepping carries him back and forth diagonally forward, his bent arms, which carry metal blades (*espada*), slash powerfully in opposition up and down in the direction of the diagonally inclined torso and in time to the quick paces of his feet. As one *mae de santo* (Olga do Alaketu, 1974) explained: "He eats raw [food] and doesn't throw anything away; he kills, eats, and doesn't throw anything away, doesn't repent for what he has done" (*Ele come cru e não lança; ele mata, come e não lança, não se arrepende do que faz*).[29] Ogun moves between the seated audience and the drums, and, when reaching one or the other, spins around forcefully and returns in the opposite direction. Olga do Alaketu called this dance *pada Ogun* (1974), perhaps "Ògún's return" (Abraham 1958:539).

There is a popular story in Yorubaland about how Ogun sank into the ground alive leaving a long chain emanating from the spot and instructing his people that, if they ever needed him to defend them, they should pull on the chain that he left anchored in the earth. To test Ogun's allegiance, one day a citizen tugged on the chain, and Ogun came out slashing with his cutlass, in the process decapitating his own townspeople. Realizing what he had done, he vowed never to return. The *pada* Ogun of Brazil may relate to this well-known Yoruba motif of Ogun's absolute aggression, for it is said to represent gestures of war (*gestos dos guerreiras*).

Another of Ogun's mimes is similar to dances for other "hot" or dueling deities, such as Xango and Oxossi, called *ecu* (Pierson 1942:304). Two people face each other: two Oguns, or Ogun and another "hot" deity or other participant. Slightly shifting the right foot backward in four counts while pivoting on the left, and then repeating on the other side, each dancer prepares for a mock duel. Then, the dancers shift their bodies slightly from side to side alternately kicking the feet backward. All the while facing each other, they thrust their cutlasses, carried in the right hand, back and forth laterally, cutting across the left wrist in a rapid cadence in time to the music.

Sometimes the preparatory steps described above can be used to lower the knees to the ground to a seated position. From that position, sitting on their knees, the dancers move their torsos in a circular direction so that, at its farthest extent backward, they are practically lying horizontally on the ground. After circling one way and then the other, the dancers slowly work their way back to a full standing position in the same fashion as they descended. Such dances express Ogun's identity as a warrior.

It is perhaps significant in the Brazilian context, where the Yoruba language is no longer well understood, that the dances are mimetic, representing Ogun in a literal way. With the possible exception of a few elders, devotees are unable to give translations of Yoruba-derived songs; rather, they prefer to explain the dances which accompany the songs (M. and F. Herskovits 1942a:12; Binon 1967:165). In the Bahian context, where the oral liturgy is only vaguely understood by its users, dance can define and characterize the deity in a more precise way than the oral texts. Thus in addition to stressing *how* Ogun operates, that is, his dynamic qualities, the dances in Bahia become more literal by miming precisely *what* Ogun does.

Bastide felt that "Ogun's persona as a brutal and aggressive warrior and beheader . . . won out" over that of hunter, blacksmith, or farmer in Brazil, where he has become more widely known as the patron deity of slave revolt (1978:254). Indeed, warrior plays and dances are traditionally popular in Brazil, where they have become odd mixtures of elements from the *cucumbys,* the *congos*, and the *quilombo*—mystery plays patterned after the Portuguese *autos* (Portuguese mystery plays)—which usually depicted battles between two opposing groups (Ramos 1939:111). An 1888 illustration (fig. 9.15) in a book by Mello Moraes Filho shows a group of Os Congos performing a war dance which appears to be quite similar to the mock battle in which Ogun mediums engage. Moraes Filho states,

> In transit, following a religious litter, a struggle ensues between the two lines of blacks, that were in dispute, defending themselves, ...
> And, fighting each other with iron swords, making complete turns and cadencing the flanks, the *Congos* advancing in procession, singing, in heat of battle, in bitterly contested combat:
>
> *Fire on the earth,*
> *Fire in the sea,*
> *That our queen*
> *Us has to help! . . .*
> (Moraes Filho 1888:95)

FIGURE 9.15. A nineteenth-century illustration shows
Brazilian Os Congos dancers performing a war dance
similar to the mock battles staged by Ogun mediums.
Adapted from Mello Moraes Filho (1888).

As in performances of the *congos* and *quilombos*, Ogun engages in mock combat in which two people face each other wielding swords. Ogun dances, as well as *quilombos* performances, symbolize slave revolt (Ramos 1939:110; Bastide 1978:254). Since these mystery plays tended to be mimetic and preceded the Candomblé by nearly a century, it is quite possible that Os Congos, *cucumbys*, and/or *quilombo* war dances were appropriately grafted onto the Yoruba war deity Ogun.[30] Further evidence for this suggestion lies in the Portuguese-inspired costumes worn by the possessed mediums. Like the older Os Congos' costumes, the vestments of Ogun, as well as other male deities, consist of a long tunic, belted by a wide sash, over full-legged pantalettes.

By the same token, the *àgèrè* dance, which is associated with hunters and is performed to honor Ògún and Eyinlè in Yorubaland, appears to have been incorporated into the repertoire of dances for hunting deities Oxossi and Yansan in Bahia. In Bahia, Inle (Eyinlè) represents an aspect or quality of Oxossi (*qualidade*).[31] Thus, as Bastide (1978:254) suggests, Ogun's persona as hunter seems to have dropped out in favor of his persona as warrior, or rather seems to have been usurped by Oxossi, who in Yorubaland is also traditionally a hunting deity.

Ògún in Western Yorubaland and Brazil: A Comparison

There are marked similarities between ritual performances for Ògún in Igbogila, Nigeria, and in Bahia, Brazil. Like those in Igbogila, cult groups or Candomblés in Bahia honor diverse Yoruba deities collectively during a single ceremony. The rites of initiation are similar too, including symbolic death and rebirth, seclusion, and practices of taking away the clothes, bestowing new names, shaving and bathing the head, and embedding medicines to stimulate possession trance. After honoring Ẹlẹ́gba, both groups dance in a counterclockwise circle to invoke each of the deities in sequence with a minimum of three songs each. In addition to Ẹlẹ́gba, other deities represented in the cult group of Igbogila which are also found in Bahia are Iroko, Omolu, and of course Ògún. Inle, the Bahian version of the Yoruba deity Eyinlè, is considered a manifestation of Oxossi—both are associated with hunting. In Yorubaland and in the more traditional cult houses of Bahia, Ògún is always invoked first after Ẹlẹ́gba, and explanations for his coming first are much the same: he "opens the way."

Devotees of Ògún in both places carry instruments symbolically associated with the deity. The sword is more common in Brazil, but in Nigeria Ògún mediums also carry iron pincers, spades, flywhisks, or miniature guns. Although Ògún is acknowledged in Brazil to be the god of iron, the cutlasses carried by the possessed mediums are made of laminated chrome, as are many of the ritual instruments of Candomblé which require metal. Emphasis on the left in the context of possession trance is not as evident in Brazil as in Yorubaland. Yet, Pierson (1942:289) notes that, when a deity wishes to take leave of the ceremony, he clasps left hands with another participant tightly.

The style of the onset of possession trance is quite similar, including the practice of greeting members of the audience individually, keeping the hands on the hips, and exaggerated stepping. In Brazil as in western Yorubaland the possessed devotees are called the horses of the gods.

A further comparison may be made in the marked distinction between dance which serves to invoke spiritual forces and dance which follows the invocation and represents the materialized force itself. Both in Yoruba country and in Brazil the distinction is made in terms of dynamics. In Bahia, when devotees invoke the deities at the beginning of the performance, gestures are minimalized. Rather than portraying the deities fully, they merely give an indication of the movements which represent them. Thus Ògún's large, forceful movements are reduced to small, vague, effortless gestures. In a subtle way, index fingers that serve as cutlasses offer a gross understatement of underlying warlike intent. This minimalization of movement conserves energy for the long service which culminates in possession trance, when the deities are given full expression. For as the horses of the deities, the devotees are ridden hard. Nonetheless, the marked difference between dances performed as invocations and as actual possession serves to concentrate energy in the part of the dance which actualizes the deity.

The important point here is that the dances, however understated, were nevertheless performed. Like liturgical texts, the import of which is not always fully understood by listeners, their significance lies in their actual performance. Whether or not the dances are literally understood, the performance is thought to carry power. What is vital, then, is the actual effort—the verbal and kinetic exertions which, when minimally stated, invoke metaphysical forces but, when fully asserted, activate and even embody those forces. Both in Brazil and in western Yorubaland, the dances which manifest Ògún indeed reinforce the verbal images of him in myths and praise poetry. They show him to exert explosive force—powerful, quick, and direct.

Conclusions

Because dance and oral performance express, and are even thought to conduct, spiritual force, an analysis of the use of dynamics in ritual is essential to our understanding of the total religious framework of the Yoruba; it allows us to perceive the gods as power personified, each embodying a particular locus of dynamic qualities which remain coherent and consistent no matter the context. By focussing on *how* deities act (the qualities of their actions) as distinguished from *what* they do (the acts themselves) it is possible to resolve apparent contradictions in their personalities. We can go beyond the creative/destructive dichotomy and examine the wellspring of power that underlies both creation and destruction: Òguń's *àṣẹ*. The dynamic configurations expressed in Òguń's dances and verbal arts serve as models of and for humans so that, as Bartenieff (1980) puts it, they may cope with the environment. Through ritual performance, people tap and use power that is appropriate for meeting life's demands.

NOTES

1. The data for this paper were gathered during fieldwork in Nigeria in 1975, 1977–78, and 1982 and in Bahia, Brazil, during the summer of 1974. The 1982 research trip was sponsored by the National Endowment for the Humanities (RO-20072–81–2184). I wish to thank in particular the *Olórìṣà* of Igbogila, Nigeria, for welcoming me at their rituals. I am also indebted to Joçelina Françisca Barbosa of Ile Olga do Alaketu, Matatu, Salvador, for teaching me the Candomblé dances for the deities, and Olga do Alaketu and Antonio Agnelo Pereira, Elemaso, Ile Caṣa Branca, Salvador, for discussing Candomblé ritual and dance with me. Special thanks also go to Juana and Didi dos Santos and to Pierre Verger for many courtesies during my stay in Bahia. I also wish to thank Rowland Abiodun for reading and commenting on this paper and Henry John Drewal, who assisted in all phases of this project.

2. In Yoruba thought, the phenomenal world is *ayé*, usually translated simply as world. *Ayé* is a domain where people reside temporarily. In addition it includes a number of spirits who can become manifest in human or animal form. The realm of the gods and ancestors is known as *òrun*, a permanent otherworldly reality. The relationship of *ayé* to *òrun* is expressed in the proverb "The world is a market, the otherworld is home" (*Ayé l'ọjà, òrun n'ilé*).

3. Egúngún refers to masquerades which honor the ancestors in Yorubaland and also to the society which produces them. Cloaked in cloth and embellished with other items such as carved masks, bones of animals, or feathers, they are thought to be spirits manifest in the world (*ayé*).

4. *Kùtùkùtù* means "early in the morning" and, in this context, also evokes the quality of the rain. It conveys the dynamic of just beginning something; it implies an initiating action which has not yet reached its full potential (personal communication, Rowland Abiodun, 1982).

5. Rudolph Laban's theories of effort are based on similar kinds of observations. Thus, "the weighty power of a rock with its visible potential for impact speaks of the tremendous impetus with which it might plunge into the valley as an avalanche. The grace of a plant speaks of the readiness to move which drives a flower out of its stem from which fruit and new seed will sprout. . . . Animal movement speaks of the fine adaptations with which a particular species has immersed itself into its surroundings to fit increasingly finer, more differentially into the workings of nature" (Laban cited in Bartinieff 1980:1).

6. For the most elaborate discussions of *àṣẹ*, see Verger (1964), dos Santos (1976), and M. and H. Drewal (1987).

7. For a discussion of behavior as it relates to concepts of inner power, see H. Drewal (1977).

8. Informants say this snake is the Black Mamba; however, Abraham (1958:153) points out that "the Spitting Cobra (Blacknecked Cobra) is often wrongly called the

Black Mamba." Indeed, salmon-pink and black cross-bars, according to Abraham, usually alternate on the underpart of the Spitting Cobra's neck and front part of its body.

9. Utterances express attitudes toward time, space, weight, and flow audibly through the combination of: 1) speed of sounds or syllables, 2) their degree of directness—whether they are voiced in a straightforward manner or are gliding, 3) their vocal force or thrust, and 4) their flow—whether the stream of energy is free-flowing or bound, held back, or restrained.

10. In analyzing movement and its corollary oral expression, I follow Laban and Lawrence, who identified four factors which, in varying degrees, combine to produce effort or dynamic qualities: exertion (from light to strong), control (from fluent to bound), time (from slow to quick), and space (indirect or direct). In the authors' view: "A person's efforts are visibly expressed in the rhythms of his bodily motion. It thus becomes necessary to study these rhythms, and to extract from them those elements which will help us to compile a systematic survey of the forms effort can take in human action" (1947:xi).

11. However, I have followed the practice of the Department of African Languages and Literatures at Ọbafemi Awolowo University (see, for example, Oyelaran 1976–77).

12. Candomblés are Afro-Brazilian cult groups organized for the worship of African deities, primarily those of the Yoruba (see Omari 1984).

13. The right hand sometimes carries percussion instruments shaken initially to invoke the god and ultimately to pronounce àṣẹ, àṣẹ, àṣẹ, "so be it," in response to prayers. As one participant in traditional Yoruba religion noted, "When townspeople hear the bells and gongs of the priest performing ceremonies inside his shrine, they will be saying in their homes as they are working, 'àṣẹ, àṣẹ, àṣẹ' to accompany the ringing in support of whatever the priest is saying." Lending efficacy to prayers and invocations, the sound of the bells helps to induce possession trance and later in the ceremony to enforce the words of the gods, spoken through the mediumship of the priest.

14. Ògbóni is a society of elders which functions as a governing body together with the king. For more information on Ògbóni, see Morton-Williams (1960) and H. Drewal (in press).

15. Ọjẹ̀ is the name given to members of the Egúngún society.

16. This holds true in the United States among practitioners of Yoruba religion who were originally trained by Cubans (Edwards and Mason 1985:iii). Thus, at sacred ritual parties (*bembe*) for Yoruba deities in the New York metropolitan area, drummers begin by saluting Ẹlẹ́gba first and then Ògúṅ. For an American practitioner's perspective on Ògúṅ, see Edwards and Mason's booklet (1985:16–20), written primarily for English-speaking initiates of Yoruba religion.

17. The cult is found in an Ẹgbádò town, but it originated among the Ọhọrí Yoruba. Thus devotees sing and pray in the Ọhọrí dialect. The Ọhọrí Yoruba live on the border between Nigeria and Benin (R.P.B.) in the area of the Kumi swamp. Because of their relative inaccessibility during the rainy season, they are considered by their neighbors to be among the most conservative Yoruba. Their dialect is quite distinct. The members of this cult group indicate that their practices had earlier roots among the Gùn (Ègùn), an Àjà-speaking people of southern Benin (R.P.B.). The deity Omolu is said to have come from Gun country and, indeed, one of Omolu's dances is called *ègùn Omolú*, meaning the Omolu of the Ègùn people, who, according to cult members, are from Àjàṣẹ́ (Porto Novo).

18. Although Ògúṅ is the dominant deity in this cult group, any medium can join, and thus conceivably any deity can be included. Other deities represented within the

group are Ṣàngó and Ọya, whose priests are no longer possessed, because they have grown too old and feeble to perform.

19. For another ceremony which features the deity Ondo, see M. Drewal (1975).

20. Western physicians refer to this movement as "winging of the scapulae," which implies a neurological disorder and a lack of control. However, these movements performed in western Yorubaland, quite to the contrary, are superbly controlled. Not only can they be performed with a wide range of dynamics, but they also can be intentionally varied rhythmically.

21. For more details on the deity Eyinlẹ (Erinlẹ), see Thompson (1969) and Babalọla (chapter 7).

22. One of the association's titleholders, Aṣípa, holds a position on the king's council of chiefs. The society was probably at its peak during the nineteenth century, when during the Yoruba civil wars hunters became warriors to defend the town.

23. The analysis of Candomblé dance comes from observations of 14 ceremonies in 6 different houses during 1974. For consistency, the English spelling of Ògún is used throughout, without tone marks.

24. *Obrigação* are analogous to *bembe* in the Cuban Lucumi, or Santeria, tradition, which are now held in the United States by Hispanic peoples as well as both black and white Americans.

25. Saint here is a euphemism for an African deity. In Brazil, Catholic saints have been syncretized with African deities. To a large extent, this occurred to mask Candomblé during a time of religious repression (Omari 1984:14).

26. For a discussion of the role of the drums and drummers in Candomblé, see Herskovits (1944).

27. This is also the case in Afro-American *bembe*, sacred parties held for the Yoruba deities.

28. Tempo is one of the factors that make up dynamic qualities thereby helping to characterize the vital force of deities. Behague notes in his examinations of Candomblé songs that "the idiosyncrasies attributed to a given orixa (whether young or old, temperamental or peaceful, and so on) influence the tempo of such songs" (1975:75). As in the Old World, the song determines the drum music, which in turn sets the pace of the dances.

29. Lépine (1981:23) presents some personality traits that are common to Ogun mediums, suggesting at the same time that after initiation they become more like the deity. It seems clear that one's personal deity licenses the expression of certain distinctive personality traits associated with that deity. And dance is one of the mechanisms through which Ogun power is expressed and felt.

30. According to Pereira da Costa (cited in Ramos 1939:106), the earliest documented date of a Congos or Cucumbys is June 24, 1706. This is found in a document belonging to a religious association in the town of Iguarassu in Pernambuco; whereas, Carneiro (1954:48) calculates a date of circa 1830 as the foundation of Candomblé. Furthermore, Ramos says of the *quilombos* of Palmares, formerly a community of runaway slaves who banned together in collective resistance, that their plays recall "the opposing camps, the dances, chants, struggles ending in capture, intrigues and trickery and finally the siege of the Negro position and with its fall, the reenslavement. . . . When the queen is introduced into the plot, there seems to be a close relationship between these plays which I have called *quilombos* and the Congo plays" (1939:110). Moreover, in a revised reprint of Moraes Filho's 1888 work, Câmara Cascudo observes (1979:72, n.28) that the performance of Os Congos is very similar in detail to that of "os 'Mouriscos'" (Moors) associated with processions on São João's Day in Portugal. Such warrior dances involving battles with swords as part of Catholic processions, he suggests, can be traced to fifteenth-century Europe.

31. These shifts in emphasis and fusions in Brazil reflect the need to systematize deities from diverse locations in Yorubaland who have similar attributes in order to show how they actually are integral parts of one unified system.

REFERENCES CITED

Abraham, R. C. 1958. *Dictionary of Modern Yoruba*, London: University of London Press.

Ayoade, J. A. A. 1979. "The Concept of Inner Essence in Yoruba Traditional Medicine," in *African Therapeutic Systems*. Z. A. Ademuwagun, J. A. A. Ayoade, I. E. Harrison, and D. M. Warren (eds.), Waltham, Mass.: Crossroads Press, pp. 49–55.

Babalola, S. A. 1966. *The Content and Form of Yoruba Ìjálá*, London: Oxford University Press.

Barnes, Sandra T. 1980. *Ogun: An Old God for a New Age*, Philadelphia: ISHI.

Bartenieff, Irmgard, with D. Lewis. 1980. *Body Movement: Coping With the Environment*, N.Y.: Gordon and Breach, Science Publishers, Inc.

Bastide, Roger. 1978. *The African Religions of Brazil: Toward a Sociology of the Interpenetration of Civilizations* (Helen Sebba, trans.), Baltimore: The Johns Hopkins University Press.

Behague, Gerhard H. 1975. "Notes on Regional and National Trends in Afro-Brazilian Cult Music," in *Tradition and Renewal: Essays on 20th-Century Latin American Literature and Culture*. M. H. Forster (ed.), Urbana: University of Illinois Press, pp. 68–80.

Beier, Ulli. 1970. *Yoruba Poetry*, Cambridge: Cambridge University Press.

Binon, Giselle. 1967. "La Musique dans le Candomblé," in *La Musique dan la Vie*, Tome 1. T. Nikiprowetzky (ed.), Paris: pp. 159–207.

Carneiro, Edison. 1954. *Candomblés da Bahia*, Rio de Janeiro: Editorial Andes (2nd ed. revd.).

Crowther, Samuel. 1852. *A Vocabulary of the Yoruba Language*, London: Seeleys.

do Alaketu, Olga, Mae de Santo. 1974. Interview, Matatu, Salvador, Bahia, August 17.

dos Santos, Juana E. 1976. *Os Nago e a Morte: Pade, Asese e o Culto Egun na Bahia*, Petropolis: Editora Vozes.

Drewal, Henry J. 1974. "Efe: Voiced Power and Pageantry," *African Arts* 7(2):26–29, 58–66.

———. 1977. "Art and the Perception of Women in Yoruba Culture," *Cahiers d'Etudes Africaines* 68(37–4):545–67.

———. In press. "Meaning in Oshugbo Art among Ijebu Yoruba," in *Festschrift*, Ethnologisches Seminar, B. Engelbrecht and R. Gardi, (eds.), Basel: Universität Basel.

Drewal, Henry J., and Margaret T. 1983. *Gẹlẹdẹ: Art and Female Power among the Yoruba*, Bloomington: Indiana University Press.

Drewal, Margaret T. 1975. "Symbols of Possession: A Study of Movement and Regalia in an Anago-Yoruba Ceremony," *Dance Research Journal* 7(2):15–24.

———. 1986. "Art and Trance among Yoruba Shango Devotees," *African Arts* 20(1):60–67, 98–99.

Drewal, Margaret T., and Henry J. 1978. "More Powerful Than Each Other: An Egbado Classification of Egungun," *African Arts* 11(3):28–39, 98–99.

———. 1987. "Composing Time and Space in Yoruba Art," *Word and Image* 3, 4.

Edwards, Gary, and John Mason. 1985. *Black Gods—Orişa Studies in the New World*, Brooklyn: Yoruba Theological Archministry.

Herskovits, Melville J. 1943. "The Southernmost Outpost of New World Africanisms," *American Anthropologist* 45(4):495–510.

———. 1944. "Drums and Drummers in Afro-Brazilian Cult Life," *The Musical Quarterly* 30(4):477–92.

Herskovits, Melville, and Francis Herskovits. 1942a. "Afro-Bahian Religious Songs," (Album XIII Notes), *Folk Music of Brazil* issued from the Collections of the Archive of American Folk Song, Library of Congress Music Division.

———. 1942b. "The Negros of Brazil," *The Yale Review* 32(2):263–79.

Hertz, R. 1973. "The Pre-eminence of the Right Hand: A Study in Religious Polarity," in *Right and Left: Essays on Dual Symbolic Classification*, R. Needham (ed.), Chicago: University of Chicago Press, pp. 3–31.

Laban, Rudolph, and F. C. Lawrence. 1947. *Effort*, London: Macdonald & Evans.

Langer, Suzanne K. 1953. *Feeling and Form: A Theory of Art*, New York: Charles Scribner's and Sons.

Leahy, J. G. 1955. "The Presence of the Gods among the Mortals: The Candomblé Dances," *Brazil* 29(4):4–11.

Lépine, Claude. 1981. "Os Estereótipos da Personalidade no Candomblé *Nàgó*," in *Olóòrìṣà: Escritos sobre a religião dos orixás*, C. E. M. de Moura (coordinator and trans.), São Paulo: Editora ÁGORA, pp. 11–31.

Moraes Filho, Mello. 1888. *Festas e Tradições Populares do Brasil*. Rio de Janeiro: H. Garnier. [Reprinted in 1979 with preface by Silvio Romero and revisions and notes by Luís da Câmara Cascudo. São Paulo: Editora da Universidade de São Paulo and Livraria Itatiaia Editora.]

Morton-Williams, Peter. 1960. "The Yoruba Ogboni Cult in Oyo," *Africa* 30:362–74.

Olúpọnà, A., Aṣògún. 1975. Interview, Ibaiyun, November 13.

Omari, Mikelle Smith. 1984. *From the Inside to the Outside: The Art and Ritual of Bahian Candomblé*, Monograph Series, no. 24, Los Angeles: Museum of Cultural History, UCLA.

Oṣitola, Kolawole, Babaláwo. 1982. Interview, Ìjèbu-Òde, July.

Oyelaran, Ọlasope O. 1976–77. *Seminar Series*, no. 1 (2 vols.), Ifẹ: Department of African Languages and Literatures, University of Ifẹ.

Peek, Philip M. 1981. "The Power of Words in African Verbal Arts," *Journal of American Folklore* 94(371):19–43.

Pierson, Donald. 1942. *Negroes in Brazil: A Study of Race Contact at Bahia*, Chicago: University of Chicago Press.

Prince, Raymond. 1960. "Curse, Invocation and Mental Health among the Yoruba," *Canadian Psychiatric Association Journal* 5:65–79.

Ramos, Artur. 1939. *The Negro in Brazil*, Washington, D.C.: Associated Publishers.

Ray, Benjamin. 1973. "'Performative Utterances' in African Rituals," *History of Religions* 13(1):16–35.

Thompson, Robert F. 1969. "Abatan: A Master Potter of the Ẹgbado Yoruba" in *Tradition and Creativity in Tribal Art*, D. P. Biebuyck (ed.), Berkeley: University of California Press, pp. 120–82.

Verger, Pierre. 1954. "Rôle Joué par l'État d'Hébétude au cours de l'Initiation des Novices aux Cultes des Orisha et Vodun," *Bulletin Institut Fondamental d'Afrique Noire* 16(3–4):322–40.

———. 1955. "Bori, Première Cérémonie d'Initiation au Culte des Òrìshàs Nàgó à Bahia au Brésil," *Revista do Museu Paulista* (São Paulo), n.s., 9:269–91.

———. 1957. "Notes sur le Culte des Orisa et Vodun à Bahia, La Baie de tous les Saints au Brésil et à l'Ancienne Côte des Esclaves en Afrique," *Mémoires de l'Institut Fondamental d'Afrique Noire*, no. 51.

————. 1964. "The Yoruba High God—A Review of the Sources," Paper prepared for the Conference on The High God in Africa, Ibadan, December 14–18.

————. 1969. "Trance and Convention in Nago-Yoruba Spirit Mediumship," in *Spirit Mediumship and Society in Africa.* J. Beattie and J. Middleton (eds.), N.Y.: Africana, pp. 50–66.

————. 1976–77. "The Use of Plants in Yoruba Traditional Medicine and its Linguistic Approach," in *Seminar Series*, No. 1, Part I, Q. O. Oyelaran (ed.), Ifẹ: Department of African Languages and Literature, University of Ifẹ, pp. 242–95.

Warren, Dennis M., A. D. Buckley, and J. A. Ayandokun. 1973. *Yoruba Medicines*, Legon: The Institute of African Studies, University of Ghana.

Henry John Drewal

10

Art or Accident:
Yorùbá Body Artists and Their
Deity Ògún[1]

Yorùbá who live and work
with iron (*irin, ògún*) are also worshippers of Ògún, the god of iron. Iron
is Ògún. Ògún lives in his followers and they in him, a reciprocal relationship
which can be documented in the lives of Ògún devotees. In considering the
attributes of Ògún, iron users, and iron itself, and then in focusing upon body
artists, this essay explores the way art, tools, and techniques express the presence and impact of Ògún in Yorùbá life and thought.

The Attributes of Ògún

A cluster of traits portrays the essence or life force (*àṣẹ*) of Ògún. Among
these are physical force, hotness, quickness, directness, sensuality, firmness,
and tenacity. For some he is known as *Ògún onígboiyà*, "Ogun the brave
one" (Ògúnole 1973). Ògún's mode of operation implies no moral connotations; it is neither bad nor good, negative nor positive. It is not how he operates, but what he does, and when, that determines whether people consider
him harmful or beneficial. On one hand, Ògún's quickness or impatience can
result in hasty, careless, irrational behavior causing wanton destruction. This
dangerous side of Ògún evokes images of hot violence, vengeance, blind
rage, and indiscriminate destruction for, more than anything, Ògún is associated with bloodshed; he is "the one who is steeped in blood," *a-mọ̀-kúkú
l'ẹ̀jẹ̀* (Oluponọn 1975). One widespread tale recounts his arrival in a town

where the inhabitants offended him by what he considered to be an inhospita-
ble reception. In a blind rage, Ògún began to destroy everything. Not until
the appropriate offerings (dog, snail, oil, and soothing leaves) were made and
his praises sung did he come to his senses and realize that he was killing his
own people.[2] Thus, when he is ignored, angered, or affronted, Ògún destroys
indiscriminately. Yet, appropriate rituals can avert destruction and calm him
by turning his àṣẹ to beneficent ends.

In other circumstances, Ògún's anger may be justified. He judges and punishes liars, thieves, arrogant fools, and others viewed as antisocial:

1   Ògún a dájọ́ b'obinrin l'oyún àbòsí f'ọkọ rè.
2   Ògún a-dá-jọ́. (Fadare 1975)

1   Ògún will judge if a woman conceives without the knowledge of her
     husband [commits adultery].
2   Ògún will judge.

He acts as arbiter of human actions, especially those involving matters of deceit. As one priest explained: "If someone stole something and that person
is in a lorry, that motor will simply kill the person. . . . Ògún will kill him
there. Anytime you see something that belongs to another, you must not take
it, otherwise you will be killed by Ògún" (Oluponọn 1975). Ògún in his better
moments is firm, forthright, and, above all, honest. He is direct and straightforward in his actions, and demands the same of his followers. Truthfulness
is one of Ògún's qualities. More than anything, he hates thieves and liars,
those whom the Yorùbá would describe as going "zig-zag."[3] Thus, in the
courts of contemporary Nigeria, òrìṣà worshippers swear their oath of truthfulness by putting their lips to a piece of iron and invoking Ògún's name.

Besides punishing wrongdoers, Ògún facilitates interactions between humans and supernatural forces. Worshippers of various cults frequently assert
that Ògún is essential for the creation of any altar to otherworldly beings (ará
òrun). "Anywhere you are going to put any idol [shrine] on earth, Ògún will
first of all work there. We Yorùbá have the proverb, Ògún lo ṣálẹ f'òrìṣà dó,
meaning 'Ògún is the one who clears the place where a shrine for the gods
is established'" (Oluponọn 1975). Ògún, in this positive, creative aspect,
symbolizes order: he makes possible the worship of the supernatural forces
as much as he allows the creation and maintenance of roads, bridges, fields,
and homes, all of which are essential for the survival and well-being of
humans.

Ògún is also involved in procreation. He gives life as dramatically as he
takes it away. Ògún presides over the beginning of life and the cutting of the
umbilical cord, and he is there at the end, for "Ògún is the hoe that opens

the earth (to bury you)," *Ògún okoko yeri ogu* (Verger 1957:193). His praise poetry is often graphically sexual in nature:

1   O ṣe'pọ̀n janna bi'mọ s'ilé Ijanna.
2   A gbọ́ s'okó lùku oko èrò ọjà! (Legbe 1971)

1   He made his penis lengthen to father a child in the house of Ijanna.
2   We heard how the penis struck those in the market!

Other, more pungent images were collected by Verger (1957:177).

1   O bu rin bu rin fi ọwọ ba okó idi rẹ.
2   Boya o ti ku?
3   O ri ki okó yi wọle ko ku kiki epọn
4   Kiki epọn o di ofo.

1   He entered deeply and touched his hand to the base of his cock.
2   Perhaps it was inactive?
3   He found that his penetrating penis was active except for his testicles.
4   Except for his testicles which were emptying.

Ògún's sexual prowess may perhaps be lauded because of his links with the origins of circumcision and excision. These are recorded in a myth from Kétu and summarized here:

> God put Ògún and a woman, Olùrè, on earth but Olùrè wanted to travel there alone. She set out and came to a large tree that had fallen across the path. She returned to God (Ọlọ́run) and asked him to have Ògún cut the tree. While he was chopping the tree, Olùrè was sitting nearby with her legs apart. A piece of wood flew up and accidentally lodged in her vagina. When the path was cleared, she continued on her way but the wood caused so much pain that she returned to Ọlọ́run and Ògún and asked that it be removed. Ògún asked if she would marry him and she accepted. If he had been more patient, it would have been women who asked men to marry them. Ògún removed the piece of wood. A scar remained and this was the origin of excision. . . . Ògún had sex with Olùrè but because his sperm did not come out quickly enough, he cut the foreskin of his penis, and this was the origin of circumcision. (Verger 1957:144)

The deity, infamous for bloodshed, violence, and destruction, is at the same time famous for taming nature, sustaining culture and the worship of the gods, and facilitating the very act of creation itself. He castrates as well as circumcises.

Ògún's personality implies certain kinds of actions. Images of his speed resound in praises such as "Ògún killed them instantly [all-at-one-blow]," *Ògún pa wón bèrè kójó*. This quickness reveals his legendary impatience. The thrust of his penis, euphemistically referred to as a knife (*òbe*), is direct and forceful. Like hard, sharp, powerful, and direct blows of a flashing iron implement, Ògún's actions are judged as negative when done without reason or justification, or positive when they intentionally ensure the survival and well-being of a person or community. Ògún is like a double-edged sword: wielded with rationality it can be an efficient tool, but when out of control it can cause mayhem. Ògún's image, like his *àse*, is multidimensional. Literally on the edge between control and irrational anger, Ògún's potentiality must be activated with caution and care. Such concerns are important for all Ògún worshippers, and they are paramount for body artists.

Iron Users and Ògún

The attributes of Ògún are, in many ways, mirrored by all his followers who live and work with iron. To a large extent, this is due to certain fundamental Yorùbá beliefs and practices concerning a person's relationship with particular supernatural forces. Two primary factors govern a person's or a group's worship patterns: divination and descent. The first, divination, discloses the forces, natural and supernatural, affecting individuals and prescribes appropriate ritual actions, including the honoring of particular divinities or ancestors. The second, inheritance, is perhaps the more common means of acquiring a god, for the Yorùbá believe that one's right, authority, and obligation to honor a particular divinity are transmitted through the blood's life force from generation to generation. Individuals explain this by saying, "It is in our life blood from the founder; it is our foundation." It is therefore assumed that anyone born into the lineage has an inherent spiritual affinity with a particular deity or group of deities. By extension, such innate affinity means that the person may exhibit some of the same propensities or capacities as the god.[4] In addition, individuals within the lineage are believed to share certain personality traits, which are often described in the lineage praise poems (*oríkì*) (see Babalola 1967) and which may derive ultimately from lineage divinities. This same logic applies to professions presided over by different divinities; Òrúnmìlà for diviners, Òsanyìn for healers, Olókun for beadworkers, or Ògún for ironworkers, for these, like worship patterns, are generally inherited. As the Yorùbá say, *Òwú ti baba ba gbòn ni omo fi o rán*, "The cotton carded by the father will surely be sewn by the children" (Olabisi 1975:23). As a group, ironworkers partake of an Ògún ethos.

Within this broad group, however, are a number of "branches" of Ògún, each with its own special concerns which arise from the nature of its iron-related activity. Carroll (1967:79) notes some of these branches and the implements which are their symbols: (1) Ògún Onìré, (2) ògún of the house (knife), (3) ògún of the farm (hoe), (4) ògún of the hunters (gun), (5) ògún of the carvers (tools), (6) ògún of the blacksmith (anvil), (7) ògún of the face-mark cutter (knives), (8) ògún of the torrent (outdoor shrine of Ògún), and (9) ògún of the lorry-driver (truck).[5]

The various branches within the Ògún complex fall into three broad groups depending upon where and how iron implements are used. They are in the realm of the forest, within the borderland between the bush and the community (the farms), and at the center of culture, that is, the bustling towns and markets. In the first group are the hunters, warriors, and palm-wine tappers, whose iron implements are varied: spears, guns, arrows, swords, spiked clubs (orukùmò), chained club (gaman), and knives, cutlasses, and axes. In the second group are the farmers, whose cutlasses, axes, and hoes first clear the bush and till the earth, and the ironworkers, who mine and smelt with their picks, shovels, prongs, pokers, hooks, prickers, and hammers. In the third group are the blacksmiths, with their hammers, anvils, pokers, tongs, and shears, who fashion all manner of utilitarian implements as well as exquisite sculpture in iron for the cults of Ògún, Ifá, Òsanyìn, Eyinlẹ, Ọṣọọ̀sì, and Òrìṣà Oko; the wood-carvers, with their axes, adzes, and knives; the barbers, with their razors; and the body artists or olóòlà (literally, "those who make marks [in human flesh]"), with their delicate blades. All are engaged in work which, both dangerous and physically demanding, requires courage and strength—attributes dominant in Ògún's imagery. Yet artists need more. They also need skills such as the ability for finesse, concentration, control, and especially dexterity. The Yorùbá define an artist (oníṣọna) as one who is a "skilled designer" (cf. Abraham 1958:522). The term oníṣọnà consists of oníṣẹ́ ọnà, "one-who-controls/presides-over-the-creation-of-art." Art ọnà, for the Yorùbá, encompasses notions of nonfunctional elaboration and enhancement of a thing (like embroidery on cloth) and craftsmanship (H. Drewal 1980:9). Nowhere is such skill more important than in the work of body artists, for they cut lines in human flesh.

The Nature of Iron and Iron Tools

Generations of Yorùbá ironworkers and users have forged a complex body of knowledge about iron, about its potential as well as its dangers, and about its properties, both physical and spiritual (see Bellamy 1904; Adéníji and Armstrong 1977). The nature of iron as a substance recalls the nature of Ògún and those who work with iron.

Iron possesses a number of inherent qualities that set it apart from other substances. Probably its most dramatic characteristic is its ability to undergo

striking transformations. It has a capacity to possess radically different properties while still maintaining its "iron-ness." As the ore responds to the intense heat of the smelter, the iron locked within it begins to emerge. During
the process of separation and purification, the metal begins to glow. It is an
intensely hot, reddish, and unstable substance that can become liquid as
quickly and dramatically as it can become white, hard, cold, and unyielding.
These changes are evocative of Ògún himself. Later, heat, hammering, and
cool water alter the metal's temper, producing objects of strikingly different
characteristics. They range from being as brittle as glass to being as pliable
as fresh wood. This dramatic capacity to undergo radical changes in tem-
perature, color, and temper constitutes iron's essence. This is its inherent
potential.

Tools fashioned and used by humans further define the inherent physical
qualities of iron. The attributes of tools and the manner in which they are
handled convey an image of overt physical force. In general, it is men who
wield instruments of iron.[6] The domain of iron is the domain of men and elaborate prohibitions prevent the intrusion of women at various stages in the
ironworking process (Adéníji and Armstrong 1977:41–43). Making and using
iron implements require actions which are direct, quick, and strong, and this
is evident in the form of the objects themselves.

Many iron tools, despite diversity in form and function, have in common
a sharp edge designed to penetrate cleanly and directly in order to accomplish
a task efficiently. For example, spears or arrows pierce the hides of animals,
hoes till the soil, and adzes cut wood. These man-made tools possess a particular duality: the more efficient the cutting edge of the implement, the more
potentially dangerous it becomes and the more control must be exerted. All
involve the potential of creation and destruction simultaneously. Like the potentials and problems introduced by computers in our own age, iron offers
enormous possibilities as well as dangers for society, alternatives which are
embodied in iron as a sacred substance.

Iron as a Sacred Substance

Iron's potential gives it a sacred status.[7] The innate qualities of iron are
a manifestation of its àṣẹ, a metaphysical concept central to all Yorùbá
thought and action. Àṣẹ is present in all that exists—things, persons, supernatural forces, sounds, and gestures (cf. M. Drewal, chapter 9). Iron possesses that supernatural force. Hence, objects made of iron are not only primary symbols of Ògún, they *are* Ògún. An Ògún devotee reveals this
philosophical concept when he describes how an Ògún altar is established:

> When a shrine is called Ògún, it is Ògún. It becomes Ògún once you have
> placed two pieces of iron together and poured oil on it. The shrine needs food
> to be active. Then you can offer prayers to it. As soon as it is put together

it stays Ògún, and will be Ògún forever after. By dismantling the iron, one takes Ògún away. (Barnes 1980:37)[8]

The essential elements are two or more pieces of iron, sacrifices, and the voiced prayers of humans.[9] The iron on the shrine is not only the "witnessing object" that, as Verger explains (1964:17), is the "support" of the altar or shrine, but also it contains the life force or àṣẹ of the divinity. Examples of other such objects hosting intensified àṣẹ are the thundercelts or neolithic axes (ẹdùn àrá) on Ṣàngó shrines, and the river pebbles (ota) on Ọya, Eyinlẹ̀, and Ọṣun altars. When iron is present on a shrine, it must be ritually "fed" with the blood of animal sacrifices, palm oil, palm wine, gin, water, kolanut, snail's fluid, or other substances, all of which activate and exalt the deity.

The importance of sacrifice is brought out in well-known praises to Ògún such as the following invocation from Porto Novo:

1   Ògún alake ni jẹ aja
2   Ògún onigbajamọ irun ẹni ni jẹ
3   Ògún olola wọn jẹ ẹjẹ
4   Ògún alapata ẹran ni jẹ. (Verger 1957:194)

1   *Ògún alake* eats dog
2   Ògún of the barbers eats human hair
3   Ògún of the body artists drinks blood
4   Ògún of the butchers eats meat . . .

Different branches of Ògún require particular kinds of sacrifices. Ògún Aláké, the Ògún of warriors/hunters, prefers dog, whose blood is poured upon the iron and stone altars of the deity. The iron razors of the barber consume human hair, while the iron instruments of body artists drink blood of a client. The same is true for the tools of the carver, for "Ògún of the carvers consumes the blood [sap] of wood" (Ògún gbẹ́nàgbẹ́nà jẹ ojè igi) (Oluponọn 1975). The term ògún in this and other verses cited earlier is used in a double sense to mean the deity *and* the iron implement, for they are inseparable. Supervised by the god of iron, the work carried out by iron-using professionals constitutes, in a sense, sacred activity since it provides nourishment for iron, for Ògún's àṣẹ.

The proper "feeding" of iron also requires prayer. These praises and invocations contain àṣẹ to assure that what is asked will come to pass (cf. M. Drewal, chapter 9). The importance of sacrifice and human voices is clear in all aspects of iron work, from mining, to the siting of a Yorùbá smelter, to the elaborate rituals required when a smelting furnace is lit. Before digging, miners place palm wine, the fluid of a snail, and kolanut on the spot and offer prayers to Ògún. As Adéníji and Armstrong (1977:11) explain, they serve to ensure success in finding good iron ore and in preventing the hole from "collapsing upon them." Additionally, the miners must bear no one ill will (literally, "bad inside") (kò gbọ'dọ̀ ní inú búburú sí ẹnikẹ́ni), not commit adultery, nor steal (Adéníji and Armstrong 1977:13).

Similar spiritual concerns emerge in siting a smelter. A smelter must not be so close as to disrupt society, yet never so far as to prevent society from controlling it. As Adéníji and Armstrong (1977:19–21) explain:

> . . . one must go to build the smelting house in the bush; but it must not be far from the place where many people live or where Ogun stays and hears (the) voices (of human beings). [The reason for this siting of the smelter is] if the sound of people's voices does not penetrate inside the hearth of the smelter, the iron which is being smelted inside it will become dumb (yó'yadi); that is that this iron will not become iron that rings but rather slag (ìdàrọ́)—which means that this iron is still-born (èyí ni pé irin náàá ya àbíkú).

In other words, earth turns to iron only through human intercession. Hands, minds, and voices transform a natural substance into a functional, "living" cultural artifact.

The rituals attending the establishment of a smelter become more elaborate when the smelting fire is lit. The smelter constitutes a shrine to Ògún and the fire, like the heat of the deity, is sacred. In the powder that ignites the furnace, the smelters mark the sign for Ògún (Ògúndá Ìrẹtẹ̀) that comes from the Ifá divination lore. This sign and its verses denote "victory" (Abimbọla 1976:30) and celebrate success in the face of danger, an association which is appropriate to a deity who revels in battle. Then the ironworker straddles the "mouth" of the furnace with a red cock in his left hand, a mixture of pepper and red and white kolanut in his mouth, and his eyes closed, and begins to recite incantations (ọfọ̀) to Ògún:

1	Ìbà Ògún, Oníporin Ayé
2	Ìbà Ògún, Oníporin Ọ̀run
3	Ìbà àgbààgbà mẹ́'ta, ìporin ìgbà ìwá ṣẹ̀
4	Ògún dá'kẹtẹ̀ ní pópó
5	Ọ́ rawọ́ agada ibéjé ibéjé
6	Iná giri-giri nínú ada
7	Oòrùn giri-giri òkè
8	Iná sunṣu àri jẹ
9	Oòrùn sunṣu àsun lòlùbọ́
10	Iná giri-giri inú ada
11	Akùkọ rẹ̀bẹ̀-rẹ̀bẹ̀ Ògún fún ọ rèé!
12	Kírin ó pò!
13	Kírin ó jiná
14	Wọnrọn-wọnrọn-wọnrọn! (Adéníji and Armstrong 1977:30–33)

1   Homage to Ògún, the Iron-Smelter of the World (3 times)
2   Homage to Ògún, the Iron-Smelter of Heaven (3 times)
3   Homage to the three patriarchs, iron-smelters when existence began!
       (3 times)
4   Ògún put on a big straw hat in an open place
5   He spun the sword as a warning, as a warning! (3 times)
6   The blazing fire in the furnace, (3 times)
7   The sun shining brightly above; (3 times)
8   Fire cooks the yam so it is edible, (3 times)
9   The sun cooks the yam so it wilts [and is inedible] (3 times)
10 Blazing fire in the furnace, (3 times)
11 Here is the red-red cock which Ògún presents to you! (3 times)
12 So let the iron be well-smelted,
13 Let the iron be well heated
14 To ring well and long! (3 times)

The cock's crow is said to carry from this world to the afterworld (*tó kọ jáyé kọ já'run*). It is likened to a palm frond (*amọ̀*) "separated from death" (*tàbí tó bákú lamọ̀*). The allusion to the palm frond (*amọ̀* or *mariwo*), an important Ògún symbol, refers to its continued life as thatching or dressing for shrines after it is cut from the tree. Amidst these invocations, the smelter sacrifices the cock and pours its blood over the Ifá sign, lights a bundle of reeds with flint, and ignites the furnace while reciting the secret names of fire over the blaze. Finally, he climbs on the furnace platform and vigorously blows pepper and kolanut over the smelter as further prayers are voiced (Adéníji and Armstrong 1977:29–31). Through the ritual, humans shape, control, and change raw power into socially useful power.

The supplications voiced by the followers of Ògún have one major theme: protection from physical harm. More specifically, they ask to be spared from "accidents" caused by iron that has gone out of control, like a careening lorry or a wayward axe blade. Essentially, these prayers appeal to Ògún to ensure that iron is used to benefit humanity. This is graphically illustrated at annual Ògún rites in Ifẹ̀ and Ileṣa known as Ìbọgún or Ìbẹjá, when devotees must sacrifice a dog by decapitating it with a single, swift stroke of a sword. They must emulate the quick and precise actions of Ògún himself, who kills instantly. Failure to accomplish this act shows a lack of efficiency and control; the rite is, therefore, unacceptable to Ògún.

The major themes from Ògún rituals are repeated in his symbols. Ògún's symbolic colors, red and white, represent the extremes through which iron goes (hot/cold, liquid/solid, brittle/pliable). Red connotes heat (fire, forge), violence (anger), impatience, and bloodshed. The leaves used in preparations for Ògún, such as *ọdúndún* and *rinrin*, are said to "cool" the heat of Ògún (Verger 1976–77:249). One Ògún devotee (Alabe 1975) explained the predominance of red in Ògún symbolism as follows: "When a man takes a blade to make marks, you won't see white water come out of the person's body. The blood will be red . . . Ògún is using something which is red." Awolalu puts it another way:

> Since Ògún is believed to be fiery, things offered to calm his anger include snail and palm oil. Before a child is circumcised . . . the body-fluid of the snail is sprinkled on him, especially on the part of the body to be incised. After circumcision, the knife used for the purpose is put in a plate in which there is plenty of palm oil. (1973:86)

Ògún's red may also refer to the lateritic soil of Yorubaland and the rust that forms on unused iron. Both connote the absence of man. In contrast, white evokes man's intercession, for Williams (1974:99) notes that iron is considered to be "worn white with use." Likewise, the white fluid squeezed from the snail soothes both the cuts made by Ògún and Ògún himself, and white semen possesses life-giving potential. Cool white balances the heat of red by symbolizing the eternal effort to control and channel the enormous powers of iron and Ògún.

Yorùbá Body Marks: Types and Significance

For the Yorùbá, lines in flesh are primordial. Pointing to the palm of his hand, one tattooer commented, "God made a proverb saying, 'open your hand, here are lines'" (*Ọlọrun pa sò'we sile pe lagba ga yin ọwọ, ilà ni*) (Fadare 1975). From this fact of creation, humans evolved the art of cutting patterns in flesh. The symbols associated with Ògún and iron resonate in the art, tools, techniques, and personalities of body artists.

Marks and Identity

Lines on a person signify many things. Some marks localize a person in time and space, indicating indelibly an individual's place and condition in a broad cultural and ontological system. The practice of using marks for this purpose, probably ancient among the Yorùbá,[10] seems to have been especially important during the nineteenth century, a period of widespread conflict between Yorùbá and their neighbors as well as among various Yorùbá ethnic subgroups who engaged in slave-raiding on a massive scale (see Johnson 1921; Ajayi and Smith 1964; Smith 1969).[11] Immediate visual identification became crucial, as one elder recalls:

> In the ancient days . . . during the wars long ago, if any children (without marks) were carried away by the enemy, we could not recognize them later if they were found because there were no marks . . . therefore if I have my own mark then I put it on my children and if I see them, I know that they are my own children. . . . This happened during the wars [which] caused them to have to make marks. (Fadare 1975)

This is of course only a partial explanation, because facial marks generally distinguish ethnic subgroups and not lineages (fig. 10.1a, b). In some cases, however, marks signified members of royal households (both masters and slaves) (Johnson 1921:106). In other cases, divination determined that a child receive no marks at all (Faleti 1977:26). Facial scarifications may therefore be remnants of religious practices or political allegiances which have, over the last two centuries, undergone significant changes.

Face and body scarifications communicate other biographical facts about a person, including conditions of birth. Children called àbíkú (literally, "those born to die"), mischievous spirit infants who plague their mothers by being born and then dying soon after, are sometimes marked with a distinctive sign such as three scars on the shoulder (Houlberg 1976). If and when they are reborn, they are recognized and treated appropriately to encourage them to remain alive. Other marks indicate the presence of younger siblings or relations. Adepegba (1976:56–57) notes the practice of sympathetic scarification (èjè gbígbà). When a child undergoes circumcision and cicatrization, his relatives have cuts made to remind them to handle the child gently.[12] The marks are also believed to ease the child's pain. Other cicatrices may indicate inherited occupations, such as three lines on one cheek and four on the other to identify a mark-maker. A person's cult membership may be evident from tattoos or scarifications, like a double thundercelt on the arm of Şàngó worshippers. Among the Ohori Yorùbá a large jagged zigzag mark from the ear to the corner of the mouth (fig. 10.1c) called òşílùmí is a "mark of sorrow" to denote the loss of someone very dear to the person (Ògúnole 1973).

Marks and Well-Being

A large variety of body markings have curative or protective associations. Two types, circumcision and excision, are performed as initiation rites in many African societies, but among the Yorùbá they are done primarily for reasons of health and procreation. The elderly olóòlà Fadare (1975) explained that dirt can collect under the foreskin, causing an infection known as èèta (cf. Abraham 1958:167). Too, he said, a circumcised penis is easily washed and "better" for intercourse. His explanations recall Ògún and the myth given above that accounts for the origin of circumcision. Excision, as explained by Yorùbá males, allows intercourse to be more "enjoyable" for the woman since removal of the clitoris (oba inú ayé, "king-inside-the-world"), which can enlarge and extrude, causing discomfort, allows the female freedom of movement (Alabe 1975). Once again, the explanation for this operation accords with the myth.

Other types of marks on the body are curative. Herbal doctors, priests of the god of herbalism, Òsanyìn, as well as body artists administer a large number of medicines via incisions on the body (see Warren et al. 1973). The placement of the incisions corresponds with the intended effect of the medicines to be inserted. Thus, short vertical marks under the eyes (gbèrè ojú) of some

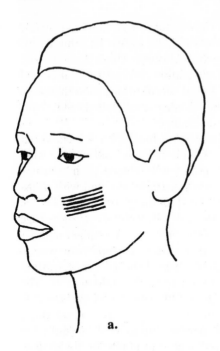

a.

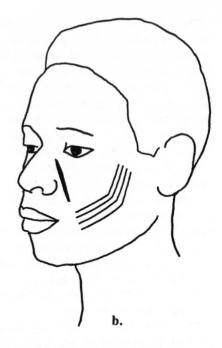

b.

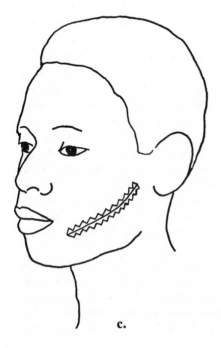

c.

FIGURE 10.1.   a—Èfòn Yorubá marks consist of many, closely spaced lines that are said to be "split open" (*là*). After Abraham 1958:301;
b—The four *kẹ́kẹ́* marks of Ọ̀yọ́ and Ẹ̀gbádò Yorùbá and the single oblique cicatrice (*bààmuń* are broad and bold. After Abraham 1958:300;
c—The Ọ̀họ̀rí Yorùbá face mark *ọ̀ṣílùmí* indicates sorrow for the loss of a loved one.

children signify that medicines have been inserted to prevent the child from trembling, a condition believed to be caused by the sight of spirits (Faleti 1977:24, 25). An *olóòlà* explains: "The mother or parents will prepare a medicine and bring it to the *olóòlà* who will then put it in the cicatrices he makes on the child and in this way prevent the child from dying" (Ògúnole 1973). The medicine *ẹrọ àgbà ì-ná*, literally "relief from that which is obtained and not spent" (i.e., the acquisition of money that disappears without producing tangible results), is rubbed into cuts made around the wrists of both hands. Medicine for severe headache is put into three cuts in the forehead (Warren et al. 1973:2, 3, 69), and medicine to prevent snakebite is put in an incision that encircles the left ankle: it must be renewed after the person kills a snake (Tereau and Huttel 1949/50:11). Medicine to protect one from the destructive invocation of another person is inserted in a "cut in front of the patient's ear" (Prince 1960:73), while medicines to make a curse effective (*àfọ̀ṣẹ*) are rubbed into a cut below the lower lip, so that "when the individual wishes to curse he licks his lower lip and whatever he says will come to pass" (Prince 1960:68). Similarly, the singer of *ìjálá* chants (for hunters) has incisions near his mouth for the insertion of medicines to give him courage and aid his memory (Babalọla 1966:68–86).

Such substances also facilitate the worship of the gods. Those initiated into cults for the gods must be prepared to receive, without danger, the spirit of their deity in order to become mediums in rituals of possession. To accomplish this, incisions are made in the cranium of the devotee and substances which activate the vital essence of *àṣẹ* of the god are inserted and sometimes signified by a patch or tuft of hair known as *òṣù*. The deity can now enter the properly prepared spiritual or inner head (*orí inú*) and possess the medium (*adóṣù*).[13] Substances inserted into the heads of devotees for Ògún, the one who clears roads and fields, "open the way" for contact between the world and the otherworld.

Marks of Beautification

The accomplished body artist also creates complex and intricate tattoo cicatrice designs known as *kóló* for men and especially for women. *Kóló* consist of very short, shallow, and closely spaced hatch marks (*wẹ́nẹ́wẹ́nẹ́*) that form linear designs into which a colorant (usually charcoal or lampblack) is inserted. The healed cuts produce a matt black pattern with a low-relief rippled texture against a semi-glossy, dark skin surface (fig. 10.2). These elaborate patterns are judged primarily in terms of aesthetic properties, that is, how successfully they enhance the appearance of the wearer.[14] They constitute the ultimate test of the visual acuity, sensitivity, technical ability, and creativity of an *olóòlà*. Informants without exception stress aesthetics when discussing *kóló*: "We are making designs, art (*A nṣe ọ̀nọ̀n*) . . . to make a person famous (*gbajúmọ̀n*) [literally, '200 faces know him']" (Ògúnjobi 1975). Another informant puts it this way: "It [*kóló*] has no reason, just for funning

. . . just to make *fáàrí*, to make *yọ̀nga*" (Fadare 1975). *Fáàrí* and *yọ̀nga* connote ostentation, showing off, or boastful behavior like strutting or swaggering (Abraham 1958:205, 688). The emphasis is clearly on the visible display of the enhanced and beautified human body. As the *olóòlà* Ògúnole remarks, *kóló* "is in order to embellish, to make one beautiful, illustrious (*a fún yín ṣọ̀go*) with marks. The women do it to enhance their beauty."

Placement

While both males and females adorn themselves with *kóló*, women have by far the most varied and numerous designs placed on different parts of their bodies. The most common sites for women's *kóló* are face, neck, chest, abdomen, back, arms (upper and lower), back of hands, calf or lower leg, and thighs. Men have *kóló* on the face, neck, and arms. These sites are not in order of importance, for the client decides where patterns should be placed. Rather, the placement of designs seems to suggest an awareness of differing degrees of visibility. Face, neck, arm, and hand designs for women are fully public and highly visible (fig. 10.3); patterns on the back, chest, and abdomen, however, are somewhat more restricted though still often visible in public (figs. 10.4, 10.5); but patterns on the upper thigh, intended for intimate friends or a spouse, are basically private (fig. 10.6a).

Motifs

The designs formed by the hatching process (*wẹ́nẹ́wẹ́nẹ́*) consist of a small number of lines and shapes that are altered and recombined to create a wide range of distinct yet subtly differentiated configurations. Zigzag lines are a pervasive element whose alteration and placement create a series of individual motifs; one is called "legs of a cripple" (*eruku arọ*). The diamond, the zigzag line flattened and mirrored, produces a design called "cowries" (*ẹ̀ṣa*). The diamond shape in a different combination with additional lines produces a motif called "lizard" (*arágba/alángba*). The triangle (sometimes referred to as *onígun mẹ́ta*) is identified by its placement, usually in a border or "closing" motif, which is then called "arrow" (*ọfà*). The hemisphere, a subtly rounded triangle, is also found in "closing" motifs. The circle, called simply "o" or "ho," may be embellished with radiating lines. The names assigned to some of the most basic lines and shapes—for example, "legs of a cripple"—seem to be based only in part on a visual correspondence with the subject represented. The primary objective of the semantic association appears to be the labeling of motifs to facilitate the identification and transmittal of imagery.

These visual units can be combined to create more complex representations of flora, fauna, and cultural objects. An early account (Burton 1863:104) describes how "The skin patterns were of every variety . . . tortoises, alligators, and the favorite lizard, stars, concentric circles, lozenges, welts. . . ." Only one example of flora, the palm tree (*igi ọpẹ̀*), has been documented (fig. 10.6b), although other motifs resemble leaf forms. Fauna are, by far, the

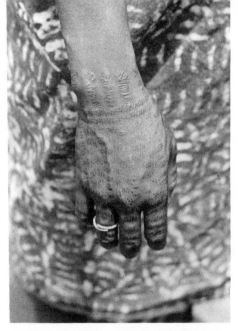

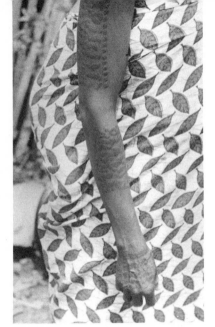

FIGURE 10.2. Tattoo cicatrice design (*kóló*) on the back of a hand showing lines of hatch marks (*wẹ́nẹ́wẹ́nẹ́*) darkened by lampblack or charcoal that produce a slightly raised, rippled texture on smooth skin.

FIGURE 10.3. *Kóló* designs on the arm and hand of a woman.

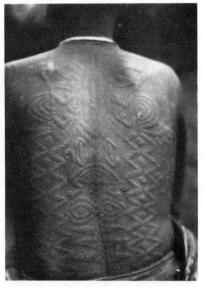

FIGURE 10.4. Elaborate *kóló* design on a woman's back showing two ostriches (*ògòngò*) at the shoulder blades. Pobe, Benin, pre-1948. Photograph #C48-1784-567 by G. Labitte, courtesy of the Phototheque, Musée de l'Homme, Paris, France.

FIGURE 10.5. Elaborate *kóló* design on a woman's back showing two ostriches (*ògòngò*) at the shoulder blades. Photograph #70037, courtesy of the Field Museum of Natural History.

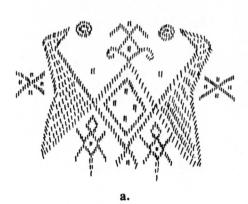

a.

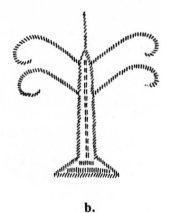

b.

c.

d.

FIGURE 10.6.
a—The *kóló* design called "husband sits on lap" (*gbókọ létan*) is usually placed on a woman's thighs;
b—*Kóló* design of a palm tree (*igi ọpẹ̀*);
c—*Kóló* design of lizards (*alángba*) and chameleons (*agẹmọ*) in a larger design;
d—*Kóló* design of a king's crown (*adé ọba*).

most consistently represented. They include specific species of birds such as ostrich (*ògòngò*), vulture (*igún*), dove (*àdàbà*), or simply a generalized form of bird in a larger composition; lizard (*arágba, alángba*) (fig. 10.6c), snake (*ejò*), chameleon (*agẹmọ*), centipede (*ọ̀ọ̀kùn*), and butterfly (*labalábá*). Cultural items include forms with religious connotations such as *ẹ̀ta Ògbóni*, the name given to a divination sign, a Ṣàngó dance-wand (*oṣé Ṣàngó*), a Muslim writing board (*wàláà*), the sign known as "moon of honor" (*oṣù ọlá*), and an amulet (*tírà*); symbols of status—a crown and title staff (fig. 10.6d); objects of everyday use like a comb (*òòyà*), *ayò* game-board, scissors, and the Y-shaped blade of the *olóòlà*; more contemporary images such as a wristwatch or an airplane (*ọkọ̀ òkè*); and calligraphy, such as the name or initials of a client or a fiancée, or proverbs and prayers.[15]

Tools of the Body Artist

The tools of the body artist are unlike those of farmers, blacksmiths, hunters, and warriors in an important way: they are extremely small and lightweight (fig. 10.7). On the far right is the blade used in circumcision. Its twisted iron shaft allows a firm grip by the *olóòlà*, and the slightly curved and wide blade allows a smooth, continuous cut of the foreskin. The blade next to it is for excision.[16] The two blades on the left are for scarification. These double-edged spear-shaped blades are suitable for longer, deeper marks. In contrast to them is the most delicate of all the instruments, the one in the center, for making the elaborate *kóló*. It is a Y-shaped tool with two sharp, narrow blades at the top.[17] The design of these instruments is suited to small, refined, and delicate effort rather than large, gross manipulation. The absence of wooden handles emphasizes this fact, for these instruments are meant to be held not with the hand, but rather with the thumb and fingers. The design admirably suits the function, allowing for precision and sensitivity, since the width of the cutting edge facilitates short, fine lines. Doubling the blades allows the *olóòlà* to work rapidly and continuously without having to change or sharpen the instrument. Another significant feature is the squared shaft, which allows the artist to maintain constancy in the alignment of the blade since the cuts are parallel marks placed close together. Thus, the very form of the body artist's implements conveys a concern for controlled manipulation of iron. But more than this, the blades embody the canons of dexterity—precision, firmness, and delicacy.

Like all iron implements, the blades of the mark-maker are sacred. The procedures used in their manufacture include certain strict rituals (Faleti 1977:26). The blacksmith is said to "create" (*pa*) the blades, a verb which connotes the performance of a magical, highly skillful act (Abraham 1958:538). The client provides a snail, a pigeon, and soothing leaves (*rinrin* and *òdúndún*). When the instruments are finished, the blacksmith bathes them in a mixture of the leaves, snail fluid, and the blood of the pigeon for three days before they are given to the body artist. The mark-maker repeats the same procedure and, on the seventh day, he polishes them white with the potion as he chants the following invocation:

1   Ògún niyi lọwọ alagbèdẹ
2   Abẹ ma niyi lọwọ oníkolà
3   Ire mi mbe l'ekulé mi. (Faleti 1977:26)

1   Ògún is here handy for the smith
2   Blades are here handy for the mark-maker
3   My fortunes are at the back of my house [with my shrine for Ògún].

The care taken with the body artist's implements also reveals their sacredness. The blades are carefully wrapped and tied in a red or white cloth, Ògún's symbolic colors (Fig. 10.7). They are kept with other ritual items that are essential for success; kolanuts (top, far left), for all invocations to Ògún, and fan-shaped objects or "badges" of the mark-makers known as atáàmù (below blades). One informant explained, "They are like a license from the ancient days. . . . If they [body artists] walk about the town [holding them] . . . people will say, 'That is the person who is making marks.' . . . If you don't have them you won't come from the foundation of [be a legitimate] olóòlà" (Fadare 1975). Blood and other scarificial residue cover these objects, both of which have large iron rings on their handles and one has iron rings around its perimeter.

Techniques of the Body Artist

Two skills are important to the body artist. The first is an ability to create marks which differ subtly yet significantly from each other. Such proficiency distinguishes the accomplished body artist from a mutilator. The second is an ability to work with speed. An accomplished olóòlà can perform a variety of cutting operations. To a large extent, the skills he uses in each operation are reflected in the terminology used to designate specific cutting techniques and distinct types of cuts.

Each cutting operation has its own term: (1) circumcision (dá'kó) and excision (dábò), (2) scarification (ilà), (3) medicinal incision (gbẹ́rẹ́), and, the most demanding of all, (4) the creation of intricate kóló patterns. In circumci-sion and excision, flesh is cut (dá). This same verb is used in the context of tapping palm wine (dẹmu, dá ẹmu) through an analogy to a cut around something and the release of fluid, whether sap, blood, or semen.

In facial scarification, different cutting techniques produce a variety of visual and textural qualities (fig. 10.8). Yoruba terminology distinguishes these

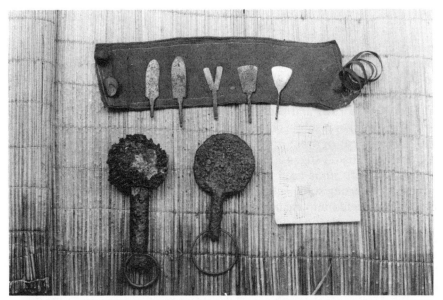

FIGURE 10.7. The tools and ritual implements of the *olóòlà*. Top left to right: kolanuts, two blades for cutting face marks (*àpálĭlá* and *ǫmǫ*), Y-shaped double blade for cutting *kóló* designs, circumcision blade, blade for making marks on the neck (*eke*). Bottom left to right: two badges of the body artist (*atáàmù*), drawings of various face and neck marks done by the artist, Y. Fadare. Ìláró, Nigeria.

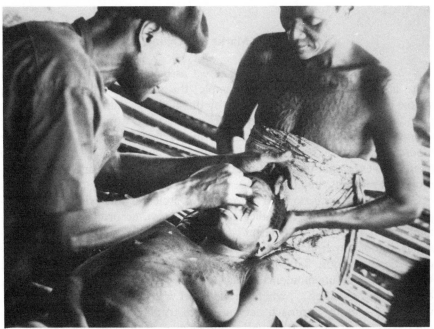

FIGURE 10.8. The body artist A. Ogúnole demonstrating how he cuts face marks on a client while she is steadied by a friend who has elaborate *kóló* designs on her upper chest. Isose, Benin (R.P.B.).

types of cuts from others and reveals that there is a high degree of sophistica-
tion in the definition of lines and linear patterns. Thus *ṣá kẹ́kẹ́*, or, literally,
"to slash *kẹ́kẹ́* marks" on a person, indicates broad, bold and highly visible
lines; making the same pattern less distinct and visible is indicated by a different cutting verb (*wà*) and a different name for the marks (*gọ̀mbọ́*). Other
verbs that distinguish subtle differences in technique are *kọ* (to cut) *turé* facial
marks, *bù* (to cut or tear) *àbàjà* marks, and *là* (to split open) Ẹ̀fọ̀n marks
(Abraham 1958:301) (fig. 10.1b). Medicinal incisions have their own terminology. The verb *sin* is used to denote cuts (*gbẹ́rẹ́*) made for the expressed
purpose of inserting some substance. This same verb is used for *kóló*, when
colorant is inserted into shallow cuts.

The tattoo cicatrices executed by the *olóòlà* require the most elaborate and
refined technique. The term for the lines formed by the hatch marks
(*wẹ́nẹ́wẹ́nẹ́*) suggests a number of visual, tactile, technical, and aesthetic qualities: slenderness (*wẹ́*), indicating short, closely spaced parallel lines (Thompson 1973:49); smallness (*wẹ́wẹ́*), implying linear delicacy; and *wẹ́lẹ́wẹ́lẹ́*, conveying a pleasing rippled texture on the skin (Anonymous 1937:228). Speed
of execution is also imperative in the creation of *wẹ́nẹ́wẹ́nẹ́* marks, for colorant must be inserted before the blood flows or coagulates and the cuts close.
As one *olóòlà* explains, "If the first one [blade] is no longer sharp we begin
to use the second" (Alabe 1975). Speed in cutting, like the swiftness of Ògún,
is crucial.

Body Marks and Ògún

Kóló motifs appear to have little direct association with Ògún, although
there are some exceptions. For example, the palm tree (fig. 10.2b) is the
source of the oil and wine preferred by this divinity. Palm-wine tappers are
devotees of Ògún. It is also the source of the palm-frond midrib, *mariwo*,
a dominant Ògún symbol. Cultural items of metal, such as scissors, the
olóòlà's blade, a wristwatch, and an airplane also appear. It seems more
likely, however, that these motifs express prestige, identity, or aesthetic preference as much as they do Ògún.

Circumcision, excision, and *kóló* all have a clearer link with Ògún as expressions of sensuality. As indicated, the first two, according to male informants, make intercourse "better" for males and more "enjoyable" for females. *Kóló* are explicitly erotic in intent. Dark, textured patterns in low
relief on a smooth, flat surface have both a visual and a tactile appeal.
Witness the playful comments of one *olóòlà*: "A woman with marks all over
her body is very fine . . . when we see a girl with marks and she is (naked),
we boys can easily approach her and begin to play and rub her body with
our hands . . . if we see [the marks] and glance at the body, the weather will
change to another thing [we will become sexually aroused]!" (Ògúnjobi

1975). Ògún is thus linked to these marks in that he ensures human reproduction not simply by facilitating intercourse but also by encouraging it.

Tattoos and scarifications evoke Ògún in another implicit but important way—as rites of passage. Although they are not ritually celebrated, the body marks indicate changes in the wearer's status. As with initiation ceremonies, they also are tests of the subject's strength. Comments about *kóló* are explicit in this regard. Sometime before puberty, a person chooses to have these marks, at least in part, because of the way society regards them. One informant describes how people praise a woman covered with body designs with words like "she is very courageous" (o ni láyà dáadáa) or ridicule one without marks with "she is a coward" (*ojo ni*). *Kóló* announce that the bearer is brave and strong enough to endure pain in order to enjoy society's admiration. Thus it is said, "With pains and aches are marks made on us, we become beautified by them only when they are healed" (*Tita riro ni a nkolà, bi o ba sàn tán ni a to di oge*) (Faleti 1977:27).

The prevalence of body markings may be due in part to concepts of the human body and of the person. According to Morakinyo and Akiwowo (1981:26, 36), the Yorùbá "concept of the person . . . , vis-à-vis body-mind relationship, is a unitary one. The body is the mind . . ." and Yorùbá assess an individual's personality from both physical appearance and behavior. In light of this, elaborate body markings are viewed as proof of courage, fortitude, and strength. All of these are highly valued. They are personified by Ògún and body artists.

Body Artists and Ògún

The *olóòlà* is an extension and manifestation of Ògún in a number of ways. First, he brings order to society by providing temporal, spiritual, and spatial markers at various points in a person's life. The severing of the umbilical cord is the initial act of defining an individual. Circumcision and excision follow after the child is named, that is, when it is regarded as part of human society. These operations define and anticipate the child's sexual role. Sometime later, divination may require other incisions to identify a special child, such as an *abíkú*. Once a child's survival seems likely, facial scarifications indicating social identity are incised, and others, indicating occupations, cult affiliations, and initiations, may be added. In making indelible signs, the mark-maker gives visual expression to Yorùbá concepts of the self as a part of an embracing cultural and cosmological system. Like Ògún, who creates order by transforming the forest into farms and cities, and who tames society by judging disruptive individuals, the *olóòlà* helps to create order by visibly placing individuals in a larger social and cosmic universe.

Second, the body artist sustains culture by providing for the physical and spiritual well-being of individuals. The curative inoculations ensure survival.

Others are designed for protection against enemies, or for facilitating contact with the supernatural realm; they enhance a person's potential for dealing with the often inexplicable forces in the world.

Third, the *olóòlà* is a cultural innovator. As an artist, he contributes his aesthetic sensibilities by embellishing human flesh with beautiful, creative patterns. Itinerancy among Yorùbá body artists, a tradition of some antiquity, fosters such innovation and leads to the rapid dispersal of motifs over a wide area.[18] Several artists recount their frequent trips to distant markets where they observe, adopt, and adapt new patterns. Some (Fadare and Ògúnjobi 1975) develop "portfolios," notebooks of motifs and patterns observed and recorded during their travels, which they carry with them and show to prospective clients. Literacy has also caused body artists to innovate. Many of them, even those unable to read, introduced calligraphy into Yorubaland. They learned to inscribe the letters of the Yorùbá alphabet, names, sentences, and proverbial expressions on the bodies of their clients. Fostering as well as responding to changing aesthetic preferences, body artists have continued to develop new patterns.

Finally, the personality of body artists expresses most clearly their relationship to Ògún. *Olóòlà* seek the qualities of patience and composure. One describes the ideal artist as having "a cool, patient character (*ìwa tútù àti súùrù*). He must not be excitable but friendly, attractive, and approachable (*ń fa ni móra*). He must not drink liquor or palm wine, because if he drinks a lot he won't be able to do the marks well. He may penetrate too deeply and instead of making a design he will just make a big wound." Precise control by the mark-maker is the difference between art and accident. Precision is possible only when an artist exhibits self-control as well as control of his medium.

The need for self-control in the face of danger is a theme that is central to Ògún. All Ògún followers confront danger, but the challenge for a body artist is fundamentally different from that faced by a hunter or warrior. The latter faces death or injury at the "hands" of his prey, be it animal or human. The former faces danger that is within himself. Carelessness and cowardice can result in disaster; they must be avoided at all costs. He must strive to emulate the finer attributes of his god—firmness and bravery—in order to achieve success. The irreversible nature of his work demands courage, confidence, and, above all, precision. An *olóòlà* is reminded of this each time he invokes Ògún with the praise:

1 Ògún, iyan kan bí ọgbẹ́
2 Anaíyà páta bi ọna

1 Ògún, the one who is like a big scar [wound]
2 The courageous one is like the road

The scar, the road, and Ògún are alike. None can be changed. An informant explains, "if the blade should turn, mistakenly turn, you can't say 'make another one' . . . it can't be cleared [removed] . . . if three or four marks are put in the place, they are there until the end of a person's life, they can't be cleared again" (Fadare 1975). Another adds, "The road is always there. It never moves. No matter what traffic comes along, truck or car, it does not budge. It is courageous."

In Yorùbá thought, the cosmic realms of world (*ayé*) and otherworld (*òrun*) are distinct but not separate. They penetrate and influence each other depending upon the quality of communication established and maintained between humans and spirits, gods, and ancestors. One affects the other, and vice versa. Such beliefs shape in significant ways people's thoughts and actions. People not only contemplate divine forces, they manipulate them—sometimes praising, sometimes emulating, other times scolding or blaming. Such closeness between devotee and deity forges a clearly definable ethos that shapes as well as reflects various facets of a person's life. The examination of those who work with iron, specifically body artists—their myths, rituals, materials, implements, techniques, and personalities—shows this to be true. Embodying many of Ògún's attributes, they boldly incise beautiful, indelible lines in human skin with firmness, speed, and precision. In thus forming their concepts of Ògún and actualizing them in their lives, body artists have helped to create the world of Ògún that in turn has shaped Yorùbá culture in distinctive ways.

NOTES

1. Fieldwork for this study was carried out among the Ọ̀họ̀rí and Ẹ̀gbádò Yorùbá in Benin (R.P.B.) and Nigeria in 1973, 1975, and 1977–78. I wish to express my gratitude to The National Endowment for the Humanities, Cleveland State University, and the Institute for Intercultural Studies for their generous financial support; the Institutes of African Studies, Universities of Ìbàdàn and Ifẹ̀, and the Nigerian Museum for providing research affiliations; Rowland Abiọdun and especially Margaret Thompson Drewal for their editorial suggestions and insights; and to the Yorùbá individuals who patiently shared their thoughts on Ògún and body arts. Unless otherwise indicated, all drawings and photographs are by the author.

2. Cf. Verger 1957:142; Beier 1956:29; and Awolalu 1979:32 for other versions. English translations from Verger 1957 are by the author.

3. Ògún's primacy in matters of honesty is evident in another of his symbols, young palm leaves, the "cloths of Ògún" known as *mariwo*. These are often tied on bundles of harvested crops or firewood left unattended along the roadside by their owners. These fronds announce, in effect, "Ògún will punish (kill) those who steal." Similarly, *mariwo* placed at the entrances to sacred sites or private places signals a warning to the uninitiated and the unwelcome that the path cleared by Ògún for a certain purpose should not be misused and that just retribution at the hands of Ògún will follow.

4. Verger (1957) has noted the same phenomenon. More recently Morakinyo and Akiwowo (1981:32–35) discuss heredity and the gods as important factors in the formation of a person's personality (ẹ̀dá ẹni).

5. Williams (1974:304) gives a slightly different list: (1) those who use knives or other iron tools within the community, (2) palm-wine tappers, (3) farmers, (4) hunters, (5) Ògún Onírè, ruler of Ìrè, (6) blacksmiths, and (7) all other worshippers of Ògún. In the Ọ̀họ̀rí community of Ibaiyun, the Aṣògún (head of the Ògún worshippers) identifies the categories as blacksmiths (Ògún Alágbẹ̀dẹ), body artists (Ògún Olóòlà), carvers (Ògún Gbẹ́nàgbẹ́nà), and towns where Ògún is the major civic deity (Ògún Ìlú, Ògún Onire, Ògún Àjọbọ) (A. Oluponọn, interview, November 14, 1975).

6. However, certain qualifications should be noted. Faleti (1977:27) states that ". . . a woman whose father is a mark maker can be taught how to and she can make marks. But the daughter of a mark maker who marries a lay man cannot teach her child to make marks." In 1975, I was told by the head of the body artists at Ìláró (Fadare) that the Ìyálóde, leader of women and a titled elder of the community, was sanctioned to perform all rites in his absence.

7. The material and spiritual aspects of any substance are for the Yorùbá inseparable. It is for this reason that persons swearing oaths of truthfulness say "May Ògún/ iron kill me if I lie" as they touch a piece of iron to their foreheads or lips.

8. See Williams 1974:78–100 and Barnes 1980:8–30 for discussions of the sacred iron complex in Africa and among the Yorùbá.

9. Williams (1974:39–40) makes the similar point that "spirit and matter are seen as coterminus. 'Simply anything can become a god,' a Yoruba informant once remarked. 'This button' (pointing to the dashboard of the car in which we were), 'it only needs to be built up by prayer' . . . all matter is dormant spirit with potential expression as a good or evil force depending on the manner of its propitiation. . . .'"

10. A number of Ifẹ̀ terra cotta and copper sculptures (ca. 1100) and Ọ̀wọ̀ terra cottas (ca. 1400) depict elaborate scarification patterns, some closely resembling nineteenth and twentieth century Yorùbá marks. An Ifá divination tray now at the Ulmer Museum and collected at Allada in the early seventeenth century (possibly Yorùbá, but probably Aja) depicts male and female figures with elaborate face, chest, and neck scarifications.

11. Based on data received from an Ìjẹ̀bu Yorùbá informant, d'Avezec (1845:55–59) recorded that the tradition of tattooing ("ella" [ilà]) and circumcision were done by a specialist known as alakila.

12. Faleti (1977:24) notes the same practice, which he calls gba ẹ̀jẹ̀ fun. A photograph by T. J. H. Chappel in the Nigerian Museum Archives (#41.1.A.30) documents a similar practice among the Egun/Ẹgbádò Yorùbá in which a large triangular pattern of keloids are made on the abdomen of an elder sibling to complement the incision of facial marks on the younger, for it is said that, "if an older child is marked at the same time, the baby will not suffer such pain." This triangular scar pattern is identical to keloid designs on abíkú statuettes of Aja people discussed by Merlo (1975).

13. For detailed analyses of the symbolic significance of Yorùbá projections from the top, see M. Drewal 1977, 1986.

14. An Ẹ̀gbá Yorùbá praise poem graphically recounts the aesthetic impact of such marks: A hunter's wife had elaborate designs known as gbegbéèmu put on her abdomen while her husband was away. When he returned, he was so taken by the sight of his wife's beauty that he stopped short, thunderstruck, and in so doing accidentally dropped his loaded gun, which exploded, killing him! (Faleti 1977:23–24)

15. For illustrations of these kóló see H. Drewal 1988.

16. Faleti notes that the difference in size of these two instruments is "to afford an easy and quick recognition during an operation," but more important they differ

because "of a taboo that the female's must not be used for a male, or the male's for a female. If this happens, the subject will be prone to promiscuity" (1977:26).

17. A similar blade used by an itinerant Yorùbá tattooer at Ìlọrin was documented in 1912: "The cutting edge was indented in the middle, thus giving the blade two sharp angles with which the incisions were made" (MacFie 1913:122).

18. For a discussion of itinerancy and its implications for African art history, see H. Drewal 1977.

REFERENCES CITED

Abimbọla, Wande. 1976. *Ifa: An Exposition of Ifa Literary Corpus*, Ibadan: Oxford University Press.

Abraham, R. C. 1958. *Dictionary of Modern Yoruba*, London: University of London Press.

Adéníji, D., and R. G. Armstrong. 1977. *Iron Mining and Smelting*, Ibadan: Institute of African Studies, Occasional Publications, no. 31.

Adepegba, C. 1976. "A Survey of Nigerian Body Markings and Their Relationship to Other Nigerian Arts," unpublished Ph.D. dissertation, Indiana University.

Ajayi, J. F. A., and Robert Smith. 1964. *Yoruba Warfare in the 19th Century*, Cambridge: Cambridge University Press.

Alabe, A., body artist. 1975. Interview, Igbeme, November 19.

Anonymous. 1937. *A Dictionary of the Yoruba Language*, Oxford: Oxford University Press.

Awolalu, J. O. 1973. "Yoruba Sacrificial Practice," *Journal of Religion in Africa* 5(2):81–93.

———. 1979. *Yoruba Beliefs and Sacrificial Rites*, London: Longman.

Babalọla, S. A. 1966. *The Content and Form of Yoruba Ìjálá*, London: Oxford University Press.

———. 1967. *Awọn Oríkì Orilẹ*, Glasgow: Collins.

Barnes, Sandra T. 1980. *Ogun: An Old God for a New Age*, ISHI Occasional Papers in Social Change, #3. Philadelphia: ISHI.

Beier, Ulli. 1956. "Before Odudua," Odu 3:25–32.

Bellamy, C. V. 1904. "A West African Smelting House," *Journal of the Iron and Steel Institute* 2:99–126.

Burton, Richard. 1863. *Abeokuta and the Cameroon Mountains*, 2 vols., London: Tinsley Brothers.

Carroll, Kevin. 1967. *Yoruba Religious Carving*, New York: Praeger.

d'Avezec, M. 1845. *Notice sur le pays et le peuple des yebous*, Paris: Librairie Orientale de Mme. Ve Dondey-Dupre.

Drewal, Henry J. 1977. *Traditional Arts of the Nigerian Peoples*, Washington: Museum of African Art.

———. 1980. *African Artistry: Technique and Aesthetics in Yoruba Sculpture*, Atlanta: The High Museum of Art.

———. 1988. "Beauty and Being: Aesthetics and Ontology in Yoruba Body Art," in A. Rubin (ed.), *Arts of the Body*, Los Angeles: Museum of Cultural History.

Drewal, Margaret T. 1977. "Projections from the Top in Yoruba Art," *African Arts* 11(1):43–49, 91–92.

———. 1986. "Art and Trance among Yoruba Shango Devotees," *African Arts* 20(1):60–67, 98–99.

Fadare, Y., head of the mark-makers. 1975. Interview, Oke Ibese Quarter, Ìlàró, November 6.

Faleti, A. 1977. "Yoruba Facial Marks," *Gangan* 7:22–27.

Houlberg, Marilyn. 1976. Personal communication, November 4.

Johnson, Samuel. 1921. *The History of the Yorubas*, Ibadan: Ibadan University Press (1969 edition used).

Legbe, A., diviner and Èfè singer. 1971. Interview, Emado Quarter, Àyétòrò, April.

MacFie, J. W. S. 1913. "A Yoruba Tattooer," *Man* 13:121–22.

Merlo, Christian. 1975. "Statuettes of the Abiku Cult," *African Arts* 8(4):30–35, 84.

Morakinyo, O., and A. Akiwowo. 1981. "The Yoruba Ontology of Personality and Motivation: A Multidisciplinary Approach," *Journal of Social and Biological Structures* 4:19–38.

Ògúnjobi, body artist and town head. 1975. Interview, Igbeme-Ile, November 19.

Ògúnole, A., body artist. 1973. Interview, Isose, Òhòrí, May 5.

Olabisi, O. 1975. In *Dimensions in Black Art*, H. Drewal (ed.), Cleveland: Cleveland State University, p. 23.

Oluponon, A., Ògún priest. 1975. Interview, Ibaiyun, Òhòrí, November 14.

Prince, Raymond. 1960. "Curse, Invocation and Mental Health among the Yoruba," *Canadian Psychiatric Association Journal* 5:65–79.

Smith, Robert. 1969. *Kingdoms of the Yoruba*, London: Methuen.

Tereau and V. Huttel. 1949/50. "Monographie du Hollidge," *Études Dahoméennes* 2:59–72 and 3:10–37.

Thompson, Robert F. 1973. "Yoruba Artistic Criticism," in *The Traditional Artist in African Societies*. W. L. d'Azevedo (ed.), Bloomington: Indiana University Press, pp. 19–61.

Verger, Pierre. 1957. "Notes sur le Culte des Orisa et Vodun à Bahia, La Baie de tous les Saints au Brasil et à l'Ancienne Côte des Ésclaves en Afrique," *Mémoires de l'Institut fondamental d'Afrique Noire*, no. 51.

———. 1964. "The Yoruba High God—A Review of the Sources," Paper prepared for the Conference on The High God in Africa, Ibadan, December 14–18.

———. 1976–77. "The Use of Plants in Yoruba Traditional Medicine and Its Linguistic Approach," in *Seminar Series,* no. 1, Part 1. O. Oyelaran (ed.), Ifè: Department of African Languages and Literature, University of Ifè, pp. 242–95.

Warren, Dennis M., A. D. Buckley, and J. A. Ayandokun. 1973. *Yoruba Medicines*, Legon: The Institute of African Studies, University of Ghana.

Williams, Denis. 1974. *Icon and Image*. New York: New York University Press.

PART THREE

Transformations of Ogun

J. D. Y. Peel

11

A Comparative Analysis of Ogun in Precolonial Yorubaland[1]

About Ogun, there seems to be a high degree of consensus on two general points: (1) that Ogun is a Pan-Yoruba deity of fairly uniform character and significance, and (2) that his cult has adapted remarkably to the conditions of the modern world and across the Atlantic. In this essay I wish, through a comparative examination of mostly contemporary evidence of the cult of Ogun as it was in the second half of the nineteenth century, to qualify the first of these points; and this should clear the way to a fuller appreciation of the second point.

The first edition of *Africa's Ogun* lacked a specifically historical account of the Ogun cult in precolonial Yorubaland, other than a number of historical references that were incorporated into Sandra Barnes's and Paula Ben-Amos's synthesizing essay, "Ogun, the Empire Builder," which covers a broad span of both time and space. It is inevitably tempting to regard the cult of Ogun in precolonial Yorubaland as providing a baseline for assessing the cult's divergent development under different conditions across the Atlantic, and I think this has possibilities, provided it is done with great circumspection. The origins of much of Ogun's cult in the New World go back to before the mid-nineteenth century, and to treat Ogun in Yorubaland as it was between 1845 and 1912 as unproblematically equivalent to what it had been a century or more earlier, implies that it could have undergone no development in West Africa. Any historical analysis must be strongly oriented to the recognition of temporal change, and thus will tend to be drawn into opposing that predilection in Yoruba cultural studies to emphasize continuity, often by the postulation of "time-binding" cultural essences. "Traditional" religion is widely regarded as the vehicle par excellence of ethnic and communal identity, and perhaps nowhere more so than the cult of Ogun, insofar as Ogun is celebrated by Wole Soyinka, the leading Yoruba man of letters of our day, as an icon both of a personal vision and of Yoruba (perhaps also African) values.[2] This makes a *historical* study of Ogun more consequential and also more difficult than that of topics that are less culturally charged.

Evidence from the CMS Journals

The great bulk of the evidence will be drawn from the journals and reports of missionary agents—in the great majority, Yoruba ones—of the Church Missionary Society, active since 1845. Without question this is the richest contemporary source for almost any aspect of Yoruba life, especially when read with the published works of such Yoruba CMS clergy as Samuel Johnson, James Johnson, and E. M. Lijadu. These men were hardly disinterested observers of what they considered to be "idolatry," and only rarely can their observations be called "ethnographic," in the sense of attempting to portray "heathen" religious practices in some detail as being significant in their own right. There is, for example, little detailed description of the rituals of *orisa* worship, or record of myths or prayers. What we have is hundreds of mostly brief references to the *orisa* and their devotees, as they came to the attention of CMS agents as they went about their pastoral and evangelistic business. They fall into several main categories: observations of *orisa* worship by individuals encountered in streets or houses; references to public festivals, sacrifices, or oracular consultations; conversations and arguments with devotees or priests about their *orisa* or about *orisa* worship in general; itemizations of which "idols" have been given up by new converts; and, very occasionally, general characterizations of particular *orisa* or of the cults of a particular community. In contrast to much of the large existing literature on *orisa,* which is strong on general characterizations of the *orisa,* drawn from oral sources such as myths, *ese Ifa,* and other kinds of religious poetry, and on analyses of their rituals, particularly the great annual festivals, the CMS data focus our attention on the more prosaic, day-to-day character of *orisa* worship. Where modern studies of "traditional religion" commonly present it as detached from the main preoccupations of daily life, the CMS journal writers, even if their accounts do not often penetrate very deeply, cannot but forcefully convey the omnipresence of the *orisa* in the lives of ordinary Yoruba in the last century. Their evidence, taken as a whole, tells us a great deal about both the settings and the occasions when Yoruba people entered into relations with the *orisa.*

So this body of source material has weaknesses, of which we must be aware, as well as strengths, which we should try to exploit. The most significant strength is the sheer number of references to *orisa* cults—in my reading of the entire archive, I have noted 778 of them, and have doubtless missed some—made under broadly similar assumptions over a large swath of Yorubaland. This makes possible systematic comparison, between different towns and regions in

Table 1.
Orisa Reported in CMS Journals, 1845–1912

	Abeokuta		Coastal Southwest		Ibadan		Other Oyo		East		Total
	n	%	n	%	n	%	n	%	n	%	n
Ogun	11	4	6	4	10	7	5	6	21	14	53
Sango	41	16	23	16	41	27	29	38	12	8	146
Oya	3	1	1	1	9	6	7	9	1	1	21
Orisa Oko	14	6	1	1	12	8	5	6	0	–	32
Obatala	30	12	4	3	11	7	2	3	8	5	55
Other white *orisa*	13	5	8	6	4	3	3	3	1	1	29
Ifa	40	16	31	22	25	17	15	19	29	19	140
Esu/Elegbara	19	8	14	10	9	6	2	3	27	17	71
Osun	15	6	6	4	8	5	0	–	13	8	42
Yemoja	12	5	6	4	1	1	1	1	0	–	20
Other water *orisa*	5	2	5	3	2	1	1	1	4	3	17
Osanyin	3	1	8	6	1	1	0	–	1	1	13
Sopona	9	4	3	2	2	1	0	–	6	4	20
Buruku	6	2	1	1	2	1	0	–	0	–	9
Ori	6	2	4	3	3	2	3	4	0	–	16
Ibeji	5	2	3	2	2	1	0	–	0	–	10
Other	21	8	20	14	8	5	4	5	31	20	84
Total	253	100	144	102	150	99	77	98	154	101	778

Notes: Abeokuta includes all Egba and Egbado towns and villages, but more than 90% of references relate to Abeokuta itself. Coastal Southwest means Lagos, Badagry and vicinity, Awori towns (Ota, Igbesa, Ado Odo). Ibadan is just Ibadan and its farm villages. Other Oyo means (in order of importance) Ijaye, Iseyin, New Oyo, Oke Ogun settlements, Ogbomosho, and observations made on journeys through the Oyo towns to the east of Ibadan. East means (in order of importance) Ondo, settlements on the Eastern Lagoon (Leke, Itebu, Ikale country, etc.), Ilesha, and parts of Ekiti.

terms of their cult profiles, and between the manifestations of particular *orisa* in different places. Through comparison, and particularly through the use of appropriate contrast cases (e.g., Sango vs. Ogun, Ogun in eastern vs. in western Yorubaland), we can make much more out of what are often rather passing observations. And just as a determined historicism is the best antidote to the tendency to essentialize Yoruba religion across time, so is regional comparison to the too easy assumption of Pan-Yoruba uniformity. It is not that pronounced continuities do not exist in Yoruba religion, across both time and space, but that they need to be seen as existing in the face of historical vicissitudes and variable local circumstances.

Table 1 presents references to the main *orisa* in the journals and letters of CMS agents organized according to five distinct regions, each of which has its own cultural character. Because of the uncertainties attaching to the figures, they are better used comparatively with one another—because the effects of the uncertainties will then tend to cancel one another out—rather than treated individually as indicators of a particular state of affairs. Moreover, because they are biased by where the CMS was active, as well as by the number of mission agents and the length of time they served—nearly a third of the references relate to Abeokuta, and just over half to the southwestern corner of Yorubaland, while Ijebu and large parts of the farther north and east are missing—cross-regional comparisons need to be made on the basis of the proportion of references that each *orisa* receives in a particular region. Thus we can compare the 4 percent of references to *orisa* which Ogun receives in Abeokuta with Obatala's 12 percent in the same town or the 14 percent which Ogun has in the east. The table needs to be read down (comparison within a region) before it is read across (comparison between regions).

Of course, these kinds of data present certain problems in their use. Most important, the aggregate references to *orisa* in the CMS agents' reports can be at best only an approximate measure of their significance in the lives of communities, since strictly speaking they do not record the actual frequency of cult observance among the Yoruba, but rather what struck missionary observers most frequently as worthy of report. Religious prejudice, as such, seems less of a problem than less obvious forms of bias, of which the authors may not have been aware, such as a tendency to give more space to what caught the eye or to neglect those aspects of religion which were private or implicit in other activities. Doubts about arguments that proceed largely from silences or thinnesses in the sources are well recognized in principle in historical methodology, but are less easy to quell in practice. I simply say that I am very aware of them, and will address them as they become pertinent at particular points in the argument.

Two Questions about Ogun

So what do the figures tell of Ogun? To begin with, they clearly confirm what is often remarked on in the literature, that the cult of Ogun is especially strong in eastern Yorubaland. From the eastern Lagoon up through Ondo to Ilesha and the edges of Ekiti, Ogun accounts for 14 percent of *orisa* reported, third after Ifa (19 percent) and Esu (17 percent). Although there are no references to Ogun's cult center at Ire[3]—most of Ekiti was evangelized only in the twentieth century—Ogun's importance at Ondo and Ilesha is strongly attested. At Ondo, unlike Abeokuta or Ibadan, the annual festival of Ogun is referred to as a major event in the public life of the town.[4] Though references to Ilesha are relatively sparse compared with the rich documentation available for Ondo from 1875 onward, the CMS agent there wrote in June 1889 of "the annual festivity of Ifa . . . which with Ogun, wh[ose] festivity is always kept about six [months] after this, make the two great idols worshipped in common by the whole town from the king to the poorest man."[5] Ifa and Ogun still structure the Ijesha year in this fashion, and the dominance of precolonial religion by these two *orisa* is strongly confirmed by the responses to a question put to household heads in a sample survey that I conducted in 1974: Ifa and Ogun each made up 26 percent of all *orisa* named as those worshipped traditionally in the household, followed by Osun at 8 percent and Orisa Onifon (the local equivalent of Obatala) at 7 percent.[6] It so happens that the CMS agents who provide us with information about the cults of these eastern Yoruba towns were themselves mostly Egba, and they clearly understood that the cult profiles of this area were significantly different from what they knew at home in Abeokuta. So the first question is: Why is Ogun more prominent in the religious systems of eastern Yorubaland?

The second question concerns the nature of Ogun's presence in western Yorubaland. My initial reaction on collating the evidence of the CMS reports was one of surprise that in the whole southwestern area, Ogun accounted for only 4 percent of references, and was outstripped by Sango in the ratio 4:1, even though Sango was a deity associated with the Oyo enemies of the Egba.[7] In Abeokuta itself, Ogun also came behind such *orisa* as Ifa, Obatala, Esu, Osun, Orisa Oko, and Yemoja. In Ibadan and the Oyo areas, Ogun came up somewhat more often, but at 7 percent still did not reach more than half the level reported for the east. This was the more surprising since Ogun appears to occur far more often as the main element in personal names than any other *orisa* (with the possible exception of Ifa). Notable examples include Ogunbona and Ogundipe, the two *balogun* (war chiefs) who successively between the 1840s and the 1880s were the chief patrons and protectors of the CMS at Abeokuta; Ogunmola, the *Basorun* of Ibadan; Ogunkoroju, the *Balogun* of Ijaye who gave quiet support to the mission there; and Ogunbiyi, the first Lagosian chief to become a Christian. The explanation I shall propose will be partly a matter of religious *realities,* that Ogun was part of a more complex cultic division of labor in the center and the west; and partly one of religious *appearances,* that Ogun was of a particularly immanent character, which reduced his saliency to the missionary gaze.

Ogun and Iron

Ogun is most commonly glossed by the CMS journal writers as "the god of iron and war," and the relations between these aspects have provided a primary focus for discussing Ogun's place in the cultural and political development of forest-belt West Africa. Ogun appears as "god of iron" in a more direct and unmediated sense than as "god of war": he is not merely "*of* iron," in the sense of being the force or principle "behind" iron technology, but virtually iron itself, worshipped as a personal force. The epithet "god of iron" sounds analogous to such expressions as "god of brass" or "god of palm nut," applied to Osun and Ifa respectively, which missionaries sometimes used to make their point that the *orisa* were *merely* "idols": inanimate material objects or artifacts taken to represent imaginary beings. Ogun is sometimes described in this way as "god of stone,"[8] which refers to the blacksmith's anvil stone, taken as one of his symbols. But with iron, it seems less fitting to say that Ogun was represented by it than that Ogun *was* it. Perhaps this would explain why Ogun, despite the very personalized way in which he appears in myth, is never portrayed in carved human form:[9] such a representation could only be inferior to iron itself. Such thoughts appear to have been in the mind of the Ibadan catechist James Barber when in a report of a deep discussion with a *babalawo* he first wrote "Ogun (the god of iron, which is of hunting and war)," and then crossed out the first "of," so that it reads simply "Ogun (the god iron . . .)."[10]

This is consistent with the common practice of Ogun's cult as CMS evangelists noted it. At Erinla near Ondo, a man worships Ogun in the form of some iron implements with a piece of skin from an elephant's tail,[11] and at Leke on the eastern Lagoon, a pastor encounters six men in an enclosure next to a house worshipping Ogun as "twelve guns arranged horizontally in a row, an animal having been sacrificed to worship them."[12] But what particularly underscores how much Ogun is identified with iron is that clear instances of Ogun worship are often described without Ogun being named as such—something that happens with no other deity. A Lagos pastor sees a dead fowl hanging over the anvil, and bits of kola lying around, in a blacksmith's shop. Asked why he doesn't eat them instead, the blacksmith replies that he must be "paying religious homage to his tools as such acts make him to be always lucky."[13] The German missionary J. A. Maser gives a fuller account of a rather similar ritual at Abeokuta:

> Abroad in the town, he encounters a family group gathered in a blacksmith's shop for an oracular consultation. Seven "country hammers," the blacksmith's tools, are set up erect, and he addresses each in turn, breaking kola as he does so. As the pieces fall, the answers are lucky or not. The sacrificial fowl is held up in front of the hammers. As Maser retires, not wanting to disturb the ceremony, the blacksmith calls him back to partake of the kola, which he declines.

Maser does not say that the ritual here is addressed to Ogun, but this obvious fact is confirmed when he calls back ten days later to find the blacksmith in the "house of Ogun" close by, "making *odun* [festival]" with his fellow worshippers.[14] Elsewhere, in the absence of the clinching presence of the blacksmith, iron objects of worship can be only presumptively attributed to Ogun, though I think the presumption must usually be very strong, as with the calabash with a plate, an old rusty sword, a mug, and a half-pair of scissors which made up the idol of a man at Palma,[15] or the "new god of iron" that Chief Olikosi of Ota set up in the center of his house.[16] A case that is less certain is a reference to people rescuing their "gods of iron" from their houses during a fire at Abeokuta, for the plural might indicate other deities, such as Orisa Oko or Osanyin, whose cult objects were also made of iron.[17]

The links between Ogun and iron appear more directly in connection with blacksmiths, who are engaged in the mysterious transformations of ore and metal, than with other occupational groups, such as hunters, warriors, and farmers, who merely use iron tools. Here I find a curious and marked bias in the CMS references. Although Ogun was more widely worshipped (both by individuals and as the major deity of the community) in the east, nearly all the references to blacksmiths, whether or not they also refer to Ogun, occur in documents relating to central or western Yorubaland. This does not seem likely to have occurred randomly, and yet obviously there were many blacksmiths in the east, so it is a real puzzle that they are virtually missing from the detailed and continuous reportage that we have for more than thirty years from Ondo.[18]

The most likely immediate reason has to do with the public saliency of blacksmiths, which would affect the frequency of missionary allusion to them. In central and western Yorubaland, blacksmiths' shops are often mentioned in reports of public preaching about the town, for they were places where people liked to congregate, like markets, thus providing the evangelist with a ready-made audience. The processes of ironworking were also a rich source of useful metaphors. In one case the evangelist affects to accuse the blacksmith of cruelty for putting the iron in the fire and inflicting blows on it—"iron being worshipped by the people as the god of iron," he adds—and goes on to ask them: "To whom then . . . should we give thanks—He who makes the iron for our use or the iron which is made?"[19] In another case, a catechist chances on the workers separating the dross from the pure iron, and likens it to sin. "As this iron was useless before you smelted it, so is our body," he tells them. "We are to be purified before we are made fit for the kingdom of heaven and there is no furnace that would make us pure, but the blood of Christ which cleanseth from all sins."[20]

These two cases come from Ota and Ibadan, and apparently blacksmiths' shops were not the same kind of public place as this in Ondo. Weavers' sheds—again a venue suitable for the evangelist to make contacts[21]—are something of a parallel case: present in Abeokuta and Ibadan, but absent in Ondo. Here there is an obvious reason—the east lacked the tradition of men's weaving that existed among the Oyo and Egba[22]—which does not help us directly, but still suggests that regional comparison may clarify things. For to the contrasts between eastern and central/western Yorubaland in the prominence of the Ogun cult and in the frequency of reference to blacksmiths in missionary reportage can be added a third: the scale of ironworking activity itself. Map 11.1 is a consolidation, with some additions, of two maps in Afolabi Ojo's *Yoruba Culture*. These show that whereas the great civic festivals of Ogun are to be found in the east, especially in its forest regions, the centers of iron mining and smelting—the real seat of iron technology—are located in an arc running from the Awori country west of Lagos up into Egbado, to a large area of north-central Yorubaland between Ibadan, Iseyin, and Ogbomosho, possibly to Ilorin.[23]

That blacksmiths' shops in the center/west appear more prominently as public venues may be related to the practice here of a wider and more elaborate range of ironworking techniques, which included smelting. Though Eugenia Herbert

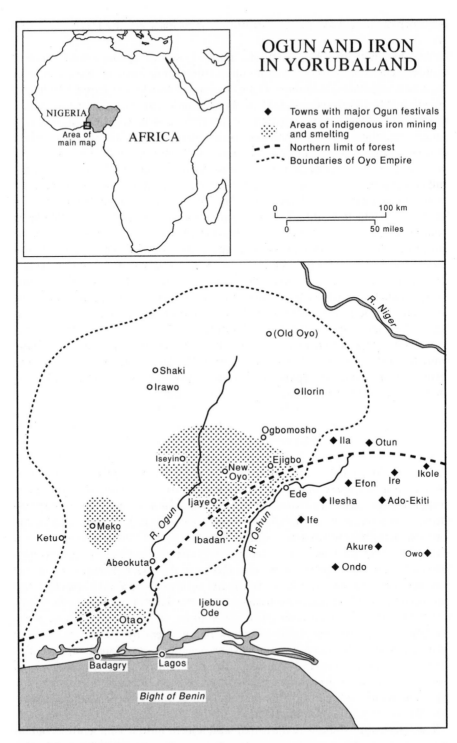

MAP II.I Ogun and Iron in Yorubaland

in her recent comparative study of African ironworking has underscored the contrast between smelting and smithing, the correlations we have found for Yorubaland rather undermine her linkage of smithing with the public and smelting with the secret and isolated.[24] It was in the Yoruba east, which lacked a strong tradition of smelting, that blacksmiths appear to have worked inside their compounds, just as women did their weaving. Yet it was also here, where iron was most scarce because it was not locally produced, and was imported from the smelting areas of the west and north,[25] that Ogun was held in the greatest honor.[26] For iron must have been particularly crucial in enabling agriculture and human settlement to take place in the formidable environment of the southeastern forests. *"Eni pe Ilaje l'oko, ko ni irin ajo Ogun ye"* (Whoever calls Ilaje a farm will not have Ogun to clear his journey's path) goes an Ijesha proverb, referring to a small village which was once the kingdom's capital before the foundation of Ilesha.[27] What this proverb declares, like the festivals of Ogun in towns such as Ilesha and Ondo, is how much the overall viability of the community depends on the use of iron. The festivals do this most emphatically through the parades of the male citizenry through the town, marshaled by their *egbe* or quarter-based bands of militia under their *elegbe* chiefs, which are such a prominent feature of them.[28] This tendency to associate Ogun with the generality of the townsfolk, rather than just with those whose work brings them into close contact with iron, is perhaps the keynote of the cult of Ogun in eastern Yorubaland.

Ogun as Snake: A Lost Cult?

Nothing that has been said so far—whether about the individual devotions of blacksmiths and others who worked with iron, or about the communal importance of Ogun in eastern Yorubaland—challenges the notion, widespread in the literature, that (as Abraham's *Dictionary* puts it) "Ogun is worshipped only by men, not by women." This might seem to make symbolic sense for a deity "of iron and war," yet it is not true. Pierre Verger has given a detailed account of women's participation as *iyaworisa*, *"femmes dediees a l'Orisa et qui chantent pour lui,"* in a festival of Ogun Igbo in the Nago villages of Ilodo and Isede, and Margaret Drewal has described women possessed by Ogun not far away at Igbogila in Egbado.[29] For a more prosaic instance of female devotion to Ogun, there was the woman butcher noted by E. M. Lijadu at Ondo in 1892.[30] As she went into her stall in the market, she gathered up her iron implements, split kola and threw the pieces several times over them, and offered some "incantations." To Lijadu's question, she said she was "consulting Aje the goddess of money through Ogun the god of iron [and that] Aje promises to send me many customers with much money to carry home after the market." This Ogun/Aje linkage is attested from elsewhere;[31] and, as a woman's ritual directed at personal wealth, it may perhaps be seen as practically analogous to the cult of Ori, which was popular among wealthy women in central and southwestern Yorubaland but apparently absent from the east.[32] As described here by Lijadu, such elements of the ritual as breaking kola over iron tools seem identical to those practiced by male workers with iron.

But the main way in which Ogun appears in the CMS journals as an object of women's worship is quite different: not as iron but as a snake. It was not exclusively a women's cult, though women were most active in it (as, indeed, in most *orisa* cults). The most dramatic account of the cult of Ogun-as-snake relates to Ijaye in 1855:

> It was the annual Ifa festival of the *Are* Kurunmi, despotic ruler of the town, and large crowds had gathered before the gate of his compound. Most of them were said to be "worshippers of the orisa called Ogun or snake," for Kurunmi's late mother had been one of its principal devotees, and this was in remembrance of her. Lots of snakes of different sizes from different parts of the town were brought to "play" with Kurunmi, but he wouldn't allow them inside his house since [says the catechist Charles Phillips] he was afraid of them. So they were displayed on a platform set up in front of it. The worshippers took them up and carried them in their arms: mild unless irritated, some were up to six feet long and as thick as a man's thigh. The people looked upon them with curiosity and praise.[33]

Kurunmi's own premier *orisa* was Sango, and a rather similar (though reversed) family linkage of Sango and Ogun came up during a pastoral visit at Ota: a female devotee of Sango has a child dedicated to Ogun, whose snake is kept in a calabash where it's fed with rats.[34]

But the cult was most commonly encountered when its members went about the town with their Ogun-snakes, offering blessings in the god's name, and receiving gifts of cowries (in essence, sacrifices) in return.[35] An African pastor in Abeokuta in 1852 met two women, "one of whom had a large snake curled round her neck, while the other as a crier went before singing and extolling Ogun the god of blacksmith [*sic*]."[36] Many years later another pastor, on the road to the Ibadan camp at Ikirun, met a "snake charmer" who had once even attended church at Ibadan with a Christian friend; he reproached him for "directing [people] to worship Ogun through the snake to earn his livelihood."[37] Back in Ibadan, a catechist told a woman sitting by the roadside with her snake and getting a few cowries from passersby that Ogun was not the true God to worship.[38] A traveling Methodist missionary was visited by a female "snake charmer" at Oyo in the early 1890s.[39] Our last glimpse of the cult is again in Ibadan, when a European woman missionary encounters "sitting by the roadside an old woman, an Ogun worshipper with a huge snake coiled round the body, and she asking alms of the people."[40] Some missionary must have photographed the elderly female *Ologun*, captioned "a snake charmer," who is shown in Figure 11.1[41]

This form of the cult of Ogun seems to have gone unremarked in the secondary literature, save for the briefest passing reference in Talbot's *Peoples of Southern Nigeria* (1926) to "snake charmers," who adore [Ogun] in the guise of a smallish snake called Mana-mana."[42] This does not sound as if it derives from any very close acquaintance with the cult, since *mona-mona* means "py-

FIGURE 11.1 A female devotee of Ogun, with a snake coiled
around her body, photographed before 1932.

thon," which better fits the descriptions of the sometimes large snakes which occur in eyewitness reports from the nineteenth century. Evidently erased from the memory of Abraham's educated informants in Ibadan in the early 1950s (along with the memory that women also worshipped Ogun), it seems likely that it died out rather rapidly in the early twentieth century. The old woman whom Mrs. Fry met with her snake near Kudeti Church in 1911 must have been one of a dwindling band. It looks likely that it died out sooner among the Egba than among the Oyo Yoruba: the sole Abeokuta reference is from the 1850s, whereas those for the Oyo areas continue into the 1880s and later. This seems supported by the confused reference to the cult in the Reverend T. Harding's summary account of Egba religion in 1888: he emphasizes the importance of Ogun in a listing of *orisa* which goes on to mention Orisa Oko and Yemoja, and right at the end notes that worship is also given "to a snake called Manumanu."[43] Harding's failure to link "Manumanu" explicitly with Ogun, if it is not due to misunderstanding or ignorance, suggests that this form of Ogun's cult was by then rare if not extinct at Abeokuta.

It is not easy, in the absence of evidence of other kinds from outside the CMS papers, to explain why Ogun's cult should take this form. But one final negative clue gives us a little help. There is only one reference to Ogun-as-snake from outside the central and western areas, but it is an exception which seems to prove the rule that this cult was exotic to the east:

> At Ondo in 1878 a man and a woman were seen to have brought from Ile-Ife several snakes which they publicly exhibited "as the god Ogun, blessing the people in its name . . . [and getting] large amounts of cowries in return." But next day one of the quarter chiefs took against them when they started their display in his street, and threatened to cut the snakes to pieces. This triggered a popular clamor against them, and the *Lisa* [Ondo's most powerful chief of the day] advised them to get out of town.[44]

Since the site of Ile-Ife was all but deserted at this time, it seems quite likely that these two religious entrepreneurs were not themselves Ifes but Oyos from the adjacent settlement of Modakeke, where the cult must have been as prevalent as it was in Ibadan or Ijaye. However that may be, the Ondos clearly took it greatly amiss that strangers should come and present one of their most important deities in such an outlandish form.

So we need to seek an explanation in terms that apply specifically to the situation in central and western Yorubaland. Dahomey might seem a possible source, since it had two notable snake deities. There was the *vodun* Dangbe, represented by a large python at its major cult center at Whydah, and also worshipped along the Lagoon eastward as far as Badagry;[45] and there was also the rainbow serpent Dan, otherwise known as Aido-Hwedo or (by the Yoruba) Osumare, whose origins were traced to the Mahi country north of Abomey.[46] But neither of these seems to have any affinity with Ogun (or with Gu, his Dahomean form). In any case, an explanation of a cult in terms of external origins is less helpful than one which deals with its intrinsic meaning.

Unfortunately, the lack of external evidence to supplement the thin accounts in the CMS journals prevents more than the most hesitant speculation. Snake symbolism in general can carry a number of different connotations, but one of the most widespread is of earth-rooted or chthonic power, and this would fit with the technologies of iron *production,* mining, and smelting, long practiced in central and western Yorubaland.[47] Ogun-as-snake evidently had its heartland in the Oyo towns where Ogun, while not attaining the degree of civic recognition that it got in the iron-hungry east, was nevertheless an ancient cult, probably more so than Sango.[48] It was at Oyo in the 1950s that Peter Morton-Williams came across the *orisa* Alajogun, a refraction of Ogun known as the deity of fighting.[49] Alajogun, unlike Ogun himself, *was* represented in human form, and in one instance was accompanied by his wife Oke Ijemori, she standing with a snake around her neck (for she was said to play with them)! Their children were hills (*oke*), and one wonders if iron-bearing hills were particularly intended. For what more appropriate as a symbol of this great power drawn from the earth than *mona-mona,* the python?

Ogun and Orisa Oko

The prominence of any one of Ogun's potential meanings or functions in a particular place depends partly on local circumstances (such as the mining and smelting operations of the center/west, or the acute iron hunger of the east), but it is also affected by what other deities are present in any local complex of cults. By "local cult complex" I mean the ensemble of cults found in a particular place, which is likely to include both a good many of the *orisa* found widely (especially those that figure in Ifa divination verses) and others of more local currency, perhaps even unique to that place. These complexes are the practical, concrete reality of Yoruba religion, rather than the Pan-Yoruba pantheons—models or idealizations which give each *orisa* a particular character, temporally and spatially uniform, and set them in a system of complementary relations with one another—which dominate the literature.[50] What is generally held to be distinctive of an *orisa* is also qualified by the fact that all *orisa* are required by their devotees to provide much the same range of general benefits: protection, health, guidance, children, wealth, etc. This means that female *orisa* (such as the gentle and fecund river goddesses Osun and Yemoja) sometimes take on "male" qualities, such as fierceness, while *orisa* with predominantly male functions (such as Ogun or Sango) can also be associated with fertility for their female devotees.[51] The mobility of *orisa,* whether as a consequence of the migration of their ordinary adherents or through the promotional zeal of their priests, also promotes shifts in the character of *orisa.* An incoming *orisa* may find its special niche (as the deity of new yams, or smallpox, or hunting) already occupied, or it may seek to carve out a new niche for itself. Even the thunder god Sango, who seems the most essentially male of deities, can come to be represented as female where he is a latecomer to communities that already have a male thunder deity.[52] The unending push and pull between the homogenization and the differentiation of cults that takes place in the Yoruba religious marketplace means that no single cult should be considered in isolation.

As the "god of the farm," whose main cult emblem was an iron stave made from hoe blades, Orisa Oko overlaps with Ogun in respect of the application of iron technology to agriculture. Though variously described as male or female, Orisa Oko is most commonly represented in myth as a hunter who turned to farming. His main cult center was at Irawo, a small town in the far northwest of the Yoruba country, where there was an important shrine for the settlement of witchcraft accusations. According to the Reverend Thomas King (himself an Egba), Orisa Oko was the most esteemed and prominent deity worshipped by women at Abeokuta; it was handed down in families, where its first acquisition "was always originate[d] from the accusation of witchcraft and sorcery."[53] Initiation was expensive, but membership carried social privileges: devotees (recognized by red and white marks on the forehead) could not be seized for debt, might cross war lines, and were exempt from tolls.[54] The interdict against their coming into contact with dead bodies suggests the relevance of the same complex of ideas about pollution and death that pertain to the cleansing role of the blacksmith's forge. But the clearest case of functional overlap at Abeokuta between Orisa Oko and Ogun was evident when, in order to promote cotton as a cash crop, the CMS introduced a roller gin. Its erection and operation aroused great interest among the Egba: some reckoned that it was "a sort of mysteriously acting fieldpiece . . . for the use of the Egbas against their enemies," while others, contemplating it in silence, took it to be a manifestation of Orisa Oko.[55] In view of Ogun's celebrated adaptation to modern technology, it is striking that in this instance from the mid-1850s it was Orisa Oko who took the part: "a god represented by iron," explains our witness.

In the CMS reports from Ibadan, Orisa Oko figures somewhat differently. There is less emphasis on the elite status of Orisa Oko's devotees, but more on the communal importance of the cult. Because Abeokuta was an amalgamation of many "townships," which each kept their cultic peculiarities, there was virtually no cult that embraced the whole town save that of Oro, the collective ancestors.[56] Ibadan's population was even more heterogeneous in its origins, but its early settlers were so scrambled that townwide festivals could coalesce more readily. The Egba pastor of Ibadan, Daniel Olubi, considered that, because "the whole town" was involved in them, the three principal deities of Ibadan were Orisa Oko, in whose honor "every gate and street are full of soup and pounded yams," along with Ogiyan (one of the "white deities," related to Obatala) and Oke'badan ("Ibadan Hill," the genius loci).[57] Orisa Oko's importance, shown by his association with the New Yam festivities, rested on the Ibadan people's recognition of his key role in the annual reproduction of their community. When the second rains of 1883, much needed and expected, arrived in a nightlong downpour in mid-August, a pastor overheard many people in the street the next day attribute them to Orisa Oko, whose feast was due at the next new moon.[58]

All this seems to be just what we would expect for the chief agricultural deity; and insofar as Ogun could also have agricultural functions, we can consider Orisa Oko to have taken some of the semantic space that Ogun occupied in the east. The exact converse has been noted by Femi Ojo in a western Ekiti town where Orisa Oko had been introduced from an Oyo source: finding Ogun already clearly associated with farming, Orisa Oko had to assume a much more general role, as healer and protector against witchcraft, etc.[59] Another illuminating case is provided by Ila-Orangun, the main Igbomina town, which stands on the border between what I have been calling the east (where Ogun is a major civic deity) and the center/west (where Sango and Orisa Oko have a strong presence). Here, according to Pemberton's careful analysis, Ogun stands in a complementary relationship to Orisa Oko as hunter to farmer, the two aspects of subsistence provision.[60] But the ceremonial placing of the New Yam ritual was not simply a matter of anchoring it to the festival of the main agricultural deity. While it *is* very widely attached to Orisa Oko in the center/west and to Ogun in the east, other *orisa* figure too: most commonly Obalufon, but also Oro at Iseyin, Ifa at Ilesha, Oramfe at Ondo, and even Sango at Ijaye.[61] Its linkage with a particular *orisa* seems to have been governed by practical convenience as much as by what was symbolically most appropriate, though in the towns of the east (as well as some old towns in the center/west, such as Iseyin and Ede) Ogun was always bound into a ceremonial sequence that linked him with collective and royal ancestors, and with the forces of annual renewal, of which eating the New Yam was such a powerful symbol.

Ogun and Sango

As a force to build empire, Ogun is challenged by Sango, the early *Alaafin* of Oyo deified as a thunder god. In a recent analysis, J. L. Matory has persuasively shown that Sango was much more than just the official cult of the regime: he was the very icon of the means and manner of the *Alaafin*'s rule, through his messengers (the *ilari*), the royal wives and Sango priests, who all stood as wives to the god-king as possessing husband.[62] Matory goes on to contrast Ogun with Sango, as a deity who was more effective as a pathfinder or culture hero than as a ruler, and whom myth represents as failing to sustain his marriage with Yemoja. This is fair enough, as far as mythic representations go, but does not capture the manner in which Ogun's cult realized its communal importance, particularly among the eastern Yoruba. The central feature is that, despite his linkage with royal ancestors, Ogun's was typically a civic, rather than a royal, cult: a deity worshipped "from the king to the poorest man," as M. J. Luke nicely put it for Ilesha in 1889.[63] A clear sign of this is the occurrence during Ogun festivals—as at Ilesha and Ila—of mock battles between palace and town chiefs, ritual dramas which present the expression and resolution of conflicts between the king and the people as lying at the heart of the public life of the community. At Ilesha, it was chiefs particularly connected with Ogun/iron who mediated the tensions between the king and the people.[64]

In the 1820s the imperial order of Old Oyo gave way to seventy years of turbulence among its successor states and their neighbors, which Matory sees as an "Age of Ogun" following an "Age of Sango." The newly dominant social forms of the period—the warlords (*ologun*) and their retainers or "war boys" (*omo-ogun*), their vast military households, their prominence in the title systems of new towns such as Ibadan, Abeokuta, and Ijaye—have been well described by historians.[65] Matory's is quite a Yoruba way of putting it, in terms of successive "ages" (*aiye*) which each have their distinct character, and there is some evidence that contemporaries could see it this way too. A *babalawo,* in discussion with an African catechist in Ibadan in 1855, put down the wars to God's having sent Esu (disorder) and Ogun (war) "to execute His vengeance on men upon the earth for their disobedience."[66] Two decades later, a rather similar diagnosis was made by another *babalawo,* also in Ibadan.[67] God had sent Ogun and Sopona into the world to "render unto everyone according to his deeds." "Ogun is armed with 4000 short swords and he goes out daily on the earth to slay, for his meat is to drink the blood of the slain." The *babalawo* ended by referring to Sango, "a very mighty god, and when he is about to go [into] the world, he is always cautioned by Ifa and Orisanla to deal gently with their own special worshippers." So both Ogun and Sango, like Esu and Sopona, are here seen as destructive deities, in contrast to the saving deities, Ifa and Orisanla (Obatala). But the overall message is less that Yoruba considered this as *uniquely* Ogun's age, than that they recognized Ogun as one of the major forces shaping it.

As far as levels of individual devotion go, there is no evidence from the CMS reports that Sango was at all displaced by Ogun. On the contrary, by the CMS evidence, Sango appears alongside Ifa as the most popular deity of late-nineteenth-century Yorubaland, though less "Pan-Yoruba" in the spread of his appeal than Ifa. Accounting for as many as 38 percent of all *orisa* referred to in other Oyo towns and 27 percent in Ibadan—a difference explicable by Ibadan's significant population of non-Oyo origin—Sango attains 16 percent at Abeokuta, and still reaches 8 percent, equal to Osun, in the east, right outside his home territory. References to Ogun run at much lower levels, except for the east (where Ogun stands at 14 percent). Though these two sets of figures for Ogun and Sango are misleading as direct measures of their relative importance, they do shed light on the social character of the two cults. The number of reports of Sango expresses not merely his popularity, but also the sometimes spectacular appearance of his cult and the zeal with which he was promoted. The cult survived the collapse of the old imperial capital where it had been based, and thrived vigorously in the new world of the *ologun.* It made its way through the belief of its devotees in its protecting power, through the way that it both frightened people and offered them relief from their fears, and through predation, in the form of the fines or purification fees which it levied after a house had been struck by lightning.[68] While priests of Ogun are never mentioned in the CMS reports[69] (except to the extent that a blacksmith might implicitly serve as one), priests of Sango are the next most frequently mentioned religious specialists after *babalawo* and Muslim *alufa*. The senior Sango priests at Ibadan were clearly formidable figures who had to be treated with circumspection by the ruling war chiefs of the town,[70] whereas the cult of Ogun does not appear as a distinct force in the politics of the town at all.

The adaptability of the Sango cult shows up equally at whichever end of its range we view it. As an instrument of rule, its potency was most evident at Ijaye, which until 1862 was Ibadan's only rival as the military successor state to Oyo. Its ruler Kurunmi—functionally a "man of Ogun," if ever there was one—took the headship of the Sango cult himself and made it a mainstay of his regime. But Ijaye was an Oyo town, whose people were already predisposed to hold Sango in awe. More impressive in its way was the extent to which Sango started to make inroads into Ogun's heartland of the east, regions which war and trade had opened to Oyo influence as never before. At Ilesha by the late 1880s, the Sango cultists were wielding a new influence over the king,[71] and their confident public praises of their god excited some popular resentment.[72] The reasons for these developments at Ilesha are obscure, but for Ondo we have a much fuller picture. From the late 1870s Ondo was afflicted by a run of acute smallpox epidemics. Though Sango was said in 1877 to be "worshipped here by only a few . . . [and] looked upon with some degree of contempt by the mass of the people," two years later he had "many worshippers" who conducted an impressive festival.[73] In 1879 and 1880 the chiefs gave large amounts to some newly arrived Sango cultists for sacrifices to expel the disease. The sheer chutzpah of the Sango people in promoting their god as the solution to the epidemic—something for which he was not previously known—can only be wondered at, especially when they called at the CMS compound afterward to mock the Ondos for their gullibility![74]

Ogun's relevance to the public sphere was realized differently from Sango's. In all areas of Yorubaland, the nexus of killing, pollution and purification, and retributory justice was fundamental to it. Kurunmi, who avoided close contact with his mother's cult of Ogun-as-snake, is reported to have turned to Ogun on two occasions, both involving the claim to righteous vengeance. An adulterous wife of his was killed and her organs were torn out "in the front of his house before his Ogu, his god of iron"; and an old woman was killed for an unspecified offense at his Ifa festival, again before his Ogun, who this time received his usual sacrifice of a dog.[75] At Ota the place for executing criminals was a little grove of trees near one of the town gates, known as Ojugun ("the face of Ogun").[76] Ogun's role as the sanction of justice, which was most universally expressed in the practice of swearing on iron, is closely linked to his role in purifying the just shedder of blood. Here every blacksmith's shop was potentially a shrine: after the Egungun at Ibadan had executed the adulterous wife of a chief, the actual killer had to sleep in a blacksmith's shop for several nights, to be released from blood guilt.[77] Both sides at the Kiriji battlefield had shrines of Ogun to which heads of the slain were taken,[78] which sound similar in their general form to the hunters' shrines of Ogun marked out by the cheekbones of elephants.[79] That of the Ekitiparapo was a grove in the middle of the camp where sacrifices were made, and there was also a smithy which could serve as a sanctuary like other blacksmiths' shops.[80] Ogun, even in relation to the butchery of war, was far from being gratuitously bloodthirsty. There is no evidence that he required human sacrifices:[81] when the war staff (*opagun*) was propitiated at the beginning of Ibadan's campaigns, it was Oranyan, not Ogun, for whom a man was killed.[82] Unlike Sango's, the cult of Ogun was not predatory.

Ogundipe as Man of Ogun

Yoruba religion is distinguished equally by the variety of its *orisa* and the reality of personal cultic choice. It has long been suggested that as a result there might be a close correspondence between the personality of the devotee and the character of his god. This idea finds striking confirmation in the case of that individual worshipper of Ogun about whom the CMS missionaries tell us the most, the Egba chief Ogundipe. A revealing little incident is told by the English missionary J. B. Wood, who reckoned him a friend and had many dealings with him.[83] Ogundipe had trained as a blacksmith, and even into his old age (he was now around 70) continued to work at his forge. Wood once called to see him, and knew he was at work from the smoke curling up in the evening air from the back of the house. Since no member of Ogundipe's house dared to interrupt him in his smithy, Wood had to wait; he finally had to leave after more than an hour without seeing him. The story discloses not only Ogundipe's commitment to his "mystery" but the awe, even fear, in which his people held him. Like other great war chiefs, he maintained a large polygynous household whose conflicts might be exacerbated by his authoritarian habits. If a wife or a slave absconded, he would pursue his rights with ferocious persistence, and on at least two occasions he killed adulterous wives.[84] His end was tragic. In failing health and fearing plots against him, he kept revolvers and a rifle always at his side, and he shot one of his wives, whom he suspected of poisoning his sleeping mat.[85] His death a few days later was suspected to be by his own hand—or perhaps someone in his household could stand his rage no longer.

If all this recalls the myths of Ogun's propensity for violence and his own fraught marriage, other sides of Ogundipe's life fit more positive aspects of the mythical template. The Methodist missionary Halligey called him "not only a brave warrior, but a very skillful mechanic—quite an artist in metal work": he made his own staff of brass, ornamented "with curious figures."[86] Ogundipe's artistic interests extended to music as well as to metalwork: he composed songs, which he set to his own music and had sung by a choir of his wives! Halligey actually met him "engaged in one of those interesting rehearsals," conducting some twenty-five women who accompanied their singing with a gentle rhythmical swaying and clapping. The words of the song, alluding to recent conflict in the town, were as follows:

> They who destroy other men's houses really destroy their own;
> The war chiefs sent their men to pull down the houses of the white men.
> The houses of the war chiefs must now come down.
> Cowards and thieves these war chiefs are.
> Strangers who visit us in peace they plunder.
> Ah! When the Dahomians come, these chiefs will flee.

We seem here to have a synthesis between the topical chants associated with the Oro cult (performed by men),[87] the Christian practice of conducted choral singing, and perhaps an element of praise poetry (*oriki*, performed by women). The expressed sentiment of retributive violence, of course, is most thoroughly Ogun.[88] And even as they sang their husband's praises, the women could not have forgotten that like Ogun he was capable of doing terrible things in his anger.

Yet despite Ogundipe's capacity for violence, in the public life of Abeokuta, insisted J. B. Wood, "he was admired, feared and *respected*. As a judge he was liked. Generally there was a fairness in his judgments much above the average, whilst his charges as a judge were moderate."[89] The Egba attributed the failure of the second rains of 1887, shortly after his death, to the passing of a great man.[90] He had first come to attention in the 1850s as the lieutenant of the enlightened chief Ogunbona,[91] on whose death he became in turn the chief patron of the missionaries. He staunchly supported them during and after the "Outbreak" of 1867 (when the Europeans were expelled from Abeokuta). Ogundipe's policy was always to keep trade routes to Lagos open and to encourage cultural innovation: when he argued, against those who wanted to maintain the blockade of the river linking Abeokuta and the Lagoon, that "the river was made by God and is for him, and that whatever is made by God is made for the Common use of all his creatures,"[92] the Ogun theme of open roads [93] converges with ideas of Christian enlightenment. Ogundipe was widely known by the sobriquet *Alatise*,[94] a name which alludes to a proverb that promotes the ideal of active responsibility: its meaning comes close to "a man's got to do what a man's got to do."[95] Toward the end of his life he modified it to the title *Alatunse* ("the one who restores things").[96] Though this seems to allude directly to his role in the installation of an *Alake* (the Egba paramount) in 1884, it also clearly echoes a recurrent missionary theme: that their preaching was about *atunse aiye*, "the restoration of the world" from its present state of confusion.[97]

Ogun in History

Of the two main ways in which anthropology can be historical—in dealing with the past as other, and in addressing the problem of change—this chapter has concentrated on the former, in attempting to give an account of the cult of Ogun as it was in the second half of the nineteenth century. The variations that have concerned us have chiefly been variations across space, not across time, and particularly as they link with variations in levels of missionary reportage of different *orisa*. The problem of Ogun's greater prominence in the Yoruba east proved less intractable than that of the apparently low level of his reportage in the center/west, when compared with that of some other *orisa*, notably Sango. To some extent, functions ascribed to Ogun in the east are taken up by other *orisa* in the center/west, such as the agricultural deity Orisa Oko. The case of Sango, however, was quite otherwise: it was a matter less of competition for the same functional niche than of a general challenge posed by a cult that was distinctly organized, aggressively promoted, and endowed with formidable sanctions. Ogun, by contrast, was a cult much more implicitly grounded in a range of mundane activities that were vital to the welfare of the community, all arising from the perceived importance of iron. These respective characteristics ensured that Sango would get the maximum "publicity" in missionary reports, while Ogun would tend to be underreported.

When the otherness of past practice is clearly shown—as here, most strikingly, with the largely female cult of Ogun-as-snake—the problem of change soon demands attention too. The conundrum here is that, while it is the differences between present and past that pose the problem, the past has to be seen as providing essential conditions for the present. The great fact about Ogun's recent history is his singular relative success, over a period in which *orisa* cults in general have been in marked decline, in adapting to the circumstances of modernity. Where Orisa Oko has declined with the marginalization of subsistence agriculture, and the Sango cult has lost its most potent sanctions, Ogun never depended on such sanctions and still possesses a large field in which he is the implicit controlling force. Though some of his areas of functional relevance have shrunk in importance—subsistence farming, hunting, local warfare, and mining/smelting operations—there has been a vast expansion in others, such as the use and repair of iron implements. If we see Ogun *qua* iron in the center of the picture, then it is a shift away from the producer to the user end of iron technology. I suggest that the demise of Ogun's snake cult was an aspect of this shift. Most notable of all, perhaps, has been the uses of iron in relation to modern travel, where Ogun's traditional connection with the open road has been reaffirmed. The nexus of mechanics, drivers, motor park touts (*agbero*), party thugs, etc.—the milieu memorably depicted in Soyinka's *The Road*—extends back to some of the values of the nineteenth-century war boys.

How far the modern manifestation of Ogun has been affected by his perception as a culture hero or as the archetype of the artist, as Soyinka has expressed it, is hard to say. Suffice it to note that, whatever his personal religious beliefs, Soyinka stands directly in a tradition that runs back to the central figures of late-nineteenth-century Egba Christianity. His great-grandfather J. J. Ransome-Kuti was very probably among the clergy and elders whom Harding assembled at Ake Church in 1888, the year after Ogundipe's death, to provide collective answers to a questionnaire about Egba religion, and who gave it as their view that Ogun was "the chief of all the many gods of the Yoruba people

. . . when other gods are consulted, their reply is 'worship Ogun.'"[98] The aggregate evidence of the CMS archive is hardly compatible with quite such a sweeping view. But perhaps we may interpret the opinion as a sign for the future as well as a statement about the past, as showing that a body of leading Christians was already prepared to regard Ogun as an acceptable symbol of some widely shared values of their culture.

NOTES

1. In preparing this paper I have been much helped by discussions with Karin Barber, Sandra Barnes, Tom McCaskie, Peter Morton-Williams, Bayo Ogundijo, Akin Oyetade, and John Picton, and by several of those who attended the Tenth Satterthwaite Colloquium on African Religion and Ritual, April 1994.

Any serious student of the CMS papers must also incur a debt of gratitude to their custodians at Birmingham University Library, particularly Dr. B. S. Benedikz and Miss Christine Penney. The documents I have cited are all from the Yoruba Mission, O (incoming papers) series, classified before 1880 under the heading CA 2 (by author), from 1880 under G3 A2 (by year).

2. Soyinka 1976:27–32, 140–60.

3. On which see Ibigbami 1978.

4. C. Phillips, Journal, 16 Sept. 1883; E. M. Lijadu, Journal, 21 Aug. 1891. On Ogun in Ondo see Olupona 1991, and further comments in Peel 1994.

5. M. J. Luke, Journal, June 1889.

6. Peel 1983:269, 326–27.

7. We can, however, assume that Sango was not as new to the southwest as to Ondo and the southeast, since his cult would have accompanied Oyo control of the trade corridor through Egbado to the coast since the early eighteenth century (Morton-Williams 1964; Asiwaju 1976).

8. Thus F. L. Akiele (letter to T. Harding, 6 May 1902), referring to a large sacrifice to Ogun by the chiefs of a village near Ogbomosho.

9. The Abeokuta church elders consulted by Harding expressly stated that no images were made of Ogun, but that anvil stones might be worshipped; they didn't even think it needed to be said that *any* iron could serve as Ogun (Harding to Merensky, 19 Nov. 1888). Kevin Carroll's judgment (1967:41) that "Yoruba people do not identify any spirit with an image; nor can it be said that they believe the spirits come to dwell in the images" would seem not quite to apply to Ogun, since iron, though the object to which the actions of Ogun worship are addressed, is not equivalent to an image which "represents" an *orisa*.

10. J. Barber, Journal, 14 Jan. 1856.

11. C. Phillips Jr., Journal, 4 Dec. 1877.

12. E. W. George, Journal, 5 June 1890.

13. T. B. Wright, Journal, 21 Jan. 1867.

14. J. A. Maser, Journal, 2 Oct. 1864. A "house of Ogun" might range in type from a thatched roof on four posts, only a couple of feet high, covering an old anvil stone or some iron implements, to a proper temple big enough for worshippers to enter. One might surmise from the time interval between the two occasions that the oracular consultation was to determine a propitious day for the *odun*.

15. M. J. Luke, Journal, 27 Apr. 1877. Palma, near Leke on the eastern Lagoon, had a very mixed population: mostly Ijebu, Lagosians of the Kosoko faction, and eastern Yoruba, Ijesha, and others, many being escaped slaves.

16. J. White, Journal, 4 Aug. 1870.

17. E. W. George, Journal, 29 Jan. 1877. On iron cult objects of other *orisa,* see Thompson 1976: chaps. 7, 10, 11.

18. M. J. Luke (Journal, 27 May 1889) met one who supported his preaching at Okemesi. In Ilesha, tradition holds that when a new quarter was founded, a blacksmith (*agbede*) was always included among the first settlers. A small area near the palace was called Odo Agbede, and the blacksmiths had their own hereditary chief, the *Sajowa* (Peel 1983:22, 34–35, 270).

19. J. White, Journal, 30 Apr. 1857, at Ota.

20. W. S. Allen, Journal, 26 June 1872, at Ibadan.

21. See D. Hinderer, Journal, 24 Sept. 1849, at Abeokuta; W. S. Allen, Journal, 7 July 1869, at Ibadan.

22. Women wove on upright looms which were set up in the courtyard or on the verandah of the house, whereas men's weaving involved long horizontal looms, set up in sheds or under awnings in public places.

23. Ojo 1966:96, 171. On smelting in Ilobi and Imeko (Egbado), see Asiwaju 1976:23. Ibadan itself should surely be included: one of its ironworking quarters, Eleta, was named after the ironstone (*eta*) found there (Falola 1984:96–98). Ilorin's name is often linked to the "grinding" of iron (*lo + irin*), as by Abraham 1958: s.v. Ilorin, but this does not seem to imply smelting. At Ile Bandele in Ilorin, a large stone is shown where this is said to have been done (Professor Stefan Reichmuth, pers. comm.).

24. Herbert 1993:12–14, 160–61, chap. 5 passim: "Smith and forge [are] much more integrated into the life of the community than the smelting furnace, and the smithy becomes simultaneously a place of asylum and an adjunct to political power." The sort of specialized smelting settlement that existed in central Yorubaland, such as Isundunrin near Ejigbo (Bellamy 1904) or the various villages called Iponrin, fits her thesis better. But smelting was clearly not limited to such places.

25. Ilesha tradition, for example, recalls that smelted iron was imported from the Ejigbo area (Peel 1983:22).

26. This is consistent with Denis Williams's linkage of West Africa's "iron hunger" with the ritualization of the metal (1974:67–86), though he does not extend his persuasive argument to intra-Yoruba variations in Ogun/iron.

27. See further Peel 1983:22–24, 270.

28. For eyewitness accounts of this at the Ogun festival in nineteenth-century Ondo, see C. Phillips, Journal, 23 Sept. 1877, and E. M. Lijadu, Journal, 21 Aug. 1891. For a certain shift in the character of the modern festival there, see Olupona 1991:chap. 5, and further discussion in Peel 1994:159–60.

29. Verger 1957:150ff.; Drewal 1992:183–84.

30. E. M. Lijadu, Journal, 11 Nov. 1892.

31. See the *oriki* to "Aje Onire Ogungunniso," collected at Kuta near Iwo by Belasco (1980:140ff.), who speaks of "the theme of interpenetrated trade and war, the inextricable unity of Ogun and Aje."

32. On Ori, see Barber 1994. E.g., Osu Daropale, "an influential woman here [Badagry], but . . . of dissolute character," is noted to "worship her head," writes S. Pearse, Journal, 2 April 1863.

33. C. Phillips Sr., Journal, 26 Oct. 1855.

34. J. White, Journal, 31 May 1855.

35. For a fuller account of this practice of sacrifice, see Peel 1990.

36. T. King, Journal, 9 March 1852.

37. R. S. Oyebode, Journal, 22 Oct. 1889.

38. F. L. Akiele, Journal, 10 Sept. 1890.

39. Halligey 1893:39–40. He does not in fact *say* she was a devotee of Ogun, but I can't see what else she would be. The Yoruba do not have "snake charmers" as such.

40. Letter from Mrs Ernest Fry, No. 25 (printed), 5 July 1911.

41. The photograph is from a series of postcards, showing local scenes, features of cultural interest, etc., sold at the CMS Bookshops up to the 1930s. It was posted in 1932, and is among the Unofficial Papers in the CMS Archive. The thatched roof in the background suggests a location in or near the savanna. I am grateful to Mr. Duncan Clark for drawing my attention to this photograph.

42. Talbot 1926:88. Drewal (1989:204) refers to a small black and red snake called *agbaadu* as a symbol of Ogun, but the point of the symbolism—that it is "quick, vicious and deadly"—seems to put it in quite a separate case from the placid *mona-mona*.

43. T. Harding to A. Merensky, 19 Nov. 1888.

44. C. Phillips, Journal, 19-20 Aug. 1878.

45. As Verger (1957:511-22) notes, of all West African cults Dangbe's was one of the most commonly described by European visitors. See, for example, Burton 1966 [1864]:73-76. For CMS reports of "Idagbe" (as they call it in Yoruba style) at Badagry, see the journals of S. A. Crowther and of H. Townsend for the three months ending 25 June 1846, and of S. Pearse, 5 Oct. 1861. The main "female" festival took place at Idale, a village four miles off, and a concluding "male" part took place at Badagry itself.

46. Verger 1957:233-38; Herskovits 1938: vol.2, chap. 32, "The Cult of the Serpent."

47. Sandra Barnes reminds me that in Camara Laye's autobiographical novel *L'Enfant Noir,* the narrator comes from a blacksmith lineage which has as its "totem" a small snake, which lives in a crack in the smithy wall.

48. Such as Ede and Iseyin. At Ede, Ogun was originally the principal *orisa* of the town, only later displaced by Sango, but is still linked with the New Yam, Oranyan, and the royal ancestors (Beier 1959:42). At Iseyin, the Oro festival (collective ancestors) began with the worship of Ogun, attended by the king in the marketplace (S. Johnson, Journal, 12 Aug. 1882). This was Johnson's first visit to Iseyin, and he quotes a proverb to show that this was an old town, never destroyed in war: *Bi a se keke ote, ki a mu ti Asehin kuro* ("If lots are cast for revolt, the Aseyin should be counted out"). Dennett (1968 [1910]:123-24) briefly describes the court in the palace at Iseyin where the king heard cases: an iron chain was stretched across it, which as Ogun received sacrifices.

49. Morton-Williams, personal communication, 1994. Alajogun was worshipped in the household of the *Asipa* of Oyo as one of the *orisa funfun.*

50. For a review of the main listings of *orisa* in a pantheon, which argues that "the variations in the hierarchical ordering make the lists untenable," see Ojo 1978.

51. Barber 1981 is illuminating on the social mechanisms involved here.

52. See Schiltz 1985 on how at Ketu and Sabe, Sango is considered to be the senior wife of Ara, the locally established thunder god.

53. T. King, Journal, 23 June 1861. This entry gives a remarkable account of the Orisa Oko cult (as far as I know, the earliest account we have). It was triggered by a devotee's renunciation of the cult (and of one of its tokens, a small ivory horn a few inches long, decorated with cowries): this was considered unusual, granted the strong devotion of this *orisa*'s followers. See too H. Townsend, "Journal of a Journey from Abbeokuta to Ijaye, Shaki and Isein," 16 Jan. 1855. The best modern study of Orisa Oko is Ojo 1973, though the case is rather atypical, since it relates to a village in Ekiti, where the cult was an introduction from the Oyo area. Also valuable is Thompson 1976:chap. 10, especially on the staves.

54. On the special status of Orisa Oko devotees, see further James Johnson, Annual Report for 1879; T. King, Journal, 2 April 1852.

55. S. Crowther Jr., Journal, June 1855.

56. As Rev. S. A. Crowther put it, in a brief ethnography—ostensibly of the Yoruba, but written from Abeokuta—"there is an established religion connected with government, which is the worship of the dead or their deceased ancestors" (letter to T. J. Hutchinson, 10 Sept. 1856).

57. D. Olubi, Annual Letter to Fenn, 28 Dec. 1875. Olubi was an Egba who first came to Ibadan as a servant to David Hinderer in 1851 and took over as leader of the

Ibadan church in 1869, continuing as its patriarch till his death in 1912. No outsider was in a better position to make this judgment.

58. W. S. Allen, Journal, 13 Aug. 1883.

59. Ojo (1973:58) says of an unnamed village in western Ekiti: "Orisa Oko . . . is not regarded as the god of farming. As far as farming is concerned, greater prominence is given to Ogun."

60. Pemberton 1977 and 1989.

61. New Yam deities: Obalufon at some households in Ibadan (J. Barber, Journal, 3 Aug. 1856) and as "god of yams" at Akure (E. M. Lijadu, Journal, 1896); the Oro ancestors at Iseyin (A. Mann, Journal, 2 Aug. 1856); a man sacrifices new yam and corn as thanks to Ifa at Ilesha (M. J. Luke, Journal, 20 Aug. 1889); Oramfe as "god of harvest" at Ondo (E. M. Lijadu, Journal, July 1895; cf. Olupona 1991:96); Sango at Ijaye (H. Townsend, 6 June 1857).

62. Matory 1994:chap 1.

63. See above, n. 4. Compare William Rea's observation on Ogun in contemporary Ikole-Ekiti: "[The] Ogun festival is the major 'civic' (as opposed to 'religious') festival of the year. As a festival it transcends the division between town and palace . . . [it] is about Ikole as a unified town" (Rea 1994:42).

64. Such as Ogboni and Salotun. Ogboni, one of the six most senior titleholders, has a sanctuary stone—symbolically Ogun's anvil—in front of his house. The head blacksmith, Sajowa, belongs to the same lineage as Ogboni, and the worship of their first ancestor Oludu brings the Ogun festival cycle to a close. The mock battle at Iwude Ogun takes place in front of the house of the Salotun, a chief who is under Ogboni (Peel 1980:231; 1983:21–22, 38, 275).

65. Ajayi and Smith 1964; Awe 1973; Falola and Oguntomisin 1984.

66. J. Barber, Journal, 14 Jan. 1855.

67. S. Johnson, Journal, 29 Feb. 1875.

68. Of many examples, one of the most eloquent is J. J. Ransome-Kuti's entry for 29–30 March in his "30th Journal of Evangelistic Work, in Gbagura [Abeokuta]." Lightning struck a house, killing a girl inside. Almost at once large crowds of Sango worshippers appeared, praising the god; and then the *Mogba* (possession priests), whom Ransome-Kuti calls "the rough, rude and robbing portion" of Sango's followers, seized the property and animals of the victims "as rich presents from their king Sango." When the fire had burned itself out, the victims were left sitting in the rain, but were required to feast the Sango people until the indemnities were complete, and they themselves impoverished.

69. Compare again Rea (1994:43) on Ikole: "If asked about the personality of Ogun as an individuated deity . . . people would suggest Ogun was all around: wherever there was iron there was Ogun. There is no Ogun 'cult' *per se* in Ikole, and no 'priest' or *aworo* of Ogun."

70. For example, if lightning struck while the Ibadan army was in the field, "the [war chiefs] are forbidden by custom to offer battle or fight until Sango is propitiated" (S. Johnson, Journal, 30 Sept. 1882). The *Are* Latosisa was then in the war camp at Kiriji, and Johnson staunchly refused to bow to custom after the Aremo mission house had been struck by lightning in a thunderstorm on the 29th. Much long-distance negotiation had to ensue.

71. M. J. Luke, Journal, 24 May 1889. It concerned a "confinement"—a ritual obligation to stay indoors—imposed on the town by the Sango cult in the king's name, like those imposed by Oro in times of crisis at Abeokuta. The circumstances at Ilesha are not described.

72. G. A. Vincent, Journal, 15 April 1885. Vincent, himself Ijesha-born, quotes a woman as saying that the Ijesha "hated those thunder worshippers by their doings."

73. C. Phillips, letter to Fenn, 23 Nov. 1877; Journal, 1 Sept. 1979.

74. C. Phillips, Journal, 17 July 1879; C. N. Young, Journal, 13 Feb. 1880. The disease continued to break out for several years, until in 1884 the chiefs turned against both Sopona and Sango, and banned them (with what long-term result, I do not know).

75. C. Phillips Sr., Journals, 3 Nov. 1853, 20 Oct. 1856.

76. E. Buko, Journal, 16 Feb. 1883: a young man is executed for murdering his master, to whom he'd been a bondsman (*iwofa*).

77. D. Hinderer, Journal, 1 Oct. 1851.

78. J. B. Wood, letter to Lang, 28 Sept. 1884.

79. C. Phillips Sr., Journal, 9 June 1853, at Ijaye.

80. Akintoye 1971:135. Matory (1994:16) cites this shrine as evidence for the diffusion of Ogun's influence as an aspect of the Ibadan military revolution. This is not plausible (1) because the shrine described was that of the Ijesha and Ekiti, not of Ibadan, and (2) because the cult of Ogun was anyway well established among the Sango-less easterners. Ogedengbe, the Ekitiparapo commander, had Ogun as a family god, being connected to chief Ogboni's lineage.

81. In two places, it might seem as if he did, but the reportage is unsound. The killing at Ota (n. 73 above) is mistakenly called a human sacrifice, since it was clearly a judicial execution. C. N. Young, the Ondo catechist (Journal, 25 May 1875), refers to human sacrifices being made annually to "Aramfe . . . and the other toward Ogun god of iron." There were two big human sacrifices at Ondo (apart from those made at the deaths of notable persons), which were to Esu and to Oramfe. Young had then been in Ondo only two months, and the time for these sacrifices had not yet come around, so his report is based only on hearsay. Presumably he attributed Esu's sacrifice to Ogun.

82. J. Barber, Journal, 26 Feb. 1854; J. Okuseinde, Journal, 21 Jan. 1873. In these reports, both from Ibadan, Oranyan (or Oranmiyan) is called "god of war."

83. J. B. Wood, letter to Lang, 18 Jan. 1884.

84. On Owode, the wife who ran off to Lagos: S. Doherty, Journal, 16 April 1882; V. Faulkner to J. B. Wood, 18 April 1882; Wood to CMS secretaries, 21 April 1882. A later incident: J. B. Wood to Lang, 12 Nov. 1885.

85. Letters of J. B. Wood to Lang, 10 and 18 Aug. 1887.

86. Halligey 1893:33. The meeting with Ogundipe described here took place in 1887, not long before his death. Most notable chiefs had their own distinctive staff (*opa*), which their messengers would carry as a token of their authorization.

87. On which see Olatunji 1975, on the Christian Egba poet Sobo Arobiodu (d.1936).

88. See Ogunba 1975, esp. 818–27, on *oriki* addressed to Ogun, who, like Ogundipe, "is intensely self-conscious, enjoys . . . flattery, for it is man's admission of Ogun's pre-eminence and a way of keeping him at a distance."

89. Wood to Lang, 18 Aug. 1887.

90. Moore 1916:92.

91. As lieutenant of Ogunbona, he was one of the three leaders of the Egba troops who garrisoned Lagos against Kosoko (E. G. Irving to Major Straith, 20 Jan 1854).

92. W. Moore (an Egba, the only priest left in Abeokuta after the "Outbreak") to Parent Committee, 27 June 1868. The name of the river, Ogun, has no connection with the name of the *orisa* Ogun.

93. As a well-known *oriki* of Ogun puts it: *Ogun, alada meji, o nfi okan sa 'ko, o nfi okan ye 'na* ("Ogun, with two cutlasses, one to clear the farm, one to open the road").

94. Whether it should be considered to be stictly a title or more like an informal surname is not certain. The Egba historian Olympus Moore (Ajisafe) writes both "Ogudipe, Alatise of Ikija" (1916:77), as if it were a title, and "Ogudipe Alatise" (1916:92).

95. The full proverb is *Alatise nii mo atise ara re* ("The one whose task is to do something he knows he has to do himself"). I am indebted to my colleague Dr Akin Oyetade on this point.

96. Halligey (1893:33) says he took the *Alatunse* title after declining the *Alake*ship for himself. Moore (1916:90-91), who merely calls him "Alatise," describes him as the most powerful man in Abeokuta during the interregnum of 1881-84 and as the main kingmaker.

97. Cf. the anonymous greeting to Hinderer (Half-Yearly Report ending Sept. 1859) while he was traveling in Ijesha country: *O ku tonse aiye* ("greetings to you, working to restore the world"); or the prophecy of Christian "light and restoration" [*atunse*] quoted by Johnson 1921:296.

98. T. Harding to A. Merensky, 19 Nov. 1888.

References Cited

Abimbola, Wande (ed.). 1975. *Yoruba Oral Tradition.* Ife African Languages and Literatures Series, no. 1. Ile-Ife: Department of African Languages and Literatures.

Abraham, R. C. 1958. *Dictionary of Modern Yoruba.* London: University of London Press.

Ajayi, J. F. A., and Smith, R. S. 1964. *Yoruba Warfare in the Nineteenth Century.* Cambridge: Cambridge University Press.

Akintoye, S. A. 1971. *Revolution and Power Politics in Yorubaland, 1840-1893.* London: Longman.

Asiwaju, A. I. 1976. *Western Yorubaland under European Rule, 1889-1945: A Comparative Analysis of French and British Colonialism.* London: Longman.

Awe, Bolanle. 1973. "Militarism and Economic Development in Nineteenth Century Yoruba Country." *Journal of African History* 14:65-77.

Barber, Karin. 1981. "How Man Makes God in West Africa." *Africa* 51:724-45.

———. 1994. "Money, Self-realization and the Person in Yoruba Texts." In Jane Guyer (ed.), *Money Matters.* New York: Heinemann.

Barnes, Sandra T. (ed.). 1989. *Africa's Ogun: Old World and New.* Bloomington: Indiana University Press.

Beier, Ulli. 1959. *A Year of Sacred Festivals in One Yoruba Town.* Lagos: Nigeria Magazine.

Belasco, B. I. 1980. *The Entrepreneur as Culture Hero: Preadaptions in Nigerian Economic Development.* New York: Praeger.

Bellamy. C. V. 1904. "A West African Smelting House." *Journal of the Iron and Steel Institute* 66:99-126.

Burton, Sir Richard. 1966 [1864]. *A Mission to Gelele King of Dahome.* London: Routledge and Kegan Paul.

Carroll, K. 1967. *Yoruba Religious Carving.* London: Geoffrey Chapman.

Dennett, R. E. 1968 [1910]. *Nigerian Studies, or the Religious and Political System of the Yoruba.* London: Frank Cass.

Drewal, Margaret, 1989. "Dancing for Ogun in Yorubaland and in Brazil." In Barnes 1989, pp. 199-234.

———. 1992. *Yoruba Ritual: Performers, Play, Agency.* Bloomington: Indiana University Press.

Falola, Toyin. 1984. *The Political Economy of a Pre-colonial African State: Ibadan, 1830-1900.* Ile-Ife: University of Ife Press.

Falola, Toyin, and Oguntomisin, Dare. 1984. *The Military in Nineteenth Century Yoruba Politics.* Ile-Ife: University of Ife Press.

Frobenius, L. 1913. *The Voice of Africa.* Vol. 2. London: Hutchison.

Halligey, J. F. T. 1893. "The Yoruba Country, Abeokuta and Lagos." *Journal of the Manchester Geographical Society* 9:28-44.

Herbert, Eugenia W. 1993. *Iron, Gender and Power: Rituals of Transformation in African Societies.* Bloomington: Indiana University Press.

Herskovits, M. J. 1938. *Dahomey: An Ancient West African Kingdom.* New York: Augustin.

Ibigbami, R. I. 1978. "Ogun Festival in Ire-Ekit." *Nigeria Magazine* 126-127:44-59.

Johnson, S. 1921. *The History of the Yorubas.* Lagos: CMS Bookshops.

Matory, J. L. 1994. *Sex and the Empire That Is No More.* Minneapolis: University of Minnesota Press.

Moore, E. O. O. (Ajisafe) 1916. *History of Abeokuta.* London and Bungay: Richard Clay.

Morton-Williams, P. 1964. "The Oyo Yoruba and the Atlantic Trade, 1670-1830." *Journal of the Historical Society of Nigeria* 3:25-45.

———. 1994. Personal communication.

Ogunba, Oyin. 1975. "The Performance of Yoruba Oral Poetry." In Abimbola 1975, pp. 807-76.

Ojo, G. J. Afolabi. 1966. *Yoruba Culture: A Geographical Analysis.* London: University of London Press.

Ojo, J. R. O. 1973. "Orisa Oko, the Deity of 'the Farm and Agriculture' among the Ekiti." *African Notes* 7:25-61.

———. 1978. "The Hierarchy of Yoruba Gods: An Aspect of Yoruba Cosmology." Unpublished seminar paper, Department of African Languages and Literatures, University of Ife.Olatunji, Olatunde. 1975. "The Poetry of J. S. Sowande, Alias Sobo Arobiodu." In Abimbola 1975, pp. 973-1029.

Olupona, J. K. 1991. *Kingship, Religion and Rituals in a Nigerian Community: A Phenomenological Study of Ondo Yoruba Festivals.* Stockholm: Almqvist and Wiksell.

Peel, J. D. Y. 1980. "Kings, Titles and Quarters: A Conjectural History of Ilesha. Part II: Institutional Growth." *History in Africa* 7:225-57.

———. 1983. *Ijeshas and Nigerians: The Incorporation of a Yoruba Kingdom, 1890s-1970s.* Cambridge: Cambridge University Press.

———. 1990. "Poverty and Sacrifice in Nineteenth Century Yorubaland." *Journal of African History* 32:465-84.

———. 1994. "Historicity and Pluralism in Some Recent Studies of Yoruba Religion." *Africa* 64:150-66.

Pemberton, J. 1977. "A Cluster of Sacred Symbols: Orisa Worship among the Igbomina Yoruba of Ila-Orangun." *History of Religions* 17:1-28.

———. 1989. "The Dreadful God and the Divine King." In Barnes 1989, pp. 105-46.

Rea, W. R. 1994. "No Event, No History: Masquerading in Ikole-Ekiti." Ph.D. thesis, University of East Anglia.

Schiltz, M. 1985. "Yoruba Thunder Deities and Sovereignty: Ara versus Sango." *Anthropos* 80:67-84.

Soyinka, Wole. 1976. *Myth, Literature and the African World.* Cambridge: Cambridge University Press.

Talbot, P. Amaury. 1926. *The Peoples of Southern Nigeria.* Vol. 2. London: Oxford University Press.

Thompson, R. F. 1976. *Black Gods and Kings: Yoruba Art at UCLA.* Bloomington: Indiana University Press.

Verger, P. 1957. *Notes sur le Culte des Orisa et Vodun a Bahia, le Baie de Tous les Saints, au Bresil, et a l'Ancienne Cote des Esclaves en Afrique.* Dakar: Institut Français de l'Afrique Noire.

Williams, D. 1974. *Icon and Image: A Study of Sacred and Secular Forms of African Classical Art.* London: Allen Lane.

Donald J. Cosentino

12

Repossession: Ogun in Folklore and Literature

The degree to which Ogun may be comprehended as a single deity with a common c.v., a particular iconography, a unique role in a complex cosmology has by no means been established by scholars of Yoruba religion(s). To be sure, the corpus of Ifa verse and other oral poetic texts, geographically rooted festivals, genealogical myths, and rituals largely controlled by initiated priesthoods have all worked to establish some consistent dimensions for the *orisha* on his home turf. But even there his uniqueness is contested, as Karin Barber noted: "Like other *orisha,* Ogun is distinct and yet not distinct, participating in a spectrum of and capabilities shared by the whole array of spiritual beings. The feature [most] commented upon, for example—Ogun's internal fusion of destructive and creative qualities—is in fact a central characteristic of all *orisha,* to different degrees and in varying proportions. Many of the specific qualities attributed to Ogun in oral poetry are attributed, in the same imagery, to other *orisha* as well. He exists in a complex shifting configuration of relationships, sometimes overlapping, sometimes separated, in some towns occupying one role, in others another" (1990:290).

If such variability describes an autochthonous Ogun, what determines his continuing evolution in non-Yoruba societies where *orisha* mythology persists? If Ogun may be considered an immigrant into Fon religion, he has been naturalized and given a sanctioned space within an official pantheon.[1] But in New World societies such as Cuba, where *orisha* worship was disguised or folklorized,[2] or Haiti, with no Ifa corpus and the easy availability of Catholic imagery, what then becomes of Ogun? And in the United States, where worshippers of Santería and of Vodou have confronted the bottomless emporia of postmodern store-bought imagery and the profound anomie of a late capitalist society, under what conditions does this West African deity persist and develop?

In the communities of the Atlantic diaspora, it is not simply that the old controls are gone, that the social and economic conditions of life are changed utterly. Rather, it is that these societies are relentlessly subject to the shaping pressures of new religions with new hagiographies, and the nearly incalculable cross-influences of new media. As Yeats suggested for twentieth-century Christianity, a rough beast is slouching toward Bethlehem to be born. But rougher beasts have stalked *orisha*-based religions in the New World since the sixteenth century, siring powerful hybrids in religion, art, and popular culture.

Other gods have slipped from the sanctified hands of the priest into popular imagination and found a new life in new media. Myths and rituals of the Virgin Mary, or Krsna, have expanded from sacerdotal care to ecstatic popular elaboration. And those elaborations continue and grow more elaborate. Just this very process may be observed in the myths and ritual arts developed about the *orisha* Ogun. Under the revolutionary social, cultural, economic, and political circumstances of the Atlantic slave trade, his already complex persona was twisted and turned into fantastic new shapes.

Reinventions of Ogun in disparate American societies have not occurred randomly. Rather, they proceed in accord with Barnes's definition of a polythetic principle in which no monotypic feature gives definition to all of a set, but a sufficient overlap in the features of each set establishes a chain of metonymic correspondences (1989:13). In the Americas, however, this principle operates without most of the political, ritual, or hierarchical referents available in Africa.[3] Each Ogun manifestation is contingent on the attributes of the last, attributes which may in fact have been aberrant or idiosyncratic. Innovation occurs outside dominant sociocultural norms, syncopated to changes in folk or pop culture. The process is centripetal, pushing out into new forms like a jazz riff. But a riff, no matter how fantastic, ultimately draws its meaning from a remembered theme. This has been the fate of the trans-Atlantic Ogun. His thematic significance has remained constant, but its modes of expression have been nearly unlimited.

The Ogou of Vodou has been resettled in the *ounfo*s of Port-au-Prince and Brooklyn. Coded as St. Peter holding the keys of heaven, Santería's Ogun may be found attractively gift-wrapped for sale in every botanica from El Monte, California, to Hialeah, Florida. Decaled on votive candles, that same Ogun is now even shelved at the Piggly Wigglies of safer, whiter neighborhoods throughout America. The Yoruba Ogun has made his literary debut in postcolonial literary canons through the writing of Nobel laureate Wole Soyinka; his American avatar has emerged as a divine hero in the pop fiction of Alex Abella and Migene González-Wippler. As a screen star Ogun possesses the demented anti-hero of the Hollywood B movie *The Believers,* and manifests during the drug lord rampages of *Miami Vice.* Not even CNN is exempt: expert academic testimony on Ogun's rage shadowed the sensational TV images of the ritual murders at Matamoros, Mexico, in 1989.[4]

The list goes on, but this point is apparent: If we want to trace the development of West African religions into world religions (for surely that is what we're discussing), then we must readjust our sights from the old votive sanctuaries to the wilds of a cosmopolitan and heterogeneous world culture. We must look particularly to those neglected margins of official culture reserved for scholars of folklore and popular culture. There we will find Ogun, and other deities, being generated anew. The sources of regeneration will not be found in oral poetry, nor in the sacred ritual which created and sustained their West African antecedents. Rather, the re-creative force resides in the allure of mechanically reproduced images and the transformative powers of the printed word. It is in those mysterious sources of the new revelation—lithography and the linotype—that the dynamos for the repossession of Ogun in folklore and popular culture will be found.[5]

The View from Turey's Spiritual Shop

My perspectives on Ogun derive from studies in African and Caribbean folklore and mythology, and field work on Vodou in Haiti. But this essay was constructed in Los Angeles (aka L.A.), where Ysamur Flores, nicknamed Samy, is a *santero* priest of Oshun and proprietor of "Turey's Spiritual Shop," from where he has kept a sharp professional eye on Ogun for the last ten years. Samy is a "crossover" *santero*. He grew up in a Santería-Catholic-Spiritist home in Puerto Rico. After abandoning earlier ambitions for the Jesuit priesthood, and a brief encounter with the Jehovah's Witnesses, he was initiated as a *santero*. His L.A. *ile* includes godchildren from the Caribbean, Mexico, and Central America. It also includes a number of African Americans, and not a few "New Age" Euroamericans from the fringes of "The Industry" (Angeleno argot for "showbiz"), and from graduate programs at the University of California–Los Angeles (UCLA) and the University of Southern California (USC). Known about town as "*santero* to the stars," Flores often speaks for the community of believers on the local media. He is also a Ph.D. student at UCLA, where he is writing a dissertation on the historical development of Santería in Cuba.

In May 1992 I visited Turey, on the second floor of the mini-mall in Hollywood, to interview Samy specifically on Ogun's California persona. We chatted in his consultation room, at the back of the botanica where he stocks the sacramental perfumes and potions of his religion. Samy is a large, imposing man who wears chains of initiation beads and the white clothes of his sacred office. On the wall in back of him hang Santa Fe Indian prints. To his right is the computer he fondly calls Eshu. A table is set up on a side wall with a white cloth, crystal goblets, and chromolithographs of the Catholic saints. It is a *mesa blanca*, prescribed in Alan Kardec's immensely influential *Book of Spirits*. In the corner by the door is a floor shrine set up for Ochossi, Eshu, and Ogun. Known collectively as "the warriors," these *orisha* work together to protect their children in the "forests" of L.A. Beads, Indian regalia, mesas, and computers may seem cacophonous assemblages to outsiders, but not to Flores, who clearly finds Ogun at home among all this votive bric-a-brac.

The L.A. Insurrection had occurred just prior to my visit.[6] Buildings all around Turey had burned, but Ogun protects his own. The mini-mall still stood across from the rubble of a Payless Shoe Store and the looted shells of Korean-Italian furniture stores. I queried Samy about the religious significance of these terrible events. As usual, he was not without a theological explanation, nor an *ebo* (propitiatory offering). "It was an Ogun event," he explained. As usual, Ogun had gotten too damn hot. He needed to be cooled down. So during the riots a friend of Samy's, a Shango priestess, got a big gourd of water and put it on Ogun's altar "to cool him down."

Samy had intimations of strife during his New Year divination: "In this year's *pataki*,[7] the earth was in a very fragmented state. So Olodumare sent Ogun down to bring it to unity. Ogun came, embraced the earth, and left his seed inside. Whenever unity needs to be achieved, he will come out. After Ogun had sex with the earth, he left his seed, and whenever there is a need, he will come out. And the signal is this: whenever Ogun comes out it will be in the desert, and the earth will shake. And then all hell will break loose. So after the Opening of the Year ceremonies we had three earthquakes, first in the desert, then Palm Springs, and then one going up to Eureka, and coming back down to L.A. After them, all hell broke loose. Following the *odu,* that's what happened. Ogun came out and said, 'You guys get together, or I get you together.' And he doesn't know the limits to anything."

"That's why these riots were out of control?" I asked.

"These riots were Ogun's business. Once he's out, you can't control him. He kills on the right, and he kills on the left. Death is on the road. You know that's what the problem was."

Samy's description of a creation/destruction matrix links his Ogun to the same deity in West Africa: "He is a force that you don't want to unleash unless you have to. People might cross a railroad track and kiss the ground as a sign of respect. But he is not that popular. He is mostly just feared. People pray to him when they go into hospitals for operations. He rules the scalpel. When you go to a hospital for an operation, you pray to Ogun. You don't want his knife to touch you. You want to cool off the knife. But you want somebody very forceful, somebody who can see beyond. When you need to unleash a power to break what is blocking everything, you deal with Ogun. Because Ogun doesn't know the line between 'too much' and 'never mind.' He will go all the way. He killed his own people. And that's the problem. You need to unleash him, but you need to cool him off when he comes back. Because he can run you over. Sometimes I have people come over who are not believers, and I say, 'We have to use Ogun,' and they say, 'Do you have to?'"

"Do you feel that way too?" I asked.

"Sometimes. But I have a very special relationship with Ogun. Every time I've gone to Ogun seeking something, he's responded. I don't fear Ogun; I respect him. I know that I can't go to him for light things. But when things call for extremes, I have to go for him. He is the only one who can open a path. He is the only one who can cut between two hairs, and never touch a single one of them. You know that's how fine he is. So he can get rid of whatever needs to be gotten rid of with a paper-thin cut. And that's what you're looking for, that finesse in a cut. But at the same time there is the Ogun that the song says: 'Ogun kills to the right, / Ogun kills to the left. . . .'"

Samy was describing a hired gun, a divine *jefe* (tough guy) to lead you through the streets he commands, an intermediary in a town you don't know, at a hospital you don't understand (and can't pay for anyway), a *jefe "muy loco"* perhaps, but "crazy" strong. Later, when I asked him which movie star he would cast as Ogun, Samy responded, "Schwarzenegger. The Terminator. Just paint him black." Then, looking at his son's toys around his desk, he modified his casting: "Have you seen the cartoon *The Tasmanian Daredevil?* He is like the Tasmanian Devil. He just roars all over the place, breaks everything, raises hell, causes mayhem. He's too rough to take to Santa Monica Pier; you'd rather take Shango. So people don't talk to me of Ogun as they talk to me of Oshun, Shango, and perhaps a little bit of Yemaya. No, not Ogun. Too rough."

There is nothing in Samy's descriptions that doesn't jibe with the Ogun of the *oriki, odu,* and *ijala.* But the details of the god's life have grown so much more elaborate, so cosmopolitan. Stories he tells about Ogun and the other *orisha* constitute a sort of hip urban apocrypha, with a richness of detail that marked the golden legends of Catholic Europe (and by extension Catholic Puerto Rico). So when I asked about Ogun's drinking, remembering the myth of his drunken slaughter at Ire,[8] Flores responded with a long psychoanalytic explanation of the deity's sex-driven excesses.

"He drinks a lot. You know that drinking for the Yoruba is one of the biggest sins because you don't control yourself. If you lose control, you're not cool. And that's when everything happens. But Ogun is the only one who can be drunk to death and still handle the machete like a kid handles a stick. You know he's good at his trade. When he commits himself, he commits himself to work day and night without rest. While the other *orisha* take five, Ogun never sleeps. That's how extreme he is."

"And is that why he's always along?" I asked.

"Part of it," Flores replied. "He is always unfulfilled sexuality. You know he's potent like fire. But he does not have a female partner. He is an absolute schizophrenic. He does not have friends. His only pal was Ossain. He met Ossain where he got the secret of medicine. And he came back. He has this partnership with Elegua and Occhosi; that's why they live together. And he's associated with these really radical types of jobs. Circumcision. Scarification. All the types of things that are so extreme. Things that are painful. They will bring you pleasure eventually, but in the beginning they just hurt like hell."

"We need to get this deity a woman," I joked, picking up on Samy's Freudian analyses.

"On no," Samy rejoined. "It's in his nature. And he is the only thing that will move the gears of society forward. Ogun is necessary. When he left and went into the forest, everything came to a standstill."

"How comfortable is he with modern technology?"

"Oh, he invented it. Ogun would be absolutely delighted with the high-tech shit we fool around with. If you talk about computers, you talk about hardware. It always refers you to the iron complex. Ogun is the driving force of technology. Because he's got all this strength inside of him. In Puerto Rico there is a seal for *Compania Fumento,* and the symbol is a man pushing a giant gear. He is going like this (*grunt*), strenuous work, that's Ogun. He needs that strength."

"There is another myth about when he tried to become a *babalawo.* You know *babalawo.* They are very refined types of people. Diviners. So he tried to become a *babalawo.* But he thought the small *opele* (divining chain) didn't do it. So he made this huge iron *opele.* And he was throwing it and *voom:* every time he was throwing it the whole earth shook. And Obatala said, 'Who's making all that noise?' And when he saw it was Ogun, he said, 'Go back to your forge.'"

The old Ogun is there, all right, and Samy analyzes him as a god tortured by sexual repression. His analysis concurs with Freud's thesis in *Civilization and Its Discontents:* the price of civilization is psychosis. And like modernist Christian apologists, Flores takes the myths, literally as he learned them from his Puerto Rican godfather, and gives them a twentieth-century spin. But he insists on the orthodoxy of his sources. When I asked him if his Ogun is the same praised in the Yoruba *oriki,* he replied, "Oh yes. We still sing, *'Ogun paa li le, Ogun paa lo la . . .'* (Ogun, the death is in the road . . .). The song still is alive here. We sing the same praises. But we do have a problem with Ogun. He's not that popular, not as popular as in Haiti, for example. Ogun in Haiti is everywhere. But not here."

For Santería, the problem is Ogun's *macho.* A drunken general, necessary perhaps in the defense of a kingdom, can cause a lot of problems in the *barrio.* So, as Flores insists, "In this religion, one tries to contain the heat, the hotness. In other African religions you're trying to heat things up in order to make them go. But in this religion we're always trying to cool things down. All the time—contain, contain. That's why in the *bembe* you start with the hot *orisha,* and you end with the cool ones. You want to contain them, you want to get rid of them quick. Because you cannot live without their force, but you need to contain them. And Ogun is the epitome of heat. Ogun is the center of the earth."

Our conversation moved finally to representations for a deity of fixed significance regenerated through heterodox elaborations. "If you want to make an altar for him, just to pay homage, an old piece of iron would do. See, the syncretism for Ogun in Cuba was St. Peter. St. Peter was dressed in green, but he is holding two keys. The keys are made of iron, but look at the symbolism of keys—keys are the things that unlock. Ogun is the roadmaker. People are confused. They say that Eshu is the owner of the road. True. After Ogun makes it."

"What other kinds of iron tools belong to Ogun?" I asked.

"A chain. Whatever comes from *El Monte* needs to be tied down. That's why a chain is always present in Ogun's cauldron. Because he needs to be brought back and tied up, or else he will just run back to *El Monte*. He dislikes the company of humanity, but he has no choice except to be ever-present. Every time he runs away, society dies. That is why he needs to be brought under control. He is not an *orisha funfun*.[9] By his nature he is unruly. So in Santería he is represented by iron. Any piece of iron will do for his worship. If you don't have an altar and you need to do something for Ogun, you can use any piece of iron and do your ceremonies for Ogun. There is no further consecration needed. And Ogun is so powerful that he doesn't need any further consecration. He just exists in his own symbol, iron. Primordial, like iron.

"Everyone says that the first *orisha* to be fed is Elegua, which is not true. He is the third. The first *orisha* to be fed is Ogun. He is the strength, the force. Whatever requires forces *is* Ogun. He is the one who takes the blood. Then the earth, the mother, receives the blood. And the third one is Eshu. If you do it with your hands, blood will flow into your hands, and Ogun is being fed anyway. So Ogun will always be the first one in sacrifice. In religious life you will always be a child until you learn to hold Ogun in your hand, and you're able to be so cool that his heat will not burn you."

Alfred Métraux said that in New World African religions, theology exists at the level of village gossip. In the case of Afro-Caribbean religions, he was certainly correct. There is a homeyness to Samy's Ogun that is missing in his West African manifestations. This is the West African god of iron rewrought out of Catholic hagiography updated through images of celluloid and video tough guys, cartoon tricksters, and advertising models. To the extent that Schwarzenegger can be cast in his role, Ogun is akin to tormented *macho* heroes as ancient as Herakles, and as modern as the Terminator. But he also remains unique. At the core of all these wild elaborations is a root metaphor which has persisted from Yoruba sacred verse through the liturgical literature of African Cuba. Ogun may be St. Peter, Mike Tyson, or Sonny from *Miami Vice,* but basically, he remains a piece of iron.

Supergod Comes to the Supermercado

The view from Turey's is idiosyncratic, but not aberrant. There is a dynamic tension between a tenacious conservatism and a boundless elaboration, which marks Ogun representations in all of Santería, and in other American realizations of the divinity. Charlie Guelprin, a powerful L.A. *santero,* establishes a new syncretism by worshipping his Ogun in the form of a Kongo *nkisi*.[10] John Mason (1989:30) reports that Afro-Venezuelans living in the San Francisco Bay area are selling 'Ogun-in-the-boot,' an army boot filled with dirt, three nails, and three rocks representing the *orisha* Ogun. For $1,200 this Ogun, and his 'now you see him, now you don't' brother, 'Invisible Elegba,' can protect your home from behind your door."

Innovation describes the ever more modish Oguns merchandised in the botanicas. It also describes the literary creations of Migene González-Wippler, an American writer who has published nearly a dozen popular chapbooks on the *orisha* tradition in Santería. Some of her titles are didactic, but others read like Gothic romances, in which the roles of virile lover, traduced virgin, and brazen hussy are all played by the *orisha*. Out of Ogun she has created a pop culture hero fit for the botanicas, where he is eagerly sought. González-Wippler is familiar with the popular hagiography of Catholicism, but more important, she has clearly browsed the racks of movie star "fanzines":

> With eyes full of lust Oggun watched Oshun disappear into the bedroom. He struggled to his feet with effort, and swerving around the room, finally managed to reach the door to his sleeping quarters. It was dark inside, but from the door he could see the shape of Oshun's body among the animal skins that covered the bed. With a savage grunt Oggun threw himself upon her. Her arms opened hungrily to receive him and within seconds they were locked in each other's arms. Not a word passed their lips. Oggun, thirsty for Oshun's kisses, spoke amply with his entire body. And she returned his caresses with wanton abandon and wild frenzy she had never shown before. (1985:61–62)

For another example of a hot new with-it Ogun, consider the character of Alex Abella's *santero* Ramon in his murder mystery novel *The Killing of the Saints*.[11] During the course of a holdup to regain the *ocha*'s repossessed jewels, Ramon becomes possessed by Ogun and kills everyone in an L.A. jewelry shop—an act of mayhem recalling the spree of the *orisha* at the battle of Ire. Abella's baroque plot revolves about a theological question that may soon become a legal question in *Los Estados Unitos*: If the *ocha* rides his horse during the commission of a crime, who is to blame? Horse or rider? A question for the *babalawo,* perhaps, because Anglo-Saxon common law doesn't comment on possession trance. Abella lays out the crime in neo-Chandleresque prose.

> The men who would carry out the carnage . . . had spent the night praying to Oggun . . . asking him for his help, his strength and his daring in the heroic deed they were about to carry out. . . . For twelve hours they knelt before the altar where they had arrayed the instruments of their devotion—.357 Magnum, .45 Colt automatic, sawed-off Browning shotgun with retractable butt, black Sten machine pistol, gray Uzi submachine gun, six sticks of dynamite, two grenades. Finally at nine the two men stripped, rubbed their bodies with oil, dressed all in white—hid their armory in the folds of their clothing and stepped out for the sacred mission at hand. (1991:6)

> Ramon was about to press the trigger to blow her brains out because it didn't matter anymore, it was just another life and now he, Oggun, would be able to add her slanty-eyed little head to the mound of skulls his followers laid before him. . . . "*Oggun nika! Oggun kabu kabu, Oggun arere alawo ode mao kokoro yigue yigue alobilona, Oggun iya fayo fayo!*" cried Ramon, raising his arms in

victory, his feet stomping the ground, a tall black man in white clothes in the guise of a god. (1991:14-15)

During the course of the ensuing trial, Ramon is asked by the prosecutor, "And you're the Christ of this new religion?" In the voice of Ogun, he answers, "I am not the new savior because we don't have to be saved. . . . But I am bringing the message of the saints down to earth" (1991:123). As the trial goes to jury, an earthquake shakes the courthouse—a literal *deus ex machina.* Ramon is found not guilty through the intercession of an anthropologist who sounds a lot like Lydia Cabrera, the author of *El Monte,* and the timely remanifestation of Ogun.

Lest one suppose that Abella's mixture of Ogun worship and modern crime is too farfetched, it is instructive to recall the ritual murders allegedly carried out in 1989 at a ranch near the Mexican border town of Matamoros. By all the media accounts (and news cameras were all over the story),[12] the cult murderers were not practicing any traditional *orisha* worship. Their practices were a mishmash of idiosyncratically interpreted Palo Mayombe ritual and New Age magic.[13] But the remains of the victims, including body parts of a University of Texas medical student, were found in an enormous iron pot maintained by the demented misinterpreters of Ogun's mythology.

Note too that the murders took place near a town called "Matamoros," praise name for Ogun's Vodou *doppelgänger,* Santiago/St. James. He is the patron saint of Spain, and divine general of the *reconquista.* Matamoros is glossed as "Slayer of Moors" (*Mata* = murder + *moros* = Moors). Santiago/Matamoros is widely celebrated through the chromolithograph of a general on a white horse trampling over the mutilated body parts of the Moorish foe. In this guise he is identified as a "kick-ass" *santo* in Santería,[14] and specifically as "Ogou" (the Kreyol version of his name) in Haitian Vodou. If indeed the Matamoros murderers were tangentially connected to Ogun through a new New Age guru's misinterpretations of Palo myth and ritual, the holy image of Santiago may have provided a powerful inspiration. And indeed in Haiti, where Santiago's chromolithograph is mass-marketed by the tens of thousands, a profound hermeneutic is derived from the glossy image.

It's All for You, St. Jacques

In no other New World country does Ogun claim a more central role in the national culture than in Haiti. In the guise of Matamoros/St. Jacques, Ogun's image is plastered in sitting rooms and on temple walls throughout the republic. Every taxi has his red ribbon tied around the base of its rear-view mirror. Unlike Santería, which treats the god like a dangerous hired gun, Vodou indulges in unabashed celebrations of Ogou. From all over Haiti, pilgrims travel by truck, car, and foot to the town of Plaine du Nord to participate in the world's largest annual Ogun festival.

Plaine du Nord is located near Henri Christophe's Citadel, an emblem of the military megalomania associated with the *orisha* Ogun. It also abuts Bwa Caiman, where Haiti's revolt against slavery began during a legendary Vodou ceremony in 1791. The Church of St. Jacques, a remnant of those slavery days, still stands in the town center. Its plain Jesuit face is painted lemon yellow. An iron fence closes off its front doors. To the right of the church is the rectory where a Breton priest lives.[15] To the left is the cemetery dominated by a tall iron cross. Running past the church compound is Centenary Road, which swerves around a series of large ruts.[16] During the summer rains, these ruts fill in to become a kind of small pond called *trou* in Kreyol. If the rains fail, Vodouisants come with pails of water to ensure plenty of mud. These muddy potholes are known as *Trou St. Jacques,* where Ogou ceremonies are held most Thursdays,[17] and day and night, nonstop, for the seventy-two hours preceding the Feast of St. Jacques on July 25.

Pilgrims arrive wearing blue dresses and red scarves.[18] These are the colors of St. Jacques, instantly recognizable from the ubiquitous chromo of the saint in blue cap with red medallion. They have come with the intentions of all pilgrims: to fulfill vows, to seek blessings, to have a good time. Pregnant women and tubercular children line up before the zinc basins of itinerant herbalists for a bath and a blessing. An ecstatic woman, declaiming in a deep male voice, rides a bony bull. Set like an altar with a red ribbon around his neck, burning candles fixed to his horns, this bull becomes a lumbering sacrifice for Ogou. After the muddy tauricide, eager pilgrims line up to be anointed by his blood.

At this festival all the disparate events seem connected. A bull falls to his knees. Nearby, pilgrims are lying face down in sludge, not visibly breathing. When one arises, she looks like a primal creature, flinging her muddied torso in ecstasy. A penitent son of the iron god wanders by with razor blades and safety pins stuck up and down his bare back. Chickens are whirled over the heads of supplicants. Three groups of drummers are situated at crosspoints around the *trou.* The music never stops. Trucks arrive with more pilgrims. Visitors gather near a *mapou* tree: a tourist, a journalist, a scholar, taking photos, gazing. Pickpockets circle like sharks.

An enormous crowd has gathered on the steps of the church near the *trou.* But they cannot enter. Iron gratings bar the doors and windows. So the pilgrims shout prayers and hurl objects—candles, pennies, cigars, rum bottles—through the gratings. They aim their missiles at an empty niche that used to contain an image of St. Jacques. The Breton pastor, Fr. Keweillant, gives specific reasons for keeping the fervent pilgrims away from their sacred target. "The Catholic Church has nothing to do with this yearly pilgrimage. These rites are for another religion. They go in front of the church because Vodou is a very synthetic religion. It searches to reconcile divinity. These Vodouisants think that an aspect of divinity is found inside the church. They call him St. Jacques, but they mean Ogou. For them, Ogou is not a saint. He is a divinity."[19]

Keweillant explains why he has kept the church doors closed against this festival since 1978. "There were constant incidents, perpetual sacrifices. The people had immodest habits. I saw a woman lift up her skirt in front of the

saint on his white horse, and say, 'St. Jacques, here I am. It's all for you.'
Another woman offered St. Jacques a piece of soap to wash her crotch (forgive
me!). I heard a woman in the dark part of the church say, 'St. Jacques, you
are a big, powerful man. The man I live with is too old. His *zozo* [penis] doesn't
work. Help me to find a younger one. . . .' I heard these sorts of things, and
decided to shut the church during the pilgrimage."

The Transforming Power of Images

The priest merely pointed out what every Haitian knows: St. Jacques *is* Ogou,
the senior brother of a military dynasty of Ogous. The process of conflating
saint and *orisha* makes a complicated gloss on two thousand years of religious
history. According to the Gospels, Jesus nicknamed the impetuous St. Jacques
"Son of Thunder." He was later martyred during Herod's first persecution.
According to Spanish hagiography, this same "Thunderer" traveled to Spain
before his martyrdom, and there his bones were translated and discovered in
the ninth century. That legend was the basis for several famous apparitions of
the saint on a white horse brandishing a flaming sword against the Moors
during the *reconquista.*[20]

By papal decree, St. Jacques became patron of Hispaniola. Several of the
earliest churches built in St. Domingue bore his name.[21] Church records indicate
that the slaves embraced his cult with great enthusiasm. The saint's popularity
rested on his fusion with the *orisha*. In turn, the development of an Ogou
theology was, and remains, profoundly affected by a continuous African rein-
terpretation of an imposed European iconography. Without *odu,* or inherited
sacramentals, the Ogun metaphor found its correlate in Catholic imagery.

Plaster representations of the saint have filled a niche in the Plaine du Nord
church, evidently from the eighteenth century until the 1970s, when the St.
Jacques frieze was removed and iron gratings were installed. A life-size statue
of St. Jacques also stood in the old Port-au-Prince cathedral (before it was
replaced with a smaller model in blue and red by the devoted scholar of applied
Vodou, Dr. François Duvalier).[22] These and similar imported representations
affected, at least sartorially, the heroes of the revolution.[23] L'Ouverture covered
his head with a red handkerchief, a sign that he "marched on the military
points of *Le Mystère,* Nago Ogou Fer" (Rigaud 1985:66). Dessalines publicly
appropriated Ogou's attributes (red clothes, avid rum consumption, sword constantly at hand). In this guise, Dessalines merged with Ogou in popular imagination, and so continues to manifest himself, as deity *and* revolutionary
general, in Vodou ceremony.[24]

The case of Dessalines offers a complex example of the effects of Catholic
imagery and the events of Haitian history on the development of Ogou theology.
Dessalines was betrayed and brutally assassinated in 1806, a fate which Vodouisants conflate with myths of the suffering Ogun *and* the passion of Jesus. Maya
Deren describes a Vodou ceremony in which these disparate myths blend and

merge in the manifestation of the deity. "Possessed by Ogou, a vodouisant sings 'I am wounded, oh I am wounded.' In this moment—with the side-stretched arms, the drooping head, the profoundly noble expression of the face, the attenuated, fallen posture of the body, and the tenderness of his two supporters, whose bodies are slightly bowed beneath his weight—he becomes the uncannily precise image of Christ being taken from the cross" (1953:131–32).[25]

Deren is aware of the complex borrowings suggested by this manifestation of Ogou as Jesus: "It is improbable that these people have anywhere seen that Christian image. Yet even if they had, and if this were an unconscious recreation of it, it would be the ultimate testimonial to their profound perception of the meaning of Christ. And if the image is not derived, but original to [Vodou], that also testifies, in another way, to an equal profundity" (1953:132). But is there need for such Jungian hedging? What Catholic church is not adorned with the Stations of the Cross, including this very image of Christ's Deposition—either as a frieze or as a chromolithograph? That image would be well known to most Vodouisants, who usually identify their religion as Catholic. The wonder is in the application, not in the source.

Sacral Fusions

It is impossible to analyze the transformations wrought upon the figure of Ogou in the last century without appreciating the profound influence of chromolithographs upon the religious imagination of Vodou.[26] All the major *lwa* are represented by these mass-produced glossy images *signifying* (in the African-American sense) correspondence between saint and *lwa*. Noting Vodou's ritual appropriation of chromos, scholars commonly assume they are employed as ruses shielding a proscribed god. But ruses would hardly have become treasured commodities, sold in abundance, and at a relatively stiff price, to eager customers. Nor would ruses be so widely and intimately employed to decorate home and *ounfo*.

The chromo trade began in the mid-nineteenth century, after a concordant was signed with the Vatican ending a schism which began in 1804. The first imports from Europe were an immediate hit. Their continuing mass popularity confirms not just the imposition but the co-optation of Catholicism. Replete with cabalistic imagery, chromolithographs have become rich food for an African religious sensibility cut off from its native sources. Far from being peripheral, chromolithographs have been central to the elaboration of Ogou theology.

The bewildering array of folk exegeses inspired by the chromo of St. Jacques indicates some dimensions of the hermeneutic treasure house offered up to the imagination of the Vodouisants. (Figure 12.1 shows a chromolithograph of St. Jacques, beaded and appliqued onto a banner used in Vodou ceremonies.) Leiris wrote the first and still most important essay on the subject:

FIGURE 12.1 Ogun's complicated role in Vodou liturgy is encoded in the chromolithograph of St. Jacques, here appliqued and beaded onto a banner used in Vodou ceremonies. Vodouists have subjected this image to intense scrutiny, evolving a new Ogun theology out of their hermeneutic practices. Courtesy UCLA Fowler Museum of Cultural History.

One sees St. Jacques on horseback, with a sword and shield, fighting the infidels and escorted by a knight in armor . . . for all my informants, the main character is the god of the forge and war, Ogoun Ferraille or Ogoun Fer (who has a sword as his essential attribute, and as with the other Ogouns, red as his color), but for some, the second character is Ogoun Badagri, brother of Ogoun Ferraille, even though for others he is more likely a Guede (spirit of the cemeteries) because the lowered visor of the helmet recalls the chin piece and other cadaverish aspects (such as cotton in the nostrils) with which the adepts who incarnate the Guedes frequently make themselves grotesque. (1952:204, my trans.)

The chromo inspires more than interpretations. It inspires narratives about the deity and his relationships, which constitute the living mythology of Vodou. The chromo thus becomes a source for revelation, open to counteranalyses like rival Christian or Muslim hermeneutics of the same sacred texts. So alternative folk exegeses of the masked knight behind St. Jacques identify him not as Guede but as Ogou Ferraille. His visor has been lowered by his father (not brother) Badagri, to prevent him from courting Ezili, the love deity, whose favors both gods are seeking (Marcelin quoted in Leiris 1952:204, n. 2, my trans.). Ezili seems to fill the mythic place of Oshun in Yoruba theology. Both deities remain unattainable objects of Ogun/Ogou's frustrated libido—a frustration which may have inspired the fervent sexual offerings to St. Jacques reported by Fr. Keweillant at Plaine du Nord.

With the folk hermeneutic explored, it becomes easier to understand why the women in the church at Plaine du Nord once confronted the image of St. Jacques like hungry lovers, and why they still revere his empty niche. By the same token, the motivations of the priests who emptied that niche, and locked the iron gratings around the church, are also clearer. So too is the animus of the fundamentalist army that marched to the *Trou St. Jacques* in 1986, planning to seal Ogou away by pouring concrete into his muddy potholes, and the resultant fury of Vodouisants who foiled their intentions to destroy the pilgrimage site with drawn machetes.

Catholics, Protestants, and Vodouisants at some level all seem to intuit the truth of Baudrillard's powerful observation:

> What becomes of divinity when it reveals itself in icons, when it is multiplied in simulacra? Do these images mask the platonic idea of God, or suggest that God himself has ever been his own simulacra—that the images concealed nothing at all? In fact they are not images such as the original model would have made them, but actually perfect simulacra forever radiant with their own fascination. . . . Then the whole system becomes weightless, it is no longer exchanging for what is real, but exchanging in itself, in an uninterrupted circuit without reference or circumference. (255)

Baudrillard analyzes the power of images to create their own self-referential world. A world that captures Ogou through lithography creates a mythology open to endless permutations.

This self-referential process seems to grow more intense. The image of Ogun is at the very heart of the political crises that arose from the election and subsequent overthrow of President Jean-Bertrand Aristide. For his political symbol Aristide chose a red cock. The bird carries many Haitian connotations. It is a Masonic, military, and sexual symbol, but most significantly, the red cock is a key character in the very popular chromo of the crucifixion. In that image, the cross is surrounded by various symbols of the Passion, including the pillar where Christ was scourged. On top of the pillar is a red cock, which for Catholics is a reminder of the cock that crowed thrice marking Peter's betrayal.

What does that chromo signify for Vodou? Haitians point out that the red cock is sacred to Ogou. Its presence in the chromo is proof of the *lwa*'s attendance at the central drama of Christianity. One Vodouisant told me explicitly that Aristide's emblem proved that he too was an Ogou worshipper. Didn't everyone see him kiss his mother on TV? And wasn't she wearing a red dress, the color sacred to Ogou? As if to prove his point, the young man then pointed to a campaign poster for Aristide. Under his slogan, and in place of his face, the poster simply reprinted the pillar and cock from the chromo. There was no need for further explanation. For children of Ogou, the message was plain enough.[27]

Revelations in Print

The Case of Milo Rigaud

Directly related to chromo-hermeneutics, and equally dependent on occult traditions, is the cabalistic scholarship of Milo Rigaud. In his 1953 book, *Secrets of Voodoo*, he fuses Ogou mythology with a wide variety of European mysticisms:

> Ogou Bhathalah is a part of the army of Ogou *loas* considered in the African tradition as the fathers of alchemy. In the universal tradition Bhathalah corresponds to the first blade of the Tarot (the Juggler). . . . Bhathalah personifies the "discipline of chaos" because it is he who directs, with the magic wand, the cosmic traffic. . . . The "swordstroke of Ogou" means that the Ogou *mystères* (*loas* of fire) or "stellar powers" are descended from heaven through a fissure shaped like the female sex organ represented by the planet Venus, who is Erzulie in Voodoo. (1953/1985:76–77)

It is tempting to dismiss Rigaud's analysis as an absurd conflation of spiritist mumbo-jumbo. To describe Ogou, he marshals the tenets of theosophy and its New Age sources: solar mythology, gnosis, alchemy. For him these occult systems are "keys" which unlock the true meaning of the *orisha*, who are, at some secret level, African manifestations of a universal mythology. Thus in one short paragraph Ogou is equated with Obatala (as he is later with Shango), the Juggler and Magus of the Tarot deck, Ezekiel's prophetic sword, the Jewish *aelohim*, the Hindu Lords of the Flame, and, through an etymological trick, the Christian devil, "Luci-Fer, whose name is also Ogou-Fer [indicating] Venus, the morning star."

It would be a serious mistake, however, to dismiss Rigaud's ideas. His work has been extremely influential in providing contemporary Vodou with a new set of referents. Many urban *ounfo*s are now covered in cabalistic imagery, especially the symbols of Freemasonry, from which Rigaud borrows heavily. Because of Ogou's work at the forge and his military leadership, many *oungan*s claim that the deity was a Freemason. The flirtation of African religions with European mysticisms has been largely unanalyzed, neglecting a major influence on the evolution of Vodou and Santería, and a fascinating field of comparison with parallel flirtations in Yoruba culture.[28]

A second comparison between Haitian and Yoruba interpreters of Ogou is prompted by Langer's observation, "[Myth] is to literature what an armature or a roughly shaped block is to sculpture—a first shape, a source of ideas" (1953:274). Certainly that is what the myth of Ogou has been to Milo Rigaud. And that is also what Ogun has been to Wole Soyinka, and to an international set of writers and artists who have mined his mythology for personal metaphors.

The Case of Wole Soyinka

Soyinka has made Ogun world-famous. He is the deity's press agent and apostle to the non-Yoruba literate world. A Nobel laureate, Soyinka is a writer whose enormous perspective has magnified the dimensions of the god he calls his muse. As artist, Soyinka is unique, but as prophet he is only the best among several writers who have sought to create a personal Ogun. Like Rigaud in Haiti, Soyinka's writing has become an important source of revelation about Ogun.

For Soyinka, Ogun exists on at least three permeable levels: the personal, the critical, and the artistic. To the query "Is there a god in your life now?" Soyinka responded, "There are several. . . . I use the Yoruba gods as creative metaphors. Sometimes as metaphors for my own experience. One in particular called Ogun. There is always a personal element towards one's deity. It's nothing unusual. I find that most people I meet, however committed they are, still display this personal element in their religion. The ones who are totally and completely enslaved by the priesthood are the dangerous ones. They are fanatics" (Soyinka 1987:512).

In his autobiography, *Ake,* Soyinka describes his consecration to Ogun. After young Wole suffers a pummeling by some older schoolboys, his ankle is injected with the *orisha's* medicine by his grandfather, who is also a priest of the god. While undergoing the ordeal, he is instructed, "Wherever you find yourself, don't run away from a fight. Your adversary will probably be bigger, he will trounce you the first time. Next time you meet him, challenge him again. He will beat you all over again. The third time, I promise you this, you will either defeat him, or he will run away. Are you listening to what I am telling you?" (1981:147).

Muhammad Ali at Ringside, 1985

For all the brilliance of his critical and artistic interpretations of Ogun, Soyinka's combative life as an engagé artist and unorthodox revolutionary seems best captured in that pugnacious blessing from his grandfather. As writer, Soyinka divides that blessing among the stubborn heroes of his fiction and the real heroes he finds in the world. Among these sons of Ogun is Muhammad Ali, whom he eulogized with *oriki*-like stanzas:

. . . Oh Ali! Ale-e-e
Black Tarantula whose antics hypnotise the foe!

> Butterfly side-slipping death from rocket probes
> Bee whose sting, unsheathed, picks the teeth
> of the raging hippopotamus. . . .
>
> Esu with faces turned to all four compass points,
> Astride a weather-vane; they sought to trap him,
> Slapped the wind each time. . . .
> Only that combination three-four calling-card,
> The wasp-tail legend: I've been here and gone. . . .
>
> Cassius Marcellus, Warrior, Muhammed Prophet,
> Flesh is clay, all, all too brittle mould.
> The bout is over. Frayed and split and autographed,
> The gloves are hung up in the Hall of Fame—
> . . . But the sorcerer is gone. . . . (Soyinka 1987:507–10)

Ogun the broken general overshadows Ali the broken boxer. Soyinka further conflates the boxer with Eshu, suggesting that the trickster must precede the hero, must indeed be incorporated by the hero. The hero emerges not from the *babalawo*'s interpretations, but from the brutalized glitz of commercial boxing. Haitians have realized a counterpart to Ali/Ogun in Sylvester Stallone's movie depiction of Rambo. A figure looking very much like that character is painted on the back of *Tap-Taps* (reconverted trucks which function as public transportation in Haiti as Mammy Wagons do in West Africa). Cradling an AK-47 and wearing Ogou's red scarf around his neck, Stallone has become an apt avatar for the *lwa* of war and the road (Cosentino 1988).[29]

Soyinka uses Ogun mythology as a master narrative for developing a manifesto on Yoruba art and culture. He appropriates Nietzsche's categories to classify Ogun as a "totality of Dionysian, Apollonian and Promethean virtues" (1969:120). Ogun is first actor ("darer and conqueror of transition"), first technician (master of the forge), first fisher (master of iron extracted from the earth "for the subjugation of chthonic chaos") (1969:123). As Soyinka's analysis develops, the Nietzschean categories expand to incorporate Hegelian arguments on the heroic will: "Ogun is embodiment of Will and the Will is the paradoxical truth of destructiveness and creativeness in acting man. . . . Nor can we lose sight of the fact that Ogun is the artistic spirit, and not in the sentimental sense in which rhapsodists of negritude would have us conceive the negro as pure artistic intuition" (1969:126).

Soyinka rejects the facile universalism of negritude. But his mythopoeic exegeses bear an unmistakable Afro-Teutonic cast, and are delivered with an Afro-Wagnerian pomposity. Indeed, there are useful analogies to be made between Wagner's recycled Wotan and Soyinka's *Sturm und Drang* Ogun:

> Alas, in spite of himself, from time to time, the raw urgent question beats the blood against his temples demanding, what is the will of Ogun? For the hammering of the Yoruba will was done at Ogun's forge and any threat of disjunction is, as with the gods, a memory code for the resurrection of the tragic myth. (1969:130)

Did Wagner "believe in" the Wotan he used as metaphor for the existential conditions of his time? Does Soyinka "believe in" the Ogun he uses in just such a way? The answer is "probably" in both cases, though not in any way acceptable to priests, or recognizable to theologians.

The Road

The most consistent metaphor Soyinka uses to evoke Ogun is the road. In Nigeria, it is the objective correlative to Ogun's existential drama. Despite the speed of the kola-chewing drivers and the dubious condition of most public vehicles, people must travel, and so commit themselves, albeit reluctantly, to the road. The metaphysical implications of this commitment are caught in the poem "Death in the Dawn" (1967:11):

> The right foot for joy, the left, dread
> And the mother prayed, Child
> May you never walk
> When the road waits, famished.

Intimately joined to this image of the famished road is that of the futile sacrifice. Each life offered to Ogun only leaves him starved for the next, in an endless series of meaningless deaths. Soyinka develops this theme, beginning with the traditional sacrifice of the dog to Ogun: ". . . And wipe your feet upon / the dog-nose wetness of the earth." When the poet begins his morning travel, a cockerel smashes itself upon his windshield. But neither dog nor cockerel can satisfy Ogun, or cancel the poet's ineluctable blood debt. For a mile down the road, he comes across a fresh corpse in a smashed car and ponders the lesson, "is this mocked grimace / This closed contortion—I?"

Although this carnage is Ogun's responsibility, the poem is not an indictment. For the road is a concentrated site of harrowing, growing only more desperate in an age of steel. So in Europe the legend of Christopher grew, a popular saint and not a winnowing of the Devil's Advocate. For in medieval Europe, as in postcolonial Nigeria (and indeed on the freeways of Los Angeles), the road is a liminal place, and in sore need of divine rationalization.

Idanre

In his complex epic *Idanre,* Soyinka reworks the myth of Ire, the story of a terrible battle in which Ogun went drunk-mad and killed his own men. In the epic, Soyinka does for Yoruba theology what Dante did for Catholic cosmography, or Milton for the biography of Satan. He creates a divine narrative which assumes the stature of revelation for future ages. What we know of Purgatory comes from Dante; Satan's rebellion gains substance in the fancy of Milton; Soyinka enormously expands Ogun's role in the work of creation.

There are limits to how far a fruitful comparison can be made between Soyinka and other epic poets. Soyinka belongs to no court, which can be considered a blessing or a curse. His sources are idiosyncratic, born out of his own hybrid religious experiences, his wide reading in comparative literatures, and his extraordinary command of the English language. His work reaches out from Yoruba tradition to a world audience, with little feedback from the original source, for whom his poetic language is an obvious barrier. What effect would a *Paradise Lost* have had on the English Protestant imagination if Milton has written it in Latin?

The epic unfolds on several narrative levels. On the literal level the poet takes a walk on a rainy night near Ogun's town of Idanre. He meets and makes love to a palm wine seller. A thunderstorm follows as he makes his way to a sacred rock. At dawn he returns to the wine seller's hut, and then he returns home. The literal journey is grid for a metaphoric trek with Ogun. Thus the palm wine girl is Oya, wife of Ogun, and the rock hill is the god's primal home. During their trek, Ogun reveals his cosmic secret to the poet: the secret of the eternal cycle of creation and destruction symbolized by the *orisha* himself.

Out of the eclecticism of Soyinka's imagery, derived inter alia from John Donne, Samuel Beckett, and the *babalawo*'s corpus of Ifa divination poetry, emerges an Ogun as newfangled and revolutionary as Milton's Satan. Ogun looms over the poem, an achronic confabulation of divine powers, including especially Sango's control of lightning, conceived in the epic as electricity:

> The flaming corkscrew etches sharp affinities. . . .
>   The fire of the axe-handed one. . . . Ogun is
> still on such
>   Combatant angles, poised to a fresh descent
>   Fiery axe-heads fly about his feet
>   . . . He catches Sango in his three fingered
>   hand
>   And runs him down to earth.[30]

Like all mythic heroes, Ogun stretches from an inchoate past to a timeless future; "His head was lost among palm towers / And power pylons." The source of the god's creativity is unbounded, amoral energy which Soyinka symbolizes in sexual imagery:

> Ogun is the lascivious god who takes
> Seven gourdlets to war. One for gunpowder,
> One for charms, two for palm wine and three
> Air-sealed in polished bronze make
> Storage for his sperms. (1967:72)

But foolish men forget the other half of Ogun. After he carved out the Road, Ogun retired to Idanre, until he was beseeched to become Oba (King) of Ire. Soyinka mocks this presumption: "we do not ask the mountains' / Aid, to crack a walnut," and the inevitable carnage that followed:

> To bring a god to supper is devout, yet
> A wise host keeps his distance till
> The Spirit One has dined his fill.
> . . . A human feast
> Is indifferent morsel to a god. (1967:76)

Ogun cannot be the epic's hero. For ultimately he is powerless to choose his destiny. He is condemned by his divine nature to a numbing recurrence: "This road I have trodden in a time beyond / Memory of fallen leaves . . . yet I must / This way again. . . ." Heroism instead belongs to the slave Atunda. In a primal act of rebellion, he rolled a stone down on Orisa nla, his unsuspecting master. And so the undifferentiated godhead was smashed into the multiple deities of *orun* (abode of the *orisha*). The existential parable is apparent: Ogun is real, but so is Atunda. We are free to rebel against fate, or be crushed by it. The models are there in *Idanre.*

Soyinka takes enormous liberties with oral tradition, of course. We might argue that such idiosyncrasies as the conflation of the deities Shango and Ogun (common also in Haiti) bastardize the tradition. But from the perspective of folklore, *plus ça change, plus c'est la même chose* is a vivifying principle. Whatever the fate of Yoruba religion in the twenty-first century, it is likely that his re-interpreted and elaborated Ogun will provide fresh material for future generations of Yoruba artists and intellectuals. Indeed, Soyinka's transformations have already caused minor reverberations in Yoruba literature. A number of parochial writers have reworked Ogun to sell in the decidedly domestic Yoruba markets reserved for "how-to" and chapbooks. These writers include Osamaro Ibie, author of *Ifism: The Complete Work of Orunmila;* Fela Sowande, author of *Ifa: Guide, Counsellor and Friend of our Forefathers;* and a host of similar Ogun interpreters published by the protean Nigerian presses. Like Rigaud in Haiti or Migene González-Wippler in the United States, these writers are anxious to pour old palm wine in New Age sacks.[31]

Postscript

When I discussed these Yoruba redevelopments of Ogun with Samy Flores, he was not impressed. "Remember that many of these Yorubas take *orisha* worship as folklore. They know it because it is folklore. Soyinka probably does not go through all the theology. He probably takes Ogun as I might take St. Lucy and do something with her."

"But his grandfather was a priest," I objected. "He was injected in the ankles with Ogun's medicine. . . ."

"That's fine and dandy," Flores shot back. "His grandfather did it. But is he doing it? Is he involved in the theology of Ogun? He's using Ogun as a metaphor, which I think is great. But remember, for the Yoruba, Ogun is a very different ballgame than for us. For the Yoruba, Ogun is the founder of the lineage. He is like George Washington to this nation. First of the line. The totem. But in our case Ogun has divorced himself from being the first of the family lineage to being the first of the divine lineage. A completely different thing. He is the first of the _orisha_. See, I don't feel that Ogun is the first of my family. So there is a different way of handling the figure of Ogun from Soyinka's standpoint to my standpoint to a Haitian standpoint."

These are the words of an American _orisha_ priest, professionally concerned with orthodoxy. He worries about sacred mythology "dwindling" into the folklore of Soyinka, González-Wippler, Alex Abella, and those thousands of pilgrims gathered around the mud pits at Plaine du Nord. Do they all worship the same Ogun? Or has that deity unraveled into a babble of unrelated manifestations? I think not. I put credence in the observation of Claude Lévi-Strauss: "the myth [consists] of all its versions . . . a myth remains the same as long as it is felt as such" (1965:92). Is there greater variance in these Oguns than there is in the Jesus of Catholicism, Mormonism, Christian Science, and the Branch Davidians? The evidence suggests there is not. Ogun, the creating/destroying, victorious/defeated, horny hero of iron technology strides polythetically, and with growing popularity, into the twenty-first century.

NOTES

1. Suzanne Blier (1995) argues that Fon religion privileges foreign deities, insisting that even those of demonstrably native origin (e.g., Mawu) speak foreign languages.

2. The Castro regime has created _Casa Africa,_ dedicated in part to the African religions of Cuba, and has encouraged folkloric troupes to choreograph _orisha_ rituals for popular audiences.

3. This is especially true in Haiti, where the theological resource represented by Ifa divination poetry was not established or maintained. In Cuba and in Brazil, forms of Ifa have been maintained.

4. My 1989 interview with CNN regarding the connections between the Matamoros murders and Palo ceremonies was broadcast on all their international cables.

5. While it may be conjectured that Ogun/Ogou myths and rituals were transmitted from Africa to the Americas with no historic break, it is my thesis that the modes of his contemporary Pan-American manifestations are so diverse and innovative that they warrant the term "repossession," signifying a second owning.

6. In 1992 the city of Los Angeles was swept by the worst civil disturbances in the United States since its Civil War (1861–65). The violence resulted from the acquittal of four police officers accused of beating black motorist Rodney King. These disturbances have been referred to as "riots," an "uprising," or an "insurrection," depending on the political attitude of the observer.

7. _Pataki_ is a narrative, usually about an _orisha,_ associated with a corresponding Ifa divination verse.

8. For a description of Ogun's generalship at the battle of Ire, see the discussion of Soyinka's _Idanre_ below.

9. _Funfun_ ("white") describes gentle or benign _orisha_ such as Oshun/Ochun.

10. Charlie is a priest of Obatala, but channels a spiritual father named El Congo Manuel, an ex–Cuban slave who died in 1670. His double spiritual heritage from Yoruba and Kongo may account for this extraordinary syncretism.

11. Abella lives in L.A. and has consulted with Samy Flores. Samy professes not to have finished the novel, but does agree with Abella's portrayal of the manifested deity, since Ogun does "kill to the right, and kill to the left" (personal communication).

12. Typical of these accounts is Jim Schutze's *Cauldron of Blood.* His was only one of several accounts (e.g., *Hell Ranch*) which were quickly published and set on the CRIME shelf of Crown and Walden and other chain bookstores within months of the press reports.

13. Of the mayhem at Matamoros, Samy said, "It had all the signs of Palo, all the signatures, everything. The only place you have a cauldron in this religion is with Ogun. And [Santería] never puts sticks in it [as they did at Matamoros]. Only iron implements."

14. Of Santiago, Samy states, "I have Matamoros on my wall, just because I like him. He is an ass-kicker. Even though I am half-Moor and sympathize with the Moors" (personal communication).

15. These observations on the ceremonies at Plaine du Nord are derived from my first field visit to Haiti in 1986. That field work was funded by the National Endowment for the Humanities and by the University (of California) Research Expeditions Program, which also sponsored the participation of ten research assistants. I wish especially to thank the Project Co-Director, Henrietta Cosentino. I also thank Fr. Keweillant for assisting us in many ways.

16. Carole Devillers has established a time line for this festival by dating the first appearance of the *Trou:* "Popular memory has it that these holes started in 1909 when the Gallois River flooded the newly built Centenary Road. Later the pond grew bigger when sand was dug from it for construction of the police station" (1985:404). This testimony adds credence to Fr. Keweillant's assertion that the festival itself began only in the 1930s.

17. Weekly ceremonies are suspended during the month of November and the season of Lent. November is dedicated exclusively to services for Gede, whose very interesting relationship to Ogou is explored by Karen McCarthy Brown in this volume. During Lent all liturgical services for the *lwa* are suspended, and their altar objects are shrouded in cloth. The practice seems analogous in form and meaning to the suspension of *Bori* services during Ramadan among the Hausa.

18. Just as at a Vodou ceremony (or a Mass in France), there were many more women than men attending this religious festival. The ratio was perhaps 3:1.

19. All quotes from Fr. Keweillant come from an interview at his rectory on July 24, 1986. He later allowed Henrietta Cosentino and me into the church to videotape the barrage of sacred offerings through the closed gratings. It seemed like a war zone. We noted that the guards posted inside were willing to accept offerings for St. Jacques and place them in the church in return for small gratuities. The resulting videotape was later stolen, along with our camera, from our living room in Los Angeles.

20. For biographic notes on St. James, see *Butler's Lives of the Saints* (San Francisco: Harper and Row, 1987), pp. 221–22.

The shrine built for the "Thunderer" over the site of his relics in Compostela became Europe's second most important pilgrimage site (after Rome, of course). The Wyf of Bathe claims to have visited Compostela during the opening lines of her prologue in *The Canterbury Tales.* Another gloss on the origins of Santiago de Compostela suggest that it may have been a shrine site for an earlier Celtic aquatic goddess, Brigitte (Beauvoir-Dominique 1991:14–15).

21. Even the cathedral in Port-au-Prince, dedicated in 1781 to Our Lady of the Assumption, was widely understood to be under St. Jacques's protection and popularly known by his name (Beauvoir-Dominique 1991:47).

22. The cathedral statue was part of a side altar dedicated to St. Jacques, which in the nineteenth century became popularly associated with statues of the revolutionary heroes erected in the nearby Champs de Mars (Beauvoir-Dominique 1991:47).

23. The dialectic works in two directions, as Beauvoir-Dominique observes: "We must guard against a unilateral vision of the relationship between tradition and history as

one of agent to product. While the collective memory of Ogou–St. Jacques worked on the heroes, the actions of history worked on the memory." (1991:62; my trans.).

24. Papa Doc reported the following manifestation of Dessalines in a Vodou ceremony he witnessed:

> I quivered with stupefaction when the personality of the *houngan* was capsized in a hypnotic state, and surging forward from the depths of his consciousness came Dessalines the Emperor. It was truly him. The wild face, the fanatic physiognomy . . . he mounted two men in order to better arch his back in the pose of a chevalier.

Although this manifestation occurred during a Petro ceremony, it seems entirely consistent with the representation of Papa Ogou as St. Jacques, seated on the back of his *hounsis* as he would mount his white horse, brandishing his sword to the right and to the left (Beauvoir-Dominique 1991:59–60).

25. In a footnote Deren remarks, "This manifestation occurred in precisely the same way several times, over a five month period, and was accepted without surprise, as if those present were familiar with it, although it does not seem to be a very common aspect" (1953:132).

26. The most significant parallel in contemporary religions is the dialectical relationship between the Indian chromolithograph of the Snake Charmer and the development of Mami Wata cults in West and Central Africa (Drewal 1988).

27. For an elaboration of the symbols used by Aristide, see Cosentino 1991:616–25.

28. Huxley's *The Invisibles* is an important exception to this observation. His conversations with Vodouisants are studded with cabalistic references. Obafemi Awolowo's intense allegiance to Rosicrucianism, and his pilgrimages to its headquarters in San Jose, California, are an example of an analogous Yoruba attraction to cabalism.

29. If one were to introduce the question of "Ogun type" heroes in African American lore, an extraordinary gallery of characters including John Henry, Stagolee, and High John de Conquer would need to be examined. The "Ogun type" hero exists in contradistinction to the "Eshu type," "a line of trickster heroes extending from Brer Rabbit to Shine to Eddie Murphy.

30. In the *Four Stages,* Soyinka gives this confabulation of Sango and Ogun a theoretical basis: "The tragic actor for the future age (already the present for Europe) is that neotechnic ancestor Sango, god of electricity, whose tragedy stems equally from the principle of a preliminary self-destruction represented (as in a later penalty of Ogun) in the blind ignorant destruction of his own flesh and blood. What, for Ogun, was a destructive penalty leading to a drama of 'Passion' was in Sango the very core of his tragedy" (1969:127).

Is there some parable of modernism lurking in this fusion: Ogun/Iron + Sango/Electric = Industrial Revolution? Pierre Boulez had a similar equation in mind with his famous production of Wagner's Ring Cycle, projecting Wotan as a sort of nineteenth-century Capitalist Robber Baron.

31. Folklorizing *orisha* mythology isn't limited to the written word. Under the patronage of Austrian expatriates Ulli Beier and Suzanne Wenger in the 1950s, Yoruba artists were encouraged to re-create the *orisha* in new media. Huge representations were constructed in concrete near the river site sacred to Oshun, and about the town's Esso Station. The productions of talented artists such as Oyelami, Buraimoh, and Twins Seven-Seven became commodities in the international market. Around these artists gathered choreographers and dancers, including Peter Badejo, who created an Ogun opera, *Asa Ibile Yoruba* (UCLA, 1979).

To appreciative critics and collectors, the gargantuan *orisha* re-created by the Oshogbo artists seem like local gods reclaimed for a world audience. But how do these repossessed *orisha* appear to those who still make *ebo?* Oshogbo art does not take its place in any ritual continuum. Nor has much of a domestic market ever developed for its peculiar Austro-Yoruba style. If we are to consider the sculpted *orisha* in Wenger's sacred grove as votive objects, then they still stand mutely, awaiting the arrival of unborn faithful: *If you build them they will come!*

REFERENCES CITED

Abella, Alex. 1991. *The Killing of the Saints.* New York: Crown Publishers.

Barber, Karin. 1990. Review of "Africa's Ogun." *Journal of Religion in Africa* 20(3):289–91.

Barnes, Sandra. 1989. Introduction: "The Many Faces of Ogun." In *Africa's Ogun,* ed. Sandra Barnes. Bloomington: Indiana University Press, pp. 1–28.

Baudrillard, Jean. 1984. "The Precession of Simulacra." In *Art after Modernism,* ed. Brian Willis. New York: The New Museum of Contemporary Art, pp. 253–81.

Beauvoir-Dominique, Rachel. 1991. *L'Ancienne Cathédrale de Port-au-Prince.* Port-au-Prince: Editions Henri Deschamps.

Blier, Suzanne. 1995. "Vodun: West African Roots of Vodou." In *The Sacred Arts of Haitian Voudou,* ed. Donald Cosentino. Los Angeles: UCLA Fowler Museum, pp. 61–87.

Brown, Karen McCarthy. 1989. "Systematic Remembering, Systematic Forgetting: Ogou in Haiti. In *Africa's Ogun,* ed. Sandra Barnes. Bloomington: Indiana University Press, pp. 65–89.

Cosentino. Donald. 1980. Review of "Asa Ibile Yoruba." *African Arts* 15(2):34–37.

———. 1988. "Divine Horsepower." *African Arts* 21(3):39–43.

———. 1991. "Titid, Mon Amour: Lwas and Saints in the Haitian Heart." *The World and I* 6(10):616–25.

Deren, Maya. 1953. *Divine Horsemen: The Living Gods of Haiti.* New York: Thames and Hudson.

Devillers, Carole. 1985. "Of Spirits and Saints." *National Geographic* 167(3):395–408.

Drewal, Henry John. 1988. "Interpretation, Invention, and Re-presentation of Mami Wata." In *Performance in Contemporary African Arts.* Bloomington: Indiana University Folklore Institute, pp. 101–39.

González-Wippler, Migene. 1985. *Tales of the Orishas.* New York: Original Publications.

Huxley, Francis. 1966. *The Invisibles.* New York: McGraw Hill.

Ibie, C. Osamaro. 1986. *Ifism: The Complete Work of Orunmila.* Lagos: Efehi.

Langer, Susan. 1953. *Feeling and Form.* New York: Scribners.

Leiris, Michel. 1952. "Note sur l'usage de chromolithographies catholiques par les vodouisants d'Haiti." In *Les Afro-Americains.* Dakar: IFAN, pp. 201–207.

Lévi-Strauss, Claude. 1965. "The Structural Study of Myth." In *Myth: A Symposium,* ed. Thomas Sebeok. Bloomington: Indiana University Press, pp. 81–106.

Mason, John. 1989. "Fundamentals: Criteria for Change." Paper delivered at a Symposium on Yoruba Culture in the New World, University of Florida, Gainesville.

Métraux, Alfred. 1972. *Voodoo in Haiti.* New York: Schocken.

Rigaud, Milo. 1985. *Secrets of Voodoo.* San Francisco: City Lights.

Schutze, Jim. 1989. *Cauldron of Blood: The Matamoros Cult Killings.* New York: Avon.

Sowande, Fela. n.d. *Ifa: Guide, Counsellor and Friend of Our Forefathers.* Yaba: Forward Press.

Soyinka, Wole. 1965. *The Interpreters.* London: Andre Deutsch.

———. 1967. *Idanre and other Poems.* New York: Hill and Wang.

————. 1969. "The Fourth Stage (Through the Mysteries of Ogun to Origins of Yoruba Tragedy)." In *The Morality of Art,* ed. D. W. Jefferson. London: Routledge, pp. 119–34.

————. 1981. *Ake.* New York: Aventura.

————. 1987. "Wole Soyinka at LSU." Edited by Jo Gulledge. *The Southern Review* 23(3):511–26.

Philip Scher

13

Unveiling the Orisha

Peoples of African descent in the New World do make of
Africa and Slavery a profound presence in their cultural
worlds, and seek rather to describe the tradition of discourse
in which they participate, the local network of power and
knowledge in which they are employed, and the kinds of
identities they serve to fashion.

—David Scott

The legacy of African American an-
thropology in the United States until recently was marked in large part by a
search for cultural survivals. From the scouring of the material and cultural
worlds of African Americans for "Africanisms" (Holloway 1990), to the more
abstract and perhaps more sensitive search for "grammars" of African origin
still operating in African American patterns of behavior and aesthetics (Mintz
and Price 1976), the task has been essentially the same: to authenticate an
African past for New World descendants of Africans.[1] It has been pointed out
that investigations into African American culture that stress authentication at
some level ignore the very real and active uses to which the past is put by
African Americans themselves.[2]

In this chapter I will try to demonstrate, by examining Ogun and the larger
Orisha tradition in which he is placed, how the past is constantly being nego-
tiated by different groups active in the Orisha religion in Trinidad and Tobago.
My object here is to outline the specifics of two historical narratives and to
show them as parts of a longstanding debate, the outcome of which is now,
at some level, the control of the future of the religion and its place both in
the national consciousness and in the rapidly growing transnational network
of Orisha practitioners. The historical narratives which are utilized by various

groups of practitioners of the Orisha faith in Trinidad have embedded in them elements which are instrumental in the presentation of each group's ethos, as well as in the struggle to find a voice for the general public via the national media. The emergence of the Orisha faith into the public eye, although a relatively new development, is in keeping with and utilizes strategies that recall the adaptive nature of Yoruba religion in general. However, instead of focusing only on the consistent qualities of Yoruba religion and its perennial ability to negotiate political terrain, as a mark of its "Africanness,"[3] I am here more interested in the contemporary "self-fashioning" that the construction of historical narratives implies, and the role that pure Africanness versus a New World character plays in that project. Toward that end I will be looking here at the contemporary condition of Orisha worship in Trinidad, with special attention to the Orisha practitioner's relationship to the general public. New developments in the religion and among individual practitioners over the past several years speak to a new commitment to bringing the faith into the public eye. This commitment has taken forms as grand as a campaign for an official public holiday for Orisha (Lord Shango Day) down to a local artist's series of t-shirts featuring, among other Orishas, a many-armed Ogun, with each hand holding an emblematic instrument of Ogun's in a sort of iconographic melding of Orisha and Hindu images.

Historical Narrative and Representation

The different versions of the history of the Orisha religion in Trinidad, in addition to being at the center of a particular local debate, are also reflected in the history of the scholarship of African religion in the New World. The main point of contention in these many narratives is how the Roman Catholic presence in New World African religion emerges. Before examining this question in greater detail, I would like to stress that the Catholic element as a specific *problem* in the narrative—that is, as something requiring explanation—is determined in this case wholly by the role that it plays in the possible future of the Orisha religion itself. In other words, the current struggle for legitimacy in Trinidad, which is currently focused, in part, on whether or not Catholic saints and liturgy belong in the Orisha religion, has made the historicization of the Catholic elements, the hows and whys of their existence within the religion, of paramount importance. In this way, a contemporary development in the Orisha religion which manifests itself as a struggle to represent itself to a global and national audience has highlighted the importance of a particular aspect of its own history. It is in the process of identity formation, and the problems inherent in any project of this nature, that facets of a history (in this case the presence of Catholicism in Orisha) are brought into relief. Most dramatically at the level of the religion's structure and organization, the influence of a national and transnational presence, and the pressures to be represented, have effected a transformation in the group's consciousness such that the nature and importance of its own history have grown and changed markedly. Until fairly recently the Orisha faith, previously known as the Shango cult, was little known and little understood. Persecuted actively in the nineteenth century, and even recently marginalized by the state and public lack of awareness, some groups within the Orisha faith have embarked on campaigns of active, positive public relations and education.

The Orisha religion's activities toward participation in the public realm have been uneven, as the religion is relatively unorganized and, again, until recently feasts and religious practices were not coordinated across the island of Trinidad. However, attempts on the part of various Orisha groups to make themselves known and, if not accepted and understood, at least tolerated have used as a strategy the national rhetoric of tolerance found in the national anthem ("where every creed and race finds an equal place"). Finding an "equal place," as it turns out, seems largely to be a result of marketing and following the protocol of public debate through the press. The presence of press coverage on Orisha activities (from almost no coverage ten years ago, to regular coverage concerning the administration of the religion today) belies the public's (or at least the press's) willingness to engage with the religion as it has come to present itself as having responsible leaders who provide interviews and write letters to the editor.

At the same time, there is still the struggle for representation. Representation requires, for national purposes—as do education programs, marketing campaigns, and public relations of all kinds—the objectification of the properties of the religion, even if those properties are emphasized as being "unrefined, unbridled, spontaneous" (*Trinidad Express,* April 29, 1994). The content of the religion, its practices, and historical narratives needs to be sufficiently standardized to be clearly identifiable. The nature of the religion must be organized for presentation to the public—in a word: objectified. The struggle for representation lies in gaining a dominant voice in the public sector. The "version" of Orisha that is most successfully presented (i.e., ultimately accepted) will have achieved for its adherents a position of power in the future direction and control of the Orisha faith.

In recent years the perceived "Africanization" of the Orisha religion (Houk 1992) has grown. Africanization is the process by which certain Orisha groups attempt to eliminate all European as well as Hindu and Kabbalah influences from Orisha religious practice. There is at least one group in Trinidad (Egbe Onisin Eledumare) for whom this is an explicit part of their self-described statement of purpose. In some other *palaix* (individual compounds) the priest might express some modified or less programmatic desire to see Catholic elements or Hindu elements removed, while at the same time wishing to preserve certain practices. In others the narrative or version of history most often utilized by the "Africanizers" will be subscribed to by a priest, but without the concomitant desire to purge the Orisha faith. Finally there are those groups which offer a different narrative of the history of Orisha, a narrative which stresses that the presence of Catholic elements is an integral part of a distinctive New World religion, the Orisha faith. It is this latter group that is the largest and arguably the most successful at organizing the disparate and traditionally in-dependently operated *palaix*. This last group has also been the most successful in making and keeping ties with other Orisha groups (including Santeria in Cuba, Puerto Rico, and New York, Vodoun in Haiti, Candomblé in Brazil, and Yoruba groups in Nigeria). Their version of the history of Orisha practices in the New World and in Trinidad stresses the inclusiveness of the religion. They have been instrumental in making sustained contacts with the Ooni of Ifé as well as with forging links across the nation of Trinidad in an attempt to bring together the independent Orisha practitioners under one umbrella organization.

Africanization Narrative vs. Ecumenical Narrative

I wish to turn now to two historical narratives which are being presented currently in Trinidad. These two versions of Orisha history have counterparts in academic and popular literature, and these versions are sometimes cited in defense of either one or the other of the narratives in question. The "African-ization" narrative has as its goal the justification of a kind of active "purificat-ion," in which the long-time association of Orisha with Catholic saints will be dismantled. Thus, Ogun, often associated with Saint Michael in Trinidad, is shedding this "cover" and emerging as a "purely" African Orisha. The stated goal in this dissociation is not to denigrate Catholicism, but to announce sym-bolically that African religions in the New World need not hide anymore. It is also not the goal of this group to impose their view of the religion on other Orisha practitioners, but to offer an alternative to the syncretized version.

The Africanization narrative utilizes the argument that Catholic saints were, in a sense, draped over African Orisha to "camouflage" them from the prying eyes of whites who had forbidden the practice of African religion and who were actively trying to destroy it (Bastide 1971, 1978). Much of the literature concerning the history and development of African religions in the New World has contended that "syncretism" was the result of this kind of political and religious persecution. Most notably the followers of Roger Bastide have pro-moted this view. What is stressed here is that Africans "forced into Catholic social and religious patterns . . . had to adapt their representations of sacred space and time to fit European patterns. At first, this was probably no more than an adaptive strategy to preserve Yoruba cultural and religious integrity amid the erosive effects of slave society" (Murphy 1988:123). This version of the narrative is also found in Houk's full-length study of the Orisha religion in Trinidad, where he argues that the presence of the Catholic saints occurred initially as a form of disguise, and then over time became fused into the everyday practices of the religion. Houk goes on to point out that "the basic structural similarities of the two religious systems [Catholicism and Orisha] provided the opportunity for a meaningful syncretism of *particular elements* of both. This does not however, explain why such syncretism occurred" (Houk 1992:118, my

emphasis, and 1995). Houk is right to point out that there are structural similarities between the two faiths, but it is possible that, at least to some extent,
the structural similarities *do* explain the occurrence of the "syncretism." In
looking at the growth of the Orisha religion in Trinidad, we find a situation
unique to the development of African religions in the New World. In this
situation, much of what has been cited as evidence to support the camouflage
or disguise theory is undermined.

The counternarrative, such as it is, emphasizes the very real relationships
that African and Catholic practices and theologies have to each other. The
supporters of this view argue that it is not a contradiction to be of the Orisha
and also a Catholic. They argue that Catholicism and Orisha have never been
considered the same thing, but that Orisha practitioners discovered analogies
in Catholicism and appealed to Catholic saints as a way of incorporating the
potential power of the saints into Orisha worship. In the words of Deren, "It
is, in fact, a monumental testimony to the extremely sophisticated ability of
the West African to recognize a conceptual principle common to ostensibly
disparate practices and to fuse . . . elements into an integrated working structure" (1953:56). It is important to recognize at this juncture that the Africanization narrative requires the presence of Catholic oppression and the forced
integration of Catholic elements in order to demonstrate a particular kind of
African resistance. This particular vision of African resistance focuses on creative uses of the oppressor's culture without any real or active engagement
with it, at least initially. It denies the New World African any role in the formation of his or her own unique cultural complex, the legacy of which exists
in the present day. As Gilroy (1993) has pointed out, such narratives, in effect,
eliminate the importance of slavery (even though they are forged by a desire
to forget slavery) and make recourse to the construction of African culture
anterior to the slavery experience. Purging Catholic elements, at some level, is
the act of forgetting.[4]

The "integrationist" narrative, on the other hand, stresses the agency involved
in the incorporation of foreign elements into existing African structures. This
process never completely sacrifices the basic African cultural forms because
the African structures remain intact, informing and changing the borrowed
elements to give them conformity within existing practices. This type of narrative
has the advantage of highlighting the elements of Orisha which are inclusive.
The highlighting of inclusive elements is a significant act in the attempt to
successfully "market" the religion to the nation (Trinidad) and the world of
African-derived religions.

Trotman gives two persuasive reasons why the disguise theory of "syncretism"
cannot fully explain the presence of Catholic elements in Orisha, at least in
Trinidad. The first of these is purely historical. Trotman points out that attempts
to prohibit the religion did not come about until 1883, although he seems to
have overlooked the Ordinance of 1868, which prohibited the practice of *Obeah,*
which, although not considered the same thing as Orisha practice by Africans,
was used by whites as a pretense for persecuting African religious practices.

Most scholars agree that the Orisha religion really took hold with the post-emancipation arrival of the majority of Yoruba in the late 1830s and early 1840s (see Houk 1992). Thus in large part the religion was established after slavery, and there was a considerable amount of time before official efforts were made to suppress it. By the time of the Ordinance of 1868, and certainly by the time of the prohibition in 1883, Catholic elements were already in place; thus the reasoning that the adoption of Catholic elements was a form of sub-terfuge is more unlikely. Trotman's idea is a good one, but relies on the fact that *official* persecution is recorded as beginning in the 1880s; it makes no mention of possible unofficial harassment by either the authorities or other parties, in which case the "disguise" theory might still be a salient one. At the same time, the relatively late arrival of the Yoruba, many of whom were free and living in often remote and ethnically homogeneous situations, would have made them a peculiar minority even within the community of African-Trini-dadians already present in the society. Hence the adoption of Catholic practices may have been as much a way to find acceptability among African Catholics as a way to avoid persecution (cf. Trotman 1976:11–13).

Secondly, the public nature of Yoruba worship with its drumming and danc-ing would never have been confused with any kind of practice of Catholicism, and these practices themselves have survived without Catholic disguise (Trotman 1976:13). Both of Trotman's points do damage to the received notions of the disguise theory. In addition to the historical evidence he puts forth, one must take into consideration the structural and spiritual similarities of the two re-ligions, which offer the most compelling evidence as to why the combination of Orisha and saints may not have been a purely pragmatic phenomenon. This, of course, does not rule out that disguise may have been a contributing factor in the syncretism, but merely indicates that it may not have been the only reason for it. The disguise theory certainly demonstrates the strength and per-severance of Africans in terms of the survival of cultural forms, but it does not take into account the fact that the Orisha faith is a welcoming one, one that is capable of incorporating new elements and changing to meet the demands of new situations. If, in Trinidad, the disguise theory was the only explanation, it would not explain the evidence that the structural similarities themselves give, namely that Catholic saints and Yoruba Orisha *do* have characteristics in common, both iconographic and substantive, and these characteristics are high-lighted in the association of Orisha with saints. It does not seem, given the evidence from Trinidad, as well as from other sites of Yoruba-Catholic mixing, such as Haiti, that Orisha priests were entirely dismissive of the efficacy of appealing to Catholic powers, especially once those powers were incorporated into a familiar system of worship.[5]

Ultimately a "synthesis" occurred, which was not haphazard. Orisha were carefully paired with certain saints in certain instances. Such a process would certainly not have made an impact on Europeans, who would not have known the difference. It would not have mattered to a European, ignorant of who Ogun was, or what his qualities were, that he was being "hidden" behind St.

Michael, who carried a sword as Ogun did. A pure masking effort would merely have seen to it that it appeared as though Catholicism were being practiced, and such an effort would most probably have been content with placing any saint in the place of any given Orisha.

The matching of specific saints with specific Orisha who shared similar qualities was not directed to the outside world of the Europeans but was done for the sake of the practitioners themselves, who would have been able to fully appreciate the spiritual metaphor. Thus, although masking might have been a consideration in some cases, the way in which the masking took shape reflected a desire on the part of Orisha practitioners to maintain the integrity of the faith *for themselves*. And in that regard there could not have been a state in which the arbitrary process of mere masking gave way to the more integrated "synthesis of ideology and meaning" that Houk mentions because the formal applications would already be that integration. In contemporary Trinidad, where the construction of a narrative of the origins of Orisha worship serves different groups attempting to legitimate their visions of the future of Orisha worship and representation, the relationship between Catholic and Orisha elements takes on a particular significance. In the case of the Africanization narrative, the specifics of the syncretic process are primarily an attempt to explain integration on the basis solely of persecution and necessity.

There is no evidence, for instance, that African religion faced with Catholicism in a less antagonistic environment would have remained aloof. To the contrary, the presence of Hindu elements in the Orisha faith, which occurred in a far more balanced cultural environment, reveals one of its most basic and intrinsic qualities: its inclusive tendencies. It is the purpose of such integrationist narratives, therefore, to offer a vision of the role of the religion in the present day. For the more integrative groups, the syncretistic narrative offers the greatest hope for appealing to a multi-ethnic, multi-faith society. In contrast, the narrative of disguise, by focusing on persecution, offers an opportunity for those wishing to concentrate primarily on the African elements to do so in a legitimated and justified fashion.

There are still other factors that counteract the disguise theory. In both Orisha worship and Haitian Vodoun, there are Orisha with no Catholic counterparts. If disguise were of primary importance, and no saint were used to cover a given Orisha, either that Orisha would be exposed and the disguise of the whole pantheon would be at risk, or, presumably, the Orisha would cease to be worshipped. But neither of these things occurred. On the contrary, the Orisha often continued to be worshipped in their African forms. This attests to the fact that the appropriateness of a given saint was of greater importance than having a saint there at all. Once again, if disguise was the only motive, there were plenty of saints to choose from, but the fact that the Orisha remained "undraped" indicates that disguise was not a complete prerequisite for survival.

When someone asks a *babaorisha* (a priest in the Orisha faith) how many Orisha there are, he or she might be told there are 1,001, or perhaps 401, or even 4,001. When it comes to counting the Orisha, there is always one more;

there is always the possibility for change, growth, and development, symbolized by the number one, which indicates that there is no necessary closure to the Orisha pantheon. It is within this spirit of adaptation, change, and continuing vitality that some groups representing the Orisha religion in Trinidad have sought to organize themselves as cohesive bodies, with increasingly standardized activities and progressive coordination of feasts around the country. The development of the Orisha religion toward this end has been a long-term process, but within the last ten to fifteen years the movement has taken certain steps to solidify the administration of the faith by legitimizing it in the eyes of a global community of Orisha practitioners. In addition to making contact with and gaining the recognition of the Ooni of Ifé in Nigeria, the religion has also incorporated itself through an act of Parliament (in two instances) and attempted to reveal its practices to the general public.

One should not, indeed one cannot, downplay the hardships suffered by Africans in relation to their religious practices. Almost universally, Africans were forbidden to create their own representations of their religious figures, forcing them to turn to acceptable alternatives. But it is also true that the Orisha faith is an accepting one, as long as new images and ideas are brought into the system in a coherent fashion. It is a testimony to the strength, not the weakness, of the African religions in the New World that they were able to incorporate outside religions, especially those of their oppressors, with the integrity that they did. One must remember, in this respect, that Catholicism did not enjoy the full sanction of the white ruling class, and one cannot make any easy connection between the actions of the church and the sentiments of those who held secular power. In fact, Catholicism was increasingly marginalized after the British captured the island in 1797.

The fact that Catholicism is, generally without reflection, linked to the slaveholders and hence to white hegemony and persecution does not take into account the politics of elite society in Trinidad in the nineteenth century, when Orisha practice first began to take hold. With the growth of British and hence Protestant superiority on the island, Catholicism was made a second-class religion, even though the majority of the island's inhabitants were Catholics in some form or another. Although this is not the place to elucidate the rife divisions between the Catholic and the Protestant camps during the nineteenth century (see Wood 1968:190–211), suffice it to say that camouflaging African practices with Catholic ones in a situation in which Catholic priests could barely afford to conduct their business, and Protestant heavy-handedness was clearly broadcasting its position as the religion of the government, would not necessarily have been the best way to distract the authorities from African religious practices. In a telling comment, then-governor Lord Harris asked what kind of message was being sent to liberated Africans who were being told that Anglicans were infidels destined for hell. Clearly the foreign and anti-Protestant message being promulgated by Catholics was no way to curry favor with the relatively new British administration, and its adoption by Africans was hardly a clever way of deflecting attention. In a particularly ironic pronouncement, British writer Charles Kingsley (himself a Protestant) claimed disparagingly that Catholicism was "suited to the tastes of the people" (Brereton 1979:157–58). His purpose in this statement was to show the relative inferiority of the Catholic church as well as of the "unimaginative and illogical Negro," but to our purposes here he has pointed to perhaps the most compelling reason why Africans consciously and purposefully adopted elements of Catholicism in their religion. Far from being unimaginative, the use of an alien religion by Africans in the New World shows the persistence of an African imagination, flexibility, and integrity, not manifested merely as a form of shallow disguise, but as a full, rich, and novel religious complex.

In a further testimony to the degree of agency involved, even post-emancipation, and post-official persecution in Trinidad, the Orisha religion sought like-minded faiths and incorporated them to some degree, even without the pressures of the dominant group. For instance, the presence in Trinidad of Hindu elements, but not of Muslim ones, or of the Kabbalah in some cases, points to an ongoing process of coherent change and adaptation.

It is interesting to note that the matching of saints to Orisha seems to have transformed the saints more than the Orisha. In the discovery and adoption of saints with similar characteristics to Orisha, it was obviously the Orisha who were being used as the models. The saints were secondary and chosen because of their likeness to a given Orisha. In some sense the Orisha and their personalities in the New World are much more consistent with their Old World counterparts than are the saints. This also seems to be the case with the changes Ogun has undergone even within Nigeria. Examples given by Barnes (1989) demonstrate that Ogun can accommodate new technologies and changing social relations. Although Ogun encompasses a wide variety of meanings, his "root metaphor" quality remains stable. Thus it is not so much Ogun that changes, but the lives of his devotees. A conversation with an Orisha practitioner in Trinidad more clearly reveals this point.

I was speaking to Oludari, an Orisha priest in Diego Martin, Trinidad, and we were discussing the characteristics of Ogun. Oludari told me that, as far as he was concerned, Ogun was not the god of iron, per se, but also the Orisha who knows how to make iron. Ogun must be a kind of scientist, a technician who understands how to turn ore into iron. In other words, Ogun is a god of the process as well as of the finished product. That is why, as Oludari told me, Ogun is also the Orisha involved with new technologies. Ogun has always known about automobile engines, factory machines, and the like; it was only for people to discover the depth of his knowledge of all technological processes. It is the people who change, not Ogun. Thus what emerges in Trinidad Orisha, indeed as elsewhere, is a deity (or set of deities) with a deep integrity that in fact allows for flexibility and change. As Barnes has pointed out, the root metaphor is specific enough to remain consistent, but broad enough to be applicable to changing situations.

I make this point because it demonstrates the persistence of the spirit of the Orisha faith embodied in the earlier example of the number of Orisha often given by Orisha priests. As I have explained, the number one represents the fact that Orisha is encompassing, and that it can appreciate and incorporate a new form of worship. As one prominent priest told an interviewer in the *Trinidad Guardian* (April 23, 1993), "[Orisha] is something you cannot join. We are all born Orisha and all that is around us is of the Orisha. So it is neither a question of joining or accepting, it is a question of what you are." It is also quite common for Orisha practitioners in Trinidad to belong to faiths other than Orisha and feel no contradiction. More than the external manifestations of the faith, such as the features of specific Orisha or the details of specific rituals, the transformative quality of the religion is what has enabled it to remain relevant to the community of worshippers. In all cases, however, the acceptability of new religious forms or new applications for the Orisha are based upon how those phenomena can be fitted into what remains a fairly consistent set of criteria. Ultimately Orisha religion survives through rather conservative means. It is the strength, ultimately, of the Orisha tradition that allows it to compare everything to itself.

The survival and growth of the Orisha religion in Trinidad cannot be attributed to the persistence of static forms, but to the underlying ethos of the value of tolerance, coupled with a fairly consistent frame of interpretation, again its "root metaphor" quality. Orisha thrives because of its relevance to a community of practitioners, and this relevance persists through change and growth, which is a fundamental aspect of the religion itself.

The question becomes, then, why is the disguise theory so persistent and so central to the story of the Orisha religion in Trinidad? The disguise theory/narrative has many properties which make it relevant to a particular kind of Orisha worshipper in Trinidad. The historicization of the "masked" quality of African religion makes it possible literally to uncover the African form from its supposed oppressor. The uncovering of the faith supposedly restores it to something like its "original" form. Although it is accepted by practitioners of this kind of Orisha worship that the religion is different in Trinidad than in Africa, this is as much a function of a desire to retain autonomous control over the faith as it is a recognition of the inevitability of religious transformation. In fact, religious transformation is clearly not seen as desirable or inevitable if the faith remains, in some form, true to its "roots." The desire to control the destiny of Orisha, as well as its past, and to make solid connections to African "tradition" as a form of legitimation is the primary goal of the "Africanization" process. Gilroy has argued that the "command of tradition . . . provides the critical bond between the local attributes of cultural forms and styles and their African origins" (1993:191). The purification of a form and the restoration of its African elements is a way of eliminating the deleterious effects of the history of slavery and smoothing the historical path.

In discussions with members of one of the Africanizing groups of Orisha practitioners (Oludari's organization called Egbe Onisin Eledumare), I heard narratives of a precolonial African idyll in which there was little conflict. This was a guiding principle in the extrareligious activities of the group, which included the running of a small school and cultural center. The group was also involved with a small garment-manufacturing business. The ethos was consistent, and stressed communality and cooperation. The group's attentions were clearly focused on Africans in Trinidad, especially the poor. An Ogun without St. Michael is, for the collective body of worshippers, a more powerful deity, one whose attributes can be solidly labeled African, not syncretic. For them, a decloaked African religion clearly has the advantage of appealing to African pride, but this necessarily has limited application to the society at large, and therefore contributes to the marginalization of this group to the mainstream of Orisha practitioners whose goal now is to be as inclusive as possible.

The actual historical accuracy of the disguise narrative does not find much support in the record; however, its saliency depends less on academic legitimation than on the efficacy it has for this group of practitioners. The active utilization of the historical narrative is what is of primary importance to all of the Orisha groups. Thus, the masking and demasking elements of the narrative serve two basic purposes. First, the presence of a certain kind of persecution (that is, religious intolerance) makes masking or disguise essential for survival and not an element of religious choice or appropriation. The idea that Africans willingly adopted certain elements of Catholicism makes the whole situation too messy and complex to serve a political purpose. Masking thus implies a temporary, pragmatic phenomenon. It also implies that once persecution is done with, it is the African's responsibility to return to the "original" form. This then leads to the second purpose, which is to make practitioners active in their own history. Demasking is a task which remains for present-day Trinidadians of African descent, who are left to restore their religion to its rightful purity. This is an empowering and sobering activity which helps motivate those people who actively participate in the Africanization movement. It is an act of liberation.

Current Developments

Recent events in the Orisha faith point to a current trend toward the globalization of and local centralization of the religion. These changes are marked by a desire on the part of some leaders within the religion to establish an umbrella organization for Orisha adherents which would be responsible not only for the administration of internal affairs, but also for the education of the public with regard to Orisha. In short, the new group is interested in establishing a public face for Orisha. Efforts toward this end have taken shape steadily over the past fifteen to twenty years, and probably date back as far as the Black Power movement in Trinidad in the late 1960s and early 1970s, when African culture in Trinidad enjoyed a great deal of attention and popularity. Since then Orisha practitioners have been concerned with forming a body that would be able to represent the coordinated voices of Orisha worshippers across the nation.

In 1988 the Ooni of Ifé visited Trinidad with the aim of overseeing the establishment of an official body to administer to the Orisha faith. During his visit he recognized a group that had been incorporated by an act of Parliament in 1981 (Act no. 35, assented to September 9) called the Egbe Orisha Ile Wa. The Ooni anointed the current head of that organization as Iya l'Orisha of Trinidad. Some founding members of the group, however, became dissatisfied with the direction in which the religion was going and decided to form another Orisha body called the Opa Orisha Shango. This group was also incorporated by an act of Parliament in 1991 (no. 7), with the express purpose of continuing the "Orisha Traditions and Practices as they are known in Trinidad and Tobago and as taught by approved experts of Africa and the African Diaspora." The aims of the Opa Orisha Shango also include fostering relations with the government and other bodies "in the promotion of National Development Activities aimed at improving the quality of life in Trinidad and Tobago" (p. 4).

The founders of the Opa Orisha Shango had been involved with the Egbe Orisha Ile Wa, but were concerned with that organization's seemingly ineffectual efforts with regard to the unification and centralization of the religion.[7] The Opa Orisha Shango, however, is concerned with the open display of the religion in the eyes of the public and the state, and is attempting to promote the religion's activities as a legitimate part of the island's religious community. Toward that end, and upon the death of the first Iya l'Orisha, Gretel Prime, in 1993, the Opa Orisha Shango, after a process of divination and consultation with the Orisha, elected Molly Ahye as Iya. Molly Ahye does not have her own *palais* and shrines where she can hold feasts, nor does she have the spiritual heredity that many of the other priests and priestesses have, in the sense that she does not come from a long line of Orisha priestesses. On the other hand, she is a well-known and popular figure in Trinidad, having been a dancer, and having been involved with the promotion of dance across the nation. She has also traveled extensively, tracing the paths followed in the African diaspora and researching African religious practices in Nigeria and Brazil. She is currently pursuing her doctorate at New York University.

Her choice as Iya l'Orisha of the Opa Orisha Shango organization makes sense from an educational and public relations point of view. In public pronouncements and interviews since her installation, Molly Ahye has stressed her role as educator and made it quite clear that the Orisha have called her to this position based not on her experiences with holding feasts and performing ceremonies, but on her skills as a teacher. This does not mean that she will not perform duties as a priestess, but that her other skills are what were required.

In an interview given in the *Trinidad Express* on April 29, 1994, Ahye bemoaned the fate of Orisha culture in Brazil, calling it "contained and controlled . . . almost like a Broadway play." She worries that Trinidad and Haiti may be the "last strongholds of unrefined, unbridled, spontaneous, Orisha manifestations." At the same time Ahye "gets vexed with Trinidadians for neglecting their history." As she points out, "It's as if you have amnesia. That's why people are able to rewrite history and tell you what they want and you have to accept it." Clearly, for Ahye, the subject of the history of the Orisha religions in the New World is no small matter, and the desire to control the production and to some degree the environment of the reception of that narrative is uppermost in her mind.

Ahye's installation as head of the Opa Orisha Shango sparked controversy in the Orisha community, which was played out briefly before the public in a series of articles and editorials. In September 1993, the then Iya l'Orisha or high priestess of the Opa Orisha Shango was buried at Claxton Bay in Trinidad. Her death left vacant the post of high priestess of one of the largest organizations of the religion. Mother Prime, as she was known, also belonged to the Spiritual Baptist church, a Protestant-derived African religion. Although the Egbe Orisha Ile Wa preceded the Opa Orisha Shango, it did not capture the public's attention with the same efficacy as the Opa Orisha.

Gaining recognition and positive press is a major goal of all of the Orisha groups. As recently as 1992, the religion was not present on the Protocol list of Trinidad and Tobago and was not recognized by the Inter-Religious Organization, a body formed to mediate in religious disputes and promote religious harmony and understanding in Trinidad. Contrast this to the high degree of organization and visibility of the Hindu body the Maha Saba, which has been incorporated since 1952 (Act 41 of Parliament), and the visibility of the Muslim community, which has its own schools and acknowledged holidays, and one can begin to understand the Orisha practitioners' desire for recognition. One particular affront for the Orisha faith was its omission from a group of stamps intended to celebrate the religions of Trinidad and Tobago. As far as the public is concerned, Orisha is still a marginalized faith.

The election of Molly Ahye as Iya l'Orisha of the Opa Orisha Shango was held after a session of divination and prayer by elders of the faith, and she was duly sworn in at a visible ceremony which was covered by all of the major press and media organizations in Trinidad. Soon after the announcement of her selection, a spokesperson for the Egbe Orisa Ile Wa questioned the authority upon which this decision was made. The disputant in this case was Jeffrey Biddeau, a respected and well-known Orisha priest who had been ordained in Nigeria, "the centre of the Yoruba nation and their Orisha religion." It is worth citing at length the wording of his objection, which was reproduced as an article by a reporter in the *Trinidad Express:*

> Dancer Molly Ahye cannot possibly be considered Iya l'Orisha (High Priestess) of the Orisha movement argues Orisha priest Jeffrey Biddeau, nor is the Opa Orisha organization which selected her representative of the religion. He states in a release that "it is against the code of ethics of the Orisha religion that anyone who does not meet the necessary requirements . . . be initiated priest or priestess of the religion." . . . "Such person must also be a devotee" explains Biddeau. "To be a devotee one must be called to belonging to the Orisha. The call comes by possession of the Orisha. Therefore, on behalf of the religion, devotees and elders who disagree with Molly Ahye's present status" says Biddeau, "we do not consider Opa Orisha

as the umbrella nor Molly Ahye as Iya l'Orisha of the Orisha movement of Trinidad and Tobago." (May 15, 1994).[8]

In 1992, Houk was able to write of the Orisha movement, "There is, in short, no particular form of worship that is considered standard or proper by the group as a whole" (Houk 1992:31). Houk points out that there is no governing body of the religion at this time either. Although there are still a few different groups vying for the position as the representative body of Orisha practitioners, the appearance of Biddeau's letter is remarkable. Even more remarkable is the fact that a basic leadership dispute is being played out in a public forum. Until very recently such a thing would have been unheard of. Traditionally there have been no centralized leadership roles, no umbrella organizations, and certainly no need to go to the press concerning a basic power struggle. Thus the entry of the Orisha movement into the public sphere is itself a symptom of the generally perceived notion that only in a public forum will legitimacy be attained. Even if the public is made aware of the religion through its disputes, it is also being made aware of the fact that it is witnessing the acts of a legitimate group.

Nearly a month later, a response to Biddeau's letter appeared in the *Express.* The headline read "Stay Out of Opa Orisha's Business." The author of the article made an appeal for religious tolerance and claimed that the Opa Orisha Shango has every right to choose its own leaders, just at the Egbe Orisa Ile Wa does. He draws the analogy that the Egbe's dissatisfaction with the Opa Orisha's choice of leader was tantamount to the Anglican church's claiming dissatisfaction with the Catholics' choice of pope and refusing to acknowledge the church or the pope as the head of the Anglicans (*Trinidad Express,* May 24, 1994).[9] The implication here is that the Orisha faith, like the Christian faith, has denominations.

Ultimately this may be the fate of the Orisha faith in Trinidad as competition grows over access to public recognition, state services, and so on. The various groups will probably be enjoined to coexist as denominations without one group gaining ascendancy. This factionalism, however, must be seen as growing out of a desire for participation in the public sphere, a participation that was seen as necessary for the group's very survival.

In a final postscript to the transformations undergone by the Orisha faith, this year's Republic Day celebrations included a tribute to Obatala, the "Orisha of pure thought and creativity," whose symbolic color is white. Republic Day, celebrating the formation of the Republic of Trinidad and Tobago, is also traditionally celebrated by the wearing of white. The *Trinidad Guardian* newspaper reported that Republic Day is observed *"by some sects of the Orisha religion"* through devotion to Obatala (September 24, 1994). The ability of African religions in the New World to accommodate other faiths clearly extends to the accommodation of national holidays, and the rhetoric of nationalist ideology. At the forefront of these celebrations, along with a full-color photograph, were members of the Opa Orisha Shango.

The full-scale participation by the various Orisha sects in the public sphere adds a new dimension to the concept of the flexibility of New World African religions. Not only do individual deities such as Ogun possess the internal integrity to shift and accommodate to changing situations, but the faith as a whole retains this as a guiding ethos. Far from being a static or, worse, disappearing body of beliefs and practices, Ogun and the Orisha in Trinidad have demonstrated an ability to keep up with new developments.[10] Public debate, marketing strategies, public relations campaigns, and other forms of self-promotion and legitimation are not merely new strategies, but new twists on elements that have always been present in Yoruba and Yoruba-derived religious practices. The contemporary manipulation of historical narratives is only one example of the political and strategic adeptness that has always been present in African religions in the New World. What marks this debate, then, is not so much the fact that it is in keeping with Yoruba religion's historical engagement with the political, but the self-conscious quality that these political moves have in relation to the negotiation of an African versus New World identity.

Notes

The research for this chapter was made possible by a Fulbright fixed-sum grant to Trinidad and Tobago. I would like to thank Sandra Barnes, Paul Hanson, and Garth Green for commenting on earlier drafts of this essay. In Trinidad I was helped by many people, but I would especially like to thank Oludari Olakela Massetungi of Egbe Onisin Eledumare for his kindness, hospitality, and patience. I would also like to thank Kay Baldeosingh, Kathleen Maharaj, and Melissa Richards at the *Trinidad Express,* and Marsha Brooks and Dr. Funso Aiyejina at the University of the West Indies, St. Augustine, for many interesting and fruitful discussions.

1. See Scott for a thorough treatment of this problem in anthropology.

2. See Scott (1991) and Gilroy (1993).

3. See, for example, Barber's "How Man Makes God in West Africa: Yoruba Attitudes towards the Orisa," in which she demonstrates a deep concern with very mundane political issues in Yoruba belief. The fact that this is a feature of the African belief system is of less concern here than the fact that it is a feature that is consistently found throughout the New World, and which is ignored at the cost of losing perspective on the ways in which Yoruba-derived religions continue to engage with political concerns in new ways all the time. This is fundamentally at the root of this chapter. As Barber says so well, "They [the Yoruba] live in a kind of society where it is very clear that the *human* individual's power depends in the long run on the attention and acknowledgment of his fellow-men" (1981:724).

4. Slavery makes itself present in certain narrative strategies within black nationalist discourse, often as a kind of negative space.

5. For a similar account of Grenada, see Polk (1993:76 and 80).

6. Houk (1995:183) gives a lengthy explanation concerning the lack of syncretism for some of the Orisha. He claims in the instance of Elefa, for example, that the characteristics of this Orisha are not "well-defined," making syncretism difficult. This appears to support my hypothesis that syncretism was carefully planned to adhere to some perceived similarity between saint and Orisha over and above other considerations in-

cluding duress. In a state of duress, it seems logical that little attention would be paid to the nature of the saint being utilized solely for protective cover.

7. Both ecumenical and Africanizing groups want to open up the religion in their own ways, and this is also conveyed through their respective choice of narratives. In the ecumenical narrative, openness means equivalence with regard to other religions such as Catholicism. In the Africanizing narrative, openness means not having to hide behind any other religious practice.

8. It is interesting to note here that in her own interview for the *Trinidad Express* (April 29, 1994), Ahye indicates that the Orisha did not call her to be a priestess in the traditional sense. I do not know, however, if this means that she was, in fact, possessed by an Orisha.

9. There seems to have been some terminological confusion here as well. Jeffrey Biddeau claimed that Molly Ahye was not considered by the Egbe Orisha Ile Wa as the rightful head of the Orisha *movement.* The Egbe Orisha is also known as the Orisha Movement, and thus the author of this response, Aldwin Joseph, was claiming that it was irrelevant for one organization to criticize another's choice of leader. However, it seems likely that Jeffrey Biddeau was not speaking merely of his own group, but of the religion in general, since he speaks of representation in the broad sense.

10. The most recent bid by the Orisha religion in Trinidad for national legitimacy has been the call for a nationally observed holiday for Orisha practitioners, to be called Lord Shango Day. Members of Egbe Orisha Ile Wa have called upon the members of the newly elected United National Congress government to fulfill a campaign promise made to the effect that Orisha practitioners would be given a separate holiday in the event of a UNC victory. Shouter Baptists, a religion close to Orisha in many ways, have been granted their own holiday already by the UNC (*Trinidad Express,* February 1, 1996).

References Cited

Barber, Karin. 1981. "How Man Makes God in West Africa." *Africa* 51(3):724–45.

Barnes, Sandra T. (ed.). 1989. *Africa's Ogun.* Bloomington: Indiana University Press.

Bastide, Roger. 1971. *African Civilizations in the New World.* New York: Harper and Row.

———. 1978. *The African Religions of Brazil.* Trans. Helen Sebba. Baltimore: Johns Hopkins University Press.

Brandon, George. 1993. *Santeria from Africa to the New World: The Dead Sell Memories.* Bloomington: Indiana University Press.

Brereton, Bridget. 1979. *Race Relations in Colonial Trinidad, 1870–1900.* Cambridge: Cambridge University Press.

———. 1981. *A History of Modern Trinidad, 1783–1962.* Port-of-Spain: Heinemann.

Deren, Maya. 1953. *Divine Horsemen: The Living Gods of Haiti.* New York: Thames and Hudson.

Gilroy, Paul. 1993. *The Black Atlantic: Modernity and Double Consciousness.* Cambridge: Harvard University Press.

Herskovits, Melville, J., and Frances S. Herskovits. 1964 (1947). *Trinidad Village.* New York: Octagon Books.

Holloway, Joseph (ed.). 1990. *Africanisms in American Culture.* Bloomington: Indiana University Press.

Houk, James. 1992. "The Orisha Religion in Trinidad: A Study of Culture Process and Transformation." Ph.D. dissertation, Tulane University.

———. 1993. "Afro-Trinidadian Identity and the Africanization of the Orisha Religion." In *Trinidad Ethnicity,* ed. Kevin Yelvington. London: Macmillan Caribbean.

————. 1995. *Spirits, Blood, and Drums: The Orisha Religion in Trinidad.* Philadelphia: Temple University Press.

Metraux, Alfred. 1959. *Voodoo in Haiti.* London: Andre Deutsch.

Mintz, Sidney, and Richard Price. 1976. *An Anthropological Perspective on the Afro-American Past.* Philadelphia: ISHI Occasional Paper in Social Change, no. 2.

Murphy, Joseph M. 1988. *Santeria: An African Religion in America.* Boston: Beacon Press.

Polk, Patrick J. 1993. "African Religion and Christianity in Grenada." *Caribbean Quarterly* 39 (3 & 4):74–82.

Scott, David. 1991. "That Event, This Memory: Notes on the Anthropology of African Diasporas in the New World." *Diaspora* 1(3):261–84.

Simpson, George Eaton. 1978. *Black Religions in the New World.* New York: Columbia University Press.

Trotman, D. V. 1976. "The Yoruba and Orisha Worship in Trinidad and British Guinea, 1838–1870." *African Studies Review* 19(2):1–17.

Warner-Lewis, Maureen. 1991. *Guinea's Other Suns: The African Dynamic in Trinidad Culture.* Dover, Mass.: The Majority Press.

Wood, Donald, 1968. *Trinidad in Transition: The Years after Slavery.* London: Institute for Race Relations; Oxford University Press.

Henry John Drewal and John Mason[1]

14

Ogun and Body/Mind Potentiality: Yoruba Scarification and Painting Traditions in Africa and the Americas

Erin Ogun ki se awada "Ogun's laugh is not a laughing matter"
Ogun a sa'le fun orisa "Ogun clears land [and heads] for the gods"
Ogun okoko yeri ogu "Ogun, the hoe that opens the earth to bury us"

—Verger 1957:187, 188, 193

Throughout the lives of persons who live according to Yoruba ways, Ogun "opens the road," helping them to actualize their *iwa,* their character, personality, and destiny. As patron of all who use iron, Ogun guides those who incise bodies, either with tattoo scarifications (*kolo*) serving principally aesthetic purposes (Drewal 1988, 1989), or those marks (*gbere*) whose inscriptions have primarily curative, protective, and empowering objectives.[2] *Gbere* include inoculations that deal with a variety of crisis situations, as well as those performed during initiations of *orisa* devotees. Initiation *gbere,* accompanied by head/body painting, attract and encourage divine forces to occupy the bodies of the devout, who then literally *embody* sacred presences and powers. Reflecting upon our own studies and experiences of Yoruba/Lukumi body arts, we offer some thoughts on how visible markings on bodies signal invisible transformations of persons.

Part I

The distinction between so-called "aesthetic" and "empowering" body arts is an arbitrary, basically Occi-centric one. From a Yoruba perspective, all corporal transformations, whether obvious, subtle, unseen, temporary, or permanent, signal *empowerment* in a variety of ways. As Yoruba say, *iwa l'ewa,* "character/essence is beauty," and vice versa. Beauty (*ewa*) possesses power (*ase*), the power to move and change us in substantial ways. This holds for *kolo* (tatoo scarifications) and the symbols and sanctified pigments of spiritual forces painted on our bodies as much as the healing substances that soothe our skin or penetrate our bodies via inoculations. This view is due in large part to Yoruba concepts of the relationship between the body and the mind. As Morakinyo and Akiwowo (1981:26, 36) have noted, the Yoruba "concept of the person . . . vis-a-vis body-mind relationship, is a unitary one. The body is the mind."

In the West, some are beginning to examine and take seriously the bodily basis of experience and knowledge (see Johnson 1987; Drewal 1994)—something Yoruba have understood for some time in their holistic approach to human capacities and sources of well-being (Ademuwagun et al. 1979). The senses— sight, hearing, smell, touch, and taste, as well as the sense of motion/movement/balance—create and respond to affective qualities in the "arts," which Yoruba define and understand as "evocative form." Logocentric approaches to the arts have limited our understandings of art on its own terms. As Drewal has argued elsewhere (1990:35), language-based approaches, such as semiotics, are just that: *language*-based, not *sense*-based. Art communicates and evokes by means of its own unique codes, and these await investigation.

Recently, a vision-based approach has been outlined by the Yoruba artist and art critic Moyo Okediji (1992:119–23), which he imaginatively terms *semioptics*—an approach that recognizes the limitations of the linguistic basis of semiotics and seeks to uncover the ways in which the sense of *sight* shapes our perceptions and understandings of the world.

Semioptics is an important step, but it needs to be part of a more comprehensive investigation of the *bodily, multisensorial* basis of understanding. Language, for example, is just one of the ways we experience and represent the world. But before language we began by perceiving, reasoning, theorizing, and understanding through *all* our senses, and these continually participate, though we may often be unconscious of them, in the ways we literally *make sense* of the world. Sensing (hearing, tasting, etc.) is thinking; sensing is theorizing. In the beginning, there was *no* word.

Three examples may suggest how specific senses contribute to experiences and understandings of art in a Yoruba environment. Take the sense of hearing. In Yoruba society, the notion of "educability" is conveyed in the term *iluti* (*ilu-eti,* "possessing a well-trained ear"), the ability *to hear well and learn* (Abiodun 1983). Examining indigenous concepts of orality might provide insights into African understandings of "understanding." Such an exercise might be one way to respond to Mudimbe's challenge "to make African thought thinkable" (1988).

A second example involves the sense of smell. At Abeokuta in 1978, I experienced a masker (Egungun) representing lineage ancestral warriors (fig. 14.1).

FIGURE 14.1 An Abeokuta Egungun masker representing lineage
ancestral warriors. Photo by Margaret Thompson Drewal.

Its powerful aura, its *ase,* resided not only in its evocative visual forms, which included power packets sewn into and attached to its costume; not only in the impressive chorus of words of praise that energized it (Barber 1994); not only in the kinetic energy of the accompanying dancers and the rushing, boisterous crowd; but also in the pervasive, overpowering *stench* that emanated from its blood-soaked tunic! Words, or a focus on visual imagery, for example, are woefully inadequate to capture such moving multi-sensorial experiences of evocative form.

A third example comes from what one might consider a "strictly visual" art form: *kolo* tattoo scarifications (cf. Drewal 1988, 1989). While the sense of sight certainly is used to perceive and appreciate them initially, it is the sense of touch (whether actual or virtual) that provokes a more profoundly sensual experience. As one Yoruba man confided to me, "When we see a young woman with *kolo,* or touch the *kolo* with our hands, the weather changes to another thing [we become sexually aroused]!"

A Yoruba view of body/mind unity underlies perceptions of the relationship between body markings and personal attributes. Yoruba assess an individual's personality from both physical appearance and behavior. Thus *kolo* are created, experienced, and understood as highly visible *exterior* proclamations of one's *inner* courage, fortitude, and aesthetic sensibilities. Other body scarifications containing inoculations (*gbere*), because of their potency and secrecy, are generally not flaunted but instead are hidden, shown subtly, or revealed in carefully monitored circumstances. Yet they too shape perceptions, interpretations, and actions concerning a person's inner essence or personality (*iwa*).[3] Thus Ogun, the highly visible civilizer/destroyer, path-clearer, leaves his mark on interior landscapes as well.

Yoruba Signs of Empowerment in Africa

As with the different kinds of *kolo* marks, Yoruba have precise terminology to denote the act of inoculation with the verb phrase *sin gbere. Sin* is the verb "to incise," and *gbere* refers to the inoculation itself. Delano (1969, 2:204–205) explains and illustrates the monosyllabic verb *sin: "o sin in,* he incised any part of his body" and *"o singbere fun un,* he is incised; *o sin mi ni gbere,* he incised me." More interesting, however, are his examples of the metaphorical uses of *sin gbere,* which reveal clearly the notion of augmented capacities, of empowerment. For example, the sentence "he incised him/her on the occiput [top of the head]: (*o sin in ni gbere ipako*) is rendered figuratively as meaning "he alerted him to the coming danger." In other words, certain inoculations make possible intuition, foresight.

Abraham (1958:590) provides similar examples: *o sin gbere fun mi,* "he incised my head or body as a charm to ward off trouble." Like Delano, he gives another figurative example: *o sin mi ni gbere eti,* literally "he/she inoculated me at the ears," which he explains as "he gave me a hint as to the likely outcome of my affair." In both Delano's and Abraham's illustrations, *gbere* allow persons to be forewarned about forces operating in particular circumstances—a kind of bodily based divination that affords a hypersensitivity to presences, an intensification, expansion, and refinement of one's inherent abilities.

Gbere provide extrasensory capacities. They extend possibilities, augmenting a person's powers by incorporating ingredients in the incisions that possess *ase*. Interior enhancement creates exterior possibilities. Thus, for example, when a singer wants to excel at hunters' songs (*ijala*) or make prayers or curses more effective, she/he has *gbere* incised on the tongue. If a hunter wants to see better at night, he has *gbere* cut under his eyes. *Gbere* are a way of having influence, of enlarging one's presence and effectiveness in the world, *aye*. Such empowerment practices seem to have contributed an ideology of resilience which, as one colleague has suggested (Yai 1994), may in part explain why Yoruba philosophical tenets have such a prominent role in African faiths of the Diaspora.

Herbal doctors/priests, followers of Osanyin, the god of healing leaves, medicine makers (*onisegun*), Ogun followers, and body artists (*oloola*) all administer a large variety of power-enhancing substances via incisions on the body (see also Drewal 1989:245, 247). Such marks are most often small and subtle, not bold or obvious, and their placement on the body generally corresponds with the intended effect of the medicines inserted. Thus, small, short vertical marks under the eyes (*gbere oju*) of some children signify that medicines have been inserted to prevent the child from trembling, a condition believed to be caused by the sight of spirits (Faleti 1977:24, 25). An *oloola* (Ogunole 1973) explains: "The mother or parents will prepare a medicine and bring it to the *oloola* who will then put it in the cicatrices he makes on the child and in this way prevents the child from dying." The medicine *ero agba ina,* literally "relief from that which is obtained and not spent" (i.e., the acquisition of money that disappears without producing tangible results), is rubbed into cuts made around the wrists of both hands. The ingredients for this medicinal relief include (1) the head of a particular type of snake, (2) a leaf of a plant, (3) a whole pod of alligator pepper, and (4) a tail of the gray parrot—all ground together and rubbed into the cuts around the wrists (Warren et al. 1973:2–3).

Medicine to enable one to eat poison with impunity includes substances ground together and rubbed into three incisions cut beneath each eye (ibid. 5–6). A preparation that activates a remedy involves the application of "medicine to sixteen cuts on the front and back of each wrist"—some herbalists said ingredients should be burned, others said they should be dried (ibid. 7). The procedure to prevent curses from affecting a person is to "cut nine incisions on the head and apply the medicine" (ibid. 11). The antidote for the medicine in which one's enemy has used a miniature bow and arrow to shoot at one's effigy (*a-pe-ta*) is to "grind and rub the medicine into three cuts on both the right and left sides of the body" (ibid. 13). To counteract bad medicine, "cut incisions around the wrists and around the ankles; apply the medicine to them" (ibid. 14, 16). Raymond Prince (1960:73) recorded "the belief . . . that if one does not answer to one's name [in a dream], the invocation will not be effective. To prevent damage by invocation the native doctor will sometimes make a cut in front of the patient's ear and rub in certain protective medicines."

The preceding examples deal with forces in the world, or *aye*. The expression *omo ar'aye*, "[dangerous] children/persons of the world," refers specifically to all those who would destroy or diminish one—one's mortal enemies and detractors. Abimbola (1976:37–40) cites an Ifa verse in which the protagonist's enemies were "mouths," that is, all those who sought by innuendo, gossip, or lies to undo and destroy him. Spoken words carry force, *ase*—performative power to accomplish things. Thus, in the example cited above, hearing one's name in a dream can signal danger. In other circumstances sounds signal victory or success precisely because voiced power and appropriate actions accompany the marking of the body and work to activate ingredients and forces.

It is not only other people who are the source of one's challenges and trials. Forces in the otherworld (*orun*), such as ancestors, *ara orun*, and deities, *orisa*, also operate in the world and must be acknowledged, respected, and dealt with. Some persons are instructed to honor and placate their forebears by participating in ancestral masking performances (Egungun); others are devotees of certain *orisa* through divination, and are expected to become vessels for divine entities so that their deities can enter and act in the world on appropriate ceremonial occasions. *Ori-sa*, "anciently selected heads" who became deified, live and act in the world via the spiritual "innerheads" (*ori inu*), the "selected heads" of their living followers. Such transcendence is made possible during the initiation rites of *orisa* devotees when they receive body markings—paintings and incisions—primarily around the head.

Prepared Heads—Sacred Colors and Cuts

Colors and substances, efficacious in ways that are simultaneously and inseparably physical and metaphysical, facilitate the worship of the gods. Those initiated into societies honoring the gods must be prepared to receive, without danger, the spirit of their deity, and to become their deity's medium during possession ceremonies. To accomplish this, colors are painted and incisions made on the top of the head of the devotee, and substances which activate the vital essence or *ase* of the god are inserted in *gbere*. This site and symbol of initiation is known as *osu*, often later signified by a patch or tuft of hair (cf. M. T. Drewal 1977). The deity can now enter the properly prepared spiritual or inner head and possess the medium or *adosu* (lit. "one-with-*osu*").

In the first step, the heads of the faithful are shaved and then painted with medicinal and evocative pigments—colors mixed with certain ingredients that actively attract and direct spiritual forces to those they will inhabit during possession trances. The following is a description of a head-painting initiation ceremony witnessed by Margaret Thompson Drewal and the author in northern Ijebu-Yoruba country in August 1986.

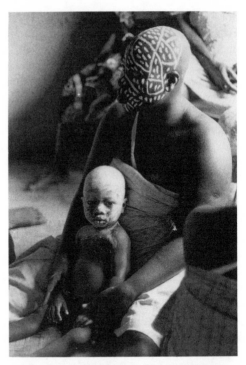

FIGURES 14.2 and 14.3 Initiates having their heads painted with the colors, patterns, and sanctified substances of certain gods. Photos by Margaret Thompson Drewal.

The initiation was hosted and supervised by an *iya Sango,* a priestess of Sango (Thundergod, who was the fourth king of Oyo), as part of a festival honoring Sango and other deities. About a dozen priestesses and seven initiates were involved, mostly female, ranging in age from about two to twenty. On the day we arrived, the novices were lined up preparing to walk to a nearby stream and shrine of Olueri/Osun, a river goddess. The eldest novice, the daughter of *iya Sango,* led the way with a gourd containing a knife balanced on her head and a chicken in her hand. All were dressed in white cloth with *osun,* red camwood powder, covering their legs and feet. *Iya Sango* explained, "We dress ourselves as we dress the gods' shrine; it's like giving food to the gods and sharing it with them."[4]

To the accompaniment of a small *bata* drum ensemble, and with serious demeanor and measured step, they first placed their left feet three times in a small pool of cool water poured between two trees that marked an ancestral founding spot (called *orisa/osi asese*) before proceeding to the river. This act was what some Yoruba ritual specialists call *aito/eto,* a segment or stage in a longer, complex process of sacred actions (cf. M. T. Drewal 1992:31, 197). It brings to mind the Yoruba adage "When one pours cool water in front, one's way will be cool, smooth" (*Ti a ba da omi tutu siwaju, aa ri ile tutu te*).

Upon their return from the river, we followed them into the shrine room, which contained the sacred witnessing objects of various *orisa* (from left to right): Osun (large lidded vessel); *ibeji* and *oro* (small wood figures set in an earthen vessel); Sango, Oluaye (Obaluaye), Aganju, Oge, and Aira (large earthen vessel painted red, holding layers of wooden dancewands, *ose,* metal *ose* painted red with white dots, a multi-headed wood staff painted white with red dots, long camwood-covered horns, and a large stone); Yemoja (large vessel with low relief design colored red); Ogun (pieces of iron) and Oya (long celts covered in red camwood), both placed in front of Yemoja; Osun (vessel); and Orisanla (several smaller white-colored vessels). Several priestesses offered prayers and blessings for the initiates as they sat in the shrine room on special mats.[5]

Two days later we returned to find the initiates with their heads shaven and in the process of being painted (figs. 14.2, 14.3). An Orisanla priestess, who had offered prayers at the shrine two days earlier, directed the painting, assisted by two others. The first step was to cover the entire head (to the upper neck) with *efun,* white kaolin or chalk mixed with sanctified water, probably from Olueri/Osun's stream. As this milky liquid dried, it turned bright, opaque white on the skin. Next she divided the head into left and right sides and covered the left with *osun,* red camwood powder mixed with water. Both the *efun* and *osun* appeared to be mixed with other substances. After this bilateral division, the priestess, beginning with the right (white) side and using a short brush made of a small, flattened wood twig, divided it with a red (*osun*) line from the top of the head (occiput) down the side to the ear, thus creating right-front and right-back quadrants. The right-front section was then further divided vertically, and a series of red zigzag lines were painted between the vertical ones. The resulting triangular areas were then filled with short slashes of red

FIGURE 14.4 A priestess points to the intersection of the lines that created the four sections of the head. Photo by Margaret Thompson Drewal.

FIGURE 14.5 The division of the head into two, then four, and then further sections recalls how diviners "open" an Ifa tray before beginning divination. Photo by Margaret Thompson Drewal.

to create a kind of patchwork pattern. A long diagonal line was made from the nose bridge across the cheek. Short slashes were placed in the area around the eye and lower face and around the edge of the ear. The right-back quadrant remained white.

The priestess repositioned the initiate and, taking the gourd containing the *efun* or white chalk pigment, began painting lines on the red camwood surface of the left side of the head (figs. 14.2, 14.3)—first a vertical one from the occiput to the ear to create front and back quadrants; next another line from the top to the cheek to divide the left-front section in half. More zigzag lines further divided this area into triangles that were then filled with white slashes. A long white diagonal line was made from the nose bridge across the cheek. Short slashes were placed in the area around the eye and lower face and around the edge of the ear. The top of the left-back section was marked off into a triangle and filled with slashes. The rest of it was divided vertically; the right half (back) side was painted with indigo (*aro*), while the left half remained red.

Each of these color sequences, areas, and color combinations signified a specific deity: red lines, patterns, and slashes on white in the right-front quadrant were for Aganju; the white right-back quadrant was for Orisanla; white lines, patterns, and slashes on red in the left-front quadrant were for Sango; the red half of the left-back quadrant was for Oluaye/Obaluaye, the blue half for Esu Laalu. At the conclusion of the painting, in a final action, the priestly painter took her stick-brush and held it at the intersection of the lines that created the four sections of the head at the occiput—the place where all spiritual roads met—thus pointing to the place where other empowering substances would later be inserted into incisions and covered by a small amalgam of sacred materials, the *osu* (fig. 14.4).[6]

The division of the head into two, then four, and then further sections recalls how diviners "open" an Ifa tray before beginning divination (Drewal 1987) (fig. 14.5). The intersection of lines signals the juncture of world and otherworld (*aye/orun*), the passage of forces between them, and the positioning of persons in this force field. Just as the diviner draws forces to the session, so too the *orisa* priestess paints sanctified colors and patterns on the selected heads of initiates in order to "open" the way for cosmic communication via possession trance. It is Ogun, through his blade-wielding followers, who makes this possible: first in shaving the head, and later in cutting the occiput for the spiritual inoculations.

After the painting was completed, the initiates were led back into the main altar room. Soon afterward, while the initiates were seated on mats beside the *orisa* shrine, all the priestesses came in. They made several elderly women come into the room to add their voiced *ase* to the proceedings, and then prayed over them, blessing them on their life's journey. In the room with them was an offering (in this instance a pig) that concluded this stage in the rites. The eldest novitiate led it out on a tether and turned it over to two men, who dispatched it with a knife at the base of the two trees marking the *orisa-osi asese* ("divine progenitors'" altar).

Later the officiants danced and sang, playing (*sire*) in honor of the gods. Several entered the shrine room, taking out various altar objects, such as twin memorial figurines (*ere ibeji*) or wands (*ose*), for use as choreographic accoutrements. The atmosphere was relaxed, filled with playful humor and impromptu performances. For example, one priestess, after looking closely at Margaret Thompson Drewal, determined that she was a child of Orisanla and proceeded to sing a series of the *orisa*'s praises while dancing with her.

Sometime later, medicines were inserted at the top of novitiates' heads and then covered by a ball of sacred substances (*osu*). The novitiates were secluded for approximately two weeks, emerging only for certain ceremonies until the conclusion of their initiation. They were thus beautified, healed, and fortified in ways identical to those used for the altar vessels and witnessing objects of the *orisa*. They were prepared as living vessels of spirit, as human altars. Each section of their heads, each color-application sequence, color combination, pattern, and placement signified an *orisa* important in their lives. With the help of the road-opener Ogun, each individual's personal essence and direction was ritually aligned with those forces that had brought her/him into the world. They were spiritual companions on the journey through life until it was time to leave for the next.

Part II: Ritual Body Markings among the Lùkùmí-Yorùbá of Cuba and the United States

Today there are no guilds or collective bodies of workers who deal with body scarification in Cuba or the United States. However, there are remnants of body scarification rituals deeply associated with Ògún which survive in both places. There are also *oríkì* to Ògún, recited by *òlòrìsà* in Cuba and the United States, that reflect on Ògún's role as *olóòlà* (body artist):

> Ògún nà ka (o) 'nílé
> Ògún nà nà 'nílé
> Ògún kóbò kóbò
> Aláajèrè rẹ́ ówo
> Ògún lu mu sun
> Ògún fĩn màlũ
> Ngbẹ́ l'ẹyín dá lọrò
> Ẹkún fẹjú
> Ta nà a wá rà àwúre
> Òṣíbíríki, alàṣẹ
> A júbà.

> Ògún points at the owner of the house
> Ògún flogs, flogs the owner of the house
> Ògún the Flogger

> Owner of people who profit from the trade of cutting boils
> Ògún pierces (a thing) to drink what oozes out
> Ògún carves/engraves the cow
> Carving with teeth that cause one to cry out in pain
> Crying with gritted teeth and wide-open eyes
> Stung, flogged, we look to buy the good-luck soap (àwúre)
> He-who-may-burst-out-suddenly, the-owner-of-authority
> We salute.[7]

In many òrìṣà houses in Cuba and the United States, the ability to address the head of a novitiate (a person entering into the process of initiation)—such as shaving, cutting the head, in the sense of incising and putting medicine into the head, even painting the head—is the domain of those individuals who have gone through the entire cycle of initiation and have received the "knife of Ògún," ọbẹ Ògún, as a sign that they are full-fledged members, adults in the community.

The knife of Ògún is not only a badge of adulthood, but also a sign that a person can lead others in prayer by being able to ritually slaughter and butcher the animals needed to make initiation possible. The owner of the knife has the authority to become a master of ceremonies. Without this knife it would be impossible to dispatch four-legged animals and very big fowl, peacock, duck. These types of animals must be dispatched with a knife, and only those people who are authorized by the community to be the "owners of knives" can work in this way.[8]

There is a tradition where people apply paint to the head. This painting is called ọṣù.[9] These geometric patterns, made up of different color series of concentric circles, serve as the sign or signature of specific òrìṣà (fig. 14.6). The painting of this design is done with specially prepared paint, paint that contains medicine. The medicine is then thought not only to permeate the scalp, but to move into those cuts that have been placed on the head, especially the cut that stands at the top or the occiput, where the ball of medicine (also called ọṣù) is placed to prepare the head for receiving the òrìṣà.

Painting the head represents other things as well. At a certain point all the priests present—in many houses only those priests who have received the knife of Ògún can touch the head—come forward and paint the ritual number for their òrìṣà in the symbolic color of their òrìṣà. The painted slashes are called fínfín (fig. 14.7). The head is decorated with fine lines and fine little dots or slashes of color so that it looks shimmeringly brilliant and beautiful in variegated colors. The priestesses of Ọṣun paint with yellow, the priestesses of Yẹmọja paint with blue, the priestesses and priests of Ọbàtálá paint with white, and Ògún, Ṣàngó, and Ọya all take red. Each of these four colors is used by all of the òrìṣà community so that, depending on the composition of the crowd at that particular initiation, the head reflects this communal touching for purposes of beautification.

Because of the language used in songs and the very fact that the head is decorated in this way, it appears that this section of the initiation used to relate

FIGURE 14.6 Head painting called
òṣù. Note the *àbàjà* marks used by
noble families of Ọ̀yọ́. Photo by
Lydia Cabrera.

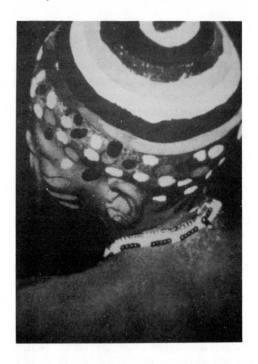

FIGURE 14.7 Initiate with *finfin* and
facial marks. Photo by Lydia Cabrera.

to scarification/decoration rituals that were later replaced by the painting of the head. Various factors may have contributed to this trend. As those Lùkùmí who were direct from Africa began to die out, elders in Cuba lost track of the proper medicines to employ, and became more and more aware of the possibility of infection, and the problems that infection might bring—unfavorable notoriety with intervention and persecution by the police. This fact is confirmed by the reluctance, observed today by many priests in both Cuba and the United States, to shave off all the hair of very prominent or famous devotees who come to be initiated. There is still, however, the fundamental tradition of making incisions at the occiput so that transformative medicine can be placed in those cuts. Those cuts are generally performed with a special razor that is definitely talked about as Ògún's tool. The *oríate* (lit.: head-of-the-divination-mat) or the priest who is working as "master of ceremonies" assumes the role of body artist and, in many cases, is joined by the *ìyálòṣà* (godmother/madrina) or *babalòṣà* (godfather/padrino), who is actually performing the initiation or has organized the initiation of the *ìyawó* (novitiate). Either the *oríate* or the *ìyálòṣà/babalòṣà* will make the incisions in the head and prepare the head to receive medicine. The incisions are always in the ritual number of the specific deity being initiated.

There are stories by older priests and priestesses that in the 1930s, 1940s, and 1950s in Cuba, not only were incisions made on the day of the initiation, but they were made every day thereafter, until the initiation was complete. As a famous old priestess of Yẹmọja, Juan Manrique Claudio, said, "By the end of the initiation your head looked like a quilt," because these incisions were set up in certain patterns, and every day medicine, new medicine, was applied to the head.

Songs are sung when the head is being prepared for these cuts. When the razor and scissor are mentioned in these songs, they are spoken of as removing obstacles—just as Ògún would remove obstacles. They even say that *irun* (hair) not only is a protector of the head, but in this case is likened to an obstacle that has to be removed in order for the planting of medicine to take place. Ògún's knife is removing this forest of hair, creating a clearing, a clearing where medicine will be planted and where it is hoped that good will sprout in the head and in the life and person of the novitiate.

As recently as 1959, a priest, whose professional work was that of a barber, came in the mornings to take care of *ìyawó*. The barber might be initiated to another *òrìṣà*, but owed Ògún special respect as his patron. He was called in especially to take care of that one job. He prepared the head for the incisions and, in many cases, then made them. He prepared the novitiate to receive the day. First the head was prepared, then the body. A barber knew how to stop a bleeding cut, and what things to apply when he nicked a person when shaving. This tradition of specialization was maintained by the Yorùbá in Cuba.[10] It has nearly died out in the United States, where now one person, either the godparent or *ojúgbònà*, does the entire job. In the Lùkùmí houses of Cuba, from the 1880s to the 1950s there were priests who had specific jobs to do as herbalists, song specialists, ritual cooks, and specialists whose job it was to create the initiation spaces where the initiates were kept.

Such head decoration is called *fínfín,* carving/decorating. The head is refashioned and covered with many raised mounds which signify the elevated status of a head that can transform itself. Devotees sing the following song:

> Fín fín òkan, wìn ní kìní dẹkùn,
> Ìyá dẹkùn, baba dẹkùn lóòní o.

> Carved, carved, one multicolored becomes a leopard today,
> Mother becomes a leopard, father becomes a leopard today O.

The head and the person are transformed into a leopard, a powerful spotted hunting animal. In many cases the spotting has a double meaning. Not only are you spotting the head of the initiate with the fine lines and cuts and decorations, but the transformed head is spotted like the leopard with the sacrificial blood of animals used in the initiation rituals of certain *òrìṣà.* All of this imagery doubles back to Ògún, the dangerous hunter in the bush, the "bad-cat" leopard in the bush. The initiated becomes more Ògún-like, more cat-like, more feline—able to see in the dark/otherworld through the act of initiation. It is the initiate's ultimate transformation into a powerful (animal) familiar: the leopard being the ultimate avatar of transformation. When possession takes place and the *òrìṣà* mounts the devotee, Ògún once again must bring his knife to clear a path. This time the path of speech must be cut so that the *òrìṣà* can communicate with their followers. The tongue of the horse is scored in ritual numbers and medicine applied so that the *òrìṣà* will be able to speak when they come to visit (*àṣẹ l'ẹnu,* "power has a mouth").

All body scarification (except that related to initiation described earlier) has gone out of use in both Cuba and the United States. Although there are published photographs of anonymous Yorùbá in Cuba exhibiting facial marks, this one (fig. 14.8) is a photograph, circa 1900, of the famous *babalawo* Adéṣínà (Remigio Herrera) which clearly shows his marks.[11]

Reminders of this practice are seen in body painting associated with certain types of *ẹbọ* (sacrifice/offering) and initiation. Painting takes place when *ẹbọ* are performed that are associated with preparing one to receive the knife of Ògún. One is marked with *ẹfun* (white chalk) as though cut with a knife. Marks are made down the length of the arm from the shoulder to the wrist, and in the back from the collarbone or the base of the neck to the coccyx or belt line, whichever comes first. In many cases, this ritual body painting, even the body painting that accompanies mounted priests of Ọbàtálá, includes decoration with *fínfín,* not just on the head, but also on the face and upper body (fig. 14.9).

Some of the old people said that at one point the priest cut the initiate and placed medicine in many parts of the body.[12] All these *fínfín* marks represented that one had been tattooed with medicine. Each dot or engraved little fine line was then covered with dots of *osùn* and *ẹfun,* each combined with medicine, acting and looking much like calamine lotion does when applied to bee stings.

FIGURE 14.8 Famous *babalawo* Adéṣínà (Remigio Herrera) of Cuba, showing Yoruba face marks. Adésínà was an Ìjèsà direct from Yorùbáland. Some Ìjèsà families have these facial markings.

One sees little slashes of color: red and white, blue and yellow. There is order, seniority, and comradeship among the colors. White is eldest, red is next, blue/black is third, and yellow is youngest. A refrain to a song sung when the head of an initiate is being painted says: *Efun ewà osùn l'àbúrò,* "Beautiful lime chalk is camwood's senior." White and red are senior among colors and when coupled with blue/black are used to represent Èṣù, Òrìṣà Oko, and Babalú, powers associated with cutting and swelling the body. In these cases devotees

FIGURE 14.9 Priest of Ọbàtálá dancing in state of possession with cane/staff of authority. Note the bent-over dance posture and fringed crown. The upper body is decorated with *fínfín* made with *ẹfun*. *Àbàjà* marks can be seen on his face.

implore Ògún to bring his healing medicine and save initiates from body decorating that swells hideously or oozes away to nothingness.

The paintbrush becomes a symbolic knife. It cuts lines, it draws lines, but it does not cause bleeding. It has become a bloodless ritual, a bloodless form of scarification, another form of masking. Devotees talk about it as though it is a mask. In other words, to become a leopard is to mask—to change one's appearance. It is like Ọya (goddess of the Niger River and the whirlwind) in the *odù* Ifá-Ọsá Ògúndá transforming from an *ẹfọn* (buffalo) into a person. She has put her mask away. Her masquerade is over, and she reveals herself to Ògún and moves back into the world of humans. In the same way, it is through initiation with Ògún's help that people transform themselves using body painting and certain *ẹbọ* that are associated with Ògún. This body scarification with paint transforms people into royal personages. Many songs talk about the head's ability to become noble. This decoration/painting ennobles you and elevates your status in the community of *òrìṣà*.

Part III: Envoi

Ògún, the way-maker, is there to cut the umbilicus that gives us life apart from our mothers; he is there as we reach the age for procreation—preparing penis and vagina through circumcision; he is there to ennoble our heads for the gods; and he is there to dig the graves at the end of one journey, and the start of another. In all this, whether with cuts or sanctified colors or both, Ògún creates potentialities for us, whether in this world or the next.

NOTES

1. The Introduction and Part I discussion of Yoruba body arts in Africa are by H. J. Drewal, and Part II on traditions in the Americas is by J. Mason. Mason writes not as an observer but as a participant and Babalòrìṣà/priest of Ọbàtálá in the Lukumi tradition. We have commented upon each other's discussions, reflecting the dialogic format of this piece. We thank Barbara Brodie for transcribing J. Mason's taped discussions; H. J. Drewal acknowledges with gratitude the NEH for a 1990 Summer Stipend to transcribe field research tapes, and The Newberry Library for a 1992–93 NEH Fellowship that provided the opportunity to research and write portions of this essay. [HJD and JM]

2. In Recife, Brazil, these inoculations are called *obere* (Carvalho and Segato 1992:29). [HJD]

3. These same reactions to scarification, especially facial, can be noted in African-American communities. When we see someone with a scarred face, as if done with a knife/razor, we tend to think of that person as violent, possibly dangerous, yet somehow provocative and alluring. Langston Hughes in his short story "Slice Him Down" gives us an excellent example of this. In a fight over a woman's honor, two best friends pull out weapons, one a knife, the other a straight razor. After a brief fight which leaves each wounded, Hughes gives us the following dialogue:

> . . . by now Terry was sitting up, a towel tied around his sliced slit cheek. "Did I kill him?" Terry moaned. "Is I done kilt my partner?" "Naw, you ain't killed nobody," the bartender barked. . . . By this time Sling's eyes unrolled. . . . Only his forearm bled a little where the fleshy part was cut. He sat up to look anxiously across at Terry. Terry looked back at Sling and then pointed to his wounded jaw.

"Say, boy, is I got me a good scar?" "Man," Sling said generously, "you got a
better scar than I got now—*'cause your'n is gonna be on your face where everyone
can see it,* and mine's just on my shoulder." "We's got something in common.
This fight's been some good after all! . . ." "Two shetlands [drinks]," Sling said
to the bartender. "For two bad men," said Terry, "cause we really bad!" "We slice
'em down," said Sling. "We really slice 'em down," said Terry. (Emphasis added)

My late uncle was a barber who plied his trade in Harlem for more than fifty years. I
spent many hours and days over the years passing time in his barber shop. Barbers
were known to be tough, streetwise men who oftentimes carried straight razors—which
were more feared than guns. The barber is a body artist whose job is to transform you
from rough and unkempt to sharp and neat. My wife, Valerie, says that the barber is
like Ikú (Death)—he attends to everybody's head. [JM]

4. In both Cuba and the United Stats, òrìṣà devotees, before and during the seven-day
process of initiation, take the novitiates to salute (with prayers and offerings) ancient
and important sites where òrìṣà and àṣẹ reside—rivers, hills, crossroads, the ocean, desolate places, markets, etc. The invisible owners of these places must consent, through
the voice of *obì* (coconut divination), to the continued journey of the novitiate. [JM]

5. In Cuba and the United States this shrine room is called *igbódù* (grove where *odù*
is obtained). Here, in the presence of òrìṣà and other unseen powers, on the ọjọ́ ìta
(second day after/third day of the initiation), the life *odù* of the initiate is cast. *Odù* are
divination verses that outline the possible fate of initiates and devotees. [JM]

6. Only the two oldest initiates were painted in this manner. All the younger ones
had their heads either divided into white/red halves, or painted white covered all over
with red dots made by the priestesses using their middle finger dipped in the osun (figs.
14.3, 14.4). These head-painting traditions re-create exactly the polychrome preparations
of much Yoruba religious sculpture and thus provide strong evidence for our understanding of figurated works as depictions of possession states in which devotee and
deity are united/become one. See the photos in Verger 1957; M. T. Drewal 1977, 1986.
[HJD]

7. For more on Ògún imagery and songs, see Edwards and Mason 1985 and Mason
1992.

8. In the Afro-Brazilian religion called Shango in Recife, the person who has the
authority to dispatch sacrifices with a knife is "a male ritual helper called *acipa* [asipa]
or *asogun*" (Carvalho and Segato 1992:29). These titles are hunter/warrior ones specifically associated with Ogun and the wielding of iron weapons. [HJD]

9. In Brazil, Yoruba/Nago painting of the head is called *efun*. Mendonca (1935:200)
cites M. Querino (1927:163) and gives in his vocabulary *efum [efun]: ceremonia do culto
fetichista dos negros . . . termo iorubano . . . imediatamente, faz-se-lhe o Efum, isto e,
pinta-se-lhe a cabeca, descrevendo circulos concentricos com as cores: branca, azul, e
vermelha* ("a ceremony in the fetishistic cult of the blacks . . . Yoruba term . . . immediately, they did Efun, that is, painted the head, creating concentric circles with colors:
white, blue, and red"). In a second reference, Jacques Raimundo (1936:152–53) gives the
following: *"efum, acto implementar com que se arma o encantamento das filhas-de-santo*
(Querino *Raca Afr.* and Ramos *Negro Bras;* 49) *do ior.* [from Yoruba] *ehfun, encantamento,
fascinacao, embelezo, atractivo"* (*efum,* "an act to implement as if to protect the possession
of the daughters of the saints [devotees] from the Yoruba *ehfun,* rapture [possession],
fascination, embellishment, attraction, enchantment"). Actually *efun* (lime chalk) refers
to the color white, which is regarded as "senior" among colors by Yoruba. [HJD]

10. Barbers had an important position in nineteenth-century Brazil as well. They
were leaders of work groups, heads of itinerant musical groups, news carriers, and rev-
olutionaries (Ramos 1944:186). [HJD]

11. Adéṣínà was an Ìjẹ̀ṣà babalawo who came to Cuba direct from Yorùbáland in
the first half of the 1800s.

12. In Recife, Brazil, Carvalho and Segato (1992:28) describe how, "in the case of *making the saint,* once the new member is taken into the *saint's room* [*pegi*] not only are sacrifices of animals performed but also *oberes* or ritual cuts are practiced in different parts of her body including the crown of the shaved head, to implant the *ases* of her saints. Yet, the latter takes place only if the person is in a state of possession. There, in the room the new *child* will remain in seclusion, and some religious knowledge will be transmitted to her, not only while she is awake but also when she is in a state of possession." [HJD]

References Cited

Abimbola, Wande. 1976. *Ifa: An Exposition of Ifa Literary Corpus.* Ibadan: Oxford University Press.

Abiodun, Rowland. 1983. "Identity and the Artistic Process in the Yoruba Aesthetic Concept of *Iwa.*" *Journal of Cultures and Ideas* 1(1):13–30.

Abraham, R. C. 1958. *Dictionary of Modern Yoruba.* London: University of London Press.

Ademuwagun, Z. A.; J. A. A. Ayoade; I. E. Harrison; and D. M. Warren (eds.). 1979. *African Therapeutic Systems.* Waltham, Mass.: Crossroads Press.

Barber, Karin. 1994. "Polyvocality and the Individual Talent: Three Women *Oriki* Singers in Okuku." In R. Abiodun, H. Drewal, and J. Pemberton (eds.), *The Yoruba Artist: New Theoretical Perspectives on African Arts.* Washington, D.C.: Smithsonian Institution Press, pp. 151–60.

Carvalho, José Jorge de, and Rita Laura Segato. 1992. *Shango Cult in Recife, Brazil.* Caracas, Venezuela: FUNDEF, CONAC, OAS.

Claudio, Juana Manrique, priestess of Yemoja. 1986. Personal communication to Mason.

Delano, Chief I. O. 1969. *Yoruba Monosyllabic Verbs.* 2 vols. Ile-Ife: Institute of African Studies, University of Ife.

Drewal, H. J. 1987. "Art and Divination among the Yoruba: Design and Myth." *Africana Journal* 14(2/3):139–56.

———. 1988. "Beauty and Being: Aesthetics and Ontology in Yoruba Body Art." In A. Rubin (ed.), *Marks of Civilization.* Los Angeles: UCLA Museum of Cultural History, pp. 83–96.

———. 1989. "Art or Accident: Yoruba Body Artists and Their Deity Ogun." In S. Barnes (ed.), *Africa's Ogun: Old World and New,* Bloomington: Indiana University Press, pp. 235–60.

———. 1990. "African Art Studies Today." In E. Lifschitz (ed.), *African Art Studies: The State of the Discipline.* Washington, D.C.: Smithsonian Institution Press, pp. 29–62.

———. 1994. "Form-words in Understandings of African Art." In *Visions of Art: The Jerome L. Joss Collection of African Art at UCLA.* Los Angeles: Fowler Museum of Cultural History, pp. 64–79.

Drewal, M. T. 1977. "Projections from the Top in Yoruba Art." *African Arts* 11(1):43–49, 91–92.

———. 1986. "Art and Trance among Yoruba Shango Devotees." *African Arts* 20(1) (November):60–67, 98–99.

———. 1992. *Yoruba Ritual: Performers, Play, Agency.* Bloomington: Indiana University Press.

Edwards, Gary, and John Mason. 1985. *Black Gods—Orisa Studies in the New World.* Brooklyn: Yoruba Theological Archministry.

Faleti, A. 1977. "Yoruba Facial Marks." *Gangan* 7:22–27.

Johnson, Mark. 1987. *The Body in the Mind.* Chicago: University of Chicago Press.

Mason, John. 1992. *Orin Orisa: Songs for Selected Heads.* Brooklyn: Yoruba Theological Archministry.

Mendonca, Renato. 1935. *A Influencia Africana no Portugues do Brasil.* São Paulo: Companhia Editoria Nacional.

Morakinyo, O., and A. Akiwowo. 1981. "The Yoruba Ontology of Personality and Motivation: A Multidisciplinary Approach." *Journal of Social and Biological Structures* 4:19-38.

Mudimbe, V. Y. 1988. *The Invention of Africa.* Bloomington: Indiana University Press.

Ogunole, A., body artist. 1973. Personal communication to Drewal, May 5.

Okediji, Moyo, ed. 1992. *Principles of "Traditional" African Art.* Ile-Ife: Fine Art Department.

Prince, Raymond. 1960. "Curse, Invocation and Mental Health among the Yoruba." *Canadian Psychiatric Association Journal* 5:65-79.

Querino, M. 1927. "A raca Africana e seus costumes na Bahia." *RABL* 25(69/70).

Raimundo, Jacques. 1936. *O Negro Brasileiro.* Rio: Record.

Ramos, Artur. 1944. *Las Poblaciones del Brasil.* Trans. T. M. Molina. Panuco, Mexico: Fondo de culturala economica.

Verger, Pierre. 1957. "Notes sur le Culte des Orisa et Vodun a Bahia, la Baie de tous les Saints au Bresil et a l'Ancienne Cote des Esclaves en Afrique." *Memoires de l'IFAN* 51.

Warren, Dennis, et al. 1973. *Yoruba Medicines.* Legon: The Institute of African Studies, University of Ghana.

Yai, Olabiyi. 1994. "In Praise of Metonymy: The Concepts of 'Tradition' and 'Creativity' in the Transmission of Yoruba Artistry over Time and Space." In R. Abiodun, H. Drewal, and J. Pemberton (eds.), *The Yoruba Artist: New Theoretical Perspectives on African Arts.* Washington, D.C.: Smithsonian Institution Press, pp. 107-15.

John Mason

15

Ògún: Builder of the Lùkùmí's House

The Lùkùmí love Ògún because he had the courage and ability to go out into the wilderness alone, armed only with his intelligence, strength, and a cutlass, and carve out a permanent and exalted place, for both himself and his followers, in the hearts and minds of men.

The term Lùkùmí (Olùkùmí—my friend) is an ancient designation still used by the Yorùbá and their descendants in Cuba. It is found on several ancient maps of West Africa, where the kingdom of Ulcumi or Lucumi or Ulcami is shown to the northwest of the kingdom of Benin. This word is also used to describe the Yorùbá language. In Cuba, the name is used when addressing African descendants who clearly distinguish themselves as having Nàgó, Ẹgbá-dò, Ìjẹ̀sà, Ọ̀yọ́, or Ìjẹbu ancestry. Since 1959, the United States has provided the latest site in the Americas where Lùkùmí-Yorùbá culture has taken hold, brought by African-Cuban, African-American, and African–Puerto Rican initiates. In the United States the term Lùkùmí is seldom used but is replaced by the designations "*Òrìṣà* worship" and "*Òrìṣà* follower."

Ògún is the clearer of the path and creator of the road that allows both men and deities to travel from one level of reality to the next. Before we employed the sharpened stone of Ògún, we used his teeth to bite through the umbilical cord, allowing a new soul to enter the world. Ògún works tirelessly against the invisible, manipulative power of Fate, and Lùkùmí songs to the *òrìṣà* are the best vehicles for exploring the hopes and expectations we look to Ògún and his fellow powers to fulfill. These songs describe not only who Ògún and the other *òrìṣà* are but also how they can transform our existence. If you have ever suffered, you realize that there is nothing you can ever do to be prepared for it except to pray for a way out to materialize instantly. Ògún is called to cut the escape path.

Figure 15.1 Ògún pot with miniature tools used to represent work
done by Ògún in the smithy, on the farm, and during the hunt.
Casa de Africa, Havana, Cuba. Photo by John Mason.

Baba wá (ò) 'ní. Baba wá 'ní.
Ìyà ó máá ọ ku o. Ìyà ó máá ọ ku o.
Ààrẹ'ré Òg̣ún baba wá.[1]

Father come today. Father come today.
Suffering is habitual; it is unexpected.
Suffering is habitual; it is unexpected.
Titleholder of Ìré, Òg̣ún, Father come.

As blacksmith and artisan, Òg̣ún is responsible for the invention and fabrication of all tools which enable hunters and laborers to pursue their livelihoods and provide us with the animal protein, medicine, produce, and finished goods that we need to survive. He and the craft guilds that look to him as their patron also create the carved, cast, and forged art that adorns our lives. (Fig. 15.1)

Òg̣ún Alágbẹ̀dẹ, Ààrẹ'ré, Alágbẹ̀dẹ.
Òg̣ún Alágbẹ̀dẹ ilẹ̀ mo kú o.
Ọmọ Òg̣ún Alágbẹ̀de ilẹ̀ mo kú o.
A wá wò ọnà Òg̣ún Alágbẹ̀de.[2]

Òg̣ún the blacksmith, titleholder of Ìré, blacksmith.
Òg̣ún, blacksmith of the land, I salute you.
Children of Òg̣ún, blacksmith of the land, I salute you.
We come to look at the art of Òg̣ún the blacksmith.

Òg̣ún is the champion of laborers everywhere, and his movements and whereabouts are carefully charted by all workers. His appearance signals the locating and procuring of the raw materials needed for production, which in turn leads to the employing of workers, and the prosperity that comes with the manufacturing and marketing of finished goods. Women who, in West Africa and the Caribbean, own and operate markets also cheer Òg̣ún's industry (Fig. 15.2).

Òg̣ún dé (i)'lé báàyìi-báàyìi. Òg̣ún dé baba ẹ rí o wõ!
Òg̣ún dé baba ẹ rí o ṣàṣàṣá. Òg̣ún dé alágbàṣe gbàṣe.
Òg̣ún dé là báàyìi-báàyìi. Òg̣ún dé gbogbo yá re Òg̣ún.
Àgò yọ̀ pã rí a t'orí 'Jẹ̀ṣà-'Jẹ̀ṣà. Òg̣ún dé là báàyìi-báàyìi.[3]

Òg̣ún has arrived at the house just this instant.
Òg̣ún arrives. Father is seen, behold!
Òg̣ún arrives. Father is seen here and there.
Òg̣ún arrives, the laborer's laborer (the one laborers obey).
Òg̣ún arrives to save us just this instant.
Òg̣ún arrives. All are ready for the goodness of Òg̣ún.
Make way. Rejoice at once. See we support on our heads,
The Ìjẹ̀ṣà of Ìlẹ̀ṣà.[4] Òg̣ún arrives we are saved,
Just this instant. (Fig. 15.3)

As hunter, explorer, and adventurer, Òg̣ún traveled and is known where none had gone before and accomplished what none were able to do. He was witness

FIGURE 15.2 Memorial bust of a Lùkùmí priestess of Ògún who danced with many colored scarves attached to her dress. This bust is kept in the Matanzas, Cuba, home of the Èṣú priest Eugenio Lamar Delgado-Èṣùdiná. The bust is cleaned and its clothes are changed twice a year. Note the collar of palm fronds, the necklace with title beads, the cutlass attached to the left shoulder, and the *àbàjà òòró* facial marks that are also worn by the Ẹ̀gbá and Ìjẹ́bu. Photo by John Mason.

FIGURE 15.3 Principal Ìjèṣà shrine for Ògún in Cuba. The shrine was established in the city of Matanzas in the early 1820s. Note the Àgèrè/Ìjèṣà/
Bèmbé drums kept on top of Ògún's house. Photo by John Mason.

to the world of bygone ages, a world of virgin beauty and simplicity. He testifies
to being enthralled by the wisdom, antics, and instructive drama of the furred
and feathered inhabitants of the woods by creating the beautiful and detailed
poems/songs of salutation known as Ìjálá. He is chief of the hunter's trio

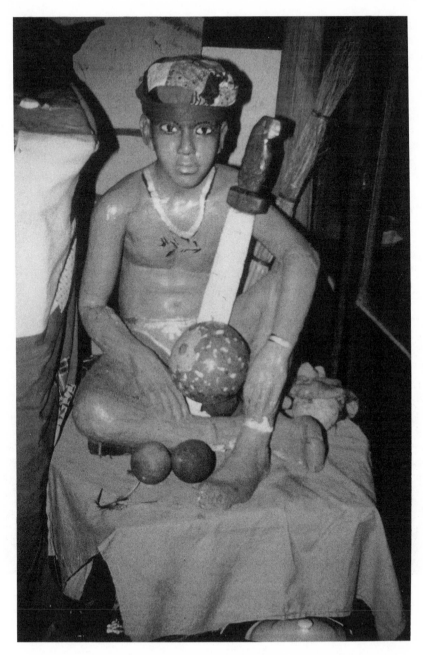

FIGURE 15.4 Commemorative statue kept in the Matanzas home of
Doña Tomasa Villamil, priestess of Ọya, that honors the Ògún of
her father, Juan Villamil. The Ògún priest Felipe Garcia Villamil is
the grandson of Juan, whose father came directly from Ọ̀yọ́ to Cuba.
Note that the *àbàjà* facial marks on the statue are also used by some
noble families of Ọ̀yọ́. Photo by John Mason.

completed by the *òrìṣà* Ọ̀ṣọ́ọ̀sì and Erinlẹ̀, and his hunter's cutlass provides them with an emblem around which they can rally after their wanderings and thereby swear to their everlasting brotherhood and solidarity (Fig. 15.4).

Ìkiri àdá Ògún ọbẹ. Ògún lò pa ọdẹ.[5]

The roaming machete is Ògún's knife.
Ògún uses it to amalgamate hunters.

Ògún is a conservationist who keeps God's law of return and replenish; he takes only what he needs to live. He not only cuts life down but guards its continuation. The hunt oftentimes takes the hunter far from home to new lands. He walks through these territories disturbing as little as possible, and taking only what he needs to live on or take back to his home. If he were to hunt all the animals today, what would he hunt tomorrow? How could Ògún, who composes beautiful songs honoring his prey, wantonly destroy that same honored animal? The same holds true for Ògún as carver, blacksmith, and body artist. Lùkùmí captives taken to work in the death camps of the Americas needed to embrace this role model if they were to survive and provide for their children yet to come.

The forest is a land of adventure and fantasy that is home to powerful and dangerous spirits. More important, it is a sanctuary that thousands of runaway slaves fled to, invoking the strength and resourcefulness of Ògún. They knew that if Ògún could survive in the forest, with his help so could they. Like the smithy, the forest is a marginal locale where alchemistic forces of transformation are at work. Both are ruled by wizards who can transform basic states of being. In the forest, water, sunlight, chlorophyll, and cellulose change into either life-preserving medicine or life-taking poison. The forest is the original medicine chest/drug/spirit store owned and operated by Ògún's mentor Ọ̀sányìn, physician hero, owner of the medicine pot that keeps us healthy and the little gourds that contain the most virulent poisons. So close is their relationship that Ọ̀sányìn had his medicine staff fashioned from Ògún's iron. Even the name Ògún has a cognate relationship with the word *ògùn,* which translates as medicine. As hunter and forester Ògún is Olóògùn, a practitioner of magic who used magical drugs. He knows intimately the secret dwelling places of his equally marginal friends, the Iwin and Ọ̀rọ̀, spirits of the earth and trees, and the favorite treetop roosts of the powerful feathered Àjé, Our Mothers, female powers which may be used for constructive or destructive purposes. Even the dreaded Ọbalúaiyé, deity of the earth who punishes wrongdoers with viral infections and who wanders the forest depths, is on friendly terms. He carries an iron-tipped spear, fashioned by Ògún, and, like Ògún, counts dogs as his most trusted and treasured companions. With Ògún as their champion, slaves, seeking refuge in a forest inhabited by such powerful and irritable spirits, could breathe easier (Fig. 15.5).

There came a time when, as a responsible parent and provider for his people, Ògún had to put aside his life as a wanderer, leave his comrades,

FIGURE 15.5 Brooklyn, New York, outdoor shrine erected to honor Ògún by the Ògún priest James Norman-Ògún Yòmi to celebrate the twenty-first anniversary of his initiation. Note upright spear mediated by horizontal cutlass with three more cutlasses standing at the foot of Ògún's pot, and the offering of a basket of cooling fruit. Photo by John Mason.

and return to the community of men with his load of knowledge, medicine, and riches. His explosive and fiery nature, oftentimes ritually symbolized by the ignition of gunpowder, is partly the rage of a wanderer tied down. His momentary insanity is caused by the siren's voice of the deep wood and the hunt that calls to him and makes him melancholy and angry. He hammers in silence as he dreams of paradise lost. I now understand what my teacher meant when he said that he could never return to his life as a seaman. If he went to sea just once more, he would never again call the land his home but would roam the waves with eyes searching the horizon for adventure. Òṣọọsì never left the forest, but Erinlè became a farmer and domesticator of animals. Ògún, never the "half-stepper," sealed his pact with society by sacrificing his most beloved possession, his dogs, to show his determination to never go wandering again. Ògún is so in love with the forest that before a devotee is initiated to him, Ògún's emblems must be fed a dog in the woods, and priestesses of Òṣun, an *òrìṣà* known for her seductive powers and great friendship with Ògún, must ritually and symbolically coax Ògún back into society, where he is dressed in a skirt of fresh palm fronds, which symbolizes cool, restrained behavior (Fig. 15.2).

> Màrìwò yéyéyé Ògún aṣọ. Alàgbà dé o.[6]
>
> Swirling palm fronds are Ògún's garment.
> The honored one arrives.

Ògún is the inventor of the war tale, of the adventure story, of the one-that-got-away tale. He keeps us enthralled and inspired by tales of his exploits and observations. He is Uncle Remus. Other *òrìṣà* associated with Ògún are also known for their storytelling abilities. Òrúnmìlà is the master storyteller. Yẹmọja, the sea, receives stories. Òṣun, the river, and Ọya, the wind, spread tales. In Cuba, priests of Òsányìn, with the aid of ventriloquism, use a doll to tell stories and give information about medicine. Èṣù-Ẹlẹgbára is called Oló-fófó (tale-bearer), whose tales cause fights and accidents so that Ògún can drink blood.

We Lùkùmí cling to Ògún because he has character, personality, status. He is not afraid to be himself. Like iron he is rigid, self-assured, and unyielding like a wall. He is an accomplisher who does something about his existence.

> Ààrẹ'ré màrìwò ya Ògún bàmbà 'laṣẹ ṣẹ.[7]
>
> Titleholder of Ìré, the palm fronds spread for
> Ògún, the stout one, who has the authority to
> accomplish things.

He is the model entrepreneur who sees and makes his own way. Ògún is economy in action—no wasted motion. Catch only what you are going to eat. You can base yourself in Ògún because, although slow, he is untiring, deliberate, and sure. This guarantees that he is victorious in the end.

Ògún-like movements form the foundation of all ritual. The aim of ritual is the successful completion of the rite. Actions which are thoughtful, economical, forceful, and repetitive provide the ritual base for forward movement and improvisation. Ògún brings the formula of 95 percent perspiration and 5 percent inspiration to all ritual procedures. The security of deliberate and repetitive actions provides the base needed for insights which promote flights of fancy and spontaneity that break through to new ground.

In his roles as Ògún Olóòlà (Ògún the body artist), Ògún Onígbàjámọ̀ (Ògún the barber), and Ògún Alápatà (Ògún the butcher), he stands at the center of the initiation ritual processes. This fact is reiterated each time the Lùkùmí recite the following *oríkì* to Ògún:

> Ògún nà ka (o)'nílé.
> Ògún nà nà 'nílé.
> Ògún kóbò kóbò.
> Aláajèrè rẹ́ ówo.
> Ògún lu mu sun.
> Ògún fín màlũ.
> Ngbẹ́ l'eyín dá lọrò.
> Ẹkún fẹjú.
> Ta nà a wá rà àwúre.
> Óṣíbíríki, alàṣẹ.
> A júbà.

> Ògún points at the owner of the house.
> Ògún flogs flogs the owner of the house.
> Ògún the flogger.
> Owner of people who profit from the trade of cutting boils.
> Ògún pierces (a thing) to drink what oozes out.
> Ògún carves/engraves the cow.
> Carving with teeth that cause one to cry out in pain.
> Crying with gritted teeth and wide-open eyes.
> Stung, flogged, we look to buy the good-luck soap (*àwúre*).
> "He who may burst out suddenly," "the owner of authority,"
> We salute.

Ògún, as owner of scissors and razors, is looked to as the director of the preparing, incising, and decorating of the initiate's head. The following songs are sung by the priests during the initiation when each of Ògún's tools is called into action:

> *Song for Scissors*
> Gbogbo ọ̀bẹ ni so ọ̀be yẹ́ erí àṣẹ[8] kà di gbó ọlá.
> Ògún ló fún wa l'abẹ o awa ni àṣẹ di gbó ọlá.

> All knives tied to knives honor the head of power
> Counted to become old with honor.
> Ògún is the one who gave us the razor.
> We have the authority/medicine to become old with honor.

Song for Razor
Irun o ìbò l'erí; l'erí àṣẹ kà di gbó ọlá.
Ògún ló fún wa l'abẹ o awa ni àṣẹ di gbó ọlá.

Hair is the cover on the head;
On the head of power counted to become old with honor.
Ògún is the one who gave us the razor;
We have the authority/medicine to become old with honor.

Song for Incisions and Painting
Fín fín ọkan kíní kíní d'ẹkùn.
Ìyá d'ẹkùn baba d'ẹkùn lóòní o.
Fín fín ọkan wìn ní kìní d'ẹkùn.
Ògún d'ẹkùn lóòní o.

Carved carved, one, little by little becomes a leopard.
Mother becomes a leopard; Father becomes a leopard today.
Carved carved, one, multicolored becomes a leopard.
Ògún becomes a leopard today.

For the Lùkùmí, the culmination of an *òrìṣà* devotee's initiation cycle comes with the receiving of the ritual sacrificial knife of Ògún. This ceremony says to the community that the recipient is a full adult priest who can lead others in ritual sacrifice and prayer. To celebrate this important occasion, the newly elevated priest oftentimes hires musicians to perform. Bàtá or Àgèrè/Ìjẹṣà/Bẹmbẹ drums are generally played (fig. 15.3). He or she must set a grand hunter's banquet, where at least three types of meat (fish, pork, chicken, beef) are served along with yams, black-eyed peas, corn, several types of liquor, and dessert. Only priests who have also received the knife of Ògún can sit at this banquet table, and a new chair is placed for the new member, their host. They all celebrate Ògún, who is the strong hand and sharp knife that provides the sacrificial feast for both *òrìṣà* and men (fig. 15.6). Ògún as the provider of the feast is the first to taste blood. Rusty iron is a sign that, even when they seem to be inactive, Ògún and his iron are at work. The rust on the iron is said to be a covering of blood. At the end of large rituals where the number of animals sacrificed has caused Ògún's knife to become overheated, a special ceremony is performed to cool Ògún and ensure that his iron will not turn against us. This ceremony ends with the Balógun (the priest who performs ritual slaughter) dancing and singing, accompanied by the entire congregation at the foot of Ògún's emblem. As he dances, the Balógun crosses and uncrosses his two knives in front of him, creating a beat and keeping time by clanking their blades together. Ògún is silent when working, save for the sound that his tools make. You don't see the accident, but you hear the screeching of tires, the crunching of metal, and the breaking of bones. His dance and songs relive mythic hunting and fighting tales. The following song tells us that Ògún is ferocious enough to come to town riding a hyena, whose jaws, like Ògún's, are powerful enough to crack and grind the hardest bones.

FIGURE 15.6 Ògún Ọdẹ-Ògún the Hunter, pin/
pendant created for John Mason by the African-
American sculptor Ògúndípẹ̀ Fáyọmi. Photo by
John Mason.

Sára ìkokò Ogún dé.[9]

On a spotted hyena Ògún arrives.

Ògún plays rough. The old Lùkùmí said that if Ògún liked you, he took
only a leg or an arm. This was a reprieve from the horror of working to death
in the cane fields. It was Ògún's test of your mental, physical, and spiritual
fitness. We only have to remember the great one-legged black tap dancer Peg-leg
Bates, who lost his leg in a southern cotton mill where he worked. But because
of his great determination to live, perfect his craft, and excel in his art, Ògún
lifted him up and gave him a long life, great wealth, and world renown and
respect. Mr. Bates was famous for his athletic ability, which he used to perform
leaps and steps that two-legged dancers could not perform. If an *òrìṣà* has
great love for you, he or she will sometimes burden you to bring out the greatness
of your character. Every member of the community, based on fitness and ability,
has an *òrìṣà* that he/she can look to as his/her dance instructor. The lame and
decrepit who are bent and slow moving can always dance properly for Ọbàtálá.
One must be strong and athletic to dance for Ògún. A lame, slow-moving
hunter can go hungry or become the victim of his quarry.

Ògún is feared because of his explosive, compulsive, and sometimes unpredictable behavior. His rage is alternately turned against himself, his children (priests of Ògún), and his followers. There is a line in one of his songs which says:

> Olójú ni s'ara yà.[10]
>
> He is the owner of eyes that make a body turn away.

An *itàn* (divination tale) associated with the *odù* Ifá Ìròsùn Méjì tells us that Ògún—the pampered son of Ọbàtálá and his wife, Yemòwó—raped his mother and carried on an incestuous relationship with her until they were discovered by Ọbàtálá. In one version of the story, Ọrúnmìlá (the divination deity) was the issue of this incestuous relationship.[11] Ògún stopped Ọbàtálá from cursing him and cursed himself to work forever without stop (in the world) performing all types of labor. Ògún is the symbol of id-directed behavior that leads to the punishment of back-breaking work that slowly wears one down. Proverbs such as "The more the knife works, the more the stone eats" speak of how Ògún is used to make others rich. Another proverb, "A knife can't be its own handle," associated with the odù Ifá Ọ̀ṣẹ́ Ògúndá, tells us that proper care must be exercised when dealing with Ògún, who is often associated with strong liquor and drunkenness.

> A sá lọ. A sá lọ. Ọ bẹmbẹ́.[12]
>
> We run away. We run away. He is cutting off (heads).

When drunk, Ògún is like a child who either can be taken advantage of or must be pampered lest he fly into a rage.

The Lùkùmí cite the love of strong drink as one of the causes for Ògún's poor record of marital success. In the divination story from the *odù* Ifá Ọsa Ògúndá, Ọya is reported to have left Ògún for the first time because he divulged the secret of her ability to transform herself into a buffalo to Ògún's senior wife, who got Ọya's secret by getting him drunk. His drunkenness and subsequent tattling led Ọya to kill the senior wife and flee to the forest. After another attempt, which failed because of his drinking, constant working, dirtiness, and fighting, Ọya left him, for good, to live with Ṣàngó. Another tale from the *odù* Ifá Ọsa Òdí also tells us that Ọya left because Ògún wanted to employ her in his smithy as his helper/slave (her job was to keep the fire going). She fled, stealing his tools of war and leaving the bellows in her place to be the slave of Ògún.[13] Noted for his strength and courage, Ògún is said to have killed another wife, Yẹmọja, because she saw him display cowardice.

Ògún is a study in extremes. When working he has little care for his appearance, is inarticulate, and has trouble communicating with people, prefers strong drink, and smells of blood and sweat. When at rest he is bathed in an aromatic herbal concoction, liberally rubbed with palm oil, dressed in a cool swaying palm garment; he also recites classical poetry set to music. Ògún is the reformed rapist who now becomes Onílà (owner of scarification marks), the circumciser of young men and castrater of the sacrificial goats given to Ọ̀ṣun and Aganjù (deity of the wilderness). Ògún is the reformed felon (murderer, wife beater, child molester) who re-enters society ever more conscious of the high ethical standard we must all strive for. We make solemn oaths while invoking his name. He breaks addictions, putting aside drink/drugs/violence, and thus offers hope to the hopeless.

> Ãrẹ 'ré a fẹ́ 're yọ̀.[14]
>
> Titleholder of Ìré we want the goodness of happiness.

My father, so many years gone as to be an ancestor, still comes to tell me stories of racism, hate, and murder. These stories make me see that there can be no true revolution, no tranquil passage or lasting transformation without the tears and pain that Ògún represents. I am possessed by Ògún. I know then that the companion of righteous, ethical, humane behavior is blind rage and bloody retribution. His sword not only seeks out our enemies but also is turned against us, for our heads choose to be accomplices in our own degradation. We must ceaselessly and ruthlessly strive to smash injustice with our intelligence and a strong right arm.

We worship Ògún because he ruthlessly and untiringly works to cut through the tangle of injustice with intelligence, technology, and two strong arms. We look for him to kill the oath- and treaty-breaker. Every day we see and hear of the rank injustices acted out against us, and we look into our culture and history, and into ourselves, to call forth that juggernaut who, armed, will go forth to smite the enemy. He is our rage that will blindly strike out until we stand ankle deep in the blood of our enemies. Without his medicine we would choke on the bile of our discontent. We must be able to touch this white-hot rage/furnace that burns in our gut or we can never cauterize that grievous, festering wound we carry. After evening the score, we open our eyes and are tempered by the cooling, healing, bitter tears of reason.

> Ògún kò mà réré; kò mà réré' kò mà réré o.[15]
>
> Ògún is not far away; he is not far away; is not far away.

NOTES

1. Song collected from Julio Marcos Suarez (Fantoma) Alaganjù, Olúbàtá, in Matanzas, Cuba, August 1992.

2. Song collected from Jesus Florensio Alfonso (Gaillego), Ọmọ Ayàn, in Matanzas, Cuba, August 1992.

3. Song collected from Julio Marcos Suarez, August 1992.

4. The Ìjẹ̀ṣà of Ilẹ́ṣà maintain a very strong relationship with Ògún, as evidenced by the two shrines for Ògún found within the palace of the Ọba. Ojo states that one

shrine is for Ògún Safe or Oni, and the second is for Ògún Owa and Ìjèṣà, that is, the Ògún of the Ọba and people of the kingdom. In Cuba, the descendants of the Ìjèṣà especially look to Ògún as their patron.

5. John Mason, *Orin Òrìṣà: Songs for Selected Heads* (Brooklyn: Yoruba Theological Archministry, 1992), p. 100.

6. Mason, p. 87, Song #1.

7. Mason, p. 92, Song #12.

8. The word *àṣẹ* in this context can alternately stand for power, authority, or the ball of medicine which is affixed to the incised crown of the initiate's head.

9. Mason, p. 93, Song #14.

10. Mason, p. 96, Song #24.

11. This *ìtàn* further states that when Yemòwó gave birth to Ọrúnmìlà, he was taken and buried up to his neck in the woods by Ọbàtálá. Ẹlégbá followed and noted the spot, and then he and Yemòwó would bring food to Ọrúnmìlà every day. Ọrúnmìlà was kept alive in this way until Ọbàtálá became very ill and lost his eyesight. No one could cure him, so Ẹlégbá suggested that he go to Ọrúnmìlà for help. Ọbàtálá was surprised to find that Ọrúnmìlà was still alive but went for help. Ọrúnmìlà agreed to help Ọbàtálá but had no tools with which to divine. Immediately, Ọbàtálá carved a divining tray and gave it to Ọrúnmìlà along with sixteen palm nuts. Ọrúnmìlà, the son of Ògún, cured Ọbàtálá and was forever indebted to Ẹlégbá and Yemòwó for his salvation.

12. Mason, p. 96, Song #23.

13. In her guise as the tornado, Ọya blows houses apart for Ògún to rebuild. He can't stay away from strong women.

14. Mason, p. 95, Song #20.

15. Mason, p. 95, Song #22.

Reference Cited

Mason, John. 1992. *Orin Òrìṣà: Songs for Selected Heads.* Brooklyn: Yoruba Theological Archministry.

CONTRIBUTORS

'BADE AJUWỌN is professor of African folklore and dean of arts at Ọbafemi Awolowo University, Ile-Ifẹ, Nigeria. He obtained the Ph.D. degree at Indiana University (Bloomington) in 1977. His research and journal publications have centered on the Yoruba hunter tradition and African diaspora studies. Ajuwọn is author of *Funeral Dirges of Yoruba Hunters* (1982) and several articles on issues central to African folklore and culture. He is currently working on *Dilemma Tales of Nigeria.*

ROBERT ARMSTRONG, an anthropological linguist, spent most of his career in West Africa. After retiring as Director of the Institute of African Studies, University of Ibadan (Nigeria) in 1983, he joined the staff of the University of Nigeria at Nsukka, where he remained until his death in 1987. Among his many writings were a *Dictionary of Idoma,* more than sixty articles, and five volumes of edited essays. In addition he translated six Nigerian books into English and produced numerous recordings of oral literature.

ADEBOYE BABALỌLA is the author of a pioneering study of oral poetic traditions in West Africa, *The Content and Form of Yoruba Ìjálá* (1966), and fifteen other books, texts, and collections, many of which are published in Yoruba. He is emeritus professor of Yoruba literature, former head of the Department of African Languages and Literatures, and a former dean of arts at the University of Lagos. In 1982, the government of Nigeria conferred the Nigerian National Merit Award on Professor Babalọla for his prolific work on oral literature, for his leadership in standardizing the Yoruba language, and for securing official recognition in Nigerian universities for degree programs in Nigerian languages and literatures. In addition to scholarly works, he has written and published in Yoruba a play, a novella, and collected poems. He is currently writing his memoirs and completing a dictionary of Yoruba personal names with more than 20,000 entries.

SANDRA T. BARNES is professor of anthropology and director of the African Studies Center at the University of Pennsylvania. Her research and publications have focused on African urbanism, religion, politics, and history. She is author of *Patrons and Power: Creating a Political Community in Metropolitan Lagos* (1986), which won the Amaury Talbot Prize, and *Ogun: An Old God for a New Age* (1980). She is preparing a study of cultural and social pluralism in pre-colonial West Africa.

PAULA GIRSHICK BEN-AMOS is on the faculty of the Department of Anthropology at Indiana University and has taught at the University of Pennsylvania and Northwestern University. She has published extensively on the cultural background, symbolism, and history of the arts of the Benin Kingdom. Her writings include *The Art of Benin* (revised edition, 1995), *The Art of Power, the Power of Art: Studies in Benin Iconography* (1983, with Arnold Rubin), and the forthcoming *Art and Politics in 18th Century Benin.*

KAREN MCCARTHY BROWN has carried out extensive research in Haiti and New York City on Haitian Vodou. She is professor of the sociology and anthropology of religion in the Graduate and Theological schools of Drew University. Brown is the author of *Mama Lola: A Vodou Priestess in Brooklyn* (1991) and *Tracing the Spirit: Ethnographic Essays on Haitian Art* (1995), as well as numerous articles on Haitian women, traditional healing, transnationalism, and migration.

DON COSENTINO is professor of African and Caribbean literature and folklore at UCLA, and coeditor of *African Arts.* He did fieldwork in West Africa in the 1970s, and is author of *Defiant Maids and Stubborn Farmers: Tradition and Invention in Mende Storytelling* (1982). He has worked in Haiti since 1986, and is curator of *The Sacred Arts of Haitian Vodou* (1995), a widely traveled exhibition, for which he edited the catalogue. He also keenly observes the progress of the *orishas* in Los Angeles.

HENRY JOHN DREWAL is Evjue-Bascom Professor in the Department of Art History with a joint appointment with the Department of Afro-American Studies at the University of Wisconsin. He has published widely on the arts of Yoruba-speaking peoples in both Africa and Brazil. His most recent books include (with Rowland Abiodun and John Pemberton) *Yoruba: Nine Centuries of African Art and Thought* (1989) and *The Yoruba Artist: New Theoretical Perspectives on African Arts* (1994). He is currently coauthoring with John Mason a book on Yoruba beadwork in Africa and the diaspora.

MARGARET THOMPSON DREWAL is associate professor of performance studies at Northwestern University. A performance theorist, she has worked among the Yoruba-speaking peoples of Nigeria and their descendants in the U.S. and Brazil. Her publications have dealt with the interconnections between the arts in ritual performance. She has authored *Yoruba Ritual: Performers, Play, Agency* (1992) and coauthored, with H. J. Drewal, *Gelede: Art and Female Power among the Yoruba* (1983). Apart from these works, she has also published on American popular culture, including spectacle and dance from Liberace and the Rockettes to George Balanchine. Her ongoing research is on multicultural dance at World's Expositions.

JOHN MASON is a Yorùbá diviner and priest of Ọbàtálá initiated in 1970. He is a graduate of City College of New York. He founded in 1977 and is the director of the Yorùbá Theological Archministry, a nonprofit research center. In the past thirty years he has been involved in the intensive and extensive study of Yorùbá culture in the Americas and West Africa. His published works include *Olóòkun: Owner of Rivers and Seas* (1996), *Orin Òrìṣà: Songs for Selected*

Heads (1992), *Four New World Yorùbá Rituals* (1985), and, with Gary Edwards, *Black Gods—Òrìṣà Studies in the New World* (1985) and *Onjẹ Fún Òrìṣà: Food for the Gods* (1981). He is completing with Henry Drewal a catalogue for an exhibit at the Fowler Museum for Cultural History, entitled *The Bead Goes On: Art and Light in the Yorùbá Universe.*

RENATO ORTIZ is professor of sociology at the State University of Campinas (UNICAMP), São Paulo, Brazil. He prepared his Ph.D. at the Écôle des Hautes Études en Sciences Sociales, Paris; entitled *La Mort Blance du Sorcier Noir,* it was also published in Portuguese in 1978. As a student of Brazil's emerging religious traditions and spokesman for its popular culture, Ortiz has published widely in Brazil, France, and the United States. His recent scholarship focuses on issues of cultural industry, modernity, and world culture. His books include *A Consciência Fragmentata* (1980), *Cultura Brasileira e Identidade Nacional* (1985). *Cultura Popular: Românticos e Folcloristas* (1985), *A Moderna Tradição Brasileira* (1985), *Cultura e Modernidade* (1992), and *Mundialização e Cultura* (1994).

J. D. Y. PEEL is professor of anthropology and sociology at the School of Oriental and African Studies, University of London. His Nigerian fieldwork has been chiefly in Ibadan (1964–65) and Ilesha (1973–75, 1979), and he has taught at the University of Ife. His main published works are *Aladura: A Religious Movement among the Yoruba* (1968) and *Ijeshas and Nigerians* (1983), which won the Herskovits Prize. From 1979 to 1986 he was editor of *Africa.* At present he is writing a book on the encounter of religions in nineteenth-century Yorubaland.

JOHN PEMBERTON III, a student of religion and art in southwestern Nigeria for more than 25 years, is the author of many articles and (with William Fagg) *Yoruba Sculpture of West Africa* (1982), (with Henry Drewal and Rowland Abiodun) *Yoruba: Nine Centuries of African Art and Thought* (1989) and *Yoruba Art and Aesthetics* (1991), and (with Funso Afolayan) *Yoruba Sacred Kingship: A Power Like That of the Gods* (1996). He is Crosby Professor of Religion at Amherst College (Massachusetts).

PHILIP W. SCHER has conducted research in Trinidad and Tobago on the exportation of Carnival and on the formation of a transnational Trinidadian cultural identity in Brooklyn, New York. His screenplay for *The Mind's Treasure Chest,* an educational feature film, won four gold awards in 1991–92 at international film festivals. His articles include "The West Indian American Day Parade: Becoming a Tile in the Gorgeous Mosaic," in the *International Journal of Comparative Race and Ethnic Studies* (Fall 1996), and writings on the relationship between Carnival and bureaucracy; the production and consumption of nostalgic Carnival forms transnationally; and the role of Carnival in ethnic conflict in Brooklyn. In addition he is completing doctoral work in the departments of Anthropology and Folklore and Folklife at the University of Pennsylvania.

INDEX